FINANCIAL FEASIBILITY STUDIES FOR HEALTHCARE

CHRISTOPHER J. EVANS, FACHE, CMPE

McGraw-Hill

New York   San Francisco   Washington, D.C.   Auckland   Bogotá
Caracas   Lisbon   London   Madrid   Mexico City   Milan
Montreal   New Delhi   San Juan   Singapore
Sydney   Tokyo   Toronto

Library of Congress Cataloging-in-Publication Data

Evans, Christopher J.

   Financial feasibility studies for healthcare / Christopher J. Evans.

      p.   cm.

   Includes bibliographical references and index.

   ISBN 0-07-022058-1 (alk. paper)

   1. Health care—Economic aspects. 2. Cost effectiveness.
3. Managed care plans (Medical care)—Finance. 4. Medical
economics. I. Healthcare Financial Management Association (U.S.).
Educational Foundation. II. Title.

   [DNLM: 1. Cost-Benefit Analysis. 2. Models, Economic.
3. Practice Management—economics. W 74 E918f 2000]

RA971.3.E876 2000

338.4'33621—dc21

DNLM/DLC

for Library of Congress   99-37338

                                                     CIP

McGraw-Hill

A Division of The McGraw·Hill Companies

1 2 3 4 5 6 7 8 9 0 BKM / BKM 9 0 9 8 7

ISBN 007-022058-1

Printing and binding by Book-Mart Press, Inc.

Cover illustration by Steve Dininno.

This book was typeset using 10 point Times Roman.

This publication is designed to provide accurate and authoritative
information in regard to the subject matter covered. It is sold with the
understanding that neither the author nor the publisher is engaged in
rendering legal, accounting, or other professional service. If legal
advice or other expert assistance is required, the services of a
competent professional person should be sought.

    —*From a Declaration of Principles jointly adopted by a Committee of
    the American Bar Association and a Committee of Publishers.*

PREFACE

THE VALUE OF THIS BOOK

So what did you pay for this book? How much time did you spend reviewing its content to decide if it is *valuable* to you? Three minutes? Five minutes? Did you see something that caught your eye? Will this book be a useful addition to your bookshelf? A colleague's? Few people in the world recognize the real value of textbooks. Given the target audience for this text, it is likely that every reader will gain something of immediate, tangible value from their investment and a bit of personal time to read it and understand its applicability to their own work life. This is the truth. I know because I make my living by consulting and advising others on matters such as those presented in this text. Of the dozen or so textbooks that I buy each year, *most of them are actually worth thousands of dollars to me* because I can turn the information into use. I convert it to economic value that I give away or sell to my clients, which results in a continual stream of work for me. You can do the same within your current work environment.

You might find the format of this book above or beneath your individual level of understanding. You might find the flow of it a bit too stilted for your liking. It isn't meant to satisfy everyone. It is meant to get across basic information on the topic and to be a reference resource for anyone on the topic. Is it *valuable*; is it worth the price you paid? If even one piece of information in this book assists you in doing your job better, understanding something, seeing a new perspective, or enhancing your knowledge base at all in an applicable manner, it has vastly outweighed its expense. The return on investment is nearly incalculable. You will reap its rewards as you deepen your understanding of the issues you see here. You may read one section and simply agree with it. What have you learned? You have reinforced your knowledge base. It may have even been written in terms that you use everyday; it might seem to have been quoted from you. In any case, readers are likely to find some tidbits of information that are of immediate value to them. As you read this text on financial feasibility, remember that your return on investment in the form of knowledge came so cheaply.

THE BOOK FORMAT

This book is designed to teach both the basic and intermediate techniques of conducting financial feasibility studies in the present day healthcare environment. Its primary audience is the nonfinancial manager such as medical practice office managers, hospital VPs, or department heads. While the book presumes a basic understanding of spreadsheet software use, it does not require mastery of skills or of financial terms. The text guides the reader through the terminology and reasons why the early assessment of financial feasibility is important in examining a proposed venture and how to identify key elements in any analysis or assignment. It borrows some issues from my previous book, *Integrated Community Healthcare: Next Generation Strategies for Developing Provider Networks* (McGraw-Hill, 1997).

The healthcare industry has become much more complex than it was 20 years ago or even 10 years ago. Patients, providers, employers, and payors have witnessed the changes and have, to a large extent, ushered in the new demands on each of the parties. Providers are seeking to evaluate alternatives that will allow them to provide care to patients in their service area or business in a more cost-effective manner. A firm grasp of market conditions, operations, and financial issues is required to understand where opportunities exist to improve service, profitability, and survival.

This book helps demystify financial analysis for readers without significant experience or formal training in this discipline. While it doesn't belittle the depth of knowledge required to produce a first rate financial analysis, it does provide a basis for nearly anyone to produce a basic analysis of existing operations or of a planned new venture.

The text is divided into three parts, and each chapter is meant to serve as an ongoing topical reference in and of itself. Part I, Chapters 1 and 2, provides the reader with an overview of basic concepts and issues in approaching financial analysis and spreadsheet modeling techniques. Part II, Chapters 3 through 7, discusses specific industry considerations and delves into a detailed presentation of financial issues on a variety of topics faced by healthcare providers and payors. Part III is a series of case studies on typical topics that lends itself to financial feasibility analysis. The case studies are from actual market circumstances and include the assumptions and market analyses as well as the financial models used to confirm feasibility. Readers should be aware that this text does not provide legal guidance in its reference to legal and regulatory issues. The author and publisher are not in the business of providing legal advice. Legal advice should be sought from a competent attorney.

Readers should remember that the text presumes readers to have a variety of educational and practical backgrounds and presents a broad range of issues on financial analysis, specifically as it relates to financial feasibility studies. Its primary goal is to familiarize readers with the basic platform for conducting feasibility analyses. In doing so, certain topics include significant depth, while others seem to examine the surface of issues. Readers should review the text and note its contents as ongoing reference materials for later use.

Chapter 1, "Overview of Financial Feasibility in the Healthcare Industry," sets the stage for the beginning reader to gain familiarity with concepts and terms of financial analysis. It is a rudimentary explanation of why financial analyses are crucial in the early decision process and how key pieces of information are structured and obtained to design the model.

Chapter 2, "Intermediate Concepts of Financial Modeling," moves into market analysis and development of key indicators of project need, which in many cases allows the analyst to determine whether further feasibility analysis is warranted. Spreadsheet design and the use of templates are discussed and examples are given that show the reader how to automate many aspects of the spreadsheet to accommodate scenario development and changes in assumptions as the project develops. Cost of capital, planning start-up costs, and capital needs are discussed. Chapter 2 concludes with a discussion of setting reasonable operating and financial targets and financial ratio analysis.

Chapter 3, "Business Valuation," presents an overview of the business valuation process, a discussion of standards of value, legal and regulatory guidance pertaining to the healthcare industry, and examples of how the business valuation process is applied.

Chapter 4, "Provider Compensation," gives readers a significant background on the legal issues and prevalent models for paying physicians and other autonomous healthcare providers (e.g., physician assistants, nurse practitioners, physical therapists, etc.) and how these different models impact both productivity and financial needs. An explanation of the fair value of provider services is provided with a detailed description of how to normalize compensation and productivity of a given model based on national comparative data. A detailed discussion of the legal implications of income distribution, including a discussion of Stark II Antireferral Law, provides the most recently held views on these far-reaching prohibitions. Automation of compensation algorithms is presented as an example of building flexibility into each analysis based on alternatives in compensation plans. This feature is of great importance when ventures may be based largely on whether providers receive enough compensation to make their participation worthwhile, while still ensuring that the project is financially feasible. Finally, a discussion of the decision to base compensation on aspects of net income distribution is provided, guiding the reader to understand the issues of how overhead and compensation affect overall project financial performance.

Chapter 5, "Selected Issues in Medical Practice Operations," presents real-life examples of situations in which financial analysis is valuable in the medical practice setting. Income modeling considering historic operating history, national comparative data, and the impact of managed care (e.g., capitation) on the income stream of a business is discussed. An explanation of cost issues and identifying cost per unit calculations (cost per patient treated, cost per procedure, percent of income, etc.) serves to identify which elements of cost measurement result in usable outcomes for planning and operations purposes. While many elements may be modeled, key indicators of performance are used to help improve operations or identify areas of real or potential weakness (addressed similarly in ratio analysis in Chapter 2). The chapter proceeds with a discussion of cost distribution in efforts to identify where, for example, cost per procedure calculations are profitable compared with income per procedure. This section has particular relevance for multispecialty medical practices and for modeling cost per product or business line. An overview of relative value unit measurement, the controversy over which system better reflects actual time expended, and some practical examples of their use are presented. The chapter concludes with a discussion of activity-based costing as a framework for identifying the specific costs of a given operation or segment of business.

Chapter 6, "Modeling Mergers," assists the reader in understanding some of the key issues in merging entities into one new business unit. This chapter begins with analyzing the anticipated scope of the merger and the range of options for the organizational structure of the new business. Consideration of what is included and what is excluded from the previous entities that will be moving forward into the new entity is discussed. An exploration of merger valuation, the amortizing of intangibles, and the decision to include portions of goodwill is presented.

Chapter 7, "Operational and Legal Issues in Healthcare Network Development," presents a discussion of provider operations networks and managed care contracting networks. Although it is not meant to be a comprehensive discussion of all alternatives available, the text provides a solid overview of the most important issues facing network developers of all types.

Case Studies

Case studies in financial feasibility are included so readers can examine one approach to a particular issue. The following studies are included: the operational pro forma for a proposed medical practice acquisition, the implementation of a hospital obstetrics service, the creation of an indigent free pharmacy program, a multispecialty (primary care) practice start-up, and an assisted living center study.

Supplementary Material

This book is more than a how-to book; a number of charts, tables, key step checklists, and spreadsheets are ready to work for many organizations. The working files for the case studies are included on the accompanying diskette, along with several surprise files. Included in Microsoft's Word 97 and Excel 97 formats, the items can be imported into many other software packages while retaining all formatting and embedded commands and formulas. Additional file formats may be available from The Health Service Group, Inc., Corporate Services Center, at (919) 460-7155.

ACKNOWLEDGMENTS

To my Lord and Savior, Jesus Christ, all glory and honor and praise. If anyone sees good or value in this text or in my work, know that it is through Christ living in me. "That if you confess with your mouth, 'Jesus is Lord' and believe in your heart that God raised him from the dead, you will be saved. For it is with your heart that you believe and are justified, and it is with your mouth that you are saved." Romans 10: 9-10

To my lovely and talented wife, Lynne, whose patience and support allowed me to complete yet another book project.

To my son, Grahame, who was too young to know that all those extra keystrokes he added while on Daddy's lap may have actually improved this book.

To my colleagues at The Health Service Group, Inc., F. Gene DePorter, CHE; Terry Dixon, CHE; and Jeff Shovelin. Many aspects of this work are related directly to their efforts and insights. The case studies are reflective of their contributions and their words. My admiration for their professionalism and dedication to going far beyond what is expected will be remembered well into the future. Without them, this book would not have happened.

To Robert L. Wilson Jr., in the Raleigh, N.C., office of Smith Helms Mulliss & Moore, LLP, attorney and friend, thanks for the use of the material on legal issues from our first book, *Integrated Community Healthcare: Next Generation Strategies for Developing Provider Networks* (McGraw-Hill, 1997). Readers, please remember that the regulatory environment is a highly complex and ever-changing area. Bob would like to extend his thanks to Patricia M. Pinkley for her assistance in updating his material.

To Michael G. Dimoff, CPA, business analyst extraordinaire and golf partner, thanks for your informal review and constructive comments, both on and off the course.

To Tom Girton, FACMPE, thanks for your review of the original manuscript and your comments.

To Patty Vogel, Management Directions of North Carolina, thank you for your insight and suggestions. I am sure my readers will appreciate your clear thoughts.

To Jim Price at MICA Information Systems in Winston-Salem, N.C., thanks for requesting the brainstorming session on information system reports; it helped me get organized in this book and in my consulting practice.

Finally, thanks to my publisher, Kris Rynne, the fine folks at McGraw-Hill, and Michael McConnell at Graphic World Publishing Services, whose diligent efforts made my job comparatively easy.

Christopher J. Evans, FACHE, CMPE
September 22, 1999
Winston-Salem, N.C.

CONTENTS

PART II

SPECIFIC INDUSTRY CONSIDERATIONS   73

Chapter 3

Business Valuation   75

Chapter 5

Selected Issues in Medical Practice Operations   161

Chapter 6

Modeling Mergers   185

Chapter 7

Operational and Legal Issues in Healthcare Network Development   201

PART III

CASE STUDIES IN FINANCIAL FEASIBILITY   223

ONE

BASIC CONCEPTS AND ISSUES IN FINANCIAL FEASIBILITY IN THE HEALTHCARE INDUSTRY

CHAPTER

Overview of Financial Feasibility in the Healthcare Industry

"I have hardly ever known a mathematician who was capable of reasoning."

Plato

THE IMPORTANCE OF ANALYZING FINANCIAL FEASIBILITY

Few people live and work in a world where cost consciousness is not a significant issue. Even in the largest of organizations, a strong financial footing is the predominant characteristic that allows for the continued existence of the entity. This book describes how financial issues impact healthcare delivery and financing and techniques that serve both as reminders and tools for organizations.

Organizations, be they as small as solo medical practices or as large as publicly traded multinational entities, require appropriate cash flow and capital for the basic operational needs in order to remain in business. For smaller businesses, the issues might be more basic such as a reasonable doctor's salary; salaries for staff, supply, and other overhead expenses; and some amount for equipment replacement. For larger organizations, millions of dollars are gained or lost simply by the management of receivables and payables. Capital for expansion and replacement reserves can be substantial and may require debt financing. On each end of the spectrum, each entity must conduct its business in a manner that allows it to meet the basic needs of the business—to continue in operation—and to allow it to weather storms in the foreseeable future.

For each of these organizations, someone needs to be supervising how business is conducted, identifying areas of immediate or potential problems, and instituting changes to mitigate unfavorable results. This book describes basic techniques for evaluating the financial health and success of business ventures, all in the construct of financial feasibility.

Financial feasibility studies allow organizations to evaluate many aspects of how a given business, product, or service might be accepted in the marketplace under specific assumptions. They attempt to quantify the results of an initiative or a process or simply to serve to identify elements that contribute to enhanced or diminished business performance. These studies tend to cast things in black and white, given the very nature of working with numbers.

The key to really understanding and conducting reasonable, probable financial feasibility studies is to understand one thing: financial feasibility is simply predicting the future. Given the absurdity of this concept, one may recognize that there are few certainties to which one may cling.[1] Therefore, the *assumptions* under which the study is conducted provide the underlying structure on which all results must be measured. If the assumptions are reasonable, probable, and defensible, then the study and its results become reasonable.

Much of the discussion in this book will center on the assumptions for performing our feasibility studies. As one becomes more proficient in these analyses, the largest amount of time is spend in defining the scope of the assignment, the market segments affected, and the operating assumptions for the study. The reader is referred to more-detailed financial management texts for a deeper and more thorough understanding of general financial management.

ANYONE CAN DO FINANCIAL MODELING SIMPLY AND EASILY

Reasonable, defensible financial feasibility can be performed by persons with relatively little financial background once the basic understanding and tools have been assembled. The scope of the project really dictates who should be conducting the feasibility study. Many individuals can adequately perform basic, first-pass analyses such as the start-up expenses of a new physician or remodeling for new exam rooms, but conducting advanced analyses such as a replacement hospital study, construction and start-up of a new multispecialty practice, or submitting a regulatory agency review report on long-term care bed usage and costs requires detailed knowledge and expertise.

This book will guide the beginning reader to an understanding of financial and operational terminology as well as how to construct financial reports that add value (make sense) to an organization's operations.[2] Beginners will find that the subject is not as daunting as it might appear initially, especially after some experimenting with some of the models. A rudimentary understanding of computer spreadsheet programs is essential and the accompanying diskette includes spreadsheets for each of the case studies in Excel 97 format.[3]

A basic understanding of the task in performing financial analyses must be prefaced with an understanding of why we are analyzing the issue and the circumstances that surround our reference points. Businesses use financial models to estimate future performance and compare past performances between time periods and among external benchmarks. Performance is profiled generally in either a short-term or long-term manner, with the indicators of performance geared by the term. Long-range decisions involve typically larger financial issues of physical plant, equipment, and overall financial viability. Shorter-term decisions often are based on actual productivity, which includes aspects of price of services, patient and payor mix, and other microelements of operations.

To familiarize readers with formats and tables, the following examples indicate methods of presentation, which facilitate rapid understanding of financial analyses.

Example 1–1

Numbers should represent the level of importance of the item they describe or represent. A medical practice clinical supply budget might be represented as 76,283. It also might look like 76283 or $76,283.45. For the sake of clarity, decimals can be omitted by using the spreadsheet function to reduce decimals to zero places. The program automatically rounds up anything from 0.50 or greater to the next whole number. This number, $76,283, is meaningful because it tells us the overall total and it can be compared with previous years; it also may be represented as a percent of revenue or a percent of total expenses. In many circumstances, it is much more meaningful to know that clinical supply expenses are 4.5% of total revenue. This number may be benchmarked more readily than straight dollars. Other examples throughout the book will develop a baseline understanding of the relative importance of numbers when used in feasibility studies.

Example 1–2

Percentages should reflect meaningful relationships. It is meaningful to begin with collected revenue as a starting point because all business must be driven off of what comes in. Understanding what percentage adjustments to revenue (e.g., contractual allowances, bad debt, write-offs) are off of total revenue is an important figure, not only to track internally but to use against national comparative data. Remember that healthy financial performance in the healthcare industry will result from the optimum interplay between provider (and staff) productivity, payor mix and relationships, and optimizing of reimbursement due the entity.

Some of these elements, such as basic demographics, may well be out of your control; others are not. They are the result of understanding your operation and improving it.

CLARIFYING TERMS

We will use several key terms throughout this book that the reader should understand from the beginning. Rudimentary financial terms such as revenue, adjustments, percentage of revenue and profit are among them. Let us begin with a definition of the terms used in this book. Much of what will be discussed will be from the position of managerial accounting, which encompasses cost and profit centers, budgets, performance reports, and financial planning.

Basis of financial statements means the accounting format used to represent the activity of the entity. The formats used most frequently in medical practices, *cash basis* and *income tax basis,* while somewhat different, often are simply called *cash basis.* Cash basis accounting recognizes income when it is received in hand and expenses when they are paid. Accounts receivable, while owed to the entity, is not considered income. Accounts receivable is considered a business asset, though not taken into consideration under the cash basis.

Accrual basis means the accounting format whereby an entity recognizes income at the time the day the product or service is rendered (though not necessarily collected) and expenses at the time they are incurred (though not necessarily invoiced or paid). It is a format of accounting used by virtually all large entities and some larger medical practices. Accrual basis accounting allows for frequent and timely appraisals of past performance of the enterprise as the basis for management decisions about the future. Some businesses prepare reconciled statements in cash and accrual formats to facilitate understanding for different individuals. As an example, the Multispecialty Primary Care Start-Up Feasibility case study is prepared on an accrual basis while the others are on a cash basis. Accrual basis provides a truer picture of business performance because it matches the revenue for an accounting period with the associated costs in order to measure net income.

Generally accepted accounting principles (GAAP) are a set of accounting standards developed over time that serve as the historical "best practices" in financial reporting. The Financial Accounting Standards Board (FASB) is the organization by which GAAP is maintained through input from accounting groups and individuals.

Income statement, profit-loss statement, or statement of income and expenses each mean the financial report that indicates gross categories of income and expenses to the entity over a discrete period of time (e.g., for the current month and/or the current year to date [YTD]). Several different formats of this report are used, often combining current month and year to date with some adding the same period comparisons from the previous year. A cash flow statement is a similar document that includes additional information about discretionary expenses (i.e., expenses that may be unrelated to direct operations so as to be captured by a business operator, e.g., depreciation) to yield the true amount of cash available to the entity (see the financial models in the case studies for add-backs to yield cash flow). Cash, therefore, is used in the business to pay operating expenses, to finance operations, and in the case of excess cash, for investments. In smaller businesses, however, at the end of the fiscal year any excess cash is returned to the business owners as compensation, generally to avoid paying corporate level taxes on the asset at the end of the year.

Fiscal year is the annual time period of the business's accounting period. In many companies, the fiscal year is the same as a calendar year. Within the fiscal year, the business may produce mid-period statements, perhaps quarterly or monthly, in order to monitor and profile its performance.

Balance sheet is the statement of assets, liabilities, and equity of the entity or organizational unit as of a specific day (*assets* are items owned by the entity, *liabilities* are items owed, and *equity* is the owner's interest to date; therefore, *assets always equals liabilities plus equity*). Much like a bank account at the end of a month, the balance sheet is a snapshot of the capital structure (the financial composition) of the entity. Therefore, we see that businesses are supported by a capital structure comprised of owner equity and long-term debt, including current maturities of long-term debt. Assets may be *liquid* or *illiquid*. A liquid asset is one that can be readily converted to use, such as cash and near-cash items such as certificates of deposit and marketable securities. Near-cash items are those that can be turned into cash within a period of three months. Furniture, fixtures and equipment of the business, while assets, are less liquid because it takes time to convert them (through sale) to their cash equivalent. In later chapters of this book we will examine various aspects of liquidity.

Related to liquidity, assets may be termed *current,* which implies their likelihood of being converted to their cash equivalent within the period of one year from the date of the statement. Similarly, *current liabilities* are those that are expected to be paid within one year of the statement date. The *current portion of long-term debt* is the amount of the total long-term liability that is due within the same one-year time period. *Contingent liabilities* are potential expenses that have yet to be resolved and require some recognition of existence (e.g., a pending malpractice suit or other lawsuit).

Given this understanding, business owners and analysts need to choose the desired structure of *long-term liabilities* and equity by which the business will be supported (i.e., how much of the business will be supported by owner equity [paid in capital as start-up funds] and how much will be supported by various classes of long-term debt [third party—bank loan, mortgage] or shareholder notes).

Working capital is the firm's short-term assets. Working capital is what allows businesses to make their payments on time and continue business operations. In smaller businesses, working capital is provided by the regular turnover or collection of accounts receivable. The general formula for net working capital is current assets minus current liabilities.

Let us now turn to financial reports and some of the terms used with them. The first several items deal with income and the remaining deal with expenses.

Gross charges and **gross revenue** mean the full charge for a product or service that is invoiced by the provider. As we know in the healthcare industry, the full charge is rarely collected.

Patient revenue and **other revenue** indicate the source of revenue that the entity generates. It is helpful to know where revenue derives, for example, patient revenue (e.g., professional services), ancillary services, other revenue (e.g., nutrition consulting, midwifery, counseling, education, etc.). The deeper you can segregate the income streams the better information you have to examine your performance. Ideally, it would be most beneficial to see income detail (e.g., in a medical practice, by each individual provider, by professional services rendered, by different types of ancillary services, etc.) in order to identify patterns in the practice and opportunities for improvement (Exhibit 1–1).

Contractual adjustments indicates the contractually negotiated difference between a payor and the provider's normal (full) fee schedule for the product or service.

Bad debt means amounts that are owed to the provider that have been deemed to be uncollectible from the responsible party and have been written off the books. These amounts are handled very differently from organization to organization and under different bases of accounting. Some businesses write off bad debt or uncollectible amounts from outstanding accounts receivable only after many years (which is why these entities have very large accounts receivable amounts over 120 days). Others never write off uncollectible accounts, thereby skewing the statements. **Returns** or **refunds** are amounts that were overcharged to payors or patients and are refunded.

Collections, net income, and **revenue-net** mean the total income (cash in hand) available for use.

Operating expenses is the broad category of items related to the cost of providing the service directly. These include items such as personnel, benefits, supplies, and rent and utilities.

Nonoperating expenses or **other expenses** is the category of expenses that are necessary but not directly related to the provision of service (e.g., interest expense, depreciation, and amortization [see below]).

Other categories of expenses might have their own subheadings such as general and administrative, clinical, physician, or provider expenses. They should be arranged ideally to communicate a logical relationship or a grouping within

E X H I B I T   1-1

Provider Production Analysis
Evans OB/GYN: Gross Charges

| Provider | Obstetrics | | | Gynecology | | | | Total | Percent Total |
	Inpatient	Outpatient	Ancillaries	Inpatient	Outpatient	Ancillaries	Ultrasounds		
Dr. Grahame Evans	210,708	148,802	14,612	342,826	166,015	35,145	76,988	995,096	45.47%
Dr. Sam Evans	192,461	203,438	15,152	326,611	129,657	29,906	54,888	952,113	43.50%
Ashley Ryll—Midwife	132,922	43,688	13,754	0	0	0	51,000	241,364	11.03%
Total	**536,091**	**395,928**	**43,518**	**669,437**	**295,672**	**65,051**	**182,876**	**2,188,573**	**100.00%**
Percent total practice	24.49%	18.09%	1.99%	30.59%	13.51%	2.97%	8.36%	100.00%	

SOURCE: Practice Monthly Production Report, 12 months ending 12/31/98.

EXHIBIT 1–2

Sample Income Statement Input Worksheet

Patient Revenue	1998	
Gross Charges	410,000	
Less Contractual Adjustments	(94,400)	
Patient Revenue—Gross	315,600	
Less Returns and Allowances	(3,997)	
Patient Revenue—Net	**311,603**	
General & Admin. Expenses		
Salaries—Staff	71,836	
Taxes & Benefits—Staff		Either one total number or
Taxes—Staff	6,493	list
Benefits—Staff	5,266	each
Insurances—Staff	2,865	individual
Other Benefits/Bonuses	982	number
Information Services	4,911	
Clinical Laboratory	10,013	
Radiology/Imaging	1,664	
Medical and Surgical Supplies	10,913	
Building and Occupancy	19,616	Either one total number or
Rent		list
Utilities		each
Phone		individual
Other (e.g., Depreciation)		number
Furniture and Equipment	3,356	
Admin. Supplies & Services	6,411	
Outside Professional Fees	2,074	
Promotion and Marketing	1,119	
Other Interest	655	
Business and Property Taxes	818	
Recruiting	218	
Miscellaneous Expenses	13,210	Last catch-all category
Total G&A Expenses	**162,420**	
Gross Margin	**149,183**	
Physician Expenses		
Owner Salaries	119,215	
Employed Physician Salaries	0	
Employed Extender Salaries	0	
Taxes and Licenses	12,294	
Benefits—Providers	9,500	
Expenses (CME, Dues, Travel, etc.)	4,000	
Malpractice Insurance	4,174	
Total Physician Expenses	**149,183**	

the particular financial statement that might provide meaningful information at a glance or in a comparison (Exhibit 1–2).

Depreciation and **amortization** are cost allocation categories for longer-term expense items. Depreciation is that part of the cost of assets (e.g., furniture, fixtures, equipment, leasehold improvements) that is deducted from revenue for asset services used in operating the business for a certain period. The amount used in depreciation is based on the type of asset, the depreciation method used, and the allowable time frame dictated by the tax code. Depreciation is used for tangible assets (e.g., furniture, fixtures, equipment, and leasehold improvements). Amortization is used for other assets such as goodwill, certain investments, and other prepaid expense items. Depreciation and amortization are referred to as *noncash charges,* because though they are recognized as expenses and they do not result in the reduction of cash or of working capital. Later discussions will involve the use of replacement reserve funds as related to depreciation of equipment and other fixed assets.

Other terms included are often in financial statements or financial models that bear at least a cursory review. Greater detail will be given throughout the text.

Pro forma means, literally, "a matter of form." In the financial world it means a financial representation of activity or a financial model. Most often a pro forma is a profit-loss statement with supporting detail to indicate the operating assumptions behind the numbers.

Profit, earnings, and **margin** mean generally the excess of income after meeting all of the operator's desired expenses for operating the business. These are confusing terms in that they can be disguised by the inclusion of owner discretionary expenses or perquisites within the operation of the business (e.g., a physician who spends $12,000 annually on continuing medical education).

Operating margin is the excess of income over expenses for the direct provision of services in a financial statement so constructed. Be aware that some people refer to this amount as the net income of the business. This issue is discussed in greater detail in other chapters.

Other terms (*return on investment, return on invested capital, contribution margin,* and *return on operations*) are discussed in greater detail later in the text.

COST INFORMATION

Costs are the monetary representation of an asset or service that has been purchased by the business. Costs are assigned to objects with which they are associated, such as equipment cost and personnel cost. They are related to their object from a historical expense perspective (i.e., the cash price paid for a pulse oximeter) and from various perspectives of cost (e.g., replacement cost, future cost, etc.). Costs may be considered in a variety of means. The following discussion highlights some of the key categories of costs.

Direct costs are those costs that are necessary for the immediate production of the good or service. *Indirect costs* are those costs related to the production of the good or service but in a supportive manner. As an example, the direct costs for an outpatient medical office visit may include the physician and nurse time allocation inclusive of benefits and expenses related to these individuals (malpractice insurance, continuing medical education, etc.), and amounts for the clinical and administrative supplies consumed by the physician and nurse. Indirect costs might include all other aspects of total business overhead that relate to the visit, such as an allocation of rent, utilities, telephone, office supplies, billing, and reception personnel and benefits. This is a simplified explanation but one that should suffice. *Cost drivers* are any factors that have an effect on costs.

Incremental costs or *differential costs* are the volume- or alternative resource-related costs of the amount of work performed. For example, if one physician assistant (PA) is capable of seeing 20 patients per day in the outpatient clinic while a physician could see 25 patients per day, the incremental costs of providing physician coverage is the difference between the total costs of the physician assistant versus the physician. Another example might be the baseline or fixed costs of operating a mammography unit (lease payment, staff person + benefits − fixed costs that must be expended to provide the service to even one patient) versus the incremental costs of treating several hundred patients with one machine and one staff person. This discussion of incremental costs touches on another dimension of costs: *fixed and variable costs.*

Fixed costs are costs that do not vary with volume of work effort. They also may be thought of as costs that must be incurred to provide the service or generate the good (asset). Fixed costs include items such as office space, personnel, telephone, insurance, and basic equipment but not necessarily the additional equipment (or staff) to handle more volume that may be categorized as a variable cost. Generally speaking, think of fixed costs as the ones you need to open and keep open the doors for business, rather than those related to how much work the business does.

Variable costs are those expenses that are almost purely volume-driven, such as clinical supplies and office supplies. Sometimes these are referred to as *semi-variable costs* or *step-fixed costs,* which reflect additional expenses, such as personnel or equipment required to increase beyond a specific volume level. Some elements of personnel and other operating categories may be more variable than fixed depending on how the business is set up.

Discretionary costs are generally considered to include advertising, repairs and maintenance, and research and development. In reality, some of these costs might be considered necessary from a business operations perspective and not truly seen as discretionary. From a business operations perspective, some other costs may be discretionary because they relate to costs over and above what is necessary for the business. These discretionary costs are more appropriately referred to as owner discretionary expenses.

Sunk costs relate to expenses that have been committed and cannot be changed. *Opportunity costs* are the return on investment or subjective value when pursuing one option over an alternative action.

A *capitalized cost* is a cost that is recorded for an item as an asset, such as a significant piece of equipment. These costs become expenses through the application of depreciation and/or amortization and are listed as assets on the balance sheet.

Allocation of Costs

Costs may be allocated in many different manners depending on the level of detail of the analysis to be performed. From a bird's eye view, analysts attempt to allocate costs to represent expenses in each major part of the business's operation. Costs may be allocated by department, operating location, subdepartmental unit, or even by physician among the entire complement of providers. Costs of one department or unit might be allocated to another based on its support or resource consumption. Cost allocation is commonly viewed as a means of general allocating overhead expenses such as rent, utilities, phone and housekeeping expenses, and central office support staff.

Allocations can get much more complex and may be combined with *cost-volume-profit analyses* to look at individual procedures. Cost-volume-profit analyses usually examine the break-even point in the production of an item or delivery of a service. For example, a typical cost-volume-profit analysis might examine the profitability of a specific procedure or diagnosis related group (DRG). Management should decide how it wants to see costs allocated before setting about with detailed descriptions of cost allocation.

Analysts also should be aware that decisions on cost allocations might dramatically alter the perspective on performance, generally at the level below overall operations. From the larger view, cost allocations lend some information as to overall business performance when considering categories of costs such as personnel, benefits, clinical or office supplies, and telephone. The more detailed allocation of costs will lend critical information on the operations of the smaller units by indicating the individual expense items within those categories.

Broad allocations of costs may be sufficient for the simplest analyses of operations but might still misrepresent operations. Analysts should interview management in order to determine the issues surrounding analysis (the goals and objectives of the analysis) in order to capture cost data in a manner that will be useful to understanding the root causes of costs.

Cost allocation should begin with a review of work effort performed and the functional units within the organization. Do the organizational units lend themselves to viewing cost allocations in a particular manner? Would it be best to allocate costs to specific physicians as it might in a small group in which the compensation formula agreement acknowledges each physician's operating overhead in a detailed manner? Analysts might attempt first to identify the functional units for allocating costs within their organization. Within each unit, certain costs might be allocated completely for that unit. For example, if the functional unit is "Dr. Grahame," the salary, benefits, and pro rata portion of continuing education expenses of his nurse and medical office assistant might be allocated completely to him, as would his continuing medical education expenses, his malpractice expenses (or pro rata portion of the group policy), and other expenses that were related to only his practice.

Other allocation of indirect expense would need to be made to cover expenses that are not readily identifiable with Dr. Grahame only, such as central billing office overhead, which might be allocated based on gross charges generated or patients seen. Analysts should remember that individual practice differences make all the difference in the allocation method. In a group of internists, allocation of certain expenses based on gross charges might not be appropriate if one of the physicians is a geriatrician with significantly lower gross charges than the others. Similarly, physicians who are highly procedurally oriented might skew such an allocation. The key is in understanding what is going on from an operations perspective and allocating in a manner that best represents activity and resources consumed and also in a manner that may be required by contractual agreements, such as compensation.

Allocation criteria might include a number of elements depending on the goal for representing costs. Expenses related to personnel include salaries and benefits, education funds, uniforms, books, dues, and consulting fees. Square footage, lease costs, utilities, telephone, equipment, leasehold improvements, upfit costs, clinical and laboratory supplies, and other identifiable costs might be related to departments that have dedicated physical space. A more general area of allocation might apply to personnel expenses (all related categories) for receptionists, transcription, medical records, billing office, administration, or other categories of expenses that serve the entire organization. The allocation base might be dollars, charges (gross or net), patient visits (perhaps segregated into outpatient, inpatient, DRGs, lab only or nurse only visits, hours of use [e.g., operating room] prescriptions, number of appointments, etc.), or relative value units.

In larger organizations, allocation of costs may be directed by the Medicare Cost Report, a federally mandated regulatory report of facility expenses. This type of reporting associates costs with revenue and support centers for both revenue and nonrevenue generating departments. Frequently, personnel costs are allocated by the percentage of employee effort whereas other elements of cost are allocated based on other forms of productivity measurement (e.g., visits, dollars, square feet used).

IDENTIFYING IMPORTANT MODELING VARIABLES

When given the task of examining the relationship between certain variables or performing a feasibility study, after understanding the basic goal of the study, one needs to begin identifying the important modeling variable that will *drive* the analysis. Drive is the operative word. Dollars, patient visits, and other items may be classified as drivers of financial models.

Ultimately, dollars (i.e., revenue-net) drives most financial models. There is little that can be done in most circumstances without cash from operations to support an ongoing venture. This may not be the case in certain health system-sponsored charitable activities or in the case of a business that is projected to require many years before profitability. Given this position, how sales or income is planned tends to dictate how the business will proceed. Let's look at some ways to consider this.

As we begin to think about the inputs to our modeling effort, it may be instructive to remind ourselves of how we are going to get where we are going in the first place. Financial success will result ultimately from an acceptable level of return on investment. How we get there is a function of many factors, discussed here and elsewhere. Of the most basic issues will be what we do to generate income and at what levels, how much it costs us to produce the income, and the flow of work which is the source of income. Analysts therefore begin to think about work volume, which is related to market share and position, and the capacity/productivity to do the work. Analysts think about how much income is associated with what type of work, and how to maximize it while meeting the mission of your organization. Analysts lastly think about the cost of producing the work and develop an understanding of the cost structure. With reimbursement continually on the decline, the reduction of costs will be of prime importance to business success.

One method of representing income is to use historical operations and the basis for future growth, as is done with the case study, Acquisition of Dr. Grahame. Medical practices and healthcare businesses such as home health agencies, durable medical equipment companies, and physical therapy and rehabilitation firms are all dependent on patient flows and managed care or direct employer contracts for revenue and business growth. Many factors affect this potential for growth including the decision to add providers or support staff. Adding overhead to any business should be evaluated carefully, especially when overhead may not produce revenue directly. The delicate balance of infrastructure needs provided by support staff and technology can have positive and negative effects on the growth of a business or practice.

Principles of Forecasting in Healthcare Planning

Analysts should remember that strategic thinking is the pursuit of the right questions.

From a broad economic analysis perspective, the following points are made by Gilbert Heebner, retired head of Core States Financial Corporation, and are referred to as Heebner's Seven Laws of Forecasting.[4]

- History repeats itself; history does not repeat itself. The future is not random, but it does not repeat itself exactly either.
- From time to time, major shocks–often unforecastable–throw the economy off course. Developments from outside the economic system are usually not anticipated by forecasts, but they may be anticipated by experienced observers.
- The consensus of economist's forecasts is more often right than wrong. It is not wise to automatically be against the consensus.
- Adherence to a single economic theory can be dangerous to your forecasting health. Theories can become less valid as conditions change.
- Economic forces work relentlessly but on an uncertain timetable. This means forecasts are more likely to be correct regarding cause and effect rather than timing.
- Be aware when something goes off the drawing board of historical experience. Abnormalities are always important!
- The road is more important than the inn. The way you arrive at a forecast is more important than the forecast itself. The reasoning behind the forecast is generally eye-opening and is sometimes of more use than the forecast, an argument for greater involvement of executives in the forecasting function.

Forecasting business growth in the healthcare industry should be based on the following general principles.

Healthcare is Changing Rapidly and Unevenly Across the Country as Evidenced by the Following

- Continual changes in reimbursement from all payors
- Overall growth, evolution, and dominance of managed care
- Governmental influence and intervention in reforming healthcare finance and delivery
- Continuing escalation in uncompensated care, especially for hospitals
- Decreasing lengths of stay and increasing technological and pharmaceutical development leading to increased outpatient treatment and therapies
- Increasing competition among all providers on cost first then on access and quality

The uncertainty surrounding healthcare delivery and financing dictates that limited, cautious judgment dictate planning efforts. Albert Einstein told us, "the kind of thinking that got us into the problem won't get us out." The modern translation might be, "If you are going in the wrong direction, speeding up won't help."

Analysts Should do the Following

- Review goals and objectives for the activity being planned.
- Draft the fixed- and variable-cost elements.
- Develop *reasonable assumptions* on rates of increase of income and expenses; indeed the basic premise of conservative estimates is embodied throughout financial accounting.
- Observe conservative growth factors (e.g., medical care component of consumer pricing index).
- Consider neutral or negative growth factors where appropriate.
- Plan and budget for contingencies (provider turnover, vacancies, business volumes).

Build Checks and Balances into Each Forecast

- Tie provider compensation to minimum production levels based on historical and/or national comparative data when appropriate.
- Ensure generation of minimum working capital requirements before entertaining any distributions.
- Create ownership of operations for all employees and contractors through incentives that are individual, tangible, attainable, and that represent commitment to the organization.
- Profile the best, worst, and most likely scenarios for each venture before deciding on forecast.
- Expect variations from the forecast; revise annual forecasts quarterly and multiyear forecasts annually.

Summary of Steps in Preparing and Analyzing Pro Forma Statements— Advanced Model[5]

1. Analyze the working capital requirements of the business based on industry sources.
2. Analyze the fixed assets of the company to determine whether an additional investment in fixed assets is necessary, or whether any existing assets are above the needs of the business and could be sold without affecting the entity's earning power.
3. Review any contingent liabilities and determine what provision needs to be made for them.
4. Determine the desired structure of long-term liabilities.
5. Summarize a pro forma income statement for the subject company.

Now before getting too far ahead, the reader will want to construct a basic financial model similar in format to the monthly or annual pro forma statements in any of the case studies in order to have a reference point from which to develop the model. One example is the Multispecialty Primary Care Start-Up Feasibility study because the supporting detail provides information on the sources of many of the key revenue and expense amounts.

Salient Considerations—Providers and Support Staff

Production volume levels should be established as a guideline to financial performance. As previously mentioned, historical volumes will yield some indication of style of practice of the physician and physician extender. It is difficult to change the practice patterns significantly for physicians, and any statements of significantly increasing volume (effort) post-sale should be taken with reservation. In such cases, production volume should be addressed contractually with the provider to give each party the clear understanding of how the practice must operate and further, to economically incentivize the provider to maintain production targets. It is easier to increase production levels for midlevel practitioners because they themselves bring little-to-no intangible value to the business. Given a PA or nurse practitioner who is producing significantly below national comparative standards, the transition plan and pro forma statements should gradually require this individual to attain median production standards as a minimum standard of job performance. In most communities, it is far easier and better to recruit a midlevel practitioner than it is to recruit a physician.

The cost of operations is one of the chief considerations in evaluating the financial success of new business ventures. The ability to add providers may become the difference to pursue the arrangement or not. From the physician's standpoint, however, the addition of new providers, especially physicians, dramatically increases overhead and reduces bonus opportunities. Employment arrangements should address the distribution of bonus dollars in consideration of the addition of new providers and their impact of the financial performance of the practice. This supports the trend for attaching to the physician employment agreement a mutually agreed upon operational pro forma. Once the physicians have agreed to the plan for provider recruitment, base income, and incentive formula, the teeth exist to hold the physicians accountable to the new effort.

Financial rewards for physicians, tangible and intangible, must be derived based on their own system of values. Simply attaching monetary value as an incentive to increase production and net revenues may not be a driving factor for a physician with young children in the home. To paraphrase *The Belief System,* by Thad Green and Merwyn Hayes, (an employee) must believe that he/she is able to perform the job (capable of achieving/making the effort), and that this successful level of performance will result in an outcome that is tied to this performance, and further, that this outcome is one that is satisfying to that employee, as an individual.[6] Tying these issues together is the goal of the employment and compensation arrangement that must be settled prior to meaningful pro forma analysis.

Business Profiling

The practice or subject business should be analyzed thoroughly based on its historic operations, its operations in relation to national and regional comparative data, documented growth plans for the business prior to sale, and anticipated growth plans post-sale. These growth plans should be on a needs-based factor to determine how the subject entity fits into the existing or growing network strategy. The business profile then becomes an excellent tool to coordinate input from various sources.

Content and Implementation

The pro forma is a typical financial-based model, usually created as an annual, year-end summary of income and expenses or as a monthly cash flow model. It may be created on a cash or accrual basis, although the accrual basis is used more frequently. The creation of the pro forma for the established operating entity is a serious annual planning activity that, after initial profile, may be administered in-house in even small practices. The model must address the existing or proposed governance structure as it impacts general business operations. It may be wise for many organizations to use external sources to develop these documents if in-house expertise is questionable or unavailable. Physician groups may feel more comfortable with external coordination of this process, and hospitals may not feel objective enough to consider all the issues.

Forecasting

The first phase of the feasibility study is the financial forecast. Forecasts allow for owners and managers to plan for the future, not to predict outcomes.[7] Therefore the goal of the forecast is planning. Although some analysts believe in beginning with the balance sheet, most readers will begin with forecasting the income statement (balance sheet issues can be addressed when planning financing and working capital needs).

The process of forecasting financial performance in the healthcare industry is often conducted over a period three to ten years and should represent the analyst's most likely scenario for the subject business. The general rule of thumb is to forecast only that which you can reasonably project. In healthcare, therefore, forecasts are most often in the two- to five-year range for medical practices, with primary care practices tending to be longer than specialty care practices. Forecasts should include detailed income and expense projections that are documented and have basis in market reality (attention to historical operations, provider productivity expectations, projections on provider recruitment, ingress of managed care, etc.) Growth rates of income and expenses should be reasonable. As one example, our consulting group recently reviewed a valuation (specifically the discounted cash flows analysis) of a primary care/surgery center with two senior physicians, each very near retirement age, performing near the 90th percentile of medical group management association (MGMA) production. The growth rates presumed no diminution of effort for the next 10 years and after a period of initial income growth of about 10%, increased revenue approximately 3% per year thereafter. This is one example of inappropriate expectations for income. The underlying assumptions become the basis of any reasonable forecast. Given the serious penalties (fraud and abuse, private benefit and inurement) that may affect both parties, a conservative and reasonable forecast based on attainable goals (and ideally tied to provider performance agreements) does indeed portray the most likely scenario. If the forecast is for a for-profit entity, be sure to include appropriate taxes—the nominal rate of 40% is typically used—on income forecasted in order to prevent overestimating profit. After income is modeled, move on to expenses.

General Technique

Pro forma analyses typically begin with the creation of a base for income and expenses that derive from the business historical operations or from national comparative data. To this base, adjustments are made for unusual occurrences or identified changes in business operations including working capital requirements, fixed asset analysis, capital expenditures, depreciation, replacement reserve, contingent liabilities, and structure of long-term liabilities (amortization of purchase price, cash advances to sustain operations, etc.). The analyst must evaluate his or her understanding and basis for growth rates (positive, neutral, or negative) for the projections. The following methods may be employed for any income or expense category.

- Business historical average
- Percentage of revenue
- Regression trend analysis of the subject business
- Regression trend of healthcare industry
- Manually adjusted rates

Other Data Elements to Consider (Including Their Cost Relationships) Are as Follows

- Number of physicians in practice
- Physicians and extenders per population served
- Severity of illness
- Risk pools of patients in practice

- Amount of managed care/capitation
- Structure of benefits plans
- Occupancy and equipment relationships to work volume
- Support staff complement
- Elements of general operating overhead
- Diagnostic clustering of workload, e.g.,[8]

    General medical examination

    Acute upper respiratory infection

    Prenatal/postnatal care

    Hypertension

    Nonpsychotic depression

    Lacerations/contusions

    Ischemic heart disease

    Acquired immunodeficiency syndrome

Avoiding Extraneous Issues

The analyst can easily get bogged down in analysis-paralysis if he or she does not take care to focus on the issues of prime importance. As an example, when projecting a ramp-up rate for patient visits for a new physician, monthly or quarterly estimates are likely to provide sufficient detail to model income. It is probably not necessary to model patient visits per day and to monitor cash flow on a weekly basis. The business needs to have some idea of the income and expenses of taking on a new provider and knows that it will need a certain amount of working capital to support the venture. Finely tuned financial models do not usually estimate weekly activity. Other issues should be treated in a similar manner: focus on the broad first then increase your level of detail until your return on effort is justified.

FINANCIAL MODEL AND SPREADSHEET DESIGN

As has been discussed earlier in this chapter, the reader may reference any of the case studies or the master files on the diskette accompanying this book in order to see how to create basic and intermediate-level financial models.

SIMPLIFYING THE MODEL TO ITS ESSENTIAL ELEMENTS

Let's take a look at one of the case studies to set up a basic financial pro forma. Using the Multispecialty Primary Care Start-Up Feasibility study, first read the case study introduction and operating assumptions for this study. Then open the file on a computer and follow along with this book. *Note:* Read the highlighted box on all the files with this book. Choose the worksheet "Assumptions." You'll see first under Income Assumptions, the provider complement (i.e., the number of physicians and PAs used in this study). If you look to the right, you see the MGMA comparative data references at the time the study was done. Below that you see three sections of month-by-month income profiles for each physician practice. Remember, the internal medicine (IM) practice was an established practice, which is why their income stream is strong. The other providers were assumed to be up and running with a full practice within 12 months, which is why the amount in Month 12 for each of them is one-twelfth of the MGMA median production (minus ancillary and technical component). The practice was assumed to generate 16% of its charges in ancillary and technical charges based on historical operations of the other practices in the network. Total adjustments to income were estimated at 20%, based on historical operations (this was a hospital-sponsored physician network). These total numbers were linked to the worksheet "5-Year Pro Forma." Take a moment and go to this worksheet and examine the links in the cells on the income side, B17:M20.

Back to the Assumptions worksheet. Below the three years of income assumptions are the key operating assumptions of provider compensation, malpractice premiums, staffing, and benefits. If a more detailed compensation model is required, you can simply build the model in. You will need to be careful about *circular references,* which are formula inconsistencies whereby at least one dependent variable is inappropriately included. For example, you cannot create a simple formula for cash flow whereby some part of provider compensation is based on a splitting of profits (never mind that a splitting of profits may cause a Stark Law violation.) Underneath the key operating expenses are the financing assumptions and the annual depreciation payments. The depreciation gets a bit detailed. At the very bottom are the annual payments for interest and principal on the start-up costs.

It is really up to the owners and operators of the entity as to how they would like to handle financing, depreciation, and other key operating assumptions. The overall profitability of the venture depends on the assumptions used in modeling the performance. Please note that this does not mean a business is, in reality, more or less profitable simply because of the way of presenting the financial reports. Owner benefit and return on investment come in many forms, and the choice of amortizing start-up expenses or financing over a longer period may reflect reduced return on investment for the privilege. Remember that owner perquisites may be included within the operating budget. The essential element is to recognize where you have flexibility in planning operations. The assistance of specialized help may be necessary in order to understand the best way to plan your activity.

Creating and Maintaining Formulas To Simplify Calculations

As the case study spreadsheets indicate, there are many ways to represent data so that they provide meaningful information. You will note that some of the cells appear to be "locked" with a cell reference to another worksheet, called linked data, and others appear to have specific cell addresses locked in place (e.g., =B155). By using the Paste-link command, a cell reference is locked in place. A good place to use this is to link data between worksheets and to link to a revenue-net figure to calculate profit and percentage of revenue amounts. An excellent way to use this technique is, for example, in modeling different benefits rates. By creating one cell labeled "fringe rate," you can have one percentage number to which all other fringe calculations are pointed. This way, any change in the fringe rate would automatically change all other aspects of the analysis dependent on the fringe rate. Similarly, the interest rate for financing could be set up the same way. Not all of the spreadsheets on the book diskette are fully linked. Examine which cells are linked and which are manual formulas. You will find that linking cells is most often the smarter way to create the model.

The goal should be to create a financial model with enough variability to make it handy to make routine changes without ending up building your own software within a spreadsheet. You can quickly spend a great deal of time building all of this flexibility into the financial model without ever needing to use it. For consultants and managers who will use one model over and over again with small changes for each new occasion, building flexibility is valuable. For the first use of a model, a modest amount of flexibility should be considered because of the time you will save. In addition, clients and managers frequently change the format on how they want to see the data represented. You can save a great deal of time by producing a basic model first, then refine from there.

Some basic guidance and questions to ask before putting together pro formas include the following.

- Cash or accrual basis
- Compensation assumptions for providers (how will incentive be handled in the model)
- Productivity assumptions for providers
- Fringe benefit rate
- Staff complement and compensation
- Financing assumptions for building/real estate, equipment, working capital

After these basic issues, the focus of the financial model will dictate the rest of the variables to be analyzed.

THE IMPACT OF MANAGED CARE AND REGULATORY ISSUES

Few readers will not recognize the changes in healthcare delivery and financing brought about by managed care. Even the most talented physicians, hospital administrators, and insurers cannot predict the level of payments or services that a given population of people might require. This concept alone has thrown the U.S. healthcare system into such turmoil that every participant from provider to patient feels its influence. These outcomes were inevitable based on the financing and delivery system that grew out of the immediate post-Medicare era. The shift from hospital and inpatient focus to covered life and outpatient focus are understood by all, yet making the change has proved to be a difficult one.

Healthcare Delivery and Financing—A Brief History

Major reorganization needed to occur in the established healthcare delivery system. The traditional fee-for-service system was generating incentives driving the overall cost of care so high that the federal government was forced to overhaul financing for the Medicare program. Beyond the move to diagnosis related groups, which was difficult enough, changes needed to be made on the physician and ancillary services components of healthcare spending. Recognizing that the vast majority of healthcare spending is physician directed, incentives to overutilize services needed to be eliminated, at least for Medicare beneficiaries. The earliest attempts in fee reduction for Medicare physician fee schedules caused many physicians to close their practices to new Medicare patients while reduction in hospital reimbursement increased emphasis in cost accounting, utilization review, and quality assurance.

While changes in Medicare, and in many cases Medicaid financing, were occurring, employers and insurance companies were growing concerned with increasing volume of medical claims. The finest healthcare system in the world had created access to higher and higher intensity of care while it still had an open checkbook. Adding to that the expectation of its public to believe that access to and provision of healthcare services was a "right" of U.S. citizens and what followed was a system of increasing use and cost that would be difficult to slow down, much less stop altogether. This fundamental shift in public opinion from healthcare as a privilege to a basic right occurred during the mid- to late 1980s as HMOs and the roles of physician extenders reached broader acceptance. Legislators accepted the condition that the government had a responsibility for the health of its people. Access to health services increased while hospital emergency rooms became busier and busier with the uninsured using them for emergent and nonemergent primary care, a trend that continues in all metropolitan areas. Arguments that millions did not have access to the healthcare system were countered that in reality, these millions of medically indigent had the nation's emergency rooms as their primary care offices, only at extreme expense and without any focus on prevention. One unidentified hospital administrator shared his feelings: "Over the last two years we have had the same individual show up in our ER four times with gunshot wounds—no insurance and each time he required hospitalization for 4 to 6 days. How do you deal with that?"

An answer came from the crowd: "A better shot." It is yet another example of the stresses placed on the nation's trauma centers. The growing use of specialty physicians and the open checkbook mentality directed more types of patient care to specialists, which today are considered vital services for many primary care physicians.

The desire of payors to shift risk to providers began as a subtle turning point when insurance companies began increasing healthcare premiums to employer groups who in turn passed some of the increase on to their employees. The initial backlash spawned the development of preferred provider organizations (PPO) or panels of physicians who, under more restrictive health plans, were the sole providers of care for plan enrollees. Most PPO plans had out-of-network options but it marked the beginning of the restriction of patient choice in favor of controlling employer healthcare expenditures. Employers were not satisfied with the relatively minor cost savings in the face of ever-increasing premiums. Insurance companies continued to control the risk, which is where all the money is in healthcare. Reluctant to give up control, premiums increased and patient utilization of services continued to rise, magnifying employer exposure.

The emergence of employer coalitions seeking to leverage their expenses and the actions of large self-funded employers began the era of direct contracting, initially with hospital inpatient and ancillary services, then with outpatient physician services. The predominant method was a discount off the standard fee schedule with wide variations based on local market issues including volume and overall fee rates. On the hospital side, contracting moved to negotiated per diem rates or per case rates similar to DRG-based reimbursement. On the physician side, discounted fee-for-service remained the method of choice.

Employers continued their demand on healthcare providers as the 1980s brought the concept of total quality management (TQM), which subsequently moved to continuous quality improvement (CQI). Employers began influencing the actual provision of certain healthcare services through strict utilization review and hospital admission precertifications. Employers demanded access to their network or participating physicians so patients would be able to see them as needed and they began insisting on quality improvement and outcomes measurement to document the scope, amount, appropriateness, and quality of treatment. In effect, employers began demanding accountability from physicians and made it clear that they would seek other providers if they were not satisfied. The extent to which the payors exerted control over providers was based largely on the options available in each market.

Fee structure changes in the form of withholds from physician fees became more prevalent in certain types of health plans. Payors exacted more and more from physicians under the fee-for-service system by making them more responsible for patient utilization of services. Abuse in the form of restriction of healthcare services to patients developed as some physicians sought to maximize the revenue potential from payor plans while desperately holding onto what indemnity insurance remained in their practice. Concurrently, capitated physician contracts emerged, which sought to place the physician, generally primary care physicians, at risk for either all healthcare expenses incurred by the enrolled patient or for all of the physician component of care. While these changes spread throughout the United States gradually, certain markets developed more rapidly than others, most notably the major metropolitan areas of Albuquerque, San Diego, Los Angeles, San Francisco, and Minneapolis. It should be noted that the spread of payor payment models is yet underway; many parts of the United States are not yet capitated, although virtually all urban markets have experienced some amount of capitated payments.

REIMBURSEMENT UNDER MANAGED CARE

In a nutshell, managed care is designed to permit greater controls on cost and quality in the delivery of healthcare by requiring healthcare providers to share the financial risk of providing that care. Health maintenance organizations (HMOs) are typically structured to provide all health services to enrollees on a prepaid basis, for a single capitated fee per enrollee per month, usually paid by the enrollees' employers. Enrollees must choose among the physicians on the HMO's panel, and a referral from a primary care "gatekeeper" physician is required for the enrollee to obtain care from specialists. HMOs are at financial risk to provide medical care required in excess of that paid for through premiums.

Variations on this model include the point-of-service (POS) plans offered by HMOs, in which enrollees are permitted to decide at the point of service whether to use physicians outside the panel for which they pay higher copayments. Another variation is the preferred provider organization (PPO), which functions as a broker of discounted health services. Payors contract with a panel of providers, directly or through the PPO, who provide care at discounted rates. Enrollees must choose among the physicians on the panel, but they are not required to obtain referrals for specialty care services. Enrollees may be permitted to obtain care from providers outside the panel, but they must pay higher copayments to do so.

Under managed care arrangements, physicians are compensated on a capitated basis, which may include withhold pools or global fee arrangements. A capitation payment is a fixed monthly fee per enrollee per month that is designed to cover a comprehensive but specific set of health services. If enrollees require more care than is paid for through the monthly premiums, then the physician is at financial risk to provide that care. If the patient requires less care, then the physician can keep the excess. Withhold pools may be included, whereby a portion of the premium is withheld from the physician's salary and set aside to cover referrals to specialists and inpatient hospital care. Depending on the plan, physicians may or may not be at risk for amounts exceeding that covered by the withhold pool. If the withhold pool is not used up, the physicians share the excess. Under a global fee arrangement, physicians agree to cover the entire course of care for certain categories of patients, such as obstetrics patients, in exchange for a flat fee. The physician is again at risk of providing excess care and has an incentive to control costs.

Under managed care, hospitals also may be compensated on a capitated basis, perhaps including withhold pools. The reimbursement methodology under capitation is the same for hospitals as it is for physicians. Hospitals also may be reimbursed on a per diem basis or on a per case basis. Under a per diem system, the hospital is paid a preset rate for each day a patient receives inpatient care. If the hospital is able to control costs well, it can retain the difference between its costs and the per diem rate. On the other hand, the per-case system functions much like the DRG system in which hospitals are reimbursed for a patient's specific course of treatment.

Healthcare providers also may be reimbursed jointly when they are integrated into one provider system, such as a physician hospital organization (PHO). In a PHO, providers may be compensated through global capitation, whereby providers are paid a global fee for rendering all hospital and physician care required by patients, and the PHO assumes the risk of excess care. To contain that risk, the PHO may purchase stop-loss insurance. On the other hand, under a bundled fee arrangement, the hospital may agree to accept a flat fee per case in a specific category, and it assumes the responsibility of compensating the physicians who provide the physician services in that category of care.

Distinctions for Integrated Delivery Systems Under Medicare

Medicare reimbursement to providers may vary depending on the structure of the integrated delivery system and on which entity is providing the reimbursable services. Examples of variances in reimbursement based on the structure of the IDS include the following.

1. Medicare considers new types of entities providing outpatient care, such as cancer centers and diagnostic imaging centers, as providing physicians' services. Thus, the facility cost is considered to be included in the physician's charges. However, if the entity is affiliated with a hospital it may obtain reimbursement under Part B as a hospital outpatient department.

2. Entities that are related by common ownership or control are limited in the manner in which they can account for transactions between themselves, and related organizations must deal with each other at cost for reimbursement purposes under Part A.[9]

3. When the ownership of a provider changes, the new owner's basis in the assets for Part A reimbursement purposes is limited to the lesser of the acquisition cost or the historical cost (the acquisition cost as of July 18, 1984). However, mergers between related parties, stock purchases, and affiliations are not considered to be a change in ownership.

4. The costs of administrative and supervisory services of hospital-based physicians are subject to special rules.[10]

5. The costs of services furnished under contracts with outside suppliers are subject to special rules.[11]

6. Start-up and organization costs and the home-office costs of multientity providers are subject to special rules.[12]

7. Compensation paid to owners is subject to special rules.[13]

8. The prospective payment rate covers all services provided within 72 hours prior to hospital admission and that are admission related if they are provided by a hospital-owned or hospital-affiliated entity.[14]

9. In regard to reimbursement for skilled nursing facilities (SNF), routine service costs are reimbursed on a reasonable cost basis, subject to certain cost limits.[15] Ancillary services also are reimbursed on a reasonable cost basis, but they are not subject to cost limits. However, if services are contracted out through an outside supplier, the SNF is reimbursed on a cost basis that is limited to the net amount actually paid to the supplier. If the SNF charges the outside supplier for billing or other administrative services, that amount must be treated as a discount to the provider and it may not be treated as income by the SNF.[16]

10. For home health services, Medicare reimburses the primary provider even though services are provided by an outside supplier.[17]

11. Reimbursement rules governing hospice services restrict which types of services may be provided by outside suppliers. Usually, "core services," such as nursing services, medical social services, physician services, and counseling services, must be provided by hospice employees.[18]

12. Outpatient surgical procedures are reimbursed depending on where the service is performed. If done at an ambulatory surgical center, the service is reimbursed based on the lesser of the facility's reasonable costs or charges or on a blend of the reasonable cost and the ambulatory surgical center prospective payment rate. If done at a non-ASC site, the service is reimbursed on a reasonable cost basis.

13. Reimbursement to a hospital for durable medical equipment (DME) depends on whether the hospital is a certified DME supplier. If it is

so certified, the hospital is reimbursed based on a fee schedule. If it is not certified, the hospital is paid on a reasonable cost basis.

14. Reimbursement for renal dialysis services likewise varies depending on whether such services are provided within a hospital or at a free-standing provider. Under the Omnibus Reconciliation Act of 1990, the secretary of the Department of Health and Human Services is required to develop a prospective payment system for more hospital outpatient services. In so doing, the secretary will review the feasibility of varying payments based on whether the service is provided in a free-standing facility or in a hospital facility.[19]

In fact, in August of 1996, the Health Care Financing Administration (HCFA) issued a clarification of its reimbursement policy regarding which hospital-affiliated entities qualify as provider-based or free-standing entities.[20] The concern is that facilities are classified as hospital based when they should be classified as freestanding, and they are thus obtaining excess reimbursement. For example, hospitals are purchasing physician clinics located far from the hospital but are claiming them as outpatient departments of the hospital. HCFA's clarification listed eight criteria that must be met before an entity can be classified as provider based.

1. The entity must be physically located close to where the provider is based, and both the entity and the provider must serve the same patient population.
2. The entity must be an integral and subordinate part of the provider where it is based, and it must be under common licensure.
3. The entity must be included under the accreditation of the provider where it is based.
4. The entity must be operated under common ownership and control.
5. The entity director must be under direct, daily supervision of the provider where it is located.
6. The clinical services of the entity and its parent must be integrated.
7. The entity must be held out to the public as part of the provider where it is based.
8. The provider and its parent must be financially integrated.

WHAT MANAGED CARE DOES TO FINANCIAL MODELING

Managed care has created new challenges for all providers in the amounts of reimbursement and the means by which it flows from patients and payors. Hospitals have responded to the changing patterns in healthcare financing and delivery through focusing on the reduction operating expenses. In the early stages of increasing fee discounts, hospitals began seeking discounts from suppliers and expanding product lines beyond hospital services. DME and pharmacy services were the most prevalent diversification strategies to bring nonoperating sources of revenue into the hospital setting. Hospitals solicited their hospital neighbors, national and state hospital associations, and began forming purchasing alliances to maximize economies of scale and share ideas for cost containment and revenue enhancement. Many supply purchasing networks diversified to serve their constituent hospital members in areas like hospital consulting; strategic planning; quality assurance; and hospital equipment lease, purchase, and refurbishment. These alliances such as SunHealth/Premier and Voluntary Hospitals of America moved rapidly into providing or coordinating quality management initiatives like TQM, CQI, clinical pathways, and physician integration/medical staff services demanded by hospital members.

Physician activities have focused on a broad range of strategies secured by differing levels of physician autonomy. Strategies for improving financial and market position within a practice sought to examine costs more closely and more aggressively negotiate with payors and managed care companies. In some markets, provider networks advanced so quickly that some practices found themselves locked out of a substantial amount of their existing patient base. Physician networking activities such as independent practice/physician associations (IPAs), clinics without walls, or PHOs sought to bring negotiating clout while allowing practices to remain independent. Other practices chose to sell outright to hospitals or to affiliate with physician practice management companies (PPMs) in efforts to stabilize income, partner for strength, or capitalize the group.

Most activities presently focus on market-driven strategies, which vary widely based on the penetration and form of managed care contracting in local areas. Since the advent of managed care, payment for healthcare services has been shifting steadily away from the government to patients and employers. Medicare reimbursement cuts continue despite the desire to change the distribution of reimbursement from specialists to primary care physicians. Indemnity insurance coverage is alive and well but nearly nonexistent in certain parts of the country. Medicare risk HMOs and provider-sponsored organizations are developing and collapsing at the same time. Medicaid, while varying state to state, is following a path similar to Medicare although some programs in some states continue to be funded well.

In summary, the following observations should be recalled when approaching financial analysis in the healthcare industry. Change is coming faster and faster than ever before with costs continuing to rise and reimbursement continuing to decrease for most payor sources. Patients and employers are seeking greater levels of accountability from providers and are expecting to negotiate based on price, access, and quality, likely in that order. Anecdotal and empirical information suggest that continued integration of healthcare entities and consolidation of markets result in minimal delivery improvements, and often in increased costs to patients and payors. Patients and payors view these changes as negative and equate them to an overall decrease in functioning of the healthcare system: quality is not improving, access is poorer, physicians are as unhappy as ever, and all of it impacts the patient.

NOTES

1. Death and taxes.
2. "Adding value" is, in my opinion, a term of great vagary. When I think of a value-added service, I immediately think of its worth in *economic value* (i.e., a conversion to earning power). If you cannot ultimately convert a value-added service to earning power, or if one cannot intuitively derive its worth in earnings, one needs to ask whether it adds value in the first place.
3. Excel uses individual worksheets within one file that may have links (cells in other worksheets or other files that are tied together and are updated automatically). Excel and Lotus 1-2-3 each support worksheets, and files are interchangeable between programs with limited exceptions.
4. Hiam, A. (1990). *The Vest-Pocket CEO,* Prentice Hall, Englewood Cliffs, NJ, pp. 30–31.
5. Pratt, S.P. et al. (1995). *Valuing a Business,* 3rd ed. Richard D. Irwin, 155.
6. Green, T., Hayes, M. (1990). *The Belief System.* Beechwood Press: Winston-Salem, N.C.
7. Davidson, W.N. (1998). *Financial Forecasting and Management Decisions.* Professional Development Institute: Denton, TX, 1–3.
8. Cave, D.G. (1994). Analyzing the Content of Physician's Medical Practices. *Journal of Ambulatory Care Management,* 15–36.
9. See Provider Reimbursement Manual § 1004.1 et seq.
10. Provider Reimbursement Manual § 2108.
11. Provider Reimbursement Manual § 2118.
12. Provider Reimbursement Manual § 2150.
13. 42 C.F.R. § 405.426.
14. See 42 C.F.R 412.2; Medicare Intermediary Manual § 3610.3.B.
15. See 42 C.F.R. § 413 et seq.; Provider Reimbursement Manual § 2300 et seq.
16. Provider Reimbursement Manual §§ 2118, 2118.1.
17. See 42 C.F.R. §§ 484.14(f) and (h).
18. See 42 C.F.R. § 418 Subparts D and E.
19. 42 U.S.C.A. § 1320b-5 note (West suppl. 1996).
20. Transmittal No. A-96-7, August, 1996, as reported in HCFA Clarifies, Tightens Rules Regarding Provider-Based Entities, in 5 Health L. Rep. (BNA) No. 33, at 1223 (August 15, 1996).

2 CHAPTER

Intermediate Concepts of Financial Modeling

"It is better to know some of the questions than all of the answers."

James Thurber

DEFINING FINANCIAL AND OPERATIONAL ASSUMPTIONS

All of our efforts will be of little practical benefit without a clear definition of our assumptions. This position cannot be stressed highly enough. Most feasibility studies require the largest amount of time in the development and refinement of the assumptions on which the analysis is based. As discussed in Chapter 1 under the general technique for pro forma development, we begin with developing base income and expense assumptions for our venture. We have already analyzed the historic operations of our business, if existing, or we have begun to collect information from empirical sources, trade associations, or consultants. We have examined the general technique through our review of one of the case studies in this text already. Now let's focus on developing detailed operating and financial assumptions for operation.

Details, Details, Details

As we examined in the previous case study, we saw under Revenue Targets in the executive summary that minimum levels of production were established by using the Medical Group Management Association's (MGMA's) national comparative data for physician productivity as the baseline for operations. The historical internal medicine practice that was in place prior to the planned expansion used

MGMA data to compare with its historical performance. From our review of the Excel file, we saw the growth rates for new providers, call them ramp-up rates, to give us an estimate on when we thought the new providers would be producing at the MGMA median. We saw that 12 months was used to develop a full practice load. Generally speaking, 12 to 18 months tends to be a good ramp-up rate. Less than 12 months should probably not be considered; better to err on the side of conservancy, and greater than an 18 month ramp-up should have a basis in (low) market demand. The key is *reasonableness*. This concept will continue to be stressed throughout this text, not only for the sake of financial prudence, but because many hospital and physician financial arrangements are impacted by a variety of regulatory requirements and laws which frequently dictate the concept of prudent and reasonable business practice.

In the case study, we see the assumption of ancillary and technical revenue at 16% of total professional charges. This amount was based on historical operations of the existing practice, the amount of MGMA survey physicians' ancillary and technical revenue, and anecdotal information. This amount should be driven first by the specialty of the practice being modeled, but also by input from the physicians' individual practice styles. We all know internists who use very little ancillaries in their practices and we all know that some internists generate 25% of their revenue from ancillaries. Business prudence should govern a most-likely scenario. Note also that the ever-increasing government scrutiny on false claims will have a significant effect on the ancillary and technical charges that will be allowable in the future. Prudent business practice would dictate that high estimated revenue from any other source should have compelling support before including it in your feasibility analysis.

Other types of additional revenue could be modeled using the same general principles. As you examine the Assisted Living Facility Feasibility Study, you will see income assumptions for personal services (e.g., barber and beauty shop, snack counter, etc.).

Once revenue assumptions for the base year are created, assumptions for future years should be made. What expansion plans are being considered? What about changes in reimbursement? All of these issues should be explored or at least considered before settling on your final income profile.

Adjustments (contractual adjustments, write-offs, bad debt, charity care, etc.) should be considered and documented. What were our historic adjustments over previous years? What were our gross charges, not just our net collected revenue? Many smaller businesses operating on a cash basis financial reporting do not examine the difference between gross and net. Without a thorough understanding of what is being billed and the real reasons for not collecting the total, it is impossible to improve financial performance. Spend the time to understand how much work (dollars) you are generating on a book or cost basis and the reasons why you are not collecting it (adjustments). Note also that you must use correct comparisons of national data. Know whether you are using gross charges or net collected revenue. If you can find only gross charge national data, you may estimate based on gross collection rate information. For example, the MGMA Physician Compensation and Production Survey lists physician gross charges with technical component and physician extenders excluded or for practices with 1% to 10% of charges or over 10% of charges from technical component. To estimate the MGMA net collected revenue, you must review the Cost Survey collection information under the appropriate specialty. While the data included in each table are not an exact match, a reasonable baseline estimate may be inferred (although some estimates are highly affected by managed care penetration).

Expense assumptions are laid out in a similar manner with the same caveats on national comparative data. Referring back to the Multispecialty PC Start-Up Feasibility Study, key expense assumptions were modeled in tables under assumptions and other general operating assumptions were built directly into the monthly spreadsheets. We will discuss key aspects of expense modeling in the next sections of this chapter. See Exhibit 1–1 for a sample income and expense profile that corresponds directly to MGMA comparative data.

Certificates of Need, Regulatory and Cost Reporting

Analysts should be aware that the preparation of legal documents for regulatory bodies is serious business. Any time you prepare financial statements or projections that are for the purpose of a regulatory filing, the business is making a formal report of its past performance and stating its plans for the future. For taxable entities, the report of historical performance must mirror tax documents, or have a reasonable statement of departure to reconcile both reports. Organizations exempt from taxes have no such burden, though audited financial statements are required.

The projection of business activity for the purpose of a regulatory filing whether that is a certificate of need to change or expand service or other report creates a position statement for the entity on its plans for the future. Regulators will evaluate the plan for financial prudence as well as issues of patient access, geographic coverage, competitor impact, and other factors. Analysts should be aware of the specific requirements of the document they are preparing including the formulas for need justification, service area description and calculation, filing time tables, and other relevant factors. Do not fall into the trap of preparing a filing in error and eliminating your opportunity for a successful filing. Discuss the issues in advance with a representative of the regulatory agency and your business officials in order to position your filing to its greatest advantage.

Capitation Issues for Income Modeling

Income flow from fee-for-service (FFS) contracts varies significantly with income flow from capitation contracts. Analysts should create a mixed income model to account for the different streams. Beginning with historical operations, if applicable, the total income is divided between FFS and capitation. Gross charges and adjustments apply only to the FFS stream. Capitated income is based on a variety of patient panel issues to yield total capitated income. In the absence of historical data the practice should request sanitized actual data from another practice in their service area (if possible) estimating patient panel sizes with monthly capitation payments. Actual usage data also should be requested to estimate, by patient visits, type of visit, relative value units, or other means, the impact of patient volume compared with the FFS population. Capitated income can then be applied below adjustments to sum to total income.

MARKET ANALYSIS AND NEED ESTIMATES

Any financial model should take into account the dynamics and demographics of the geographic area in which the business is planned. The level of detail used in this area should be based on the size ($–$$$$) of the venture planned, the changing nature of the market, and the competition for the service, as general drivers for the analysis. Community demographics might play a key role if the service was geriatric in nature (assisted living, skilled nursing beds, older adult day health services, perimenopausal clinics), market segment in nature (women's health services, pediatric, etc.), or based on the geographic position of the community (suburb of a larger city, retirement, resort/vacation, rural, etc.)

For many analyses, rudimentary analysis or recognition of market issues may suffice. For larger studies that impact broader geographic areas, larger segments of the population, or have more capital at risk, an in-depth analysis should be considered. While the need for understanding the market is not reflected in great detail here, readers should be aware of the source of patients and payors when preparing financial forecasts of any type.

Data sources include local resources, physicians, hospitals, businesspeople, state departments of commerce and other offices, trade associations, Claritas, AMA Physician Characteristics and Distribution in the United States, and other sources.

ADVANCED DESIGN ISSUES

Income Considerations

Advanced design issues in spreadsheets and financial analyses might be an issue of debate, considering that this text has in mind the nonfinancial manager. We saw in Chapter 1 that we prepare financial analyses (profit-loss analyses) on a cash or accrual basis, generally speaking. Let's begin by defining the major difference in presentation. On a cash basis financial model, income is posted as it is collected and expenses are recognized when they are paid. Accounts receivable and accounts payable, balance sheet items, make up the difference in work performed but not yet collected and expenses incurred but not yet paid. Many smaller businesses operating on a cash basis may feel they need to model actual cash in hand in order to account for sufficient working capital. In these models, a model for the flow of accounts receivable is necessary (Exhibit 2–1). The flow or ramp-up of accounts receivable is based on the projections of net income but further adjusted for the rate of payment from different payors. It is possible to segment by payor mix the estimated income and then create payment estimates by payor to create the accounts receivable ramp-up. Actual cash collections come typically in a cycle of three months or more depending on the different payors. A rule of thumb tends to be to look from six to eight months for cash to be flowing equally from accounts receivable. Similarly, if an established business changes its collections agent or otherwise disrupts the normal flow of account collections, use the six- to eight- month estimate to project normal cash income. Attractive accounts receivable turnover rates (days that accounts are outstanding in accounts receivable) range around 40 days, although they are affected significantly by payor mix and contractual arrangements.

Accrual-based statements are arguably faster to prepare although the ultimate cash needs are accounted differently under the cash flow section of the analysis. In accrual-based statements, income is reported when the service has been rendered and expenses are recognized when they are incurred. A general format for accrual-based financial model is found under the Multispecialty PC Start-up Feasibility case study. In this format, charges are posted, reduced by adjustments to yield net revenue. Provider expenses, a subset of general operating expenses, indicate all of the expenses directly related to providing the service and unrelated to the financing of the service. The result indicates total operating expenses. The excess of total revenue over total operating expenses is called the unit's *operating margin* or *contribution margin*, as in the operating unit's contribution to overall entity margin. Noncash, nonoperating charges such as amortization and depreciation are then added to indicate total expenses for the operation. The excess of net revenue over total expenses is called *net income* or *profit*.

A cash flow statement often accompanies (or is attached to the bottom of) accrual-based income statements indicating the sources and uses of cash for the unit. Total sources of cash include the net income from the operation plus depreciation, amortization, and internally financed interest usually as they represent total cash available at the owner's discretion. Total uses of cash include principal reductions on loans, capital expenditures to fund future growth, and funded depreciation. Note that depreciation is often modeled as an expense using allowable limits from the tax code. Such depreciation allowances often allow for depreciation of assets at a rate much faster than the economic working life of the assets. In this case, we see often that depreciation using tax allowances are made for tax reporting but an equipment replacement reserve charge is taken in internal cash flow statements to reflect only the amounts of depreciation necessary to replace

EXHIBIT 2–1

Accounts Receivable Estimate

YEAR 1—Months 1–12   A/R Turnover Rate (Days): 89

	Month 1	Month 2	Month 3	Month 4	Month 5
A/R Beginning of Month	0	20,042	33,755	38,256	40,225
Charges Added	21,097	21,097	22,504	22,504	22,504
Charges Collected	1,055	7,384	18,003	20,535	22,293
A/R End of Month	20,042	33,755	38,256	40,225	40,436
Total Collected Revenue	**1,055**	**7,384**	**18,003**	**20,535**	**22,293**
Total Year One Revenue	**265,309**				

YEAR 2—Months 13–24   A/R Turnover Rate (Days): 77

	Month 13	Month 14	Month 15	Month 16	Month 17
A/R Beginning of Month	64,908	66,142	67,610	66,198	63,697
Charges Added	36,981	38,171	35,783	34,593	38,171
Charges Collected	35,747	36,704	37,195	37,094	35,844
A/R End of Month	66,142	67,610	66,198	63,697	66,024
Total Collected Revenue	**35,747**	**36,704**	**37,195**	**37,094**	**35,844**
Total Year Two Revenue	**503,133**				

YEAR 3—Months 25–36   A/R Turnover Rate (Days): 61

	Month 25	Month 26	Month 27	Month 28	Month 29
A/R Beginning of Month	105,660	101,669	98,338	88,228	81,563
Charges Added	54,045	54,045	44,221	44,221	54,045
Charges Collected	58,037	57,376	54,332	50,886	46,186
A/R End of Month	101,669	98,338	88,228	81,563	89,422
Total Collected Revenue	**58,037**	**57,376**	**54,332**	**50,886**	**46,186**
Total Year Three Revenue	**662,089**				

Month 6	Month 7	Month 8	Month 9	Month 10	Month 11	Month 12
40,436	41,843	44,093	50,563	57,395	60,290	62,417
23,910	25,317	30,942	33,989	33,989	35,451	36,912
22,504	23,066	24,473	27,157	31,095	33,324	34,422
41,843	44,093	50,563	57,395	60,290	62,417	64,908
22,504	**23,066**	**24,473**	**27,157**	**31,095**	**33,324**	**34,422**

Month 18	Month 19	Month 20	Month 21	Month 22	Month 23	Month 24
66,024	70,317	74,610	83,495	90,886	97,022	102,323
40,556	42,940	50,097	52,478	56,053	58,434	59,628
36,263	38,648	41,212	45,087	49,916	53,133	56,291
70,317	74,610	83,495	90,886	97,022	102,323	105,660
36,263	**38,648**	**41,212**	**45,087**	**49,916**	**53,133**	**56,291**

Month 30	Month 31	Month 32	Month 33	Month 34	Month 35	Month 36
89,422	95,317	97,955	105,081	109,260	110,243	110,550
54,045	55,271	61,417	61,417	61,417	61,417	61,417
48,151	52,633	54,290	57,238	60,434	61,109	61,417
95,317	97,955	105,081	109,260	110,243	110,550	110,550
48,151	**52,633**	**54,290**	**57,238**	**60,434**	**61,109**	**61,417**

equipment. The remainder, often 20% to 40% of the depreciated amount, reverts to owner cash flow. The difference between total sources of cash and total uses of cash is the increase or decrease in cash of the operation.

The concept of *economic life* plays a role in this decision. The economic life of a piece of equipment or an office system upgrade is generally related to the time period over which it will produce revenue. Certain types of assets will have a longer economic life than others. For example, the economic life of a set of built-in cabinets in exam rooms may be easily 30 years, whereas the economic life of office carpeting may be only 15 years. For ease of modeling, a general replacement reserve rate of perhaps 50% or so off the depreciated amounts may suffice, though individual circumstances should direct the analyst.

Cash Flow Issues

While this text is not designed to deeply explore financial management, readers should find a review of key issues in business cash flow instructive. In modeling and evaluating the income and cash flow of the business prior to evaluating owner return on investment, the income assumptions play the key role in the reasonableness of the analysis. Specifically, the quality of earnings is what drives the likelihood of growth of the income stream and its tendency to strengthen. In evaluating historical operations and cash flows, watch for one-time events such as improved cash flow from the sale of assets or reduction of investments. These events are nonsustainable and do not relate to the overall economic health trend of the business. The stability of the earnings stream therefore leads one to evaluate the strength of the business. Stable earnings come from increasing business volume and increasing business transactions. These are often discerned through the use of ratio analysis, discussed later in this chapter.

The goal of any improved cash flow operation is to increase the flow of cash coming into the business and to control or time the flow of cash going out in payables. Continually increasing income or accounts turnover by a day at a time will greatly improve operations. For businesses with large amounts of cash on hand, sweep accounts are a useful tool. A sweep account is a short-term investment tool that makes your funds ($100,000 minimum usually) available for investment overnight only, your funds are swept at the close of the business day and restored on the next morning. Interest rates yield about $14 per day at 5% interest. Delaying the payment of receivables requires a balancing act with vendors. Businesses should strive for a balance to avoid alienating suppliers and customers. Some vendors offer a discount for prompt payment of accounts. For businesses with significant purchases, these should be explored. An early payment offer of a 2% discount for payment within 10 days instead of 30 days results in the loss of about 36% annual interest for the vendor on the funds. In general, set up your business to make payments to you as easily and quickly as possible, and negotiate payment terms with time on your side. Let's review the cash flow cycle introduced in Chapter 1.[1]

Cash Inflows Result from
- Equity investments
- Borrowings
- Sale of products or services
- Investment returns

Cash Outflows are Made for
- Purchase of raw materials and inventory
- Purchase of human resources
- Purchase of operating resources
- Purchase of plant capacity
- Payments of principal and interest

Net Positive Cash Flow is
- Reinvested in the business
- Distributed to owners

Cash Reinvested in the Business is Recycled by
- Buying more raw materials and inventory
- Buying more human resources
- Buying more operating resources
- Buying more plant capacity

Generating Additional Net Positive Cash Flow

The check and balance is that net positive cash flow must be at a rate of return that is acceptable for the business risk use of the funds.

The Financial Accounting Standards Board (FASB) Statement 95 requires a Statement of Cash Flows in a complete set of Generally Accepted Accounting Principles (GAAP) basis financial statements. The statements must provide information on the sources and uses of cash for operating, investing and financing. That being said, there is *usually* no set standard requirement for producing basic financial statements and pro forma analyses, however following FASB and GAAP is good practice.

Having established this basic premise for showing financial analyses, let's look at some specific opportunities to create flexible, meaningful financial models.

Template Development and Use

Computer-based spreadsheet models may be used one time to examine a specific issue or may be used for periodic operational and financial reporting. Spreadsheets quickly calculate numbers and can be changed more readily than manual calculations. As discussed previously, certain spreadsheets may be used only one time for brief analysis. Such models pay little attention to formats, headers, lines, and shading. Other analyses will be for more formal presentations and require careful thought in design and layout, both visually and structurally. Some models will be used again and again as the basis for unrelated financial analyses. The author uses two basic models, cash and accrual, for the general reporting of information, each supported by detailed assumptions both in table and text formats.

As you begin to lay out your analysis, begin, shall we say, at the beginning. What are you trying to represent ultimately? Review your goals and objectives for the study. This should guide you in the presentation of the summary report, be it the 10-year pro forma or a one-page summary of the financial analysis. Note that this differs from the executive summary of the analysis, which is a text statement supported by a limited amount of key financial information. Once you have decided what you need to represent, decide on the basis, cash or accrual, which likely is dictated by how the parent organization prepares its statements. Still, it is best to clarify this first.

Once the overall representation format is established, the key assumptions and variables should be listed. For the modeling of opening a new physician office, a listing of key issues, though not all inclusive, to be identified might include the following.

Income Issues

- Provider complement—established or new
  Ramp-up rates for new practice
- Ancillary income
- Adjustments to income

Expense Issues

- Compensation and benefits issues
  Providers
  Staffing complement
- Operating expenses
  Historically based?
  What categories of expenses will differ at this new location?
  Are all expenses captured?
  Provider recruitment and relocation?

- Equipment needs
    Lease or purchase?
- Construction or leasehold improvements
    Construction interest, taxes, site development costs, etc.
- Moving expenses
- Depreciation and other noncash charges
- Capital equipment/capital for growth needed
- Financing arrangements

Template Layout

The key to template layout is in its potential for reuse and adaptation for other uses. As you become more familiar with the uses of spreadsheets, you will find more and more opportunity to use them in the course of daily work. For people who use spreadsheets daily, it is often quicker to build a new spreadsheet from scratch than to adapt an older one, though this depends greatly on the type of analysis to be undertaken. Once you have developed several different styles of spreadsheets and have seen other layouts of financial data, you will begin to gain some favorites and you will find yourself creating and updating your analyses again and again.

Beginning with your intended purpose and audience, put together your spreadsheet based on showing either annual or monthly columns; revenue on top followed by expenses. You might want to total each row category at the end of the year; totaling at the end of 5 or 10 years may or may not be meaningful. You might also consider showing components of revenue as a percentage of total charges or as a percentage of net revenue. Expenses are most commonly represented as a percentage of net revenue, and many data comparisons (e.g., MGMA) may be made from these figures. The ability to track expenses as a percentage of revenue over the years is also a valuable business diagnostic tool. Certain expenses tend to have a direct relationship to income (supply budgets are an excellent example) whereas others might have greater flexibility (staffing is highly flexible, so is telecommunications). In a clean and neat presentation, you should use your design to accommodate such references.

The overall summary or multiyear annual analysis can be easily established and modified. Indeed, many a supervisor or client takes the liberty to request that the analysis or data be represented in a different format based on their personal preference. For the analyst who is new to this field, expect to make these kinds of revisions. For established analysts, once you hit on a good format, it is less likely that different people will want you to change it.

The supporting data and tables behind the summary pages are what make the analysis flexible. The case study spreadsheet files are examples of different styles of spreadsheets for different purposes. Many of these files contain simple formulas and cell links to make changes in the model easily. None of these files are what may be deemed to be the ultimate adaptable spreadsheet because none of the analyses behind them supported that need. The two files that are among the most flexible are the Multispecialty PC Start-Up Feasibility Study and the Assisted Living Feasibility Study. In future iterations of these topics, more refinements will be made. In the case of the assisted living study, a single data entry worksheet that indicates all the significant variables subject to change will be implemented. Consider having only one group of questions to ask and having a 36-page detailed financial model as the output. Your modeling efforts may not ever require this level of flexibility or of reuse. Focus on creating meaningful representations of data and simple formulas, addition, subtraction, multiplication, and division as the basis for your analyses. Building flexibility saves you time in certain circumstances, you just have to guess when the extra effort is worth it up front.

Exhibit 2–2 show another example of a template for evaluating bed day volumes and revenues from skilled nursing and intermediate care beds. The model is very simple with limited inputs. This particular example was cost data from another worksheet for revenue beyond room revenue and operating expense information. Such a model could be created also to examine procedures among different payor classes.

PLANNING START-UP COSTS

Start-up costs of a new venture are best modeled under a separate worksheet as part of the supporting documentation of the analysis. The key issues under start-up costs, depending on what you are modeling include the following.

- Hard assets (furniture, fixtures, and equipment) including leases and deposits
- Initial supplies
- Preopening costs
    Staffing including recruitment and relocation costs
    Rent and other occupancy costs (utilities, telecommunications, insurance, etc.)
    Promotion and marketing
- Interest and principal payments
- Building costs including construction interest and property taxes
- Recruitment
- Any other costs incurred before doors open for business

To model start-up costs accurately, you must capture all expenses that will be incurred prior to opening, and reduce Year 1 operating expenses that are offset by those captured in preopening. Financing assumptions should be estimated in the early stages of the analysis and finalized before the final presentation of the analysis. Similarly, depreciation and equipment replacement reserve should be determined.

To review the process for determining start-up costs, let's review the case study on the Multispecialty PC Start-Up Feasibility Study. Open the Excel file and open the Assumptions worksheet. Cell A127 begins the financing and start-up section. Note the format of capturing costs *that the client requested.* Remember that even if you choose to model costs and categories comprehensively, your client may redesign it based on his or her desires. After looking at the start-up section, look at the cell formulas for the depreciation. These are a bit cumbersome and could certainly be made clearer.

Now open the worksheet named Equipment. Read through the worksheet and notice the sections for depreciation. Note also that smaller medical and office equipment was not depreciated. This is a judgment call. The default is to group each category into depreciation; this client chose not to. The summary at the bottom of the file provides the information to be linked back to the Assumptions worksheet.

Practical advice for equipment planning is as follows.

- Use clinicians and medical equipment specialists to assist you in developing your equipment needs; vendors are particularly helpful.
- Determine the lease-buy decision.
- Determine your depreciation and replacement reserve position.
- Leave some contingency amount for Year 1; use capital equipment budget for Year 2 and beyond.
- Have someone look over your complete equipment and start-up supply list before you complete the analysis.

MODELING THE COST OF CAPITAL

As we discussed in Chapter 1, businesses are supported by a capital structure, which is made up of equity, or the paid-in contributions of its owners and debt, a variety of financial instruments to provide capital for operations. The cost of capital varies greatly as to its origin, either equity or debt. Without getting into great detail in a basic financial text, debt capital is less expensive than equity capital. For most small businesses, the sources of income are either equity in the form of a loan from an owner (stockholder) or a recapitalization of the business with the addition or redistribution of ownership, or debt financing through a business loan or line of credit, most often from a lending institution. For larger entities, different subclasses of capital may be available to support business operations and different options for debt capital exist.

Strictly speaking, the use of money comes at a cost. Businesses that choose to expand do so by reinvesting income (profit) back into the business or by taking

EXHIBIT 2–2

Year One Payor Mix/Utilization Calculation

Patient Days of Service	Total Days of Care Year 1		Net Cash	
	Skilled 10,220	Intermediate 18,250	Charge per Day SC	Charge per Day IC
Private Pay—Private Room	N/A	N/A	—	—
Private Pay—Semi-Private Room	365	3,650	$119.00	$93.00
Commercial Insurance	N/A	N/A	—	—
Medicare—Semi-Private	3,650	N/A	$180.20	—
Medicaid—Private Room	N/A	2,920	—	$97.01
Medicaid—Semi-Private Room	6,205	11,680	$116.02	$87.01
Veterans Affairs	N/A	N/A	—	—
County Assistance	N/A	N/A	—	—
Other (Specify)	N/A	N/A	—	—
				TOTAL:

Intermediate Cash Receipts	Intermediate Care—Days per Quarter				Cash Receipts SC + IC TOTAL
	90 1st Qtr	91 2nd Qtr	92 3rd Qtr	92 4th Qtr	
Private Pay—Private Room	$ —	$ —	$ —	$ —	$ —
Private Pay—Semi-Private Room	$ 83,700	$ 84,630	$ 85,560	$ 85,560	$ 382,868
Commercial Insurance	$ —	$ —	$ —	$ —	$ —
Medicare—Semi-Private	$ —	$ —	$ —	$ —	$ 657,651
Medicaid—Private Room	$ 69,847	$ 70,623	$ 71,399	$ 71,399	$ 283,269
Medicaid—Semi-Private Room	$250,589	$253,373	$256,157	$256,157	$1,736,130
Veterans Admin.	—	—	—	—	—
County Assistance	—	—	—	—	—
Other (Specify)	—	—	—	—	—
	$404,136	$408,626	$413,117	$413,117	$3,059,918

Skilled Care—Days per Quarter			
90	91	92	92
Projected Cash Receipts			
1st Qtr	**2nd Qtr**	**3rd Qtr**	**4th Qtr**
$ —	$ —	$ —	$ —
$ 10,706	$ 10,825	$ 10,944	$ 10,944
$ —	$ —	$ —	$ —
$162,161	$163,962	$165,764	$165,764
$ —	$ —	$ —	$ —
$177,498	$179,470	$181,442	$181,442
—	—	—	—
—	—	—	—
—	—	—	—
$350,364	**$354,257**	**$358,150**	**$358,150**

Year 1 Projected	
Room Revenue	$3,059,918
Medicare Pen Revenue	$ 8,000
Ancillary Revenue	$ 43,064
Bad Debt Recovery	$ 46,239
Total Income	$3,157,221
Total Operating Exp	$3,101,845
Cash Flow	$ 55,377
Profit Margin	$ 1.75%

on business debt. Small business owners do this through reduced personal compensation or through a business loan. In some cases, smaller businesses sell a portion of their equity (a piece of ownership) in order to gain capital for expansion. This type of sale, a dilution of ownership interest, is pursued usually in cases in which business performance has been poor or speculative and debt financing is unavailable or when succession plans or other business reasons of the owner drive them to reduce their equity holdings in the business. The use of funds therefore must come with a cost of debt financing (interest) or in terms of using internal capital reserves, at an internal cost of capital.

Most smaller businesses have available to them business debt financing at a rate of interest no better that the prime rate available to banks and frequently at a rate somewhat greater than prime, typically prime plus 1% or plus $1/2$%. When producing the financing assumptions for financial analyses for smaller businesses, the current prime rate plus 1% tends to be a reasonable number to use. Analysts should confirm this assumption before completing the analysis because of the potential for other issues to affect this assumption.

Larger entities have at their disposal capital reserve accounts from which they internally finance business activity. These entities, through their established financial and operations policies, have certain guidelines for the use of reserve and operating funds. The internal cost of capital for a medium to large hospital may be as low as 4% or 5%; a substantial difference from prime plus 1%, running 8.75% at this writing.

Whatever the cost of capital assumptions determined by the organization, application of this finance cost to financial projections is a key decision point. Some organizations choose not to model a cost of capital at all. This choice creates a somewhat skewed picture from economic reality. An outlay of even $50,000 in cash should include the impact of a conservative investment return (certificates of deposit, treasury bonds, etc.) from the use of funds. Still, it is the client's choice how the analysis should be constructed.

Capital budgeting therefore requires a look at the return on investment that a financial outlay will bring. There are several methods for analyzing return on investment including the internal rate of return and the payback period methods. Among those methods used frequently by small businesses, the payback period is used most often. The payback period measures the time, usually in years, for the activity to create a return on investment. Frequently payback period is used to measure how soon an expense pays for itself. The cost of the activity is divided by the savings, or by the net income stream associated with it. Simply speaking, if the payback period of the asset is greater than the return generated by the asset, the investment is poor. The problem with the payback period method is that it does not consider the time value of money and the impact of cash flows after the payback period. In many aspects of healthcare, investments may be practically necessary or even viewed as a necessary fixed cost of operation. The decision to add new clinical equipment or open a new office will likely involve more detailed analysis of return on investment, even if only to assuage owner's concerns about the expense outlay. Several of the case studies presented in this book include basic return on investment formulas. The reader is referred to a general financial text for a detailed discussion of return on investment.

AMORTIZING ACQUISITION AND START-UP COSTS

To amortize means to put money aside at intervals for the gradual payment of a debt.[2] For our basic purposes, to amortize start-up costs or acquisition costs means to allocate a portion of the total expense over a period of years. When businesses expand or, for example, when a hospital acquires a medical practice, the accompanying cost is applied to the future financial performance of the business to reflect a recouping of the expense. In business valuation we speak of these expenses as part of profiling the debt service of the business postacquisition to ensure that cash flow is sufficient to support the debt and therefore the purchase price. In this section we will address basic issues of how to apply amortized payments in our financial projections.

Typical expenses that are amortized over a period of years often include preopening expenses for a new business and acquisition costs. We do not consider financed capital, whether for working capital or loans, or mortgages or equipment lease/purchase arrangements under the same category as amortized expenses. Generally speaking, think of the major costs incurred to begin the new business or line of business.

The length of time over which to amortize costs can vary greatly, dictated principally by the owner of the firm. Investor time horizons differ by investor and class of asset amortized, usually not exceeding the economic working life of the asset and normally a much shorter period. You will see from the Multispecialty PC Start-Up Feasibility Study that the amortization period for start-up costs was 12 years. This is probably on the far end of the spectrum for most smaller healthcare business projects. The investor is saying that they are in this venture for a reasonably long haul and are willing to spread the start-up costs over this period of time in order to achieve certain business performance targets for the venture.[3] One factor that may determine the amortization period, be it 5 years or 12 years, is the need for net income of the venture. In some cases partnership interests and compensation arrangements are based on a distribution of net income or other allocation of income before net. The existence of income to be distributed can be an integral component to the operation of the business. In these cases, agreement on the amortization period should occur between interested parties.[4]

Survey indications of the profitability of hospital-owned physicians versus medical practices or physician practice management companies (PPMs) is based largely on the reasons and expectations of the physician coming into the network and on accounting conventions.[5] Physician practice management companies routinely amortize intangible assets over 40 years. This certainly assists them in looking more profitable than hospitals that often try to recoup acquisition costs over 3, 5, or 10 years.

Hospitals that attempt to amortize the purchase and other related acquisition costs of a medical practice within the practice's financial statements over a short period of time (less than 7 years) should recognize that operations will likely run at a deficit. If a medical practice or other healthcare business is profitable and acquired at fair market value, the resulting annual cash flow is the maximum amount that may be amortized on an annual basis (see Justification for Purchase Test, p. 110). Insistence on spreading costs in excess of this amount presents an undue burden on the business and skews the operating results. Hospitals, buyers, and governing board members should be aware that it might not be appropriate to allocate 100% of all costs to acquired businesses. Hospitals in the process of building provider networks are keen to allocate network costs to practices, but they frequently create financial reports that make provider incentive opportunities disappear. The network must absorb certain costs and parent organizations must understand that these costs cannot deprive the practices from their true operating performance.

The allocation of costs in financial models then becomes an issue of how long the owner chooses for the allocation period. In many financial models, time periods of 7 to 12 years are used. For smaller businesses planning small scale (less than $100,000 cost) expansions, 4 or 5 years could be used. The main issue is that the owners and stakeholders understand the issue and the options.

RATIO ANALYSIS AND COMPARISON[6]

In assessing the financial performance of any business enterprise, William Cleverly, Ph.D., of the Center for Healthcare Industry Performance Studies (CHIPS), suggests there are four critical questions which must be answered.[7]

- What are the primary criteria by which financial performance is measured?
- What critical factors affect the primary measures of financial performance?
- Which specific measures should be used and how are they defined?
- What peer groups should be used to provide relevant standards for benchmarking operations?

Cleverly states that financial performance, in any dimension, most routinely comes back to return on equity, which in itself is a function of total margin, investment productivity and capital financing. It is never an absolute measure of profit.

Cleverly indicates a composite of micro and macro drivers of financial performance to be considered related to the healthcare industry (Exhibit 2–3).[8] The

E X H I B I T 2–3

Micro and Macro Drivers of Financial Performance

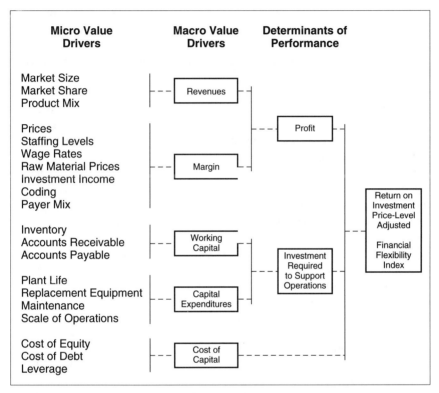

Source: The Center for Healthcare Industry Performance Studies.

primary measure of financial success used in the CHIPS study is return on investment–price-level adjusted (ROIPLA), defined as net income plus depreciation and interest divided by the replacement cost of the firm's total investment. They use also a financial flexibility index, a composite measure of financial performance, which derives from profitability, debt, cash and reserves, and age of plant.

While most analysts will not pursue such a detailed evaluation, the approach should be considered for analyses of strategic importance.

Analysis of financial performance by ratio analysis has become a widely used financial management technique, providing it expresses the proper relationship between factors. For example, the clear and direct relationship between long-term debt and tangible net worth, a capital structure measurement expresses the amount of fixed assets financed through long-term debt, and the relative security to invest in greater debt for growth purposes. Ratios are investigative tools, but watch out for issues such as changes in accounting methods and cost classifications, industry or market trends that render past performance a poor predictor, which may cause improper interpretation. Ratio analysis also can be valuable in evaluating base financial and operating strength. Ratio analysis is most widely used in comparing performance between time periods and to examine trends. It is not used more often than monthly unless you are addressing some specific aspect of operations. Most firms that do ratio analyses perform them annually or quarterly.

MGMA has been including survey results of financial and operating ratios for medical groups in their comparative reports. The reader is advised to examine these data with some reservation because data are reported at book value, (i.e., directly off the balance sheets and income statements of the groups, which we now know contain information that is affected by owner discretionary actions). These discretionary actions (whether to liquidate capital, assume debt, etc.) skew results significantly when attempting to compare businesses with each other. We will see more about discretionary operations in Chapter 3. Suffice to say that ratios are useful tools for those who understand what they truly represent.

Liquidity Ratios

Liquidity refers to the ability of the business to meet its short-term obligations such as accounts payable, payroll expenses, current portion of long-term debt, and federal withholding taxes. The *current ratio* (current assets/current liabilities) is the basic index of financial liquidity. The higher the ratio value, the easier the business is able to meet its obligations. A current ratio of 2:1 is usually considered adequate, meaning that for each $1 of current liabilities there should be $2 in current assets. Limitations are that it is a static tool that measures the present level of current assets and current liabilities; it fails to consider prospective cash flows, positive and negative; and overall liquidity may be misinterpreted because of the mix of greater or lesser liquid assets.

The *quick ratio,* also known as the *acid test ratio* (cash + marketable securities ÷ current liabilities), is the most stringent test of liquidity, recognizing that accounts receivable and inventories, while current assets, are not as liquid as cash. The higher the ratio value, the easier the business is able to meet its obligations. Limitations include that it highlights present balances and ignores prospective cash flows, positive and negative.

Days cash on hand (cash + marketable securities + board designated funds for capital × 365 ÷ total operating expenses less depreciation and amortization).

The *collection period,* also known as *days in accounts receivable* or *accounts receivable turnover* (net accounts receivable ÷ average daily operating revenue), is a measure of the length of time in days that accounts receivable is outstanding. It is a measure of the firm's ability to collect on its sales. A lower number indicates a more rapid turnover, which means improved cash flow. A healthy number for this ratio is in the 40s to low 50s. This ratio should be compared with a similar ratio measuring payment period for patient and nonpatient care accounts receivable. It also is an activity measure.

Coverage (funds flow) ratios directly measure the relationship between cash available to pay debts and the debt payments that are coming in (funds flow). Comparing some measure of income with some measure of the fixed debt charges that must be paid does this. The limitations that arise include the inclusion of non-cash revenue and expense items (long-term credit sales or depreciation charges), unusual or one-time income items, income tax effect where applicable, after-tax cash payments, and preferred stock dividends.

The *times interest earned ratio* (income before tax + interest expense ÷ interest expense) compares income to interest expense. The higher the coverage, the greater the ability to make debt payments. Limitations include that it does not adjust income for any fixed charges except interest.

The *internal funds flow to fixed charges ratio* (funds from operations − fixed charges ÷ fixed charges) overcomes the limitations of the *times interest earned ratio*. Note: This ratio provides the most accurate long-term view of the internally generated cash of the firm available to cover its long-term fixed charge commitments. (Fixed charges include interest and principal on long-term debt and capital lease obligations and required debt sinking funds payments.)

The *long-term debt to total assets ratio* is a measure of the asset protection creditors have in the firm. It provides a measure of how well the firm is able to weather losses without compromising the ability to pay creditors.

Leverage Ratios

Leverage ratios are used to evaluate the capital structure of the firm (i.e., the configuration of liabilities and equity that finance the assets of the business). Leverage ratios may concentrate on a static amount of debt and equity and financial leverage effect (i.e., the effect they have on company profits through financial leverage or on the ability to generate cash to pay debt). With more debt, the firm can increase its total assets, or earning power, without raising equity. This creates profit potential but also the additional risk of having to meet the interest and principal payments, and ultimately, bankruptcy.

The *debt to equity ratio* (total debt ÷ total debt + equity) measures debt as a percentage of total capitalization. Variations of this ratio include long-term debt ÷ total debt + equity and total debt ÷ total equity. A reciprocal relationship (total equity ÷ total debt) with a ratio over 100% indicates that investors have more risk funds at stake in the business than creditors. This ratio also can be interpreted to indicate the amount of assets available as security for creditors. For example, a normal industry ratio of 1:1 (≥100%) indicates that creditors have $2 in assets available as collateral for every $1 of credit loaned to the business (asset values plus equity.) Note: Debt configuration and tax motivation may affect these ratios dramatically.

Activity, Operating, and Profitability Ratios

Activity and operating ratios measure how effectively the company manages various assets under its control. This is achieved by comparing asset accounts with the sales they generate and liability accounts with the purchases that they generate.

Total asset turnover (total revenue ÷ total assets – depreciation) is used to reflect the relative efficiency of the use of assets. The higher the ratio, the higher the level of performance. Note: This is generally the best measure of overall operating performance. Variations of this ratio include fixed asset turnover and current asset turnover. This efficiency measure also should be compared with other measures including occupancy rates, age of plant and design, and payor mix.

Inventory turnover (total operating revenue ÷ inventory) measures a business's investment in inventories. Low values imply overstocking—an excess investment and inappropriate use of assets. Potential costs and risks include financing, insurance, storage, handling costs and damage, and theft and obsolescence risk.

Operating margin (total revenue – total expenses ÷ total revenue) is a measure of profitability (net income ÷ total revenue).

Return on assets (net income + interest expense ÷ total assets) is an overall measure of the ability of the firm to use its assets to generate income. Interest is added back to eliminate the bias due to method of financing the assets.

Return on equity (net income ÷ total stockholder's equity) is a measure of the amount of return gained on the net ownership interest. Note: the difference between the business's return on assets percentage and return on equity percentage is the effect of financial leverage.

The use of ratio analysis can be a helpful tool in evaluating the financial stability of a business. In a recent article on the top 100 performing hospitals, the standards by which they were judged were as follows.[9]

Financial Management

- Expense per adjusted discharge: total operating expenses ÷ the number of discharges, adjusted for case mix and wages
- Cash flow margin: net income + depreciation + interest expense ÷ net patient revenues + total other income
- Asset turnover ratio: net patient revenues ÷ total assets

Operations

- Average length of stay: adjusted for differences in severity of illness at admission

- Proportion of outpatient revenues: compared with total facility revenues
- Index of total facility occupancy: the sum of two measures—total occupancy rate during 1997 and the average of the percentage change in occupancy rate from 1996 to 1997 and from 1995 to 1996

Clinical Practices

- Mortality, risk-adjusted: number of actual deaths ÷ the number expected, given the condition of each patient admitted
- Complications, risk-adjusted: number of actual complications ÷ the number expected, given the condition of each patient admitted
- Average length of stay by diagnosis related group (DRG) and by provider for each DRG: adjusted for differences in severity of illness at admission

Smaller businesses might consider ratio analysis compared to MGMA data, some of which require calculation from other data, Robert Morris Associates' data by standard industry classification code, or other sources. Analysts might consider accessing MGMA's new report, "Performance Practices of Successful Medical Groups." Perhaps the best method is to create financial and operating ratios that seem to make sense for your business. Find the best industry benchmarks you can find, then monitor your own progress periodically toward your own goals. As with ratio analysis, comparison with annual and seasonal patterns will help you understand better how your business operates.

RETURN ON INVESTMENT

As we have come to understand in the preceding pages, the operation of a business or the decision to move in one direction or another is based on a return on investment. The return, what the owner receives, is usually in monetary terms, though nonmonetary benefits are often considered. The return on investment is based first within the context of how the owner chooses to operate his or her business and what discretionary decisions are made on operations. Financial decisions are rarely made in a vacuum, though fortunately for the analyst, straightforward analysis will usually suffice.

As we discussed above under cost of capital and ratio analysis, return on investment is a function of the benefits that flow to the owner as the result of investment decisions. Investment decision may be in the form of purchasing equipment, adding a new provider or service offering, or opening a new office. The investment is the total cost associated with the project including a reasonable return on the use of the funds. The reasonable return on the use of the funds is related to the fact that if cash were used to purchase equipment, the cash would have otherwise been available to the owner for profitable use, whether as owner compensation or as an investment. Therefore, the interest gained on the funds used is part of the formula for determining whether a specific investment is favorable or not.

Investment decisions are based on either short-term or long-term goals. The decision to replace existing equipment, add new equipment, add staff, automate manual functions, or other actions should be evaluated in terms of cost, investment alternative, and return on investment. As a practical matter, many business decisions for the small business owner are a reality and not a theoretical or even a serious piece of business analysis. If the chemistry analyzer breaks beyond repair, a new one is needed or outsourcing is required. How much is the new analyzer? How do the lease-purchase terms compare with outright purchase or with bank financing rates? If we outsource, what is the impact on our practice from a delivery-of-service perspective and what personnel and other costs are saved? What income do we generate from outsourcing? Does the entire outsourcing versus continuing in-house leave us better or worse off financially, and how does it affect our practice? This is the line of thinking for smaller practical challenges in the healthcare industry. The general approach is really the same for larger issues, only the interplay between activities is greater. More individuals and departments are involved, each impacted by the decisions made by operating departments individually.

Return on investment also has basis in the time value of money. Strictly speaking, the value of $1 today is greater than the value of $1 in the future. Not only are the allegorical issues of "a bird in the hand being worth two in the bush" relevant, but the overall impact of risk and return and inflation are at play. The reader is referred to Chapter 3 for a more detailed discussion of the time value of money. Readers also should be aware that the timing of cash flows affects return on investment. Income that comes to the firm in steady or monthly amounts provides a different perspective on return on investment than income that is highly varied.

Investors therefore must plan through the use of financial projections or a pro forma analysis to estimate the annual profit after all expenses and determine whether that amount, the return on their investment, is sufficient to support the planned venture. Readers will build their understanding of this concept through readings also in Chapter 3 and a review of many of the Case Studies, particularly the formulas in the accompanying spreadsheets.

ADDING PROVIDERS, OVERHEAD, AND OTHER MAJOR CHANGES

Analysts should remember that major changes in the delivery of clinical services must be a cooperative decision between clinical and administrative personnel. Administrative staff may recommend changes based on observations and application of comparative data (benchmarking); however, the final arbiter is the soundness in its clinical application. As Paul A. Sommers, Ph.D., indicates, "The essence of teamwork between administrators and physicians lies in understanding what collective outcomes are desired and in agreeing on definitions of the main targets. Once goals are set, at the level of the board and for/by the whole organization, individual style and technique will follow."[10]

Having now become aware of the key issues in preparing financial projections and analyses, it is time to turn toward modifying baseline financial models. Approved and conceptually sound financial models can be adapted for a variety of future operating scenarios once the baseline financial model is created. The model has been built to accommodate changes in different categories of income and expense assumptions, financing and amortizing, depreciation, capital expenses, equipment purchases, leases, and start-up costs. At this point, the analyst can develop more detailed input tables within the file or expand the original.

If multiple scenarios are necessary, a simple copy of the file under a new name allows the analyst to change certain aspects of the analysis for comparison with another set of assumptions. Be aware to avoid the desire to run too many comparisons lest you become confused. Even in simple financial models, such as are presented in this book, the sheer volume of numbers can make the most proficient analyst dizzy. The best route is to begin with the basic analysis and discuss the issues with the business stakeholders. Then begin to make changes and comparisons judiciously.

Capacity Issues

Adding providers or contracts depends on understanding the capacity for business volume that a business can sustain. *Capacity analysis*, a general business term, is the means for determining the benchmark activity of a business or work unit. In the healthcare industry, capacity often deals with revenue per work unit (e.g., patient visit) or physical unit (e.g., bed) or per staffing unit (e.g., physician or other staff). We measure capacity by our actual historical production as well as by comparative data. In this book, we often use the example of medical practices although the concept relates to any business or subunit.

Capacity analysis might look at revenue or visits per physician and benchmark against MGMA or AMA physician productivity data as one element. The capacity analysis profiles individual physicians with benchmark productivity in dollars and visits. Exhibit 2–4 indicates a capacity analysis for three gastroenterologists using gross productivity data. The three physicians' actual productivity is compared against comparative survey data for the mean and 75th percentile. The comparison suggests that when considering average productivity, the amount of charges generated by these three physicians equate to only 1.43 full time equivalent physicians.

EXHIBIT 2–4

Capacity Analysis

| | | | | *XYZ Gastroenterology* |
Physician	1998 Production	XYZ Average	Survey Mean	Production Mean
A	365,026			54.5%
B	353,551			52.8%
C	242,100			36.2%
Total	960,677	320,226	669,597	47.8%

Source: Theresa Raczak, MedComp.

Individual practice issues also may need to be considered. Analysts should perform the second phase of the capacity analysis by substituting patient encounters for charges. Depending on the specialty, encounters may be broken down by evaluation and management visits, procedures, hospital visits, and so on, in order to examine the actual practice issues and make reasonable comparisons with survey data. As a guideline, Exhibit 2–5 indicates a physician-need profile per 1,000 population. Readers should recognize that these amounts vary considerably based on managed care penetration and market trends. Information for most purposes can be gained from performing capacity analysis with survey data and collecting information from specialty trade groups. For more detailed analysis of performance and analysis of large dollar contracts, actuarial assistance may be required.

Capacity analysis may be done at two levels for providers with prepaid income from HMOs or capitated plans. Simply segregate the productivity percentages for fee for service and prepaid activity and make comparisons. Additional information on this technique is discussed in Chapter 4.

In performing capacity analysis when considering overhead expenses, remember to capture all relevant costs, particularly when using comparative data as the benchmark. Transcription costs, for example, are considered staffing expenses by MGMA but may not be staffing expenses for a medical group that outsources its transcription. Be aware also that certain specialized duties, such as transcription, may have highly variable benchmarks. Individual employee compensation levels should be considered in benchmarking costs. Smaller businesses fall into the trap of excessively high compensation for lower level staff as a result of years

Clinic Production, 1998			
Physician Capacity	Survey 75th	Production 75th	Physician Capacity
		45.6%	
		44.1%	
		30.2%	
1.43	801,079	40.0%	1.2

of service. It is not unusual for medical practices to have receptionists performing only receptionist-level duties earning $12 to $14 per hour. While there may be no easy answers to some of these issues, smaller businesses should be aware of the impact of these decisions.

TAX ISSUES

This book would be remiss not to address issues of taxes on the profiling of financial models of business activity. We will not address actual tax issues as it is beyond the scope of this book and varies greatly with organization structure. Suffice to say that taxable entities should discuss tax ramifications and financial model representation with a competent tax consultant, typically the corporation's accountant. Organizations exempt from income taxes should have a tax consultant or individual knowledgeable in this area review any aspects of business that may have untoward tax consequences in the areas of taxable lines of business, gains and losses, unrelated business income tax, and other issues.

CAPITAL FOR GROWTH

Accessing capital for growth is one of the main challenges for smaller businesses. Medical groups have turned to PPMs in greater numbers over the years to fuel this need. The recent crash of several high-profile PPMs and the resulting physician lawsuits has dampened the PPM firestorm.

E X H I B I T   2–5

Average Physician Need per 1,000 Population

Specialty	Ratio
Primary Care	
Family Practice	0.26
Pediatrics	0.12
Internal Medicine	<u>0.16</u>
Subtotal	0.54
Medical Specialties	
Allergy	0.02
Cardiology	0.03
Dermatology	0.03
Endocrinology	0.02
Gastroenterology	0.02
Hematology/Oncology	0.01
Infectious Disease	0.01
Nephrology	0.01
Neurology	0.01
Psychiatry	0.06
Pulmonology	0.01
Rheumatology	<u>0.01</u>
Subtotal	0.22
Surgical Specialties	
Cardiothoracic Surgery	0.01
ENT	0.04
Neurosurgery	0.01
OB/Gyn	0.13
Ophthalmology	0.03
Orthopedics	0.05
Surgery	0.08
Urology	<u>0.03</u>
Subtotal	0.37
Hospital-Based Specialties	
Anesthesiology	0.06
Emergency	0.04
Pathology	0.04
Radiology	<u>0.06</u>
Subtotal	0.20
Other (Plastic Surgery)	0.01
Total	**1.35**

Source: Theresa Raczak, MedComp.

It is without question that physician autonomy and direct control is reduced when parties outside the firm hold an equity stake or when physicians sell their practices entirely and become employees. On one end of the spectrum, simple debt financing through business loans are employed by many small businesses with personal guarantees signed by the business owners, sometimes with personal property as collateral. Further along the debt-equity continuum, other debt or equity arrangements begin to place greater restrictions on the business. A restrictive agreement might infuse some capital in the form of a right of first refusal to acquire the business, an option to purchase, or in some markets, more defined network participation agreements. These various restrictive agreements have some opportunity for providing necessary capital and may not be unattractive options for some businesses. Outright sale of a minority interest or the sale of certain assets (frequently hard assets only) with a hospital or PPM may provide greater capital but with some very hard operating realities. Partnering with a PPM or other entity to provide management services integrates your business within another's. The loss of control over certain aspects of business decisions and operations is immediate. The complete sale of all tangible and intangible assets accompanied by an employment agreement and restrictive covenants (e.g., not to compete) completes the continuum of integration and autonomy.

Businesses should begin to lay out their plans and opportunities for growth and estimate the cost of such actions. In some cases, simple debt financing may suffice; in other cases, survival may dictate that more drastic measures be taken. Groups should engage appropriate business counsel to discuss and advise them on these issues if unfamiliar. Beyond debt financing, a joint venture arrangement with a capital partner would likely provide capital at the next lowest cost. Further movement along the autonomy-capital continuum may be the only route for some groups in some markets.

Larger entities have greater avenues for capital through reserves if the project is small or public markets for larger ventures. Like smaller entities, public financing brings with it purse strings that must be tolerated, chiefly in the form of restrictions on uses of funds and on future debt obligations. Furthermore, some forms of public financing, bonds for instance, have interest rates dictated by organization financial performance, which may create other issues in the future. From the perspective of this text, choice of capital sources should be balanced based on larger institutional goals and other desired uses of finds.

SETTING AND ATTAINING INTERNAL TARGETS

Performance Improvement

Analysts can begin to develop a sense of operations through the research into historical performance and industry standards. The initial setting of internal targets of financial and operational performance, as discussed previously under ratio analysis, should be the result of applying industry best practices to your local operating conditions. Individual businessowner desires or perquisites may create a less than optimal operation in some aspects. It is up to the analyst to understand all of the inputs, and the issues they represent, to the financial model in order to identify areas for improvement.

Improvement does not come all at once, usually. It is gradual and it is the result of paying attention to detail. It has been said that luck is what happens when preparation meets opportunity. Try for that kind of luck. Once the analyst understands the relationships behind the numbers, the industry target performance, and the desires of the business owners, performance improvement becomes an issue for management. Rick Majzun of the Henry Ford Medical Centers suggests a three-step process to clinic improvement. To return Henry Ford's clinics to profitability, step one indicates that employee and physician satisfaction lead to patient satisfaction. Step two says that once patient satisfaction is achieved, a growth in revenues occurs and combined with step three, changes in cost structure management, growth in income results.[11]

Performance improvement is only partially related to knowing what you need to attain; it is also knowing how you need to get there. Some of the structure and process is technically oriented from a business or clinical perspective and some, perhaps the most crucial part, involves interpersonal communication and employee motivation. Work toward a clear identification of the issues that you believe will lead to improved performance. After you have a list of issues to address, identify the individuals impacted by these issues, the stakeholders, the persons who have the capacity to influence them. The key to setting and attaining internal targets is the cumulative effort of all stakeholders in the process. Seek first to understand the perspective of these people. Take just a few minutes to consider this point. If you can understand how your requests impact them then you can be prepared to address their concerns as they arise. No guarantees; no one is saying that everything is possible. Many issues will have conflicting positions and may not be in the best interests of some individuals. Management should make decisions based on the greater good for the organization, which may be the greater good for the owner. Work logically and patiently and you will succeed. **Above all, know your numbers and be able to defend them.**

Operating Scenarios

By this point, analysts have likely started their project and may be nearing completion. One key aspect in pro forma analyses is in settling on the most likely scenario for your operations. One technique is to rigorously plan your analysis to include the most likely scenario for your project. Another favored technique is to create different scenarios with varying assumptions for operations and financing in order to consider their impact.

From a mechanical point of view, once the primary financial model is created, you can modify assumptions and let the computer do the rest. If you haven't built a friendly spreadsheet, it may take more time. Analysts should be as careful in making changes in a financial model as in the initial creation of the model for fear of missing a change in the spreadsheet itself. The more complex the spreadsheet is, the more opportunity to miss how the cells relate to one another. This is a matter of experience and caution. It is very easy to miss changing information in a cell and be completely unaware. Complex financial models must be double-checked constantly when revisions are made. The safest way is, of course, to build your model with one worksheet for data input, or create discrete areas where data are input. Paste-link all other cells for calculation to these input cells. By this method, you eliminate any error in source data. You must, of course, create the correct formula relationships with the data.

C. Ralph MacNulty is credited with developing the Shell Scenario Forecasting approach to examine strategic planning and financial decisions. The scenario analysis section is of particular interest in how it profiles outcomes. The model, in summary is as follows.[12]

- *Collect historical information.* Quantitative forecasts should be based on historical data extending at least as far in the past as it does in the future.
- *Identify organizational objectives.* Technical objectives and goals provide a context for scenario development. Scenario building is a frustrating process without clear objectives to keep it focused.
- *Select key variables.* What variables affect the organization's pursuit of its objectives?
- *Evaluate variables.* How do these variables affect the organization' performance? How might these variables interact? Keep variables focused on what objectives are important to your organization.
- *Select scenarios.* Analysts should develop the following scenarios:

    Surprise-free scenario based on current trends continuing.

    Two extreme scenarios representing the most extreme deviations from the surprise-free scenario in either direction. These should be based on reasonable assumptions from variable evaluation.

    More moderate assumptions. While the two extreme scenarios are fairly unlikely, events are likely to deviate from the surprise-free scenario and toward one of the extremes over time.
- *MacNulty's Matrix Analysis.* MacNulty suggested a complex formal procedure for generating scenarios using the following scale: high increase, medium increase, low increase, no change, low decrease, medium decrease, and high decrease. The answers are compared and any significant differences are worked out in discussion. The method produces a wealth of information about the specific impact of variables, though most applications of variable development are more rudimentary.

- *Study the implications of each scenario.* Each scenario suggests possible outcomes from the venture and provides insight into how the organization might best tolerate impact under each scenario. Market strategies can then be modified to make the organization less vulnerable to a scenario.

Once you have created the ability to make changes in assumptions, you can simply save the entire file under a new name indicating the changes in assumptions. For example, one file might be called "New office start-up internal financing model" and another might be called "New office start-up full financing model." You can indicate in the body of the spreadsheets the changes made by using the comment feature to insert in each cell affected. You could also type text next to the area affected, but outside the print zone, highlighted to get your attention.

Your spreadsheet's data should be linked to an executive summary table area displaying the results of the analysis for your report. You could link the data directly to a word processing file if you like, though linked files easily lose their relationships if you change storage locations or names. It is best to keep data linked only within the same file as this facilitates the easiest re-use of the financial model for other purposes. Once you are satisfied with your scenario analysis, create a summary table of operating scenarios, which you can support with executive summary text assumptions (Exhibit 2–6). This table, and the analysis in its entirety, creates the supportable opinion for the work.

Decision Tree Analysis[13]

Decision trees are used to identify the options and potential outcomes of a decision or series of related decisions. The models may be simple or complex, using probabilities or higher level mathematical tools for evaluation. Broadly speaking, the decision tree assigns probabilities to events and calculates the likely returns from alternative decisions. Analysts begin with identifying decision alternatives and alternative situations. These alternatives are diagrammed on a decision tree, and possible financial returns or costs are calculated and assigned. The payoffs are totaled and evaluated for each combination of decisions. A further step includes the assignment of probabilities to each combination of decisions. Figures 2–1 and 2–2 show sample decision trees.

THE IMPORTANCE OF EMBRACING QUALITY IN OPERATIONS

Quality is a quantitative fact. Take, for example, a judicial proceeding: the judge, as the tryer of fact, ultimately makes a determination of the facts of the matter. Experts discuss their presentation and interpretation of the issues with the result being the court's opinion of the facts of the matter. Quality, therefore, should rightly be considered a noun first. In examining the existence and economic value

FIGURE 2–1

Decision Tree

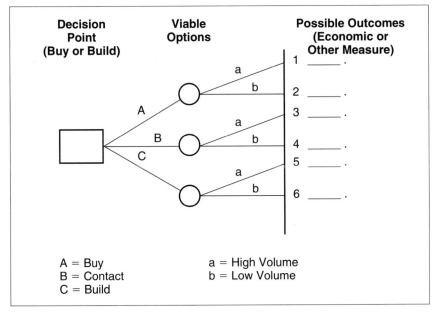

Source: Adapted from Alexander Hiam.

FIGURE 2–2

Decision Tree Adapted to Healthcare Model

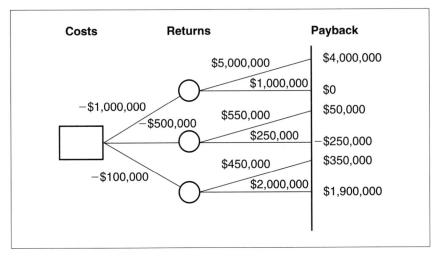

Source: Adapted from Alexander Hiam.

E X H I B I T   2–6

Lakeway Internal Medicine Financial Summary
Operating Scenarios

Scenario	Total Net Revenue (Years 1-4)	Provider Expenses (Years 1-4)	Operating Expenses (Years 1-4)	
1. Status Quo	625,000	394,800	255,470	
	646,875	395,160	266,529	
	669,516	395,542	278,139	
	693,949	395,946	290,326	
2. Adding PA/NP	675,000	445,800	267,470	
	721,875	452,254	277,554	
	794,516	458,528	289,715	
	867,949	447,359	322,481	
3. Locum Tenens/ Physician Recruitment	581,665	446,625	257,470	
	675,938	372,420	268,629	
	734,758	398,912	280,344	
	760,474	399,519	292,642	
4. Increasing Physician Productivity and Adding PA/NP	750,000	445,800	274,970	
	875,000	452,254	296,804	
	935,000	458,528	311,128	
	1,013,350	447,359	325,185	
5. **Most Likely**— Increasing Physician Productivity, Recruiting, and Adding PA/NP	708,750	467,800	281,970	
	827,500	428,794	294,548	
	944,000	461,136	307,888	
	1,022,665	464,284	321,684	

ªCumulative Discretionary Funds includes Depreciation and Amortization.
Cumulative Depreciation over Years 1–4 = 7,321, 14,642, 21,963, and 29,284.
Cumulative Amortization over Years 1–4 = 25,278, 50,556, 75,834, and 101,112.

Cumulative Cash Flow (−)	Provider Bonus Dollars Paid (Years 1-4)	Cumulative Repayment/ Discretionary Funds[a]
(57,869)	24,000	32,599
(105,281)	24,000	65,198
(142,045)	24,000	97,797
(167,968)	24,000	130,396
(70,869)	24,000	32,599
(111,400)	27,328	65,198
(97,727)	27,680	97,797
(12,214)	27,827	130,396
(155,029)	12,000	32,599
(152,739)	22,400	65,198
(129,836)	24,000	97,797
(94,121)	24,000	130,396
(3,369)	24,000	32,599
89,975	27,328	65,198
132,745	27,680	97,797
208,207	27,827	130,396
(73,618)	24,000	32,599
(2,058)	25,728	65,198
140,320	27,680	97,797
204,099	27,827	130,396

of quality, worldwide authority on the value of business assets, Shannon Pratt, provides the description of an intangible asset.[14]

What *economic* phenomena are necessary for an intangible asset?

1. It must be subject to specific identification and recognizable description.
2. It must be subject to legal existence and protection.
3. It must be subject to the right of private ownership, and this private ownership must be legally transferable.
4. There must be some tangible evidence or manifestation of the existence of the intangible asset (e.g., a contract or a license or a registration document).
5. It must have been created or have come into existence at an identifiable time or as the result of an identifiable event.
6. It must be subject to being destroyed or to a termination of existence at an identifiable time or as the result of an identifiable event.

As the result of these requirements, we see that quality, in and of itself, does not fit the definition of an intangible asset completely. But as we look further, with the mind of the financial analyst, we see that quality manifests itself in earnings (a traditional concept in business goodwill, discussed more fully in Chapter 3) for the profitable business.

The next question we ask is what economic phenomena are manifest or are indicative of value in an intangible asset?[15]

1. It must generate some measurable amount of economic benefit to its owner. This economic benefit could be in the form of an income increment or of a cost decrement.
2. This economic benefit may be measured in any of several ways, including net income or net operating income or net cash flow, etc.
3. It must enhance the value of other assets with which it is associated. The other assets may include tangible personal property and tangible real estate.

Having now muddied the waters with an alleged link between quality and economics, the reader should recognize that in describing a "quality" program or service, one should be able to defend such a claim relating the economic impact or how it relates to other aspects of business to enhance the economic position of the firm.[16] The IRS claims that a business's value is a matter of fact, indicating by inference that different opinions on a business's value are patently incorrect.[17]

Quality then, as an economic phenomenon, is a range concept. It spans from low quality to high quality, although it is not an independent variable. An "average" quality physician practice (one with no special or distinguishing features, location, or ambiance) might earn either above average or below average earnings depending on market conditions that may be wholly unrelated to quality. They may again be related directly to quality. From the analytical perspective, these variables could likely be adjusted to determine whether the level of actual quality is related to business success or not, although the scope and cost of such a study might well be astronomical. Quality of healthcare services, as most readers know, is very difficult for patients to discern. Rightly or not, quality is perceived most often in terms of the patient's perception of satisfaction of the clinical visit. Quality perception continues to suggest that it is based more on the quality of marketing than of actual care delivery. Patients gravitate toward lower price health plans. This has been well established in the literature and is best defended by the proliferation of point-of-service health plans. In point-of-service plans, patients choose the copayment option each time they seek care, from the low copay primary care physician visit to the highest out-of-network visit. Actuarial data show that patients will return to the network for routine care and comprehensive care, opting out of network usually for second opinions only. This supports the perception that superb quality itself may not be a factor; average quality is fine for most people.

All this talk about quality and economics drives to one point. Being in business is challenging enough that we must remain cognizant of how we serve our markets. Quality management suggests that managers monitor their operations assiduously in order to capture opportunities for improvement, which lead to better market position and better operational and financial performance. For larger organizations, the embracing of quality improvement began years ago; for many smaller businesses, it is either subconscious or nonexistent.

The following outline from the work of Wendy Leebov, Ed.D., summarizes the process of continuous quality improvement.

What Is Involved in a Continuous Quality Improvement Strategy?[18]

- Leadership commitment
- Management for quality
- Process improvement and problem-solving strategies with an emphasis on prevention
- Identification of customer requirements
- Measurement and feedback
- Accountability
- Employee involvement and empowerment
- Staff development and training
- Recognition and incentives
- Communication and teamwork
- Resources allocated to quality

Organizations should be attuned to their actions in improving operations to enhance quality; however, organizations do need to begin the process from the bottom up. Quality operations must be embraced by all employees for a program to be successful. The following outline provides such a single-employee focus on continuous quality improvement.

How Can One Person Improve Quality?[19]

- Role 1: Do it right the first time
- Role 2: Listen to your customers and aim to meet their expectations
- Role 3: Treat your coworkers and other departments as customers
- Role 4: Confront poor quality when you see it
- Role 5: Stretch, don't settle
- Role 6: Seize opportunities to get involved
- Role 7: Look for solutions
- Role 8: Appreciate quality when you see it
- Role 9: Pursue continuous improvement in yourself
- Role 10: Become a quality associate

SOURCES OF DATA

The following sources are among the most frequently used in the analysis and preparation of healthcare financial feasibility studies. The items followed by asterisks (*) are the author's personal favorites.

- American Medical Association (Socioeconomic Characteristics of Medical Practices,* Physician Characteristics and Distribution in the U.S.)
- Medical Group Management Association (Physician Compensation and Production Survey* and Cost Survey*)
- Practice Management Information Corporation (PMIC) (Physician Fees,* Coding,* and Reimbursement Education materials)
- St. Anthony's Publishing (Coding and Reimbursement Education materials)
- Dun & Bradstreet (D&B MarketPlace,* Dun's Review and Key Business Ratios*)
- Robert Morris Associates (Annual Statement Studies,* Almanac of Industrial Financial Ratios, Industry Norms, and Key Business Ratios)
- Standard & Poor's (Industry Surveys and Industry Reports)
- Claritas Older Adult Survey*

- U.S. Census Bureau (Census of Retail Trade, annual volume of the Statistical Abstract of the United States)
- U.S. Federal Reserve*
- Securities and Exchange Commission (Electronic Data Gathering, Analysis, and Retrieval* [EDGAR] system—10-K reports)
- The Wall Street Journal Interactive Edition (http://wsj.com)
- Dow Jones News Retrieval Publications Library

For valuation-related information, the following are excellent sources.

- *Basic Business Appraisals and How to Price a Business,* Raymond C. Miles
- Continuing Professional Education Technical Instruction Program Textbook, U.S. Internal Revenue Service, 1994, 1995, 1996
- *Integrated Community Healthcare,* Christopher J. Evans, et al
- *Mergerstat Review,* Houlihan Lokey Howard & Zukin
- Physician Compensation and Production Survey, Cost Survey, Medical Group Management Association
- *Socioeconomic Characteristics of Medical Practice,* American Medical Association
- Stocks, Bonds, Bills, and Inflation, Ibbotson and Associates
- The Institute of Business Appraisers Market Data File
- Internal Revenue Service Revenue Rulings 59-60 and 68-609 primarily
- *Valuing a Business: The Analysis and Appraisal of Closely-Held Companies,* Shannon P. Pratt, et al.
- *Valuing Small Businesses and Professional Practices,* Shannon P. Pratt, et al.
- Business Valuation Update
- Valuation—American Society of Appraisers

NOTES

1. *Cash Flow Analysis for Internal and External Decision Making.* New Jersey: Loscalzo Associates Publishing Corp., 1977, pp. 3-14.
2. *Webster's New World Dictionary of the American Language.* New York: Warner Books, 1984, p. 20.
3. Over the last 5 years or so, most smaller business investor horizons tend to be approximately 20 years. This figure should reflect an individual investor's time horizon, not, for example, a hospital or medical practice's time horizon.

4. Be aware that interested parties may not actually have input into the amortization period; a senior partner or owner may choose a shorter period to inflate the amount charged and reduce the income available for distribution.

5. Cleverly, W.O. (1997). Factors Affecting the Valuation of Physician Practices, *Healthcare Financial Management,* Vol. 51, No. 12, pp. 71-73.

6. Comments derived from *The Financial Management of Hospitals* (7th ed.), Howard J. Berman, et al. (Eds.). Chicago: Hospital Administration Press, pp 687-695; "Strategic Operating Indicators Point to Equity Growth," by William O. Cleverly, *Healthcare Financial Management,* July 1988, pp. 54–64; and "How to Read Your Company's Financial Report," by Frank C. Evans, *Management Solutions,* Chicago: American Management Association, 1986.

7. Cleverly, W.O. (1998). The 1998-1999 Almanac of Hospital Financial and Operating Indicators, The Center for Healthcare Industry Performance Studies, Columbus, Ohio, 1998, p. 5.

8. Ibid., 7.

9. Morrisey, J. (1998). All Benchmarked Out. *Modern Healthcare*, December 7, p. 39.

10. Sommers, P. (1998). *Medical Group Management in Turbulent Times*, Binghampton, New York: The Hawthorne Press, p. 126.

11. Majzun, R. (1998). *Three Steps to Clinical Process Improvement.* Presented at the Americal College of Healthcare Executives 1998 Congress on Healthcare Management, March 11, 1998.

12. Hiam, A. (1990). *The Vest-Pocket CEO,* Englewood Cliffs, NJ: Prentice Hall, pp. 284-290.

13. Hiam, A. (1990). *The Vest-Pocket CEO,* Englewood Cliffs, NJ: Prentice Hall, pp. 438-441.

14. Pratt, S.P. (1994). *Valuing a Business.* Chicago: Irwin, pp. 536-537.

15. Ibid., 537.

16. My wife suggests that our son's nanny enhances the quality of his upbringing although such an example does not lend itself well to estimating the economic impact of nanny-ing on later life.

17. U.S. Internal Revenue Service, IRS Appellate Conferee Valuation Training.

18. Leebov, W. (1991). *The Quality Quest.* Chicago: American Hospital Publishing, pp. 8-11. (Analysts are strongly urged to read this publication for an excellent, succinct presentation of this topic.)

19. Leebov, W. (1990). *The Quality Quest.* Chicago: American Hospital Publishing, pp. 32-36.

P A R T **TWO**

SPECIFIC INDUSTRY
CONSIDERATIONS

3

CHAPTER

Business Valuation

"If making money is a slow process, losing it is quickly done."

Ihara Saikaku

Integrated systems of healthcare derive value through the many functions performed within the system and from their existence in the community as a whole. If one accepts the role of the healthcare provider as serving the health-related needs of the community, then any definition of value must include measures of social and community health as well as the economic health of the integrated system. This chapter delves into financial modeling in a specialized manner, the realm of the business appraiser. Readers may find the discussion interesting but may also find the modeling more advanced. Economic measures are discussed a bit more deeply than simply an overview; however, a substantial body of knowledge has been published on the subject of business valuation in general, and as pertains to healthcare in specific.

THE DIFFERENCE BETWEEN VALUATION INCOME PROJECTIONS AND ACTUAL OPERATION

When income projections are prepared for the purpose of valuation, certain assumptions are made that may not necessarily be true in the actual operations of the business. This is due primarily to the process and technique of business valuation. Under the valuation standard of fair market value (FMV), the appraiser examines the business under certain guidelines for historic and future operations, and many of the appraiser's decisions and techniques are related solely to the maintenance of the concept of FMV. While much has been written already about these issues, the reader should understand that financial projections prepared for an appraisal should be reviewed carefully and adjusted to reflect how the acquiring entity expects to operate the business.

Chief issues to review include the following.

- Baseline income (normalized earning capacity of the business) and how it was derived
- Adjustments to historic income and their impact on the normalized earning capacity of the business
- Expense adjustments made for the purpose of valuation (discussed later in this chapter)
- Provider and staff compensation assumptions and adjustments—to be sure that they are in conformance with your personnel management system
- Other normalizing adjustments made to historic performance
- Projections in income and expenses used in the valuation
- Capital expense needs of the business

After a thorough review of these issues, acquiring entities should examine the following.

- Changes planned for the business and their impact on financial needs and income projections
- Depreciation, amortization, and equipment replacement reserve policies
- Time frame for amortization of the purchase price and other costs associated with acquisition
- Any other issues on business operation that will change from how the business operated prior to acquisition

After review of these issues, the acquirer will be much better positioned to understand and project the future financial picture of the business.

The remainder of this chapter will give readers an overview of financial issues in modeling the economic value of business entities.

THE PREMISES OF VALUE IN HEALTHCARE

Ask an art dealer what he means by value and you're likely to get a response based on the buyer's desirability of a particular treasure. Ask a realtor what he means by value and he'll say it's based on the selling price of other properties in the area. Ask a Wall Street investor and he'll say it's a function of return on investment (ROI). Ask the IRS about the taxable implications of a healthcare acquisition and they'll say it is the price at which a willing buyer and seller would agree, neither being under any compulsion to buy or to sell and both having a reasonable knowledge of the relevant facts—a standard definition of FMV.[1] Who's right? They all are, depending on your perspective. Taking this concept one step further, the subject of price also has a significant impact on value. Is "price" always an issue in discussing value? There are many circumstances when the price of a business or venture does not reflect its value as in the case of a below-market sale. Indeed, businesses or products may have significant value even if no willing buyer exists, at least in the traditional sense. In the healthcare environment, value may be any or all of the above in any given situation.

One must begin the process by asking the reason a valuation of a given healthcare entity or component is needed. The most common reason for valuation of smaller healthcare businesses, such as medical and other professional practices and small service companies, is to obtain financing or to determine a price for shares of ownership. Larger entities, such as hospitals, nursing homes, and retirement centers, use valuations almost exclusively for financing purposes. With increasing merger and acquisition activities, the purpose and function of the valuation often changes.

There are several items to keep in mind as we examine the issues of establishing the value of a discrete business or business line.

- All value is the expectation of future benefit.
- The best indicator of future performance is usually the performance of the immediate past.
- The seller sells the past while the buyer buys the future.
- Changes in healthcare delivery and financing may make reliance on historical data somewhat speculative, especially in certain medical subspecialties.
- The likelihood of realizing benefits must compare with other measures of economic and/or political risk in evaluating acquisition/network initiatives.

The most often cited *standard of value* used in healthcare business valuation is fair market value. Many buyers, however, may consider the value of a given acquisition or merger based on what it might bring to the organization in terms of synergies, positioning, or market power. In most cases, buyers are interested in quantifying the economic benefit based on certain perceptions about the subject business's income, earnings, or benefits stream. These instances exemplify the value of a strategic initiative or an investment. In most instances, we are concerned with the economic value of a business entity or business transaction when we examine the value to a healthcare delivery system.

While value may be in the eye of the beholder, the IRS's Office of Appeals, Office of Appraisal Services, Financial/Engineering Branch considers the value of a business to be a question of fact.[2] The inherent variability in perceptions of value and the potential for fraud and abuse have driven the federal government to establish statutes addressing business valuation as early as 1920 with the U.S. Treasury Department's Appeals and Review Memorandum Number 34 (ARM 34), derived to assist in the determination of intangible value of breweries forced out of business during prohibition (ARM 34 was incorporated into IRS Revenue Ruling 68-609, a.k.a. the Excess Earnings or IRS method). The IRS and Office of the Inspector General (OIG) have established guidelines for their reviewers in evaluating the potential for private benefit, inurement, and fraud and abuse in the development of healthcare integration activities.

Any buyer's goal is to acquire goods or services at the lowest price; sellers aim to sell at the highest price. These needs usually define the market price, or the price at which a good or service is likely to be sold or purchased. In assessing the motivations of a willing buyer, the classic example of an auction sale comes to mind. The final price is determined when the last willing buyer, the high bidder, exists. Hence, value is also a question of perception. The principle of substitution plays a strong role in determining value. This concept states that the value of a given activity (any economic or operational activity) is equal to the cost of acquiring an equally desirable substitute, or one of equivalent utility. The belief is that a purchaser would not pay more for something of equal value or utility, all things held equal. This concept drives much of contemporary thinking on establishing the value of entities or in assessing the feasibility of alternative scenarios.

We must think also of value in terms of a willing buyer even when no actual transaction may occur. One example includes establishing the value of a professional practice for marital dissolution. Divorce court seeks the equitable distribution of marital property. In divorce valuation, no sale actually occurs; however, a willing buyer does exist—it is the current business owner. The standard of value is that which pertains to the marital community (i.e., the current owner, based on perceptions of risk and other criteria). In strategic investment analysis, discussed later in this chapter, we presume a similar willing buyer.

In *Newhouse* v. *Commissioner*, 94 T.C. 193 (1990), the U.S. Tax Court accepted four classes of willing buyers for consideration: a control investor, an active investor, a passive investor, and a public investor. This decision shaped the perception that the value of an asset (or the corporate stock of business) may differ significantly based on the classification of the willing buyer. This concept has major impacts on the value perceptions in business acquisition and the financial and feasibility analyses of differing healthcare network development strategies.

The term *valuation* (often synonymous with *appraisal*), as used in business valuation, usually means the process by which an appraiser determines a reasonable approximation of the true economic value of a business, sometimes referred to as *business enterprise value* (BEV). This basic definition may be augmented or reduced depending on the degree of precision one ascribes to the concept and the matter at hand.

In examining the key issues in a valuation, the issues most often referenced include the following.

- A description of the property to be valued
- The purpose of the appraisal
- The function of the appraisal
- Any components of the property that are specifically included or excluded (e.g., accounts receivable, personal effects, artwork, etc.)
- The official date of appraisal (e.g., December 31, 1998)
- The applicable standard of value to be used

     Fair market value

     Investment value

     Book value

     Liquidation value

The Valuation Assignment: Purpose, Function, and Report Format

Clients use business valuations for many different needs. The *purpose*, or reason a valuation is needed, and the *function*, or how the valuation will be used, dictate several key issues the appraiser needs to begin the valuation. In healthcare, the predominant standard of value used is fair market value. Incumbent to this definition is that the property or collection of assets is deemed to have been exposed for sale on the open market for a reasonable period of time, in effect, allowing opportunity for multiple potential buyers to evaluate the offering and make bids. Hence, FMV assumes a hypothetical buyer from a universe of buyers able and willing to make the acquisition for determining the value of a hypothetical business in the geographic location of the business on the date of appraisal (Exhibits 3–1 and 3–2). Other standards of value, such as investment value (used to evaluate investment return) or liquidation value (used often to obtain financing), may also be used depending on the purpose and function of the valuation.

The purpose, function, and standard of value will dictate therefore how the valuation is conducted and the type of reports that are appropriate. It is inappropriate, for example, to use a valuation developed for estate planning purposes to value a partnership interest or to value the business, or any part of its assets for sale, because many of the techniques employed by the appraiser and dictated by appraisal methodology are applied based on the purpose and function of the appraisal. Valuations of businesses are either appraisals of the business assets or of the corporate stock of the business.

EXHIBIT 3–1

The Universe of Buyers in the Healthcare Industry

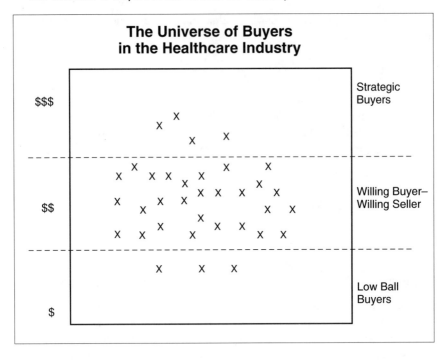

Independent third-party appraisals are performed on a nonadvocacy basis and appraisers must assume an independent position in rendering these opinions. Appraisal fees cannot be based on the amount rendered in the opinion of value.

Appraisals should conform with the Uniform Standards of Professional Appraisal Practice (USPAP), the American Society of Appraisers (ASA), and The Institute of Business Appraisers (IBA) business appraisal standards and codes of ethics. Qualified appraisers are often bound by their professional associations to adhere to specific guidelines in appraisal practice. Appraisal analysis also may be performed on a consulting basis for the purpose of evaluating or negotiating on behalf of a client, much like a business broker assists clients in the sales of businesses. These analyses are not deemed to be independent appraisals generally and most often include a statement of departure identifying this relationship.

Valuation analyses may serve many purposes and functions in the following.

· Acquisitions and mergers
· Corporate reorganization

E X H I B I T   3–2

Disparate Universe of Healthcare Buyers

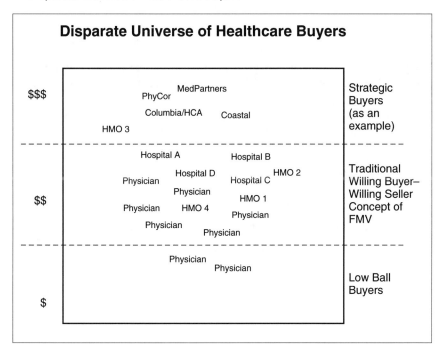

- Estate/gift/tax planning
- Financing
- Partnership agreements
- Eminent domain
- Buy-sell agreements
- Divorce settlement
- Feasibility studies
- Litigation support
- Physician recruitment
- Second opinions

Business valuations are either limited or complete valuations of the subject business, with the resulting outcome and report format prepared accordingly. The following sections summarize the nature of limited and complete business valuations and the types of reports used most frequently.

Limited Valuation

Limited valuations or desktop analyses of businesses are based on a preliminary review of business operations, and often without a visit to the business location. The resulting value of these reports may be a single figure or a range of values, depending on the preference of the client. These reports should contain statements regarding the nature of analyses based on such a limited review of data, and that the results of a complete valuation analysis may differ materially from the results of a limited valuation. Limited valuations may be used by owners or buyers to obtain a rough estimate for the value of the business or to assist clients in evaluating offers. Limited valuations are not "upgraded" generally to complete valuations, as the techniques used in a complete valuation may differ significantly. Limited valuations generally use oral or letter report formats described below.

Complete Valuation

Complete business valuations are the result of a comprehensive analysis of the operations of the subject business. In the healthcare arena, these analyses must contain specific elements of consideration in arriving at the BEV to maintain conformance with guidelines for the use of tax-exempt funds and for issues of potential fraud and abuse. The IRS guidance implies that full written reports of complete valuations be used as documentation of the fair market value of the subject business for acquisition by not-for-profit entities.[3] Investor-owned (for profit) entities may require full written reports for their internal use or as a safeguard against fraud and abuse issues under Stark laws. Complete valuations may be presented as oral, letter, or full written reports, though the resulting value does not differ by report format. The main reason for different report formats is to reduce the expense to the client by foregoing the time and effort to produce a formal written document. The appraiser must maintain documentation on all aspects of the assignment. Oral and letter reports are often converted into full written reports in the event that the buyer decides to complete the transaction.

Report Formats

The three main types of reports are oral, letter (also known as basic narrative or short-form reports), and full written (also known as comprehensive narrative or long-form reports) reports. Oral reports, though quite rare in healthcare, should always be documented in writing, typically one to two pages in length. Letter reports may be the result of a limited or complete business valuation but in an abbreviated report format to reduce the expense of creating a formal report document. Letter reports may range from five to ten pages in length and describe the purpose, function, standard of value, approach to valuation, methods employed, discounts and/or additions to value, valuation conclusion, assumptions, and limiting conditions. Letter reports are often used by buyers to assist in purchase negotiations and are often upgraded to full written reports once negotiation on the purchase is completed. Similarly, business owners may use letter reports as evidence of independent appraisal for negotiating with a potential buyer. Full written reports are comprehensive business documents, usually 70 pages or more. Specialty report formats exist for given situations dictated by client preference.

Business valuation has made great strides in the past several years, most notably with the delineation of standards of practice in the appraisal field. Consider the following from Shannon P. Pratt, an international authority on business valuation.

> It is absolutely imperative that those responsible for preparing, reviewing, and using business appraisals be aware of both the existing standards and also the development of future standards as they evolve.[4]

The ASA and The Institute of Business Appraisers (IBA) have published definitive standards for appraisal practice in the field of business valuation.

LEGAL AND REGULATORY CONSIDERATIONS

Much of the topic of discussion over the past few years has surrounded the payment or nonpayment of goodwill and the risk of jeopardizing the tax status of the tax-exempt buyer. In light of all the analysis, it is unlikely that anyone considering acquisition is not somewhat familiar with the concept of goodwill. Hence, we will dispense with an elementary discussion and target several key issues.

Goodwill

One of the first questions to address is whether or not goodwill exists in a given business. If we define goodwill as the sum total of intangible assets of a business, then any component of total BEV that exists beyond the net tangible value of the hard assets of the business (equipment and furnishings, inventory, supplies, and accounts receivable) is intangible value, or goodwill. While there are many elements that may suggest the existence of goodwill, the following describes the most prevalent components in the healthcare field.

- Stature of individual provider or provider organization within the industry
- Extent and nature of referring physicians, hospitals, employers, and health plans
- Length of time in operation of business and identification in the community
- Publicized relationships or affiliations with hospitals and other institutions
- Advertising campaigns, community acceptance, and reputation of the entity

- Revenue streams
- Proprietary interests, if any
- Reimbursement profiles and managed care penetration of the market
- Employment contracts, favorable leases, and noncompete covenants

The existence of goodwill is only the first step in identifying and allocating value to goodwill. The U.S. Tax Court enumerated three methods of identifying and valuing business goodwill: the bargain method, the residual method, and the capitalization method. Consider the following excerpt from *UFE, Inc.* v. *Commissioner* 92 T.C. 88 (1989).

> The bargain method allows us to recognize the parties' arm's-length bargain as the appropriate measure of intangible value. To use the bargain method, however, the parties must have specifically bargained for the various items of intangible value from adverse tax positions in arm's-length negotiations . . . The second and most well-known method is the residual method. The residual method subtracts the value of cash, cash equivalents, and tangible assets from the purchase price, and the remainder constitutes aggregate intangible value . . . The third method of valuing intangible value is the capitalization method, also labeled the 'excess earnings' method. The capitalization method compares the earning potential of the tangible assets to that of an industry average. To the extent that the purchased assets generate greater earnings than the industry average, the difference is considered goodwill.

The residual method is the required method for identifying and valuing goodwill in purchase price allocations for income tax purposes.[5] The excess earnings method, although used extensively, is fraught with problems in application, determination of nominal income levels, appropriate return on net tangible assets, and appropriate capitalization rates for intangible earnings. We will examine this method in greater detail later in this chapter.

The Thornton Letter

In December, 1992, Associate General Counsel D. McCarty Thornton, Inspector General Division (OIG) of the Department of Health and Human Services, responded to an inquiry by T.J. Sullivan from the IRS Office of Employee Benefits, Exempt Organizations, regarding the application of the Medicare and Medicaid anti-kickback statute to certain types of situations involving the acquisition of physician practices.[6] This letter created something of a precedent in opinion of the OIG toward the payment of any amounts for intangible value in the acquisitions of medical practices. The letter response from the OIG questioned how certain arrangements between selling physicians and acquiring tax-exempt hospitals could adversely affect the payment for and amount of services rendered to Medicare (and Medicaid) beneficiaries. The net effect of the letter was to curtail payments of amounts previously identified as goodwill in practice acquisitions by tax-exempt organizations. In subsequent years, the IRS and OIG have softened their position through guidance issued in various internal and external documents.

Despite the threats of the Thornton letter, goodwill is paid any time something is acquired at greater than the net tangible value of the hard assets. Regulatory guidelines on the content and quality of practice valuations appear to leave a broad path for assigning value to intangibles. Hospitals and other organizations are paying goodwill and other physician incentives with the approval of the IRS, as documented by numerous private letter rulings requested on the integration of providers.

REQUIRED CONTENT OF VALUATIONS

Medical practice valuations must comply with federal fraud and abuse statutes in content, though no strict format has been required. The IRS published recommended elements of a medical practice appraisal in the 1993 (for FY94) Exempt Organizations Continuing Professional Education Technical Instruction Program Textbook (a.k.a. CPE textbook) and updates in its 1995 and 1996 versions. The following elements are specifically prescribed.

- "Whether the valuation placed on an asset represents fair market value (FMV) depends on the quality of the appraisal."
- "Applicant (tax-exempt organization) represents that all assets acquired will be at or below FMV and will be the result of independent appraisals and arm's-length negotiations." (clarification added)
- "The business enterprise value (BEV) is defined as the total value of the assembled assets as a going concern (the value of a company's capital structure.)"
- ". . . requested that in all IDS applications that the valuation provide *all recognized approaches* for determining BEV, including *the income approach, the market approach, and cost approach.* The income method is the most often relevant, as it includes the *'excess earnings method'* described in RR 68-609, 1968-2 C.B. 327, and was approved for the valuation of the intangible assets in Rev. Rul. 76-91. . . ." (emphasis added)
- Income approach must include a discounted cash flow analysis
- Financial statements must be adjusted or "normalized" for extraordinary occurrences
- ". . . *reasonable assumptions* are made regarding rates of revenue increase, patient volume, and rates of expense increase based on current market conditions, growth, and best estimates of inflation trends." (Italics in the original)

- Base income for income-based methodologies must be on an *after-tax basis*
- All three methods (income, market, cost) must be included in appraisal
- ". . . the valuation must be based on a discount rate supportable by market transactions"
- "To ensure a correct valuation, the results of the income approach should be tested against other approaches such as market and cost."

Also referenced in the CPE textbooks is the reference to IRS Revenue Ruling 59-60, which prescribes the content for business valuations. This ruling has become a standard by which all competent business appraisers base their approaches to a specific engagement. Revenue Ruling 59-60 mandates that a thorough analysis of the following areas are required in the content of complete business valuations.[7]

- The nature and history of the practice or business (subject)
- The general economic outlook of the geographic market and the healthcare industry
- The book value of the subject's stock, hard assets, and financial condition
- The subject's earning capacity
- The subject's dividend-paying capacity
- The estimated value of intangible assets
- The subject assets (a listing or other wording indicating the assets to be valued/transacted)
- Comparable enterprises and their market value, where applicable

PRACTICAL REALITY IN HEALTHCARE BUSINESS VALUATION

The For-Profit Buyers

It sometimes seems as if the healthcare arena has been divided into those who can pay top dollar and those who cannot. This is the cry of the tax-exempt integrated delivery system (IDS) bemoaning the idea that they cannot compete with the for-profits because of issues of fair market value and tax status. The reality is that the for-profits may have some leniency from lesser IRS scrutiny; however, fraud and abuse components still exist.

For-profit buyers must be careful about paying inordinate amounts (amounts beyond reasonable) in asset and stock acquisitions that may reflect a payment for a continued stream of Medicare and Medicaid referrals. Physician employment contracts also may be the subject of scrutiny when total compensation far exceeds the prevailing rate in the community for a given specialty. An example might be a medical practice negotiated selling price of $1.5 million when the FMV appraisal indicates a value of $1 million and a physician employment contract of $175,000 when the prevailing rate for family physicians in the community is $125,000.

Do the for-profits have it easier? Perhaps. Their ability to acquire stock more readily and to include stock as one component of the purchase price allows more opportunity for creative/better physician (seller) deals. Equity arrangements with physicians are easier, generally given the for-profit's predisposition to investment strategies as compared to the more conservative posture assumed by many of the governing bodies of many tax-exempt organizations.

Does all this mean that the for-profits have a distinct advantage over the tax-exempt organizations or that the playing field is so far off level that you might as well pick up and go home? Not at all. An overwhelming number of physicians believe that partnering with the for-profits is akin to selling your soul to the corporate devil. The early acquisitions of Caremark, MedPartners, PhyCor, and others sent such a wave through the physician ranks that most physicians, all things being equal, would rather partner near home with folks they know and trust (somewhat). It's the old adage, better the devil you know than the devil you don't. Furthermore, the arrangements they make with the selling practices typically include equity, something many developing IDSs haven't yet embraced. On the recent downside, since January 1998, the PPMs have lost their luster on Wall Street with numerous bankruptcies and stock price crashes. Stocks that once traded at over $40 per share were trading at $7 or less in October 1998. MedPartners, the nation's largest PPM, has moved out of the physician practice business entirely. The volatility will continue in the PPM and for-profit section, though it will likely play a dominant role for years to come.

VALUATION OF MEDICAL PRACTICES AND HEALTHCARE BUSINESSES

Financial feasibility studies, appraisals, and evaluations normally precede a buyer's decision to purchase a medical group. The IRS documented in the 1993 (for FY94) CPE textbook that in an evaluation for tax exemption status (and probably fraud and abuse as well), technical documentation in the valuation should answer the following questions.

- What is the amount of the medical group's capital reserve account?
- What is the liquidity ratio (the current assets divided by current liabilities) of the medical group?
- What is the medical group's current working capital to revenue ratio (working capital divided by revenues)?
- What is the medical group's debt-to-assets ratio (total debt divided by total assets)?

- What is the medical group's long-term debt-to-equity ratio (total debt divided by equity)?
- What is the medical group's pretax return on asset ratio (pretax income divided by total assets)?
- What is the medical group's pretax return on equity ratio (pretax income divided by equity)?

The valuation report should, at a minimum, provide the data from which to calculate these ratios. A ratio analysis section, profiled by each year analyzed in the valuation, should be provided. A note of caution: Ratio analysis may serve as a useful tool in some circumstances, however, lack of comparative data may limit its transference to certain geographic areas. Some respected sources of financial and operating ratios include the Robert Morris Associates studies, MGMA, Financial Research Associates studies, BIZCOMPS, and the IBA Market Data File (available to IBA members only). Analysts should be cautioned that comparison of the subject business with comparative data uses a book value approach. The comparison of book value ratios yields limited benefit due to the numerous opportunities for discretionary operating decisions. The best way to use the ratio analysis is from the subject firm's adjusted financial statements, discussed later in this chapter.

Recent IRS Guidance for Medical Practice Valuation

These additional elements were described in the 1996 CPE textbook.

- OBRA requires that valuation appraisals of medical practices do not reflect indirect referral value to hospitals.
- Private benefit and inurement are prohibited.
- It is the organization's burden to establish the facts of a FMV acquisition.
- Organizations must establish that the methodology used to arrive at the price is reasonably likely to result in a final sales price consistent with exempt status.
- The existence of arm's-length bargaining may be questionable when a hospital acquires the practice of a physician on its medical staff.
- Factual assumptions upon which the valuation is based should be reviewed carefully to ensure that they are realistic, and if the valuation uses the income approach, it should be confirmed by the cost and market approaches.
- The allocation process combines the use of cost, market, and income approaches.

- Replacement cost is fair market value in use (FMVIU).
- Market comparisons of actual sales should be evaluated, adjusted, and applied to operating data of seller's business to arrive at FMV.
- Weighted average cost of capital (WACC) should be used.
- Terminal value is discounted by the capitalization rate.

METHODOLOGIES AND APPROACH TO VALUATION

The following section discusses the prevalent valuation methodologies used to determine the value of medical practices, other professional practices, and small healthcare businesses.

There are three broad theories to valuation: cost or asset, income, and market approaches. The cost theory states that the value of a business is directly related to the value of the business assets and the cost to create the business in the marketplace. The income theory states that the value of the business is directly related to the earnings of the business. The market theory states that the value of the business is directly related to other businesses that have sold (i.e., comparable sales). In the healthcare industry, a significant volume of data exists on the sales of medical practices. There exist few data on the sales of hospitals and medical centers and what little are available are most often anecdotal and incomparable to a given situation. In addition, transaction data may not be based on arm's-length transactions.

Value may be recognized also as incremental benefit. Under the Principle of Substitution, the value of a thing tends to be determined by the cost of acquiring an equally desirable substitute, and under the Principle of Alternatives, in any contemplated transaction, each party has alternatives to the transaction.[8] Given this conceptual framework, the value of an entity or collection of assets may be viewed as that which accrues to the assets given comparable alternatives in the marketplace. The incremental benefit possessed by one set of assets (e.g., the subject business) can be said to equal the cost of obtaining an equally desirable substitute (i.e., replicating it from start-up). In many cases, market activity may prevent any meaningful analysis using a cost to create (reproduce) approach; reproducing the asset may be impossible due to existing competition and other market conditions. In reality, if the market, while real and hypothetical at the same time, cannot support the use of one particular methodology, then other methods are de facto more appropriate.

Comprehensive methods of valuation consider several elements of value in arriving at an overall conclusion. Book value and economic value consider the value of the practice's assets. Income methods that include the capitalization of earnings, the capitalization of excess earnings, and discounted future benefits, among others, concentrate on income flows as the principal determinant of value.

Valuations should include an extensive review of employment and other covenants that may appear to cause speculation in the valuation of the subject entity.

Book value represents the value of the entity as its accounting value and can inflate the value of the business as an economic concern, while it cannot generally consider the FMV of the underlying assets. Book value does not address personal and professional goodwill and may not be an appropriate measure of the value of a given entity.

Economic value, or the FMV of the net tangible assets of the firm, may include greater than market values for fixed assets and is strongly affected by forces such as purchasing power and decisions made in a closely held business. Economic value may be a good proxy in some cases, depending on the debt service of the concern and the intangible and referral nature of the practice.

Liquidation value represents wholesale closure of the business and is typically the lowest value obtained, while not representing FMV necessarily.

A summary of a tangible asset analysis indicates the presentation of these three estimates of value (Exhibit 3–3).

Normalizing Income and Expenses

Because the income statements in most professional practices are prepared in a presentation format required for tax reporting rather than to report a true economic picture of the practice performance, adjustments to the statements are sometimes necessary.

The adjusted income statement assists reviewers in appraising the economic value of the business by establishing guidance on what constitutes expected, probable, historic, and future earnings of the concern. Normalizing adjustments remove unusual or one-time expenses and owner perquisites that are not indicative of the true economic operation of the business. They yield a bottom-line amount that reflects a new owner's income stream that may be taken from the business after meeting all of its operating expenses. It is the owner's annual ROI. This figure is referred to as the *normalized earning capacity* of the business and is the basis for projecting income into the future. It is by no means, as a rule, the complete baseline from which to form the final opinion of value. The adjusted income statement may be manipulated further under specific appraisal methodologies to reflect net income, debt-free income, net-free income available for distribution, base income for future cash flows or future earnings, or any of a number of other income streams to be capitalized or discounted. Exhibits 3–4 and 3–5 show an example of a historic and adjusted income statement.

Risk Rates of Return—Income Models

As a rate of return comparison to other investments, discount and capitalization rates quantify the business owner's efforts. Discount and capitalization rates vary among particular types of professional practices and from one period to another.

EXHIBIT 3–3

Tangible Asset Analysis
Evans OB/GYN: 12/31/98

Assets	Book Value	Adjustment	Economic Value	Adjustment	Liquidation Value
Current Assets					
Cash in Bank— Checking + Petty	8,851	(8,851)	0	0	0
Accounts Receivable	108,788	(24,174)	84,615	(37,255)	47,360
Supplies	3,623	(1,811)	1,811	(1,087)	725
Total Current Assets	121,262		86,426		48,085
Fixed Assets:					
Medical Equipment	83,162	(24,948)	58,213	(43,660)	14,553
Office Equipment	10,099	(3,030)	7,069	(5,302)	1,767
Furniture and Fixtures	37,461	(11,238)	26,223	(19,667)	6,556
Capital Lease— Norwest Computer	21,139	(12,683)	8,455	(5,073)	3,382
Capital Lease— Software	7,400	(1,480)	5,920	(4,440)	1,480
Capital Lease— Telephone System	6,966	(3,483)	3,483	(2,090)	1,393
Capital Lease—Copier	5,475	(2,738)	2,738	(1,643)	1,095
Capital Lease— Dataflow Software	3,450	(690)	2,760	(2,070)	690
Accumulated Depreciation	(127,292)	127,292	0	0	0
Accumulated Amortization	(37,987)	37,987	0	0	0
Total Fixed Assets	9,873		114,861		30,917
Total Assets	131,135		201,287		79,001
Current Liabilities:					
Notes Payable—CCB	4,739	0	4,739	0	4,739
Accrued Payroll Taxes	11,702	0	11,702	0	11,702
Total Current Liabilities	16,442		16,442		16,442
Long-Term Liabilities:					
Notes Payable—Officer	38,479	(38,479)	0	0	0
N/P—Citicorp	0	0	0	0	0
CCB Capital Lease—Telephone	0	0	0	0	0
Norwest Cap Lease Obligation	6,562	0	6,562	0	6,562
Konica Cap Lease—Copier	2,536	0	2,536	0	2,536
Dataflow Capital Lease	1,822	0	1,822	0	1,822
Total Long-term Liabilities	49,399		10,920		10,920
Total Liabilities	65,841		27,362		27,362

Book Value of the Firm: **$ 65,294**

Plus Medical Records: 95,000   18,027

FMV of Net Tangible Assets of the Firm: **$268,926**

Value of the Firm in Liquidation: **$ 69,666**

EXHIBIT 3–4

Historic Income Statements
Anytown Physical Therapy: 10/28/97

Income	YTD 1997	Annualized 1997	Year Ending 12/31 1996	1995	1994	1993	Notes
Patient Service Revenue	572,063	686,476	686,338	642,251	560,022	587,374	1
Expenses							
Owner Comp.—Mr. A	50,495	113,017	101,487	93,600	84,826	109,603	2
Owner Comp.—Mr. B	50,495	113,017	101,487	93,600	84,826	109,603	
Salaries—Staff	143,556	172,267	183,694	169,291	141,831	122,497	
Repairs and Maintenance	4,265	5,118	4,389	5,542	9,339	12,507	
Rent	55,000	66,000	66,000	66,000	67,594	63,200	
Taxes and Licenses	21,218	25,462	10,222	27,540	23,906	22,868	
Interest	466	560	857	135	—	—	
Charitable Contributions	250	1,500	2,262	44	—	—	
Depreciation	16,200	19,440	20,160	24,439	11,124	17,474	
Advertising	2,450	2,940	1,772	1,609	2,453	3,093	
Retirement Plan Contribution	770	40,000	43,087	38,266	40,605	40,590	3
Contract Labor	29,907	35,888	26,786	13,738	1,088	3,859	
Temporary Help	3,884	4,661	11,567	12,209	7,129	5,291	
Insurance	21,204	26,700	32,104	30,139	28,968	24,496	3
PT Net Expenses	3,000	3,600	2,531	14,500	14,500	11,643	
PT Net Fees	—	—	231	184	456	473	
Equipment Rental	1,183	1,420	256	—	—	—	
Legal and Accounting	5,090	6,108	5,897	4,235	3,124	3,440	
Utilities	4,411	5,293	5,423	5,353	5,901	6,324	
Dues and Subscriptions	2,700	3,000	1,528	1,817	2,397	1,249	3
Janitorial Services	2,475	2,970	3,300	3,025	—	—	
Supplies	10,887	13,065	21,349	17,776	12,304	13,222	
Postage	2,560	3,072	3,900	3,840	3,540	3,335	
Telephone	3,702	4,443	4,595	4,236	4,229	4,031	
Education	399	479	380	250	2,329	1,635	
Automotive Expenses	152	182	347	2,310	2,766	535	
Travel Expenses	4,155	5,000	8,799	3,031	4,347	3,126	3
Bank Fees	573	688	796	946	1,103	1,190	
Gifts to Physicians	—	400	370	486	722	1,119	3
Other Miscellaneous	7,912	9,495	3,032	2,878	3,268	1,897	
Travel and Entertainment	3,216	3,500	977	815	2,280	1,305	
Total Expenses	452,576	689,284	669,585	641,834	566,955	589,605	
Interest Income	2,107	2,809	3,658	4,555	2,361	2,231	
NOL Carry-over	—	—	58	4,572	—	—	
Net Profit/Taxable Income	**121,593**	**0**	**20,353**	**400**	**(4,572)**	**—**	

Sources: IRS Form 1120 plus attachments and Unaudited Income Statement dated 10/27/97 and Balance Sheet dated 10/28/97.

Notes:

1. All 1997 Annualized amounts equal (1997 YTD/10) × 12 for all categories unless noted. YTD is through 10/27/97.

2. 1997 Annualized amount estimated.

3. 1997 Annualized amount based on owner's estimate of total expense.

Expressed as a percentage, the more speculative the practice's income stream, the higher the discount rate and the capitalization rate. Conversely, the more stable the income stream the lower the discount rate and the capitalization rate. This stability or instability is referred to as risk, and it manifests itself in the greater or lesser return of the time value of money.

One generally accepted risk rate build-up methodology used in healthcare business valuation is based on a WACC as representative of the risk or return for the business.

Risk Rate Build-Up and Weighted Average Cost of Capital

As the income stream to be discounted or capitalized represents return on net-free cash flow, the returns are considered to be available to holders of debt and equity of the business. Therefore, a WACC approach is appropriate using the cost of financing for the amounts of equity and debt. (For additional reading on WACC, see both of Shannon P. Pratt's books, *Valuing Small Businesses and Professional Practices*, 2nd ed., Business One Irwin, 1993 and *Valuing a Business*, 3rd ed., Richard D. Irwin, 1996.)

The two basic components of a capitalization rate are the discount rate and a growth factor. The discount rate may be broken down into the risk-free rate of return and a risk premium return. The risk-free rate of return includes the rate of return required by an investor for the riskless use of their funds and a factor for expected inflation. The rate of return earned on long-term U.S. government bonds is considered to be a good proxy for the risk-free rate of return. Let's say at the date of our hypothetical business valuation, the rate of return on a 20-year U.S. Government Treasury Bond was 6.5%. Therefore, for the purpose of building up a discount rate, the risk-free rate of return is 6.5%.

The risk premium return is the additional rate of return required by investors in the market to compensate them for the additional risk in investing in a stock security as compared to a long-term U.S. government security. In a study published by Ibbotson Associates ("Stocks, Bonds, Bills, and Inflation Yearbook—SBBI"), it was calculated that since 1926, the average total annual returns earned on large corporate stocks, known as the market *equity risk premium* has been approximately 6.9% higher than the total annual returns on long-term U.S. government bonds (this rate is determined by the most current SBBI Yearbook available).[9] Therefore, we have added an additional required return of 6.9% to the risk-free rate of return to compensate investors for this market equity risk.

In addition to the 6.9% market equity risk, the same Ibbotson Associates' study indicates that the smallest block stocks traded on the New York Stock Exchange (defined as the tenth decile) earned an additional 5.3% premium over the larger stocks traded on the Exchange. This small stock risk premium has been added to the risk-free rate of return (6.5%) and the equity risk premium (6.9%). Summing the risk-free rate of return with the equity and small stock risk premium

EXHIBIT 3–5

Adjusted Income Statements
Anytown Physical Therapy: 10/28/97

Income	YTD* 1997	Annualized 1997	Year Ending 12/31				Notes
			1996	1995	1994	1993	
Patient Service Revenue	572,063	686,476	686,338	642,251	560,022	587,374	
Total Revenue	572,063	686,476	686,338	642,251	560,022	587,374	
Expenses							
Owner Comp.—Mr. A	50,495	113,017	101,487	93,600	84,826	109,603	
Owner Comp.—Mr. B	50,495	113,017	101,487	93,600	84,826	109,603	
Add Back: Excess Owner Salary		(90,414)	(70,312)	(59,606)	(48,951)	(99,837)	1
Salaries—Staff	143,556	172,267	183,694	169,291	141,831	122,497	
Repairs and Maintenance	4,265	5,118	4,389	5,542	9,339	12,507	
Rent	55,000	66,000	66,000	66,000	67,594	63,200	
Taxes and Licenses	21,218	25,462	10,222	27,540	23,906	22,868	
Interest	466	560	857	135	—	—	
Charitable Contributions	250	1,500	2,262	44	—	—	
Add Back: Contributions		(1,500)	(2,262)	(44)	—	—	2
Depreciation	16,200	19,440	20,160	24,439	11,124	17,474	
Add Back: Excess Depreciation		(9,951)	(10,094)	(14,659)	(6,012)	(11,702)	3
Advertising	2,450	2,940	1,772	1,609	2,453	3,093	
Retirement Plan Contribution	770	40,000	43,087	38,266	40,605	40,590	
Add Back: Excess Ret. Contribution		(20,000)	(20,000)	(20,000)	(20,000)	(20,000)	4
Contract Labor	29,907	35,888	26,786	13,738	1,088	3,859	
Temporary Help	3,884	4,661	11,567	12,209	7,129	5,291	
Insurance	21,204	26,700	32,104	30,139	28,968	24,496	
PT Net Expenses	3,000	3,600	2,531	14,500	14,500	11,643	
Add Back: Normalized Expenses		5,755	6,824	(5,145)	(5,145)	(2,288)	5
PT Net Fees	—	—	231	184	456	473	
Equipment Rental	1,183	1,420	256	—	—	—	
Legal and Accounting	5,090	6,108	5,897	4,235	3,124	3,440	
Utilities	4,411	5,293	5,423	5,353	5,901	6,324	
Dues and Subscriptions	2,700	3,000	1,528	1,817	2,397	1,249	

			Year Ending 12/31				
Income	YTD* 1997	Annualized 1997	1996	1995	1994	1993	Notes
Janitorial Services	2,475	2,970	3,300	3,025	—	—	
Supplies	10,887	13,065	21,349	17,776	12,304	13,222	
Postage	2,560	3,072	3,900	3,840	3,540	3,335	
Telephone	3,702	4,443	4,595	4,236	4,229	4,031	
Education	399	479	380	250	2,329	1,635	
Automotive Expenses	152	182	347	2,310	2,766	535	
Travel Expenses	4,155	5,000	8,799	3,031	4,347	3,126	
Bank Fees	573	688	796	946	1,103	1,190	
Gifts to Physicians	—	400	370	486	722	1,119	
Other Miscellaneous	7,912	9,495	3,032	2,878	3,268	1,897	
Travel and Entertainment	3,216	3,500	977	815	2,280	1,305	
Total Expenses	452,576	573,173	573,741	542,380	486,847	455,778	
Remove: Interest Income	2,107	(2,809)	(3,658)	(4,555)	(2,361)	(2,231)	6
Remove: NOL Carry-over	—	—	(58)	(4,572)	—	—	7
Net Profit/ Taxable Income	121,593	113,302	112,597	99,872	73,175	131,596	
Taxes at 40%		45,321	45,039	39,949	29,270	52,639	8
After Tax Income		67,981	67,558	59,923	43,905	78,958	
Weighted Average After-Tax Income 1993-1997		63,778					

Notes:

1. Excess owner compensation added back.

2. Contributions are added back because they are a discretionary expense.

3. Depreciation in excess of economic useful life is added back. See detail.

4. Excess retirement contributions based on excess owner compensation is added back.

5. PT Network expenditures are averaged (normalized) to reflect more even cash flows. See detail.

6. Interest income is removed because it is nonoperating income.

7. NOL Carry-over is removed to reflect actual owner business expenditures in the year they were incurred.

8. After tax amounts are used per IRS Exempt Organizations CPE Text 1994–1996.

*Adjusting YTD is not meaningful.

equals the average total return required by investors to induce them to invest in the smallest stocks traded on the New York Stock Exchange.

Here is where the professional business appraiser adds his expertise in assessing the appropriate level of risk for the subject business. One school of thought indicates that investing in the stock of a closely held business involves additional elements of risk that must be compensated by offering a higher rate of return. Additional levels of risk may be due to specific risks associated with the industry or the company as compared to the entire marketplace. This is called *company specific risk*.

The appraiser may choose to sum the risk-free rate of return with the equity and small stock risk premium as the total required ROI, thereby indicating that the small stock risk premium is sufficient for the risk inherent in the business being valued. The appraiser may choose alternatively to identify and quantify additional depth of risk to be applied to the subject entity. This risk element synthesis is one of the most crucial aspects of the job of the professional business appraiser. The appraiser must identify clearly how they came about their conclusion and why the defined risk rate is consistent with the standard of value under which the appraisal is being conducted. The appraiser cannot simply and arbitrarily state a risk rate to be X amount without support. This is one of the predominant errors in business appraisal by the inexperienced.

It also should be noted that this build-up technique is only one method for developing a market-based risk rate for a given entity. There are several other acceptable methods that may be perceived as having greater and lesser degrees of subjective analysis. The appropriate assessment of risk must be conducted by an individual trained in investment concepts and with a firm grasp of the operations, financial performance, and geographic conditions of the subject entity as pertains to the investment climate of the economy in general and healthcare industry in specific. Remember, the final outcome of an appraisal is a supportable opinion of value. Other methods may include comprehensive assessments of industry-specific business risk that are supported by the appraiser and are appropriate to the engagement, form of organization, standard of value, and capital structure. As an example, the range of discount rates observed in the healthcare marketplace between 1993 and 1998 for WACC, debt-free analyses has been generally between 13% and 50%.

The following charts and tables present some examples of the process in developing financial risk rate. The first table, Exhibit 3–6, adapts information from The Center for Healthcare Industry Performance Studies (CHIPS) as a rudimentary look at a buyer's perception of risk. This approach, along with Exhibit 3–7, Risk Assessment Table for Company-Specific Risk–Acute Care Hospital Model, shows great promise in more narrowly defining the subjective nature of

E X H I B I T 3–6

CHIPS Value Drivers—Perception of Risk

Factor/Dimension Considered	Buyer's Perception Level of Risk		
	Low	**Normal**	**High**
Revenues			
Market Size	1		
Market Share	1		
Product Mix		1	
Margin			
Prices		1	
Staffing Levels	1		
Raw Material Prices		1	
Investment Income		1	
Coding			1
Payor Mix		1	
Working Capital			
Inventory	1		
Accounts Receivable	1		
Accounts Payable		1	
Capital Expenditures			
Plant Life		1	
Replacement Equipment			1
Maintenance			1
Scale of Operations	1		
Cost of Capital			
Cost of Equity	1		
Cost of Debt		1	
Leverage	1		
Liquidity	1		
Number of Ratings	9	8	3
Subjective Risk Weight:	0.45	0.40	0.15

Source: Adapted from The Center for Healthcare Industry Performance Studies

E X H I B I T   3–7

Risk Assessment Table for Company-Specific Risk
Acute Care Hospital Model
Dimensions of Risk—Likelihood of Achieving the Forecasted Income Stream

| | Buyer's Perception Level of Risk | | |
Factor/Dimension Considered	Low	Normal	High
Operational Performance			
Profitability		1	
Price and Cost Position		1	
Patient Days and Census	1		
Length of Stay		1	
Case Severity Mix and Performance		1	
Wage Index and Staffing Efficiency		1	
Financial Position and Management			
Growth in Assets and Equity		1	
Asset Productivity		1	
Growth in Revenues		1	
Liquidity		1	
Return on Invested Capital		1	
Market Position and Risk			
Managed Care Impact		1	
Payor Mix		1	
Market Proaction		1	
Competitor Impact		1	
Long-Term Competitive Position		1	
Service Mix Risk			
Inpatient—Outpatient Mix		1	
Participation in Care Continuum		1	
Available Technology		1	
Demographic Trends	1		
Number of Ratings	2	18	0
Subjective Risk Weight:	0.10	0.90	0.00

company-specific risk. Exhibit 3–8 uses the weighting factors from the Risk Assessment Table for Company-Specific Risk–Acute Care Hospital Model for the initial creation of the cash flow equity discount rate. Exhibit 3–9 shows the direct build-up method. In this approach, the appraiser has made a qualitative and

EXHIBIT 3–8

Discount and Capitalization Rate Build-up—Market Factors

		Buyer's Perception Level of Risk		
Notes	Discount Rate Components	Low	Normal	High
1	Safe Rate	6.27%	6.27%	6.27%
2	Investment Alternative	7.8%	12.2%	14.15%
3	Healthcare Industry Closely-Held Business Risk Adjustment	5%	7%	15%
	Initial Overall Rate	19.1%	25.4%	35.4%
4	Subjective Risk Weight	10%	90%	0%
	Weighted Result	1.9%	22.9%	0.0%
	Cash Flow Equity Discount Rate by this approach:			24.79%

Notes:

1. Safe Rate is based on returns long term (20 year) T-Bond yield to maturity rates on the date of valuation.

2. Investment Alternative Low rate is the 72 year Ibbotson arithmetic mean Market Equity Risk Premium; the Normal rate adds the Small Stock Risk Premium, 10th decile; the High rate adds 2.0%.

3. An adjustment to equal return rates based on stability and likelihood of the business achieving a return; a component of company-specific risk.

4. Company-specific risk adjustment from risk assessment table.

quantitative judgment on the 6% company-specific risk factor. As stated previously, the appraiser's job is to create a supportable opinion of value, not a simple pronouncement. The detailed analyses and opinions behind the 6% adjustment are significantly detailed and are beyond the scope of this book.

The final exhibit in this section (Exhibit 3–10) displays the iterative process for developing the WACC. Analysts should recognize that the WACC is made based on weightings of debt and equity made at market value, not book value. This requires a substitution of debt to equity weightings at book value through an iterative process. In the first section of the exhibit, the debt at book value was 24% and the net free cash flow to invested capital was $10,000,000. The initial cash flow equity capitalization rate developed was 16.78%. The initial iteration of the value of equity after debt was $43,869,586, suggesting a market weighting of 26.4% debt and 73.6% equity. In the second iteration, the debt amount was substituted to 27%, which resulted in a second iteration of the value of equity at $42,801,447, and a capital structure weighting at market value of essentially the same. This process is necessary to avoid over or under valuing the firm by using only the capital structure weightings at book value. If we had not implemented the iterative process, we would have over-valued the firm by

EXHIBIT 3–9

Discount and Capitalization Rate Build-up—Direct Build-up Method
Cost of Capital Rates—WACC

Equity Risk Premium	7.8%	
10th Decile Ibbotson	4.4%	
20-Year T-Bond	6.27%	
Base Rate	18.4%	
Company-Specific Risk	6.0%	
Cash Flow Equity Discount Rate	**24.42%**	

Capital Structure Percentages at Book Value on 9/30/98	**Debt**	**Equity**
	24%	76%
Cost of Capital: Subject Firm	8%	25%
Tax Rate		40%
WACC—Direct Build-up Method		**19.78%**
Chosen Method		
WACC—Direct Build-up Method		**20%**
Rounded		

$1,000,000, and although this is only 2% off, a million dollars is a pretty good chunk of change for any organization.

Direct capitalization methods such as the capitalization of earnings or capitalization of cash flow are best applied in a sole propriety practice or single ownership because of the capability for the owner to exert total control over the growth and direction of the practice from the financial and operational perspectives. This method provides a snapshot of how expected, probable, future earnings of the concern are capitalized into value by a market-derived divisor for ROI (capitalization rate) of businesses representing similar financial risk. It presumes a steady growth rate into perpetuity (Exhibit 3–11).

The capitalization of excess earnings (a.k.a. IRS formula method after Revenue Ruling 68-609) is a hybrid asset and income approach to valuation wherein the tangible assets and intangible assets of the business are independently valued. The tangible and intangible assets are then combined to determine the total fair market value of the business. Tangible assets are comprised of the fair market value of total operating assets minus total liabilities at the date of valuation. Intangible assets are calculated by capitalizing excess earnings. Excess earnings represent adjusted net income reduced by some reasonable industry return on

E X H I B I T   3–10

Cost of Capital—Weightings Based on Market Value
Implementing the Iterative Process

	Iteration 1			Iteration 2		
Book Value				**Capital Structure Weightings**		
Capital Structure				**at Market Value**		
LT Debt	$ 15,737,557	24%		Debt	$ 15,737,557	**26.4%**
Equity	$ 48,838,447	76%		Equity	$ 43,869,586	**73.6%**
Total Debt				**Reweighting of Capital Structure**		
and Equity	$ 64,576,004			Capital	Debt	Equity
NF Cash				Structure	27%	73.1%
Flow to IC	$ 10,000,000			Cost of Capital	8.00%	21.60%
				Tax Rate		40.00%
Initial WACC—				**2nd Iteration**		
Cap Rate		16.78%		**WACC**		17.08%
Capitalized Value	$ 59,607,143			Capitalized Value		$ 58,539,004
Minus Debt	$(15,737,557)			Minus Debt		$(15,737,557)
1st Iteration				**2nd Iteration**		
Equity	$ 43,869,586			**Equity**		$ 42,801,447
Capital Structure Weightings				**Capital Structure Weightings**		
at Market Value				**at Market Value**		
Debt	$ 15,737,557	**26.40%**		**Debt**	$15,737,557	**26.9%**
Equity	$ 43,869,586	**73.60%**		**Equity**	$42,801,447	**73.1%**

net assets (i.e., earnings from tangible assets are subtracted from total earnings to arrive at earnings from intangible assets: excess earnings). Similar to a straight income capitalization, the excess earnings method presumes steady growth into perpetuity (Exhibit 3–12).

There is considerable confusion in application of the excess earnings methodology, particularly in the application of two different rates of return. To clarify these issues, remember the following things.

- The rate of return on net tangible assets depends on the risk of the asset mix. A range of reasonable rates for most medical practices should be somewhere between 12% and 20%.
- Earnings should be representative of "what the practice should be earning." The focus is expected or probable future earnings, not simply an average of previous years. This is why the approach of normalized earnings works well.

EXHIBIT 3–11

Capitalization of Earnings
Anytown Physical Therapy

"Normalized" Earning Capacity	63,778
(Weighted Average After-Tax Income 1993–1997)	
Multiplied by 1 + Growth Rate	× **1.04**
Equals Total Earnings to Capitalize	66,330
Divided By	
Earnings Discount Rate minus Growth Rate	**÷ 19.03%**
Equals Capitalized Value of the Firm	348,630
Minus Liabilities	− 4,348
Equals Indicated Value of the Business	**$ 344,282**

For all the discussion about RR 68-609 by the IRS's Office of Appeals, Office of Appraisal Services, Financial/Engineering Branch, which reviews valuations of medical practices related to acquisitions by IDSs, consider this excerpt from the IRS Appellate Conferee Valuation Training Program (1980) denouncing the use of the excess earnings method of valuation:

One of the most frequently encountered errors in appraisal is the use of a formula to determine a question of fact, which on a reasonable basis must be resolved in view of all pertinent circumstances . . . ARM 34 has been applied indiscriminately by tax practitioners and members of the Internal Revenue Service since it was published. On occasion the Tax Court has recognized ARM 34 as a means of arriving at fair market value. The latest and most controlling decisions on valuation, however, relegate the use of a formula to a position of last resort . . . By such a formula (ARM 34) the same value would be found in 1960 as in 1933 although the values per dollar of earnings were very different in those two years. The basic defect is apparent; the rates of return which are applied to tangibles and to intangibles are completely arbitrary and have no foundation in fact . . . All that can be said for ARM 34, or a similar formula method of capitalization using two rates of interest, is that you hope to get a good answer based upon two bad guesses. It is difficult enough to get one reasonably accurate rate of capitalization using normal appraisal methods . . . To get two fairly accurate rates, one for tangibles and one for intangibles, other than by the use of pure guesswork, is impossible . . . Any capitalization of earnings must take into consideration the economic conditions prevailing at the specific date of appraisal, including those conditions controlling in the industry in this company's area, and even in the national economy.[10]

E X H I B I T   3–12

Excess Earnings Method
Anytown Physical Therapy

"Normalized" Earning Capacity	**63,778**
Market Value of Operating Assets	275,780
Reasonable Return on Tangible Assets	× 15.00%
Multiplied by Earnings Attributable to Tangible Assets	**$ 41,367**
Normalized Earning Capacity	63,778
Less: Reasonable Return on Assets	− 41,367
Equals Excess Earnings From Intangible Goodwill	**$ 22,411**
Divided by Excess Earnings Capitalization Rate	÷ 33.22%
Equals Value of Intangible Goodwill	**$ 67,463**
Add Market Value of All Assets Net of Liabilities	+296,367
Equals Indicated Value of the Business	**$ 363,830**

The basic misconception is that RR 68-609 suggests absurdly low capitalization rates of 8% to 10%. These low rates do not nearly approximate the amount of risk in investing in a closely held business such as a medical practice, home health agency, nursing home, or other investment with questionable liquidity, in a potentially volatile market, in the 1990s. The best adaptation of the excess earnings method is to make two best guesses (documented analyses) on capitalization rates, based on some foundation of belief of risk and liquidity, and to use this value as a supporting value to be considered along with values determined from other methods.

Discounted Cash Flows/Discounted Future Benefits

The discounted cash flows analysis is an income technique of valuation wherein the total value of the business entity is determined by discounting projected cash flows back to the date of valuation. Then the cash remaining at the end of the projection term flows (a.k.a. residual, terminal value, or reversion) are reduced to present value, summed with the value of the stream of cash flows, and any liabilities are subtracted to indicate total business enterprise value (Exhibit 3–13). The theory behind the discounted cash flows method is that an entity is worth the present value of its expected cash flow. The theory of the valuation method is sound, but the application of the approach presents some difficulty. Primarily, it is difficult to project expected levels of cash flows. The steps involved in a discounted cash flows analysis are as follows.

E X H I B I T   3–13

Discounted Cash Flow Analysis
Anytown Physical Therapy

Year	Projected Increase	Projected Cash Flow	Present Value Factor	Present Value
1	4.0%	68,122	0.809454428	55,142
2	4.0%	70,847	0.655216471	46,420
3	4.0%	73,681	0.530367873	39,078
4	4.0%	76,628	0.429308623	32,897
5	4.0%	79,693	0.347505766	27,694

Cash Flow Discount Rate: 23.54%

Present Value of Future Cash Flows   201,231

Capitalize Residual Value into Perpetuity

Stabilized Future Cash Flow—Cash Flow in Year 5 × (1 + LTGR)   82,881

Divided by Cash Flow Capitalization Rate   ÷ 19.54%

Capitalized Residual Cash Flow   424,161

Discounting Capitalized Residual Cash Flow to Present Value

Capitalized Residual Cash Flow   424,161

Multiplied by Present Value Factor in Year 5   × 0.34751

Equals Present Value of Residual Cash Flow   147,398

SUMMARY

Present Value of Future Cash Flows   201,231

Plus Present Value of Residual Cash Flow   + 147,398

Minus Liabilities   (4,348)

Equals Total Indicated Value   344,282

- Develop a risk-adjusted discount rate.
- Develop an adjusted pro forma cash flow statement.
- Discount the projected cash flows by the discount rate.
- Capitalize the nth year projected cash flow into a residual value and discount it to the date of valuation (typically three to eight years in healthcare, 10 years in less volatile industries).
- Sum the discounted cash flows and the discounted residual value to derive the operating value.
- Add or subtract nonoperating assets and liabilities.

In using the discounted cash flows methodology, the most critical step, beyond the calculation of an appropriate and supportable discount rate, is the projection of the business income and expenses. While several different means exist for projecting these data, including historical average, business regression trend line, industry trend line, percentage of revenue, and manual predictions, the best approach requires a detailed understanding of the directions planned for the practice, future revenue growth, provider productivity, and salary expectations (or contractual commitments). Although it is impossible to predict the effect of all forces on healthcare systems, conservative, realizable estimates provide the basis for modeling various outcomes.

Lastly, with continuing change in the healthcare industry itself, and understanding the nature of the healthcare professional practice as a closely held business, it is wise to project future earnings over only a three- to eight-year period to account for myriad of unknown factors that may disrupt projections from becoming reality. Most healthcare appraisers would agree that primary care practices are considered more stable than specialty practices and that companies with short operating histories are less stable than businesses with five or more years of experience. The more realistic and accurate the projections, the more likely the discounted cash flows technique represents the true value of the business. Furthermore, the discounted cash flows method is considered by many to be the best proxy for the upper end of FMV.

Market-Based Methods

The market approach uses capitalization rates and/or comparative multiples that are extrapolated from reported market transactions to derive the value for the subject business. Under the market theory, three methods of valuation are usually considered: actual prior transactions that have occurred within the subject entity, such as a previous sale of the business or a buy-in or pay-out of owners (Exhibit 3–14), comparison with aggregated data of private multiples from comparable business sales (Exhibits 3–15, 3–16), and comparison of private multiples from specific, identified sales of public guideline companies deemed as reasonably comparable to the subject entity. One word of caution: It is difficult to compare practices or businesses with similar earning histories and locations. There are many tangible and intangible factors that affect these comparisons and in many cases, sufficient data are not available to establish reasonable direct comparability between businesses. The appropriate application of this technique to a given comparable business requires that the guideline company financial statements be adjusted (as one would normally do with any valuation) and comparisons made to the subject entity. This normalizing of data provides the most substantial basis for comparison. Other methods include utilizing large numbers of market transactions of reasonably comparable

EXHIBIT 3–14

Market Method—Prior Transaction

Previous Value (12/31/94)	160,000
Divided by: Previous Revenue	÷369,706
Equals Price to Revenue	0.43
Multiplied by: Current Adj. Rev.	×551,145
Equals Current Value	**238,522**

businesses to derive multiples for comparison. The large blocks of transactions normalize outliers and provide considerable power to the application of this technique. As an example, the IBA Market Data File has transaction data on over 500 dental practice sales. Even after excluding outlier and obvious incomparable transactions, these data provide considerable insight into the overall market value of dental practices. As one may imagine, many obvious intangible elements may be impossible to compare including patient friendliness, location, years in practice, small town acceptance, etc.

The Allocation of Purchase Price Technique: Tangible and Intangible Assets

Business enterprise value (i.e., FMV) determined under an income approach is often greater than the combined fair market value of equipment, furnishings, and fixtures determined under a cost approach because it includes the intangible value of the business as a going concern (i.e., the goodwill of the business). The value of goodwill can be allocated to the specific intangible assets using the residual method; the value of the latter limited to the value of the former, as calculated under the income approach.[11] In many cases, the value of the net tangible assets of the business are identified in the appraisal and the remaining value tends to be allocated toward goodwill in general. Under some cases, amounts of intangible value are allocated to goodwill, employment contracts, covenants not to compete, and other items, as in the following example.

Allocation of Purchase Price

Fixed assets and supplies	113,367
Accounts receivable	11,649
Goodwill and medical records	
(net liabilities of $1,507)	224,983
Covenant not to compete	50,000
Total purchase price	400,000

EXHIBIT 3-15

Market Approach Summary
Anytown Internal Medicine

Business Type	Annual Gross $000's	Annual Earnings $000's	Owner's Comp. $000's	Sales Price $000's	Price/ Gross	Price/ Earnings	Location	Yr/Mo of Sale
Selected Transactions								
General/ Family Practice	487	250	250	155	0.32	0.51	NC	Oct-98
General/ Family Practice	1,068	125	125	298	0.28	0.12	NC	Oct-98
General/ Family Practice	1,702	168	168	860	0.51	0.10	SC	Apr-98
General/ Family Practice	955	252	183	590	0.62	0.26	NC	Feb-97
General/ Family Practice	1,332	485	400	900	0.68	0.36	NC	Aug-96
General/ Family Practice	321	160	130	160	0.50	0.50	NC	Dec-94
General/ Family Practice	1,100	330	290	487	0.44	0.30	NC	Dec-94
General/ Family Practice	935	535	495	385	0.41	0.57	NC	Nov-94
General/ Family Medicine	340	121	121	225	0.66	1.86	TX	Nov-93
Internal Medicine	473	169	169	141	0.30	0.36	NC	Oct-98
Internal Medicine	551	200	205	240	0.44	0.36	VA	Jun-98
Internal Medicine	406	153	176	161	0.40	0.38	NC	Mar-98
Internal Medicine	285	128	130	105	0.37	0.45	NC	Jul-96

Mean P/G:	**0.46**
Median P/G:	**0.44**
Subject Firm's Adjusted Gross Income:	**551,145**
Times Market Comparable Mean P/G:	× 0.46
Initial Indication Value of the Firm	**251,407**
Upper Point Estimate of Grouped P/G	0.66
Upper Point Indication of Value	**363,755**
Lower Point Estimate of Grouped P/G	0.30
Lower Point Indication of Value	**165,343**
Times Chosen Indicator:	× **0.66**
Indicated Value of the Firm:	**363,755**

E X H I B I T   3–16

Market Observation of Price—Gross Range of Medical Practices

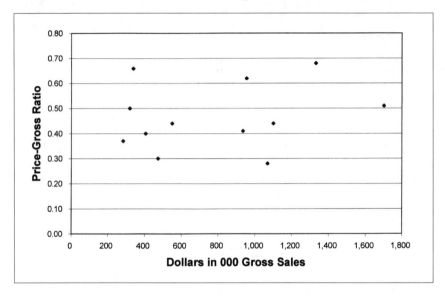

Valuation Synthesis

Appraisers expect a range of values when applying numerous valuation methodologies. The expected outcome occurs when these amounts fall in a narrow range of values.[12] Outlier estimates do occur for several reasons, each worth examining in its own right, and the reasons for these values should be understood by the appraiser.

Discounts and Premiums for Control and Marketability

The overall value of the business in the specific marketplace may be more or less than initially determined by any individual appraisal method as a result of factors affecting the marketability of the business. Marketability deals with the liquidity of the asset. Additionally, each owner's individual value may not be directly related to the percentage of ownership because of the existence of, or lack of, control.

Minority Discount

The minority discount is a reduction in value of an individual owner's share of the business due to lack of control to direct business decisions such as declaring dividends, liquidating, going public, issuing or buying stock, directing management, etc. In many practices and businesses in which owners maintain equal positions and control over management decisions, minority share discounts are rare. Minority discounts are usually seen when the purpose of the valuation is to estimate the value of a minority position such as seen in the circumstances of a divorce, a minority partner buy-in, or a financing arrangement. Interestingly, though, minority discounts are rarely experienced in the healthcare industry.

Control Premium

A control premium is an addition to value of an individual owner's share of the business for the right to make corporate decisions such as declaring dividends, liquidating, going public, issuing or buying stock, directing management, etc. Control premiums also may be an issue when a specific position contains the ability to effect a swing vote in the governance of the business. For example, when a third partner joins a group and the final ownership is an equal third of the business, the new partner has the ability to team up with another partner to make corporate decisions. Similarly a 10% or 20% partner may have this swing position, which may increase their overall percentage of value greater than face value.

Marketability Premium or Discount

The marketability premium is an increase in overall business value due to the attractiveness and ready market of the business. It is reflected most often in initial public offerings of securities and is rarely seen in the purchase of a closely held business. The healthcare field seems to be a growing exception as hospitals, health networks, provider organizations, and managed care organizations are acquiring provider practices. Marketability premiums are then an additional "bump" in value, often in the range of 10% to 20% for a specific, highly desired business in a very active marketplace. Quantifying, documenting, and supporting marketability premia are very difficult, reflecting the fact that they are seen rarely.

The marketability discount is a reduction in overall business value due to a stock restriction or prohibition such as no ready market, security law restrictions, buy-sell agreements, rights of first refusal restrictions, and shareholder agreements.

There have been numerous studies detailing statistics on lack of marketability that have pertinent bearing on the valuation of medical practices and healthcare businesses.[13-18] From these studies, the average discount for lack of marketability for restricted shares of publicly traded companies was 35%. John D. Emory conducted a series of studies on the discount for lack of marketability as the result of the value of private transactions before an initial public offering and the publicly traded prices.[19] The results of his research (the IPO studies) indicated an average discount for lack of marketability of 45%.

There is strong evidence to suggest that closely held businesses suffer much more from lack of marketability than do publicly traded entities.[20]

In a debt-free calculation, it is inappropriate to apply a full discount for lack of marketability, which we see may be as high as 35% or greater. The preferred approach is to apply the discount on a debt-free basis, although it is generally recognized that no data exist to make this adjustment. Under most circumstances, discounts for lack of marketability range from approximately 10% to 25%. This general statement is not meant to be taken lightly. The essence of a proper business appraisal is its ability to convey a supportable opinion of value.

JUSTIFICATION FOR PURCHASE TEST

A justification for purchase test uses the projected income flow amounts from the valuation (adjusted income statement and the discounted cash flows analysis) to use as a basis for funding the debt service on the total purchase price at market terms. If the business income stream cannot support its debt service, you have a hard argument to suggest that the purchase price is at FMV. Simply put, you take the total purchase price of the business, say $400,000, and profile the debt service on that amount. Conservatively speaking, use the prime rate plus .5% and amortize the purchase over 10 years for your debt payment. Using a prime rate of 8.25% (plus .5%) indicates an annual debt payment of $56,684. Going back to the valuation, the normalized earning capacity of the business was $65,819 and the net free cash flow was $59,686. This indicates that the business could support its reasonable debt service out of its most stringent cash projections. These numbers came from a recent medical practice sale of a very busy solo internal medicine practice. The interpretation is that a new physician could finance the $400,000 purchase price over 10 years while paying himself a fair market salary of approximately $200,000 per year. After 10 years, he owns the practice free and clear. All forms of valuation for business acquisitions should use a justification for purchase test to confirm value (Exhibit 3–17).

QUESTIONS AND ANSWERS

Areas of Dispute in Valuation

Business valuation is far from an exact science. The idiosyncrasies of each business, marketplace, and the experience and preferences of the appraiser contribute to the final opinion of value rendered. This discussion addresses each method of traditional valuation and highlights areas for dispute and/or abuse in practice and interpretation.

> **Q.** What are the most important issues in adjusting the balance sheet and income statements?
>
> **A.** Place yourself in the shoes of the prudent businessman. To examine the economic operations of a business, the prudent businessman does the following.

E X H I B I T 3–17

Justification for Purchase Test

Total Asset Acquisition Cost	**400,000**
Normalized Earnings	65,819
Payback from Earnings (Years)	**6.1**
Net Free Cash Flow	59,686
Payback from Free Cash Flow (Years)	**6.7**
Debt Service Capacity	
Total Payment Required	55,196
(Assets amortized over 10 years at 8.0%)	
Out of Net Free Cash Flow	59,686

- Reduces physician/owner compensation and benefits to FMV for physician professional services only
- Includes appropriate management oversight expenses
- Reduces staff compensation and benefits to local market rates for the classification of employee and job actually performed
- Add all excess compensation back to income
- Adjusts any unusual or one-time expenses, such as periods of double rent or other expenses charged or categorized not consistent with Generally Accepted Accounting Principles (GAAP), to derive representative income
- Allows expenses typical of the business (automobile, cellular phone, computer expenses) deemed to be legal and appropriate as business-use only
- Allows depreciation at rate of economic decline—expect 10 to 15 years for most assets
- Adjusts all leases to fair market rate (not at favorable rates obtainable by owners or potential buyer) as required
- Removes nonoperating assets, income, and liabilities from adjusted asset and income statements
- Adjusts for non–business-related sales or acquisitions (e.g., gain or loss on sale of equipment)

Q. Mechanically, what types of adjustments should I see under hard assets?

A. Watch for the following adjustments.

- Cash and other highly liquid assets not typically sold are usually removed (reclassified as nonoperating excess cash) as long as accounts receivable (A/R) provides sufficient working capital
- A/R adjustments are appropriate and reasonable; poor A/R aging or nonexistent aging schedules are believed to represent poor A/R and should be discounted significantly
- Any booked intangibles are removed
- Liabilities will likely carry over at full value (except in unusual circumstances in which the business has not refinanced an unusually high interest rate on an outstanding note)
- Cost methods are reasonable, and any intangible components are supported by revenues

Q. What are the key areas to watch in the methods of valuation themselves?

A. The following issues are the subject of most of the complaints or scrutiny in business valuation.

Income Methods

- Capitalization and discount rates have demonstrable bases in market transactions reflecting rates of return for similar investments and are applied to the correct benefits stream
- Earnings methods use and appropriately estimate a representative earnings flow number
- Excess earnings return on equity has basis in fact and is balanced against reasonable liquidity of the existing asset mix
- Discounted future benefits methods often are contested because of the numerous component variables; nevertheless they may be an excellent means to profile future returns
- Income projections should be realistic and profile the most likely growth scenario for the business
- Rates of growth of revenue and expenses should be supported by market observations (e.g., medical care component of Consumer Pricing Index) and established plans for expansion or development of the business
- Income projections must support amortization of purchase price in FMV appraisals. Inability to do so may indicate excessive physician compensation for business income, incorrect budgeting, and/or excessive purchase price. Use a Justification for Purchase Test

- Discounted future benefits should consider only future income streams that are reasonably definable (i.e., income beyond five years becomes more speculative, and a client's insistence on this period may require a risk calculation that obliterates business value)
- The income residual should be capitalized into value by the capitalization rate (not the discount) rate before being discounted to present value

Market Methods

- Prior transactions within the previous five to seven years should be considered valid unless highly significant changes in business operations have occurred as evidenced by trend analysis or if intangibles were excluded
- Market (private) comparisons, if used, should be of similar type businesses (i.e., specialty, geographic locale or population density, size, revenue, owner compensation)

Adjustments for Control and Marketability

- Be sure not to double count for any control adjustment; control is often accounted for in the valuation process
- Discounts for lack of marketability of either owner's shares or of the entity as a whole should be carefully scrutinized under all conditions
- The presence of multiple potential buyers in a given market in an acquisition valuation may be evidence against a marketability discount unless previous restrictions exist (e.g., existing right of first refusal to purchase, certain buy-sell and shareholder agreements, security law restrictions)
- Stock, ownership, and partnership dissolution valuations may have significant marketability discounts

Valuation Conclusions

- Asset methods should serve as guidelines, especially when the business appears to have no significant intangible value
- Liquidation value should be used in rare cases
- Reliance on rules of thumb should be avoided
- Earnings methods (capitalization of earnings and excess earnings) are used appropriately with the type of business (e.g., sole proprietorship, partnership, etc.)
- The excess earnings method is a method of last resort; in the healthcare industry, it should be used only in divorce appraisal[21]

- Discounted future benefits is always considered (except when excluded by law) when using the standard of FMV
- Private comparison value derivatives should fairly represent subject practice—out-of-date comparisons should be discarded
- Valuation synthesis by weighted average may consider all valid approaches for the subject entity but has no empirical basis in fact
- Final opinion of value using FMV should be supported by post-sale, after-tax cash flows with business purchased under market terms, within a reasonable period of time. General rule: Business flowing cash from operations independently within one to two years and payback of amortized expenses within five to seven years (depending on the size of the business)

STRATEGIC INVESTMENT VALUE IN HEALTHCARE

A Model for Quantitative and Qualitative Analyses of Investments

The cost of capital, either debt or equity, varies from one buyer to another. FMV dictates that capitalization and discount rates should be representative of market consensus. In healthcare, Medicare fraud and abuse and Stark laws and use of certain tax-exempt funds further dictate that acquisitions use FMV as the standard for appraising entities for acquisition and other types of integrated activities.

In analyzing the value of an investment, such as acquiring or affiliating with a healthcare provider organization, the capitalization and discount rates are based on the buyer's cost of capital, risk perceptions, and other relevant factors (e.g., interest rate, outlook for business, etc.). The difference between discounting future returns of a business based on market perceptions and the internal cost of capital or investment interests of a large (buyer) organization may be substantial. This difference in perceived benefit by a specific buyer, combined with an investment risk profile using capitalization and discount rates perhaps 10% less, significantly affect the ROI profile.

Return on Investment

Equity refers to the owner's interest in a business or property. Most businesses are financed by a combination of equity and debt, which represents the total investment, or invested capital. As an example from a valuation calculated to support a fair market opinion of value:

Return on equity (ROE) is defined as follows: Earnings divided by Equity

Example: Our practice has pretax earnings of $35,261 and equity of $256,852; the ROE would be

$$\$35,261 \div 256,852 = 14\%$$

Return on invested capital (ROI) is defined as follows: EBIT divided by Investment

Example: Our practice has $50,000 of interest-bearing debt and $256,852 equity, and it paid $5,000 in interest on the debt and had $35,261 of pretax earnings, the ROI would be

$$\frac{\$5,000 + \$35,261}{\$50,000 + \$256,852} = \frac{\$\,40,261}{\$306,852} = 13\%$$

To view the investment return as total cash available from the investment, that is, including depreciation, we have:

ROI for total investment is defined as follows: EBDIT divided by Investment

$$\$50,495 + \$25,500 = 75,995 \div \$340,000 = .224 \text{ (or } 22\%)$$

where $50,495 is pretax net income, $25,500 is depreciation, and $340,000 is the total purchase price.

This calculation takes into account total cash available, which dictates an unfunded depreciation account. While most small businesses do not fully fund depreciation, some allowance for replacement should be considered. Note: Any unused contingency amounts also should be added back.

Appropriate Rate of Return on Tangible Assets

Consider the following two statements from *Valuing Small Businesses and Professional Practices*:[22]

> There is strong consensus among valuation professionals that the appropriate return rate for tangible assets in the earnings-based methodologies depends on the asset mix in each case. Assets that are highly liquid, low risk, and/or readily acceptable as loan collateral require lower rates of return than assets that are less liquid, more risky, and/or less acceptable as collateral.

This is certainly the case when applying methods such as the capitalization of earnings and excess earnings methods.

> Asset values play a large role in determining collateral. Since loans are not usually made for 100% of collateral, and since there are some costs to borrowing money that are in addition to the basic interest rate, *the rate of return on net tangible assets used must be at least a few points above the rate at which bank loan money is available to them.* (emphasis added)

As we have stated previously, the internal rate of return desired by the buyer for its investment purposes varies from buyer to buyer. A company desiring a minimum ROI of 6% to 8% may choose to project its income targets to reach this goal. They may also choose wisely to tie the physician/provider employment contracts to achieving these minimum thresholds. Capital financing rates may vary accordingly.

An analysis of investments should include profiling the value of any acquisition or start-up venture, the simple and ultimate cash flow requirements, the purchase terms including cost of financing, amortization of purchase price, and appropriate ROI desired. This modeling effort is not complicated, although it is detailed. Most of the income-based valuation analyses should be recast under various sets of assumptions to obtain the most likely scenario of outcome. The ultimate consideration of strategic investments includes the specific consideration of market activities and the cost of not pursuing a given option (e.g., acquisition, start-up) or of alternative actions.

Internal Strategic Investment Analysis

Reassess the value opinion. Recall that a valuation made using the standard of FMV must be recast to address investment issues. In examining the strategic value of an investment, we take several issues into consideration.

- Adjusted financial statements are accepted as with FMV standard, or preferably post-sale pro forma cash flow statements are used.
- The buyer establishes the following.

    The internal rate of return for tangible assets and/or the business as a whole.

    The required rate of return (discount rate).

    The purchase terms and cost of debt and equity capital (usually internal rate plus hurdle rate, if any).

    Details in employment, compensation, capital, and operational budgeting.

In strategic investment analysis, we ask the following.

- Could you generate this ROI from other sources?
- Could you invest these funds elsewhere and get the same ROI?
- What community benefit results from this acquisition or affiliation?
- Can you afford *not* to pursue this venture due to other network plans?

    Managed care initiatives—preparation or reaction

    Employees/dependents require more network physicians

    Physicians leaving community

    Physicians retiring

    Physician bonding

    Counter competitor overtures or ingress into market

- Are there alternatives that will yield similar, positive postsale/affiliation outcomes?

    Other forms of physician integration activities

    Other forms of community service activities

Internal Strategic Investment Analysis—Acquisition of a Primary Care Practice

Business: Lakeway Family Medicine
The buyer has established the following.

- Rate of return for the business based on operating pro forma
- Required rate of return (discount rate): 12%
- Internal cost of capital: 8%
- Cash flows examined for 10 year-term at 8% (recognizing speculative nature of years 5 through 10)
- Taxable or tax-exempt entity under following scenarios

    Cash sale

    100% internal financing at 8% interest over 12 years

    20% down payment with balance at 8% over 12 years

    50% down payment with balance at 8% over 12 years

- Recommended level of capitalization profile
- No changes from pro forma employment, compensation, capital, and operational budgeting details

Changes in Valuation Opinion
The present value of the future income stream will be calculated by substituting a 12% discount rate as the buyer's required rate of return for this investment. By assuming a 12% discount rate, the buyer believes the following.

- The pro forma performance of this investment is considered to be an in-house operation (for a hospital, another source of nonoperating revenue), and its operational efficiency is evaluated as any other in-house operation is evaluated.
- This investment is worth $X to the buyer based on their justification of how they choose to use internal funds (taking into account the opportunity cost of capital).
- The ROI profile over the five-year period, plus the residual value of the business is satisfactory to pursue this business acquisition. Note: The market value of the business may not change significantly; it does not parallel any internal strategic value.

• The indirect benefit to the organization is consistent with the mission and goals of the institution and good business practice.

Internal Strategic Investment Analysis Results

Using a 12% discount rate, the present value of the five-year projected income stream increases from $348,616 to $878,250. To restate this, the buyer judges the present value of the future stream of income to be worth up to $878,250 in 1996 dollars based on their own internal needs and expectations for investments, yet they are purchasing this income stream for only $348,000.

Conservative business practice in healthcare would seek total ROI within five years due to uncertainties in managed care growth and changes in healthcare in general. In this example, the yield on financing of 8% on the original investment is in addition to overall ROI, any retained earnings of the business, and the residual value of the business at the end of the term.

Importance of Community Benefit in Strategic Investment Analysis

The area of community benefit and the use of certain tax exempt funds that contribute directly and substantially to the purpose for tax exemption should be considered. Healthcare organizations must include these often indirect benefits and weigh them accordingly. These local community issues are as individual as the communities themselves. Following are some examples.

• Improved access to physicians and/or healthcare services
• Retention or recruitment of providers
• Improvement in treatment modalities
• Pooling diverse areas of expertise (e.g. telemedicine/subspecialty consultations in rural areas)
• Lower cost services for patients
• Improved patient convenience

It is possible to profile myriad of circumstances to determine the best alternative in any given network venture. The scope of this type of analysis is limited principally by time and effort.

DETERMINING THE VALUE OF HEALTHCARE FACILITIES, NETWORKS, AND INTEGRATED DELIVERY SYSTEM COMPONENT ENTITIES

As stated previously, the existence of market data on actual transactions of the sales of hospitals, nursing homes, ambulatory, intermediate, long-term or assisted living facilities, and their holding companies is scarce, at best. We have seen that market comparisons may be made from actual transactions from within the subject entity, from a large number of transactions of comparable entities, or from specific identified guideline companies after adjusting financial and sales multiples. Using these criteria and given the dearth of data, it is nearly impossible to accurately apply market models of appraisal to the sales of these entities. Yet this appears to be a significant benchmark, if not the predominant method of valuation in the marketplace.

The June 17, 1996, issue of *Modern Healthcare* reported the price/earnings multiple method of valuation used by Wall Street investors when examining the value of hospital companies. The data suggest that the preferred method for valuing the Columbia/HCA, Health Management Associates, OrNda HealthCorp, Tenet Healthcare, Quorum Health Group, Universal Health Services, and Community Health Systems was a multiple of earnings before interest, taxes, depreciation, and amortization (EBITDA) ranging from 6.1 times EBITDA to 14.8 times EBITDA. Four companies (Columbia/HCA, OrNda, Tenet, and Quorum) ranged from 6.9 to 7.5 EBITDA. Readers may assume correctly that these amounts reflect some belief of investment value in the future earnings of these companies. The question is, how do we evaluate whether or not these amounts are "right"?

Consider the following real example. A hospital sought to purchase a skilled nursing facility (SNF) in a community. SNFs are controlled by most state's Certificate of Need laws, thereby eliminating the "make" option and severely restricting the "buy" option to only those who will sell at FMV. One SNF facility in the area was interested in selling at 10 times EBDITA ($5,400,000 on earnings of $540,000) because that was what it felt was the selling price for SNFs, and because the owner signed a long-term management contract for the facility (management needs to buy out the contract upon sale). Breaking down the issue, the appraiser consultant used/determined 1) $540,000 was expected, probable future earnings; 2) an appropriate risk rate representative of market consensus (FMV standard); 3) an estimated capitalization rate; 4) a market appraisal (guideline company) and range of market transactions, nationally and from that state; and 5) an estimate of liabilities, capital expenses, and depreciation. The result was that the appraiser determined that 10 times EBDITA was equivalent to a capitalization rate of 10%. A discounted cash flows analysis with a 20% (debt free) discount rate indicated a BEV of $3,200,000 (recall that the discounted cash flow [DCF] is generally a good proxy for upper end of FMV). The guideline company method indicated a BEV of $3,500,000. The market method using the price-to-earnings ratios and price-per-bed ratios for SNFs across the state (as reported from actual sales by a national trade organization) yielded a BEV of $3,700,000.

From these results, it is likely that the SNF seller is actually basing their value of the facility not on an earnings multiple of 10, but on some predetermined amount plus the buy-out of the management contract. From a valuation perspective, FMV determines the value of an entity free and clear of encumbrances or liabilities; the value of the SNF is after owner's reduction of the management agreement buy-out. But this raises another issue: What is the value of a highly regulated, capital-intensive business with a high asset book value with a generally good projected financial performance? The difference is the long-term care market. It is more stable than most other components of the healthcare delivery system, its revenue projections are more stable, its regulation and entry into the marketplace are arguably more stable, it is a growing industry. The question becomes, is this industry, and is the subject SNF facility, a reasonable candidate for a marketability premium? Working in individual situations, the professional appraiser consultant will guide the client through this understanding and develop a supportable opinion of value based on the circumstances surrounding the subject business, including all aspects of business and market analysis indicated in IRS Revenue Ruling 59-60.

Recall that an investor's decision to pursue may be based on factors other than strict performance of a given entity, or group of entities as in a health system purchase. In the acquisition, merger, partnering, or affiliation of healthcare entities, organization vision and goals dictate the need for embarking on strategies of system growth. From a value perspective, the vision and needs of the healthcare system guide the decisions that determine the options it must take to be successful, be it a local hospital, regional primary care integrated delivery network (IDN), or regional network of all levels of care. This is the principal reason for the development of taxable lines of business within exempt organizations. As these institutional providers move along the integration continuum, different structures and organizations will emerge that will allow investment strategies broader entry to serve system goals.

One of the most compelling arguments on building value is supported by Richard Normann and Rafael Ramirez—the secret of creating value lies in an organization's ability to build a "value creating system, within which different economic actors—suppliers, business partners, allies, customers—work together to co-produce value."[23] Robert Kaplan and David Norton suggest organizations develop a "balanced scorecard" linking financial perspectives with those of internal business (At what must we excel?), innovation and learning (How can we continue to improve and create value?), and customer perspective (How do customers see us?).[24] The challenge for the rest of us is to make informed decisions based on where we want to go and the means we have to get there.

NOTES

1. U.S. Internal Revenue Code. U.S. Government Printing Office: Washington, DC, Section 20.2031-1(b).

2. U.S. Internal Revenue Service. (1980) *IRS Appellate Conferee Valuation Training Program.* Commerce Clearing House: Chicago, 82–86.

3. U.S. Internal Revenue Service. (1993). *IRS Exempt Organization Continuing Professional Education Technical Instruction Program Textbook.* U.S. Government Printing Office: Washington, DC, 235, 236.

4. Pratt, S.P. et al. (1993). *Valuing Small Businesses and Professional Practices*, 2nd ed., Business One Irwin: Chicago, 4.

5. U.S. Tax Code 1.338 (b) -2(T).

6. IRS (1994). *Exempt Organization Program,* 185–190.

7. U.S. Internal Revenue Service. (1960). *Revenue Ruling 59–60.* Commerce Clearing House: Chicago.

8. Miles, R.C. (1984). *Basic Business Appraisal.* Southeast Business Investment Corporation: Boynton Beach, FL, 22.

9. Ibbotson Associates. (1996). *Stocks, Bonds, Bills and Inflation Yearbook.* Chicago: Author.

10. U.S. Internal Revenue Service, *IRS Appellate Conferee*, 82–86.

11. IRS Exempt Organization Program, 1996, 428.

12. Pratt, S.P. et al. (1993). *Valuing Small Businesses and Professional Practices,* 2nd ed., Business One Irwin: Chicago, 280.

13. U.S. 92nd Congress, 1st Session, House. (1971). Discounts Involved in Purchases of Common Stock. *Institutional Investor Study Report of the Securities and Exchange Commission.* Government Printing Office: Washington, DC, March 10, 5:2444–2456, Document No. 92-64, Part 5.

14. Gelman, M. (1972). An Economist-Financial Analyst's Approach to Valuing Stock of a Closely Held Company. *Journal of Taxation*, June, 353–54.

15. Trout, R.R. (1977). Estimation of the Discount Associated with the Transfer of Restricted Securities. *Taxes*, June, 381–85.

16. Moroney, R. E. (1973). Most Courts Overvalue Closely Held Stocks. *Taxes*, March, 144–154.

17. Maher, J.M. (1976). Discounts for Lack of Marketability for Closely-Held Business Interests. *Taxes*, September, 562–171.

18. Pratt, S.P. et al. (1993). *Valuing Small Businesses and Professional Practices,* 2nd ed., Business One Irwin: Chicago, 4.

19. Pratt, S.P. et al. (1993). *Valuing Small Businesses and Professional Practices,* 2nd ed., Business One Irwin: Chicago, 4.

20. Pratt, S.P. et al. (1993). *Valuing Small Businesses and Professional Practices,* 2nd ed., Business One Irwin: Chicago, 4.

21. In states where it is allowed.

22. Pratt, S.P. et al. (1993). *Valuing Small Businesses and Professional Practices,* 2nd ed., Business One Irwin: Chicago, 4.

23. Normann, R., Ramirez, R. (1993). From Value Chain to Value Constellation: Designing Interactive Strategy. *Harvard Business Review* 71(4):65–77.

24. Kaplan, R.S., Norton, D.P. (1992). The Balanced Scorecard—Measures That Drive Performance. *Harvard Business Review* 70(1):71–79.

4

CHAPTER

Provider Compensation

"The first sign that we do not know what we are doing is an obsession with numbers."

Goethe

Provider compensation issues are at once straightforward and highly complicated. In any event other than one physician deciding on his or her own compensation from net income, decision points are created involving finance, business economics, legal issues, and politics. This chapter is meant to provide analysts with a strong framework on compensation issues for a variety of settings. Increasingly, provider compensation is not simply for full-time employment or for income distribution models within medical groups. Provider compensation is coming to mean the entire spectrum of benefit that physicians (mainly) received from their *business transactions.* Providers are involved in an ever-widening variety of business relationships with each other, hospitals, and other for-profit and not-for-profit entities. The laws and regulatory guidance that address these relationships all derive from the nature of the provider's financial relationship with the entity with which they do business. Typically, as discussed in Chapter 3, the standard of value is fair market value (FMV). Moreover, the regulatory guidance in many cases requires ascertainment of the nature of FMV by an independent appraiser or financial advisor. The broadening nature of such business relationships suggests that a review of the legal issues pertaining to all aspects of compensation relationships be discussed.

The first part of this chapter deals with a lengthy overview of legal issues in compensation and income distribution. This section provides the reader with the legal and structural basis for most decisions on compensation. The second, more practical part deals with operational issues on provider compensation.

Please note that for clarity of presentation, much of the legal context is presented in this chapter and Chapter 7. Some areas may seem to overlap; however, it was thought to present the issues in total under the relevant legal setting rather than in two separate areas in both chapters. Note also that in some cases, it is important to differentiate physician from provider, as in the larger context of direct healthcare providers, such as physicians and physician extenders (usually physician assistants and nurse practitioners although nurse anesthetists and midwives might be considered).

LEGAL IMPLICATIONS OF COMPENSATION AND INCOME DISTRIBUTION

Fraud and Abuse and Antireferral Laws

The primary concern of the fraud and abuse and antireferral laws is the avoidance of fraud and overutilization in the Medicare and Medicaid reimbursement programs. A 1989 study by the Department of Health and Human Services, Office of the Inspector General, found that patients of referring physicians who invested in independent clinical laboratories ordered 45% more tests for their patients compared to Medicare patients.[1] This finding became the impetus for enacting the Stark Antireferral laws.

Violation of these statutes incurs severe penalties, including criminal charges for violation of the anti-kickback statutes. To compound these severe penalties, many commonplace activities in the healthcare arena would be prohibited by these laws but for the application of statutory and regulatory "safe harbors," which protect these activities from prosecution. While the federal laws govern only payments for items or services by Medicare and Medicaid, many state laws have similar prohibitions that apply to all third-party payors with varying safe harbor protections.

Medicare Anti-kickback Law[2]

The Medicare anti-kickback law prohibits the filing of false claims and the payment of illegal remuneration to receive Medicare benefits or payments. The illegal remuneration prohibition specifies that persons in violation of the statute will be found guilty of a felony and fined up to $25,000 and/or will be subject to prison for up to five years. Culpable conduct under the statute is considered the following.

1. Knowingly and willfully soliciting or receiving *any remuneration* (including kickbacks, bribes, or rebates), directly or indirectly, overtly or covertly, in cash or in kind

    a. In return for referring an individual to a person for the furnishing, or arranging for the furnishing of, any item or service for which payment may be made in whole or in part under Medicare or Medicaid; or

    b. In return for purchasing, leasing, ordering, or arranging for or recommending purchasing, leasing, or ordering any good, facility, service, or item for which payment may be made in whole or in part by Medicare or Medicaid

2. Knowingly and willfully offering or paying any remuneration (including any kickback, bribe, or rebate), directly or indirectly, overtly or covertly, in cash or in kind to any person to induce such person

    a. To refer an individual to a person for the furnishing, or arranging for the furnishing of, any item or service for which payment may be made under Medicare or Medicaid; or

    b. To purchase, lease, order, recommend, or arrange for purchasing, leasing, or ordering any good, facility, service, or item for which payment may be made in whole or in part by Medicare or Medicaid

The Medicare anti-kickback law is intended to prohibit "actions in which the defendant intends to exercise influence over the reason or judgment of another in an effort to cause the referral of program-related business."[3] Unlike the Stark II antireferral law, the anti-kickback law is a criminal statute that requires the defendant to have "knowledge and willfulness," in other words, the defendant must have "acted with knowledge that his conduct was unlawful."[4] In *United States* v. *Greber,*[5] the defendant paid a referral fee of 40% to physicians referring patients to him for diagnostic services, which the defendant called "consulting" fees, even though some of the referring physicians performed no services for him. The court held that the anti-kickback statute was violated if *any* purpose of the payment was to induce referrals. The court reasoned that Congress intended the word "remuneration" to include situations in which a service was actually rendered in addition to a referral. Similarly, in *United States* v. *Kats,*[6] the defendant owned a 25% share of a clinic that sent specimens to a lab for diagnostic purposes. The defendant's clinic received a 50% kickback of fees for tests that it referred to the lab. The court held that the government need not show that compensation for referrals was the primary purpose of a payment. Even if only one purpose of a payment was to induce referrals, the statute was violated.

The Stark law, in contrast, is a strict liability type of statute in which the defendant's state of mind is not relevant. Similar to the Stark law, however, the anti-kickback law interprets "remuneration" very broadly and it has several safe harbors.

Safe Harbors

As with the antireferral statute, the anti-kickback statute also provides safe harbors, many of which are similar to, but not exactly like, the antireferral safe harbors. These safe harbors protect certain payment and business practices from criminal prosecution or civil sanctions under the statute.

Employment Relationships Safe Harbor

For employer-employee relationships, the safe harbor simply defines remuneration not to include amounts paid by an employer to an employee who has a bona fide employment relationship with the employer, for employment in the furnishing of items or services payable by Medicare or Medicaid. This safe harbor has fewer requirements than the related safe harbor under Stark II.

Personal Services Contracts Safe Harbor

This safe harbor defines remuneration not to include any payments made by a principal to an agent or independent contractor as compensation for the agent's services if the following criteria are met.

1. The agency agreement is in writing and signed by the parties.
2. The agreement specifies the services to be provided by the agent.
3. If the services are to be part time or sporadic, and not full time for the term of the agreement, the agreement must specify exactly the schedule of such intervals, their precise length, and the exact charge for such intervals.
4. The term of the agreement is for at least one year.
5. The aggregate compensation paid over the term of the agreement is
   a. Set in advance.
   b. Consistent with FMV in arm's-length transactions.
   c. Not determined in a manner that takes into account the volume or value of referrals or other business generated between the parties for which payment may be made by Medicare or Medicaid.
6. The services to be provided under the contract must not involve the counseling or promotion of a business arrangement or other activity that violates any state or federal law.

It is important to note that the aggregate compensation must be set in advance under this safe harbor, unlike the Stark II safe harbor. Thus, in managed care contracts, the contract must specify the total amount to be paid under the contract for all the services to be performed.

Sale of Practice

Another safe harbor defines remuneration as not including payments made to one practitioner by another practitioner for the sale of his or her medical practice. The two requirements that must be met under this safe harbor are as follows.

1. The period between the date of the first agreement pertaining to the sale and the completion of the sale is no more than one year, and

2. The seller will not be in a professional position to make referrals to the buyer of the practice where such services would be paid for by Medicare or Medicaid.

Referral Services

Remuneration does not include payments or the exchange of anything of value between a participant and a referral service if the following occurs.

1. The referral service does not exclude participants or entities that meet its qualifications.

2. The participant's payments must be

    a. Assessed equally and collected equally from all participants.

    b. The payments must be based on only the cost of operating the referral service, not on the volume or value of referrals.

3. The referral service cannot impose requirements on the manner in which the participant provides the services to a referred person, but it may require that the participant charge at the same rate it charges nonreferred persons, or it may be charged a reduced fee or no fee.

4. The referral service must make five disclosures to each person seeking a referral, which it must maintain in a written record signed by either the referred person or the discloser. These disclosures must address the manner of selecting the group of participants to whom the referrals are made, whether the participant pays a fee to be listed, the manner of selecting a particular participant, the nature of the relationship between the referral services and the group of participants, and the nature of any restrictions that would exclude a person or entity from being a participant.

Stark II Antireferral Law[7]

The Stark II antireferral law was enacted in 1989 and is named after its sponsor, Representative Fortney "Pete" Stark. The Stark law generally prohibits referrals by physicians to entities in which they have a financial interest. Stark I originally applied only to payments for clinical laboratory services in which the referring physician owned a financial interest in the referred-to laboratory. Stark II became effective on January 1, 1995, and expanded the prohibitions to eleven "designated health services."

General Rule

The general rule of the antireferral prohibition provides that physicians or their immediate family members who have a financial relationship with an entity cannot make a referral to that entity for the furnishing of designated health services for which payment may be made by Medicare or Medicaid. The referred-to entity cannot bill Medicare, any individual, or other entity or third-party payor for any designated health services provided from a prohibited referral.[8]

Definitions

A *financial relationship* is defined as an ownership or investment interest in the referred-to entity, or a compensation arrangement with the entity. An "ownership or investment interest" can be through equity, debt, or any other means, and it includes an interest in an entity that holds an ownership or investment interest in an entity providing the designated health service. A *compensation arrangement* is any arrangement involving any remuneration between a physician or immediate family member and the referred-to entity unless it involves only insurance payments, debt forgiveness for inaccurate tests or procedures, or the provision of items or devices used solely to collect, transport, process, or store specimens for the entity providing the item, device, or supply. A compensation arrangement therefore normally would include payment of salaries, rental or lease payments, and any other type of remuneration being exchanged.

Immediate family is defined in the regulations as the range of relatives who could be in a position to influence the pattern of a physician's referrals. More specifically, the definition includes husband or wife; natural or adoptive parent; child or sibling; step-parent, step-child, step-brother, or step-sister; father-in-law, mother-in-law, son-in law, daughter-in-law, brother-in-law, or sister-in-law; grandparent or grandchild; and spouse of a grandparent or grandchild.[9]

With regard to physician services, a *referral* is the request by a physician for an item or service payable by Medicare Part B, including a request for a consultation by another physician and any test or procedure ordered by or to be performed by or under the supervision of the other physician. With regard to items other than physician services, the request or establishment of a plan of care by a physician that includes the provision of designated health services under Medicare Part A or Part B is also considered to be a referral. An exception to the definition of referral under the statute involves services that are integral to a consultation by certain specialists. If the following services are furnished by or under the supervision of the specialist pursuant to a consultation requested by another physician, then they are not "referrals" by a referring physician: a) a request by a pathologist for clinical diagnostic lab tests and pathological examination services, b) a request by a radiologist for diagnostic radiology services, or c) a request by a radiation oncologist for radiation therapy.

As of January 1, 1995, the referral prohibition applies to 11 "designated health services." Between January 1, 1992, and January 1, 1995, the prohibition applied only to clinical laboratory services, but 10 more services were added effective in 1995.

The designated health services to which the referral prohibition currently applies include the following services.

1. Clinical laboratory services
2. Physical therapy services
3. Occupational therapy services
4. Radiology services, including MRIs, CAT scans, and ultrasound services
5. Radiation therapy services and supplies
6. Durable medical equipment and supplies (iron lungs, oxygen tents, hospital beds, and wheelchairs used in the patient's home)
7. Parenteral and enteral nutrients, equipment, and supplies
8. Prosthetics, orthotics, and prosthetic devices and supplies
9. Home health services
10. Outpatient prescription drugs
11. Inpatient and outpatient hospital services

Reporting

Any entity furnishing items or services payable by Medicare must submit information on its financial relationships to the Health Care Financing Administration (HCFA) unless the entity provides 20 or fewer Part A and Part B items or services per calendar year. Information that must be reported includes the names of physicians and their immediate family members who have a financial relationship with an entity, the nature of that financial relationship, and the covered items or services provided by the entity. The information must be filed within 30 days after notification from the carrier or intermediary, and within 60 days after any changes in the submitted information. Entities also must retain documentation of the information submitted and furnish it to HCFA or the Office of Inspector General upon request.

Effective June 1, 1996, HCFA is mandating the use of a single new-provider application form that increases the amount of information required on the applicant's operating locations, ownership, and affiliations.[10] HCFA also has indicated that it has contracted with data verification firms to ensure that information listed on the applications is truthful, and the agency also is increasing its on-site visits to providers to ascertain whether providers are actually providing the services for which they are billing.[11]

Sanctions

Sanctions for violating the referral prohibition are somewhat severe and include denial of payment for designated health services rendered through a prohibited referral, mandatory refunds of claims paid, civil monetary penalties, and exclusion from the Medicare and Medicaid reimbursement programs. Civil monetary penalties for filing prohibited claims are up to $15,000 for each service billed. Civil monetary penalties for circumvention schemes, such as a cross-referral network, are up to $100,000 for each arrangement. Sanctions also apply for failure to report information, in the form of a civil monetary penalty of $10,000 for each day beyond the deadline that the information remains unreported.

Safe Harbors

There are several safe harbor provisions that protect common activities in the healthcare industry from sanctions. There are three safe harbors that apply to both types of financial relationships—ownership/investment interests and compensation arrangements. These three safe harbors relate to physicians' services, in-office ancillary services, and prepaid plans. Safe harbors applying only to ownership/investment interests are for publicly traded securities, shares in regulated investment companies, hospitals in Puerto Rico, rural providers, and hospital ownership. Safe harbors applying only to compensation arrangements are for office space rental, equipment rental, bona fide employment relationships, personal service arrangements, unrelated remuneration, physician recruitment, isolated transactions, group practice arrangements with a hospital, and payments by physicians for items and services.

Exceptions to Ownership and Compensation Arrangements

Physician Services.　An important safe harbor protects referrals among physicians in the same group practice. If physician services are provided personally by, or under the personal supervision of, another physician in the same group practice as the referring physician, then the activity does not constitute a prohibited referral.

The statute defines a *group practice* as a group of two or more physicians legally organized as a partnership, professional corporation, foundation, nonprofit corporation, faculty practice plan, or similar association. To qualify as a group practice, the association must meet the following requirements.

1. Each physician member must substantially provide the full range of services that the physician routinely provides, including medical care, consultation, diagnosis, or treatment, through the joint use of shared office space, facilities, equipment, and staff.

2. Substantially all of the services of the physician members are provided through the group and billed under the group's billing number, and amounts received are treated as group receipts. "Substantially all" means at least 75% of the total patient care services of the group practice members.[12]

3. Overhead expenses and income are distributed in accordance with previously determined methods.

4. No physician member receives compensation based directly or indirectly on referrals unless for a productivity bonus.

5. Group members must conduct personally at least 75% of the physician patient encounters of the group practice.

6. The arrangement must meet other requirements that may be imposed by the Department of Health and Human Services (DHHS) from time to time.

An important aspect of this definition is that an entity whose individual physicians bill in their own individual names does not qualify as a group practice. The group must attest in writing, on a yearly basis, that it meets the requirements of the group practice definition. Additionally, *the group practice may pay its physician members a productivity bonus or profit sharing if the bonus or share is based on services personally performed by the physician or services incident to personally performed services, and if the bonus or share is not calculated based on referrals.*

In-Office Ancillary Services. Another important safe harbor applies to in-office ancillary services. To qualify for this safe harbor, the arrangement must meet the following requirements.

1. The ancillary services must be furnished personally by
   a. The referring physician,
   b. A physician in the same group practice (as defined above) of the referring physician, or
   c. Individuals directly supervised by the physician or a physician in the same group practice.

2. The services must be furnished in a building in which the referring physician furnishes services unrelated to the designated health services. If a group practice is involved, the services may be furnished in another building used by the group practice for some or all of the group's clinical lab services, or for the centralized provision of the group's designated health services; and

3. The services must be billed by
   a. The physician performing or supervising the services, or
   b. The group practice through the group's billing number, or
   c. By an entity wholly owned by the physician or group performing the service.

Services excluded under this safe harbor are for durable medical equipment and supplies, but those included are infusion pumps, and parenteral and enteral nutrients, equipment, and supplies. The final regulations issued for Stark I in August 1995 define *direct supervision* to mean "supervision by a physician who is present in the office suite and immediately available to provide assistance and direction throughout the time that services are being performed."[13]

Prepaid Plans.   Referrals made under managed care plans also are protected by a safe harbor if certain criteria are met. The services must be furnished by an organization having a contract with an enrollee in which the organization is a federally qualified HMO or in which it receives prepaid payments under a federal demonstration project.

Exceptions Limited to Ownership and Investment Interests
Ownership of Publicly Traded Investment Securities.   Ownership of a publicly traded investment in a large company is protected under a safe harbor if certain requirements are met. The ownership may be in the form of shares, bonds, debentures, notes, or other debt instruments. The requirements for this safe harbor are

1. The terms of the investment must be those that are generally available to the public;
2. The interest must be publicly traded, and must be listed on NASDAQ, AMEX, or a foreign or regional stock exchange publishing daily quotes; and
3. The average shareholder equity in the company must be greater than $75 million over the previous three years.

Ownership of Shares in a Regulated Investment Company.   This safe harbor protects investment interests in regulated investment companies, as defined in Internal Revenue Code Sec. 851(a). To qualify for this safe harbor, the company must have had average total assets exceeding $75 million over the previous three years.

Designated Health Services by Puerto Rico Hospitals.   Designated health services provided by hospitals located in Puerto Rico are also protected by a safe harbor. The designated health services are limited to the 11 services defined above.

Rural Providers.   Another safe harbor protects designated health services that are furnished in a rural area. A rural area is defined as an area located outside of a metropolitan statistical area, or similar urban area, as defined by the federal Office of Management and Budget.[14] In addition to the requirement that the services be furnished in a rural area, substantially all (75%) of the designated health services must be furnished by the rural provider to individuals residing in that rural area. With regard to laboratory services, testing must be performed on the premises of the rural laboratory. If not, the laboratory performing the testing must bill Medicare directly.

Hospital Ownership. The final safe harbor relating solely to ownership and investment interests is for hospital ownership. Under this safe harbor, for designated health services provided by a hospital, the ownership or investment interest must be in the hospital itself, not in a subdivision of the hospital. In addition, the referring physician must be authorized to perform services at the hospital. If an entity, such as a joint venture, is jointly owned by a hospital and another entity, then this safe harbor will not apply because there is no ownership interest in the hospital.

Exceptions Limited to Compensation Arrangements

The remaining safe harbors apply only to compensation arrangements and are commonly relied on to protect many common activities in the healthcare industry.

Space Rental and Equipment Rental Safe Harbors. The office space rental and equipment rental safe harbors are similar and thus are considered together here, although applicable differences are noted. To fall under the office space or equipment rental safe harbors, seven criteria must be met, as follows.

1. There must be a written lease signed by the parties that specifies the premises or equipment covered by the lease.
2. The space or equipment rented must not exceed that which is needed for legitimate business purposes.
3. As applied only to the space rental safe harbor, the space must be used exclusively by the lessee when it is being used by the lessee, but the lessee can pay for common areas based on its pro rata share owed for the common areas, calculated as a ratio of the lessee's space to the total space.
4. The lease term must be for at least one year.
5. The rental charges over the term of the lease must be
   a. Set in advance.
   b. Consistent with FMV.
   c. Not determined in a manner that takes into account the volume or value of any referrals or other business generated between the parties.
6. The lease would be commercially reasonable even without any referrals between the parties.
7. The lease complies with any other requirements that may be imposed by new regulations.

Fair market value (FMV) is defined as the value in an arm's-length transaction, which is consistent with the general market value. The value cannot be adjusted to reflect the additional value that either party would attribute to the proximity or convenience to the lessor in which the lessor is a potential source of patient referrals.

Bona Fide Employment Relationships Safe Harbor. Employer-employee relationships are not considered to be referral arrangements and will fall under a safe harbor if five criteria are met.

1. Amounts are paid by an employer to a physician or family member who has a bona fide employment relationship with the employer for the provision of services.
2. Payments are made for identifiable services.
3. The amount of remuneration is
   a. Consistent with FMV for the services.
   b. Not based on the value or volume of referrals. A productivity bonus is permitted if it is for services personally performed by the physician or family member.
4. The agreement would be commercially reasonable even without referrals.
5. The arrangement meets any other requirements imposed by new regulations.

This safe harbor is very often relied on and is somewhat easy to comply with. An important consideration is that the payments must be for identifiable services, not a subterfuge disguising payments for referrals.

Personal Services Contracts Safe Harbor. The personal services contract safe harbor is similar to the employment relationship safe harbor except that it applies to independent contractor arrangements. Such arrangements will fall under this safe harbor if eight criteria are met.

1. The remuneration must be from an entity under an arrangement or a contract.
2. The arrangement must be in writing and signed by the parties, and it must specify the services covered.
3. The arrangement must cover all of the services to be provided by the agent to the entity, such that there are no "side agreements."
4. The aggregate services contracted for must not exceed that which is reasonable and necessary for legitimate business purposes.
5. The term of the arrangement must be for at least one year.
6. The compensation to be paid over the term of the arrangement must be

>   *a.* Set in advance.
>
>   *b.* Must not exceed FMV.
>
>   *c.* Must not be based on referrals.

7. The services to be performed do not involve the counseling or promotion of an illegal business arrangement.

8. Other requirements that may be set forth in new regulations.

Under the Stark laws, the compensation may be specified on a per-service or a per-hour basis, unlike under the comparable anti-kickback safe harbor. A physician incentive plan is permitted, which is defined as any compensation arrangement between a physician and an entity that may have the effect of reducing or limiting the services provided to enrollees of the entity. Compensation can be referral-sensitive, such as with capitation, withholds, bonuses, and the like, if two criteria are met.

1. No specific payment is made to a physician or group to induce them to limit medically necessary services as to a specific individual.

2. If the plan puts the physician or entity at substantial financial risk, as defined in 42 U.S.C. § 1395mm(i)(A)(ii), the plan must comply with any requirements set forth in the regulations.

Unrelated Remuneration.   Another safe harbor protects arrangements in which remuneration is provided by a hospital to a physician for services unrelated to the provision of designated health services.

Physician Recruitment.   Incentives provided to physicians to induce them to relocate to a hospital's service area will fall under a safe harbor if certain requirements are met.

1. The remuneration must be provided to the physician to induce him or her to relocate to the hospital's area so that the physician can be on the hospital's medical staff.[15]

2. The physician must not be required to refer patients to the hospital.

3. The remuneration must not be based on referrals.

4. The incentive must meet other requirements as defined by DHHS.

In *Polk County, Texas* v. *Peters,*[16] the court held that a physician recruitment agreement violated the Stark laws because the physician agreed to refer patients to the hospital in exchange for an interest-free loan, free office space, rent and utility subsidies, and reimbursement for malpractice insurance.

Isolated Transactions.   The Stark law also exempts isolated transactions from its coverage if certain criteria are met. Specific isolated transactions include the one-time sale of property or a medical practice. The requirements that must be met are the following.

1. The remuneration paid for the practice must be consistent with the FMV of the practice.
2. The remuneration must not be referral-sensitive.
3. The agreement would be commercially reasonable even without the possibility of referrals.
4. The agreement must meet other requirements that may be imposed by DHHS.

The August 1995 final regulations issued on Stark I partially clarified this safe harbor. The new rule requires that there be no additional transactions between the parties for six months after the isolated transaction except for transactions that are specifically excepted under other safe harbors. The new rule defined *transaction* to involve a single payment, and not long-term or installment payments such as a mortgage. Each installment payment would constitute a transaction for purposes of this rule, and thus this safe harbor would not apply. If additional transactions fall under a safe harbor, then the initial transaction would still qualify as an isolated one.[17] The concern with extended payments is that the physician would be under a continuing obligation to refer patients to the purchasing entity in order to continue receiving payments.

Group Practice Arrangements with a Hospital.   Group practice arrangements with a hospital will fall under a safe harbor if several requirements are met.

1. The arrangement must be between a hospital and a group practice, as defined above.
2. The designated health services may be provided by the group practice but must be billed by the hospital.
3. For services provided to an inpatient of the hospital, the arrangement must meet the requirements in 42 U.S.C. § 1395x(b)(3) as to the provision of inpatient hospital services.
4. The arrangement must have begun before December 19, 1989 and must have continued without interruption.
5. Substantially all of the designated health services covered by the arrangement and furnished to patients of the hospital are furnished by the group practice.
6. The agreement must be in writing, and it must specify the services to be provided along with the compensation to be paid.
7. The compensation paid over the term of the contract must be consistent with FMV and not based on referrals.

8. The compensation per unit of services must be fixed in advance and must be commercially reasonable even if no referrals are made.
9. The arrangement must meet other requirements as set forth by the DHHS.

Payments by Physicians for Items and Services. The final safe harbor applicable to compensation arrangements relates to payments by physicians for items and services. This safe harbor has not been clearly defined in regulations to date, but the DHHS has promulgated two requirements.

1. The payments must be by a physician to a lab for clinical services; or
2. The payments must be by a physician to an entity for other items or services and furnished at the FMV price.

Discounts. Discounts that a seller gives to a buyer on goods or services for which a claim may be submitted to Medicare or Medicaid are not defined as remuneration as long as several criteria are met.

1. Buyer's Duties
   a. If the buyer reports costs on a cost report:
      1. The discount must be earned based on the purchases of that same good or service bought within a single fiscal year of the buyer.
      2. The buyer must claim the benefit of the discount in the fiscal year in which the discount is earned, or the following year.
      3. The buyer must fully and accurately report the discount on the cost report.
      4. The buyer must provide the information given by the seller to the DHHS upon request.
   b. If the buyer is an HMO or competitive medical plan (CMP) with a risk contract under federal or state law, then it need not report the discount unless required by the risk contract.
   c. If the buyer is neither of the above:
      1. The discount must be made at the time of the original sale of the good or service.
      2. If the item or service is separately claimed for payment with the DHHS or the state, the buyer must fully and accurately report the discount.
      3. The buyer must provide information supplied by the seller to the DHHS or the state upon request.

A CMP is a state-licensed entity that provides healthcare on a prepaid, capitated basis through physicians employed by the CMP. The CMP assumes full financial risk and must have reserve protections similar to HMOs. It also must meet federal requirements for open enrollment, grievance, and quality assurance procedures.

2. Seller's Duties
   a. If the buyer is an HMO or CMP with a risk contract, the seller need not report the discount to the buyer.
   b. If the buyer is any other individual or entity, the following rules apply.
      1. The seller must fully and accurately report the discount on the invoice or statement submitted to the buyer and must inform the buyer of its duty to report the discount, or
      2. If the discount is unknown at the time of the sale, the seller must fully and accurately report the existence of a discount program on the invoice or statement submitted to the buyer and must tell the buyer of its duty to report and give the buyer documentation of the calculation of the discount when it becomes known. This information must include identification of the specific goods and services bought to which the discount applies.

The discounts safe harbor defines a *discount* to mean a reduction in the amount a seller charges a buyer for a good or service based on an arm's-length transaction. The buyer may buy either directly or through a wholesaler or group purchasing organization (GPO). A discount may be in the form of a rebate check, credit, or coupon directly redeemable from the seller only to the extent that such reductions in price are due to the original goods or services bought. A discount is defined not to include the following.

1. Cash payments
2. Free or reduced charges in exchange for an agreement to buy a different good or service
3. Reductions in price applicable to one payor but not to Medicare or Medicaid
4. Reductions in price given to beneficiaries, such as routine reductions or waivers of coinsurance or deductibles owed by the beneficiary
5. Warranties
6. Services provided under personal services or management contracts
7. Other remuneration in cash or in kind not explicitly described in the safe harbor

Group Purchasing Organizations. Payments by a vendor of goods or services to a GPO as part of an agreement to furnish such goods or services to an individual or entity are defined as not comprising remuneration, if certain criteria are met. A *GPO* is defined as an entity authorized to act as a purchasing agent for a group of individuals or entities who are furnishing services payable by Medicare or Medicaid, and who are neither wholly owned by the GPO nor subsidiaries of a parent corporation that wholly owns the GPO, either directly or through another wholly owned entity. The criteria for this safe harbor are as follows.

1. If the entity receiving the goods or services is a healthcare provider of services, then the GPO must disclose in writing to the entity at least annually, and to DHHS on request, the amount received from each vendor as to purchases made by or on behalf of the entity.

2. The GPO must have a written agreement with each individual or entity for which items or services are furnished that provides either

   a. The contract states that participating vendors, from which the individual or entity will purchase goods or services, will pay to the GPO up to only 3% of the purchase price of the goods or services provided by that vendor; or

   b. If the fee paid to the GPO is not fixed at 3% or less, the contract must specify the maximum amount the GPO will be paid by each vendor, where the amount may be a fixed sum or percentage of the value of the purchases made from the vendor by the group members under the contract between the vendor and the GPO.

Waiver of Beneficiary Coinsurance and Deductible Amounts. Under this safe harbor, remuneration is defined not to include a reduction or waiver of a Medicare or Medicaid program beneficiary's obligation to pay coinsurance or deductibles if the following criteria are met.

1. If the amount is owed to a hospital for inpatient hospital services payable through the prospective payment system

   a. The hospital may not later claim the amount reduced or waived as a bad debt or otherwise shift the burden of the reduction or waiver onto Medicare or Medicaid, other payors, or individuals.

   b. The hospital must offer to reduce or waive the coinsurance or deductible without regard to the reason for admission, the length of stay, or the diagnosis-related group for which the claim is filed.

   c. The hospital's offer to reduce or waive the coinsurance or deductible amounts must not be made as part of a price reduction agreement between a hospital and a third-party payor, unless the agreement is part of a contract for the furnishing of items or services to a beneficiary of a Medicare supplemental policy issued under the terms of the Social Security Act, section 1882(t)(1).

1. If the amount is owed to a federally qualified healthcare center or facility under the Public Health Services Act and is owed by an individual who qualified for subsidized services under the Public Health Services Act or under titles V or XIX of the Social Security Act, then the healthcare center or facility may reduce or waive the coinsurance or deductible amounts for items or services payable under Part B of Medicare or Medicaid.

Increased Coverage, Reduced Cost-Sharing Amounts, or Reduced Premium Amounts Offered by Health Plans.   Another safe harbor defines remuneration not to include the additional coverage of any item or service offered by a health plan to an enrollee, or the reduction of some or all of the enrollee's obligation to pay the health plan or contract healthcare provider for cost-sharing amounts such as coinsurance, deductibles, or copayment amounts, or for premium amounts attributable to items or services covered by the health plan, Medicare, or Medicaid, if certain criteria are met.

1. For risk-based HMOs, CMPs, prepaid health plans, or demonstration projects, the plan must offer the same increased coverage or reduced cost-sharing or premium amounts to all enrollees unless otherwise approved by HCFA or the state.

2. For HMOs, CMPs, healthcare prepayment plans, or prepaid health plans that have executed a contract with HCFA or a state to receive payment for enrollees on a reasonable cost or similar basis:

a. The health plan must offer the same increased coverage or reduced cost-sharing or premium amounts to all enrollees unless otherwise approved by HCFA or a state.

b. The health plan must not claim the costs of the increased coverage or reduced cost-sharing or premium amounts against Medicare, Medicaid, or other payors or individuals.

Price Reductions Offered to Health Plans.   A reduction in price, which a contract healthcare provider offers to a health plan under the terms of a written agreement between the provider and the health plan for the sole purpose of furnishing to enrollees items or services covered by the health plan, by Medicare, or by Medicaid, is defined as not comprising remuneration as long as the following criteria are met.

1. If the health plan is an HMO, CMP, or prepaid health plan under contract with HCFA or a state under the Social Security Act, section 1876(g) or 1903(m), then the contract healthcare provider must not claim payment in any form from DHHS or a state for items or services furnished under the contract except as approved by HCFA or the state, and the provider may not otherwise shift the burden of such an agreement onto Medicare, Medicaid, other payors, or individuals.

2. If the health plan is an HMO, CMP, healthcare prepayment plan, or prepaid health plan that has executed a contract with HCFA or a state to receive payments for enrollees on a reasonable cost or similar basis:

   a. The term of the agreement between the health plan and the contract healthcare provider must be for at least one year.

   b. The contract must specify in advance the covered items or services to be furnished to enrollees along with the methodology for computing the payment to the contract healthcare provider.

   c. The health plan must fully and accurately report, on the cost report or other claim form filed with DHHS or the state, the amount it has paid the contract provider under the agreement for the covered items or services furnished to enrollees.

   d. The contract provider must not claim payment in any form from DHHS or a state for items or services furnished under the agreement except as approved by HCFA or a state, and the provider may not otherwise shift the burden of such a contract onto Medicare, Medicaid, other payors, or individuals.

3. If the health plan is not described above, then both the health plan and provider must meet the following requirements.

   a. The term of the agreement between the plan and provider must be at least one year.

   b. The contract must specify in advance the covered items and services to be furnished to enrollees, which party is to file claims or requests for payment with Medicare or Medicaid for such items and services, and the schedule of fees the contract provider will charge for furnishing such items and services to enrollees.

   c. The fee schedule contained in the agreement must remain in effect throughout the term of the contract unless a fee increase results directly from a payment update approved by Medicare or Medicaid.

   d. The party submitting claims or requests for payment from Medicare or Medicaid for items or services furnished under the contract must not claim or request payment for amounts in excess of the fee schedule.

   e. The contract provider and the plan must fully and accurately report on any cost report filed with Medicare or Medicaid the fee schedule amounts charged under the contract.

f. The party who is not required to file claims under the contract must not claim or request payment in any form from DHHS or a state for items or services furnished under the contract, and it may not otherwise shift the burden of such a contract onto Medicare, Medicaid, other payors, or individuals.

TAX-EXEMPTION ISSUES UNDER SECTION 501(C)(3) OF THE INTERNAL REVENUE CODE

The rationale for tax exemption was stated succinctly in *Geisinger Health Plan* v. *Commissioner* in which the court reasoned that "charitable exemptions from income taxation constitute a quid pro quo: the public is willing to relieve an organization from paying income taxes because the organization is providing a benefit to the public."[18]

Unlike other statutory categories of tax exemption, section 501(c)(3) status gives its holders the ability to accept donations that are tax-deductible to their donors. Concurrent with this ability is an additional level of responsibility placed on such organizations. To receive and maintain section 501(c)(3) classification, such organizations must meet several requirements.

1. The entity must be organized exclusively for charitable purposes—the "organizational test."
2. The entity must be operated exclusively for exempt purposes—the "operational test."
3. No substantial portion of the entity's activities can be for a private benefit. The entity must serve a public rather than a private interest.
4. No part of the entity's net earnings may inure to the benefit of an "insider."

These requirements are deceptively simple and may function as traps for the unwary in certain circumstances. As for the first requirement, the IRS held that the promotion of health is a charitable purpose under I.R.C. §501(c)(3) in Revenue Ruling 69-545.[19] A hospital is engaged in the promotion of health if it meets the "community benefit" test, as follows.

1. The class of persons benefiting from the hospital's activities must be reasonably broad.
2. The hospital must operate an emergency room open to all persons without regard to their ability to pay.
3. The hospital must provide hospital care to everyone in the community who is able to pay directly or through private or public reimbursement.

4. The hospital must be governed by a board of trustees composed of independent civic leaders, as opposed to physicians or others with a private interest in the organization.

5. The hospital must maintain a medical staff open to all qualified physicians.

Other factors that the IRS has considered since the 1969 ruling include the following.

1. Whether the hospital provides specialized services if it does not operate an emergency room.

2. The hospital's provision of charity care, medical research, and educational activities.

3. The hospital's compliance with other laws, such as the Stark antireferral laws and the Emergency Medical Treatment and Active Labor Act.

To meet the "organizational test," a hospital's articles of incorporation must indicate that its purposes are limited to exempt purposes, such as charity. The hospital's organizational documents must also prohibit it from engaging in activities unrelated to its charitable purposes. Finally, the organizational documents also must indicate that the hospital's assets will be distributed to charitable organizations or for charitable purposes upon dissolution of the hospital.

The entity also must be operated exclusively for charitable purposes. No private benefit is permitted—no more than an insubstantial portion of its activities may further nonexempt purposes. No private inurement is permitted—no part of the entity's net earnings may inure to the benefit of an "insider." Any private benefit conferred by the organization must be qualitatively and quantitatively incidental to the charitable purpose of the activity or arrangement.[20] To be qualitatively incidental, the private benefit must occur only as a necessary concomitant of the activity that benefits the public—the benefit to the public cannot be achieved without necessarily benefiting private individuals. To be quantitatively incidental, the private benefit must be insubstantial when viewed in relation to the public benefit conferred by the activity. The analysis covers only the public benefit of that particular activity, not the overall good accomplished by the organization.[21]

Organizations that are tax-exempt under section 501(c)(3) may engage in profit-making activities that are unrelated to their exempt purposes only if such activities are an insubstantial portion of their activities and such activities will be subject to the unrelated business income tax. An activity is subject to this tax if it is not substantially related to the entity's exempt purpose and if it is regularly carried on. Examples of activities in the healthcare field that have been held to be subject to the unrelated business income tax include outpatient pharmacies and outpatient laboratory services sold to the general public as opposed to hospital inpatients, parking lots serving physicians' private patients, laundry services, and hospital resale of supplies and medicines. Other activities have been held to be nontaxable, such as the operation of a gift shop for the convenience of patients, the rental of office space to physicians on staff, income from volunteer activities, and income from the cafeteria or parking lot if the activity primarily benefits patients or employees.

While an insubstantial amount of private benefit transactions is permitted and subject to the unrelated business income tax, no private inurement in any amount is permitted. Private inurement commonly involves the exempt entity's overpayment for property, goods, or services to an "insider." Conversely, private inurement may involve the entity's undercharging for services it provides to an insider. An *insider* is one who has the opportunity to control or influence the organization's activities because of his or her particular relationship with the organization. Medical staff members are generally presumed to be insiders.[22]

Private inurement commonly arises in the area of physician recruitment. Generally, recruitment incentives are permitted if certain requirements are met.[23]

1. The recruitment is necessary to further the hospital's exempt purposes.
2. The total compensation to the physician is reasonable and necessary to further the exempt purposes.
3. There is a demonstrable benefit to the hospital compared to the incidental benefits received by the physician.

Typically, violative arrangements involve excessive physician compensation based on comparisons to similar positions demanding similar skills. Percentage compensation arrangements are generally scrutinized, and percent of net revenue arrangements are usually viewed as de facto private inurement. However, percentage of gross arrangements are sometimes permitted. Private inurement also may involve the exempt organization's overpayment for the purchase of a physician practice, income guarantees, rent subsidies, provision of hospital support staff for a physician's private practice, or below-market loans or leases to an insider.

Following a dearth of guidance for nearly 10 years in the area of physician recruitment, the IRS made public the contents of a closing agreement it entered with Hermann Hospital in Texas. Under the terms of the closing agreement, only new physicians or practitioners new to a hospital's service area could be permissible recruits. No incentives were permitted under the closing agreement to retain existing physicians. In addition, the IRS emphasized the requirement that the hospitals demonstrate a community need for the physician's services where they planned to use recruitment incentives.

In March 1995, the IRS issued a proposed revenue ruling in the area of physician recruitment that permitted the recruitment of physicians already in the area to serve specific, identified community needs, such as for the indigent population or for a distinct specialty.[24] Once again, the IRS emphasized the need for hospitals to demonstrate the community need motivating the recruitment incentives.

Other activities implicating the private inurement prohibitions involve joint ventures between exempt entities and taxable entities. In 1991, the IRS held that a hospital would jeopardize its exempt status if it were to form a joint venture with members of its medical staff and sell to the joint venture a portion of its gross or net revenue stream from operations of a hospital department for a specified period of time.[25] The IRS's reasons for so holding were that the joint venture would cause the organization's net earnings to inure to private individuals, that it would benefit private interests more than incidentally, and that the joint venture may violate the antireferral laws.[26] On the other hand, joint ventures are permitted if the venture expands existing resources for healthcare in the community, if it adds new healthcare providers to the community, if it improves treatment modalities, or if it reduces the costs of treatment.

Recently, the only express remedies available for violations of the tax-exemption requirements included revocation of the entity's tax-exempt status, and imposition of the unrelated business income tax on certain activities. On July 30, 1996, Congress enacted legislation to enhance these penalty provisions.[27] The legislation applies only to sections 501(c)(3) and 501(c)(4) organizations, and its primary focus is on the payment of excessive compensation, which of course must still be reported on relevant tax forms, such as Forms 990, 1040, W-2, and 1099. These modifications include imposition of intermediate sanctions and allow penalizing the recipients of excess benefits as well as any participating "organization manager."

The new legislation operates retroactively to September 13, 1995 to apply an excise tax of 25% of any excess benefit accruing to a disqualified person or insider after that date, subject to special transition rules for transactions before 1997.[28] Such penalties are in addition to possible revocation of an entity's exempt status. Organization managers who knowingly permitted the organization to engage in such a transaction are subject to a 10% penalty excise tax. Failure to correct an excess benefit transaction before notification by the IRS will result in an additional penalty of 200% of the excess benefit. However, if the violation was not caused by willful neglect and has been corrected within the allotted time period, then the IRS must refund the penalty tax.

Another issue faces hospitals whose facilities were financed with tax-exempt bond proceeds. Nonprofit hospitals that are financed in part with tax-exempt bonds are restricted from using bond proceeds for private purposes. Generally, private use of tax-exempt bond proceeds is prohibited unless the arrangement meets the criteria set forth in IRS Revenue Procedure 93-19.[29]

1. Compensation for the use of the facilities must be based on a reasonable, periodic, flat fee.
2. The maximum term of the contract must be up to five years.
3. Automatic increases in compensation must be determined by reference to an external index such as the Consumer Price Index.

4. The exempt organization must have the right to cancel the contract at the end of any three-year period.

Private use would include the use of bond-financed facilities by persons unrelated to the exempt facility, such as independent contractor physicians. Generally, interest on the bonds will remain tax-exempt if the private use of bond proceeds is limited to 5% for tax-exempt organizations. Additionally, no more than 20% of the voting power on the private entity's board may be vested in the hospital or its employees or shareholders.[30] In a foundation model PHO with a tax-exempt organization, insider physicians may not have majority control on the foundation board, nor may they set their own compensation through a board committee.

In December 1994, the IRS issued proposed regulations that when final, will liberalize the provisions of Revenue Procedure 93-19. The proposed regulation expands the categories of qualified management contracts to include the following.

1. Contracts with terms not exceeding the lesser of 15 years of 50% of the useful life of the property if all the compensation is based on a periodic fixed fee

2. Contracts with terms not exceeding the lesser of 10 years or 80% of the useful life of the property if at least 80% of the annual compensation is based on a periodic fixed fee

3. Contracts with terms not exceeding five years if at least 50% of the compensation is based on a periodic fixed fee

4. Contracts with terms not exceeding three years if all of the compensation is based on a per-unit fee

The proposed regulations also provide clearer information on public use, and they also specify *de minimis* exceptions to the private business-use test that are normally disregarded. For example, leases and other arrangements that are not renewable with terms of less than one year are usually disregarded. In addition, temporary use by developers of property to be sold to the public is also disregarded, as are incidental uses of a financed facility and qualified improvements to a facility.

OVERVIEW OF DIFFERENT METHODS OF PROVIDER COMPENSATION

Many issues, as mentioned in the opening paragraphs of this chapter, drive provider compensation. The remainder of this chapter is dedicated to understanding and implementing the practical aspects of provider compensation.

One of the first matters of practicality deals with the financing mechanism for provider payment. When business income is highly restricted as a result of managed care penetration or competition, the available amounts for business expenses, provider compensation included is limited. Exhibit 4–1 indicates the

EXHIBIT 4–1

Evolving Generation of Compensation Systems

	Fee-for-Service		Managed Care
	First Generation	Second Generation	Third Generation
% Capitation	0–25%	25–75%	75%+

Business objectives	Increase encounters
	Increase anciliary $
	Individual physicians
		Managed care contracts
		Physicians begin to work
		  together as a group
			Defined patient
			  population
			Group profitability

Compensation system	Individual revenue "Eat what you kill"	Production-based incentive plans	Salary Performance incentives

Performance measures	Production
	Quality
		Production
		Contribution to
		  group performance
		Utilization management
		Quality—medical
		  appropriateness
			Performance of group
			Clinical outcomes
			Quality—protocols

Patient interaction	Frequent encounters
	Lots of referrals
	Wants/receives
	  multiple services
		Moderate encounters
		Primary care
		  "gatekeeper" to
		  specialists
			Wellness programs
			Limited encounters

Source: Theresa Raczak, MedComp.

evolving generation of compensation systems for physician groups. In larger groups, particularly multispecialty groups, work effort is very different among providers. Coming to some conclusions about how to structure a fair, equitable, and legal compensation system becomes the goal of effective compensation planning efforts.

Analysts should determine the flow of income into the business as a starting point. Does it flow based on fee-for-service (FFS), direct contract (and the idiosyncrasies of payment), or capitation, or with some hybrid approach like pseudo-capitation or withholds? In many markets, the income flow is mixed, hence the term *mixed model compensation*. Mixed model compensation means that part of the business's income derives from, for example, FFS and part from capitation. The key issue is what percentage comes from each. Exhibits 4–2, 4–3, and 4–4 indicate examples of the two-tiered plan concept. In mixed model environments, two-tiered compensation plans profile productivity (by dollars and visit productivity) by FFS and prepaid patient indicators. This method allows the analyst to

E X H I B I T 4–2

Two-Tier Compensation Plans

Example:	Family Practice		
Visit/comp std:	4,700 HMO Visits	=	$128,000
Dr. Smith:	2,100 HMO Visits	=	57,088
FFS production:	$200,000 @40%	=	80,000
Total physician compensation:		=	$137,088

Source: Theresa Raczak, MedComp.

examine payor source and practice complexity issues as well as the direct work aspects of each provider. The examples are meant only to stimulate thinking on how to approach compensation issues, and like others discussed here, are not the solutions in all cases.

Business managers and providers recognize that productivity and availability drive income flow in a FFS market. As providers see and treat more patients, income increases as long as there are patients to treat: productivity and availability. In a capitated environment, with a fixed amount of income for each patient, the practice generates costs each time a capitated patient is seen. Providers easily fall prey to developing a mind-set of care that can limit the amount of interaction between provider and patient because the physician has a negative financial incentive through the payor relationship. This does not mean that the system is tragically flawed or that all providers will respond in this manner. It does change the provider's perspective. In a mixed model income stream, the initial response of many providers has frequently been to consciously limit care to capitated patients while continuing to maximize visits and charges for their FFS patients. The system is a "business schizophrenia" of sorts.

Analysts need to determine what drivers affect the business and the business's desires for future performance before settling on an approach to compensation. Issues include FFS vs. direct contract vs. capitation income streams, participation in payor networks, access to care of certain patient classes (particularly important in regulatory filings), capacity or volume issues, and patient/payor/ system satisfaction issues.

Analysts also must determine the need to control expenses and referrals based on the mix of payors within their business. As a general guideline, capitation levels below 20%—or perhaps 25%—need cause little change in operation within a group from a behavior perspective. Compensation is based typically on provider production as compared to group or other benchmarks, often including

E X H I B I T   4–3

Two-Tier Compensation Plan—Primary Care

Primary care
- FFS collections × _____%
- PCP capitation (_____ PMPM)
- Referral management distribution
- Hospital distribution
- Quality/customer service bonus

Less: direct expenses—overhead
- PA costs
- Payroll taxes
- Health, life and disability, dental insurance
- CME
- Dues and licenses
- Other (401(k), cafeteria plan items, etc.)

Equals: physician pay

Source: Theresa Raczak, MedComp.

E X H I B I T   4–4

Two-Tier Compensation Plan—Specialist

Specialty care
- FFS collections × _____%
- Managed care treated as FFS (multiple of RBRVS)
- Referral management distribution
- Hospital distribution
- Quality/customer service bonus

Less: direct expenses—overhead
- PA costs
- Payroll taxes
- Health, life and disability, dental insurance
- CME
- Dues and licenses
- Other (401(k), cafeteria plan items, etc.)

Equals: physician pay

Source: Theresa Raczak, MedComp.

bonus or incentive arrangements. Overall savings gleaned from effective management at these levels are marginal, although the experience gained by the group in understanding and beginning to manage its costs is invaluable.

At capitation levels up to about 70% of income, a true mixed model system is required. Mixed model systems have the effect of separating FFS and capitated income streams and driving compensation from each stream to yield total compensation. One way or the other, production continues to play a role in these models, although certain types of compensation models may use proxies for production other than dollars, for example, relative value units (RVUs).

At capitation levels over 70%, production and utilization drivers are dominant in the various compensation algorithms. In all systems, individual performance should be the focus within the model, although a growing trend is to consider group performance as well.

PROVIDER COMPENSATION

Physician compensation for owner, partner, and employed physicians must be driven by a number of factors including the specialty of physician, predominant payment mechanisms for the practice, payor mix, and group/system status. The business's desires for physician compensation will be dictated by the status of each physician in the group, whether they are owners receiving group profit distribution, employees of physician-owned groups under compensation formulas, or employed physicians of healthcare networks with more stringent legal requirements for compensation. Physician payment mechanisms should include components of a base salary (or salary draw on an established amount) and a bonus or incentive, which can be variable based on specific, objective targets established for the physician, group, and system. A difficult issue to overcome is the concept of equal compensation for unequal physicians. Two internists may have similar practices and years of experience but drastically different work habits reflecting unequal workload. Manuel Valsquez, professor of management at Santa Clara University and business ethicist, notes with uncanny clarity, "The fundamental principle of distributive justice is that equals should be treated equally and unequals, unequally."[31]

Groupness also is a business operational trait that should be supported by the compensation model. The goal should be to foster the growing together of the practice as a group in a manner that supports individual provider growth. These models commonly have the peer-review effect helping to reduce clinical variation as well.

While no one algorithm can work in all circumstances, the following guidelines should be considered.

Essential and Value-Added Physician Functions—an Example

Essential Physician Functions

- Maintain office hours for $4^1/_2$ days per week
- Provide call coverage for practice/hospital with other medical staff members
- Conduct patient rounds as time beyond office hours
- Complete medical records within time frame established by employer
- Attainment of budgeted number of patient encounters and/or revenue targets as established in operating budget/pro forma for the practice
- Provide service outside office setting through community health provider entities that the hospital and physicians deem as a significant contribution to the community
- Achieve positive scores (number is negotiable) on patient and employee satisfaction surveys

The goal is to establish a set of performance items that reflect how physicians normally go about their scope of work. National comparative data suggest that physicians routinely work 55 to 60 hours weekly in a combination of clinical and administrative activities. This is the operational benchmark for full-time service along with patient encounters and revenue. Systems that require less actual time for guaranteed compensation at comparative levels may well be committing an excess benefit transaction either under Stark or tax laws. Similarly, retirement and other benefits should be analyzed as well.

The FMV of provider services must be established for a variety of contractual arrangements involving physicians. In fact, perhaps the only time physician compensation does not need to be at FMV is for internal physician organization compensation plans. As the reader has seen, any type of contractual arrangement between a physician and a hospital (or similar entity) must be based on the valuation standard of FMV, which is established frequently by an independent third party. When comparing national physician data to local medical groups, the key areas of comparability are affected by the following.

- Production levels
- Gross charges for professional services
- Net collected charges
- Ancillary income
- Nonfinancial measures of productivity (patients seen, procedures, surguries, etc.)
- Payor mix

- Amount of time spent
- Clinical and administrative duties—typically measured in hours per week
- Continuing medical education (CME)—weeks per year
- Working weeks vs. vacation weeks

Normalizing Physician Compensation Example

Dr. Grahame is a general internal medicine physician in Anytown, N.C. He works no more than 40 hours per week, takes four weeks of vacation and one week of CME (leaving 47 work-weeks/year). His gross charges are $450,000, net collected charges of $325,000. He earns $160,000 in direct compensation; is allowed $5,000 for CME, dues, journals, and books; and has an employer-paid retirement plan contribution of $18,000 annually. National comparative data suggest that general internal medicine physicians bill $450,000, collect $325,000, work 56 hours per week, 48 weeks per year, are paid $140,000 in direct compensation, are allowed no more than $5,000 for CME, and received retirement contributions of $10,000.

Dr. Grahame's production is right in line with national comparative data, as is his CME allotment. His time at work is significantly less than the median comparison, reflective of either more efficient personal habits (providing his patient satisfactions scores are positive), a better payor mix, or an aspect of general goodwill. His practice overhead might be lower than the comparison in order to allow for his increased compensation, but we don't know this. We do know that he is working fewer hours for the same dollar level of production. Generally speaking, good for him. We should compare gross and net production dollars and align the compensation rate with the national data of $140,000. Dr. Grahame is working less hard than his sample group, so that benefit remains with him. If he worked the same number of hours and weeks as the sample, his production would be greater and result in greater compensation. Similarly, his retirement benefits are significantly greater and should be adjusted downward to either the median figure or to an amount considered reasonable for the employer's qualified retirement plan.

Readers may disagree with aspects of this analysis. The premise is based on FMV, not fair value. Fair value would require a deeper look at Dr. Grahame's existing practice in order to determine if his compensation package were fair. It could easily be fair. Even upon a more detailed analysis, which would normally be pursued, his existing direct compensation might be considered FMV, although the retirement plan contribution appears very high. The focus should be at understanding the relationship of the physician (employee, contractor, or business-owner) and what type of compensation is reasonable to flow to the individual given the specific circumstances. These issues will help determine when to adjust compensation downward or upward when using comparative data.

Other compensation areas to consider are as follows.

Value-Added Physician Functions

- Serve as medical director (e.g., Rural Health, Community Outreach Clinic)
- Serve as medical student/residency preceptor
- Provide contract services to Department of Public Health
- Provide contract services to read EKGs, Holter monitors, stress tests, etc.
- Attain outstanding scores on patient and employee satisfaction surveys
- Proactively manage utilization of healthcare services and operating expenses of inpatient and outpatient services Enhance administrative-clinical interface in providing higher quality, cost-effective care

Compensation Formula Review

The compensation formula should be based on specific physician production targets in the form of revenue for physician professional services unless the mix of revenue is such that a more detailed model is desirable. Historical practice performance can be the baseline for establishing revenue targets that may be monitored against national comparative physician production data (e.g., Medical Group Management Association physician productivity). Input can be derived from practice physicians and management to assess realistic levels of revenue from which to base the compensation plan. Monthly reports keep physicians and management appraised of performance. The practice physicians and management participate in performance reviews bi-annually in conjunction with payment of incentive pool dollars. The formula should be reviewed annually by the hospital and practice governing board.

Two-Tiered Incentive. The incentive might be based on an assessment of progress in achieving annual performance (based on the annual operating budget/pro forma) and by measuring progress toward value-added physician functions and three- to five-year strategic objectives.

Incentive Pool. The incentive pool might be based on attainment of revenue targets and variable indicators of performance.

Incentive Pool Dollars. As the incentive plan example is based initially on the attainment of revenue targets, the first part of the incentive pool will be dollars that are paid to physicians based on performance at the end of each month for attaining identified revenue targets. These amounts are carried in the operating budget/pro forma as line-item expenses with the assumption that they will be attained. The second part of the incentive pool, paid after the close of the fiscal year, are those dollars remaining after meeting practice operating expenses (as defined by the budget or actual incurred expenses) and net of payback of the annual contribution for the hospital's purchase price for the practice or other negotiated overhead expenses. Any dollars remaining will constitute the second-tier incentive pool dollars for distribution to the hospital and physicians. These dollars will consist of a maximum amount to the physician of X% of his of her base salary draw and be paid according to specified goals in practice performance, quality of care indicators, patient and staff satisfaction, resource utilization, and medical records maintenance.

An important distinction to make to remain in compliance with Stark laws is that splitting of net income is generally considered to be impermissible by law. Compensation should be based on benchmark comparative data, established in advance. This could be accomplished by developing a compensation to production ratio for physician performance based on comparative data. Careful consideration should be given to the development of the plan in format and in the specific wording. It is strongly advised that a competent health law attorney be involved in the process.

Incentive Funds Distribution. Incentive funds are often distributed approximately 45 days after the close of the mid- and end-of-fiscal-year periods. Each physician has a period to review individual and group financial reports, request clarifications, and approve the reports. If a physician cannot accept the baseline reports before the close of the review period, payment is automatically deferred, with no financial penalty to the practice, until agreement is reached.

The best, though most costly, way to handle incentive payments is to pay physicians their incentives on a monthly basis. Keeping physician income high on a month-to-month schedule maintains provider relationships while allowing the group or employer to retain high levels of control. Consider the following example for an established physician (i.e., having a full-time practice).

Physician compensation begins with a compensation draw (never salary—it implies the wrong concept) at perhaps 60% of the annual target compensation level (for example, a $140,000 target would have $84,000 as its base, or $7,000 as the monthly base compensation). The physician is paid only the $7,000 for the first month of employment. The second month, the physician draws the $7,000 base plus a variable incentive based on actual production (or other more complicated algorithm) from Month 1, thus establishing a base plus incentive payment model on a monthly basis. This compensation model is a full 40% at-risk, a veritable requirement for sound financial planning in this instance and discomforts the physician for only the first month. The business has a full 30 days to calculate the incentive payment each month before the payment is due. It is a bit of work to do the calculations each month but it does three key things: it keeps the physician whole on monthly cash flow, it maintains the risk-reward relationship of a productivity based plan, and it provides immediate feedback to the physician on his performance. A harsher plan along the same lines would put the physician 100% at risk for production with each paycheck. While this might sound fine to the employer, few physicians like this plan.

Permutations of physician compensation models are the rule rather than the exception. Business and system goals and objectives will drive incentive plans, as well they should. Physicians, as a group, will perform according to how they are incentivized to perform, provided that their basic professional and personal needs are being met. It is important that win-win relationships be established in order to satisfy the needs of each party. In most cases, creativity in structuring the arrangement can accommodate each party's needs and result while establishing control of the arrangement.

Capitated Income Concerns. Treat capitated income differently from noncapitated income and pay it out differently. For example, one may treat the distribution of the capitated income stream by a share formula or by a performance-based formula.

Share-Based Distribution. Income may be divided based on equal shares or pro rata shares in the event of significantly disparate number of assigned patients or workload distribution.

Performance-Based Distribution. Income may be distributed by absolute or relative performance of each physician (e.g., the ratio of actual to expected member costs, or the total dollars of member costs of care rendered compared to the expected cost of care [by age and sex]). Other means might profile actual costs compared to some benchmarked amount or comparing actual costs (or encounters) compared with an established treatment corridor based on encounters. As an example of the corridor model, a range of expected treatment (encounter, referral, etc.) can be established based on utilization assumptions for a given patient population and specialty of practice (e.g., a general surgery estimate may be 17 to 23 procedures per 1,000 population). The amounts distributed to the physician may be a function of actual to expected encounters derived from this range. Indeed, this model, and derivations, have been used by Kaiser Health Plans and others to establish capitated payment amounts and reconciliation formulas.

Balancing Productivity and Time. Providers, managers, and analysts will need to understand under which circumstances dollars should act as the activity measurement and when other measures of productivity should be considered dominant. Consider a 10-person general internal medicine group with 2 physicians acting more as geriatricians and two handling high complexity, high acuity, perhaps even infectious diseases (HIV positive). The income profile of these physicians may vary greatly based initially on payor mix (particularly for the geriatricians with their high Medicare population) and secondly on time spent (RVUs). In this instance, productivity for the group might be based on an algorithm that considers RVUs, patient visits, and revenue to derive an equitable distribution formula. The formula is still performance-based but recognizes the net effort of different practice populations as well as practice styles.

Data Analysis: Run the Model Before Implementing the Plan

Data capture and management is the critical element in compensation systems in the healthcare clinical environment. Providers are data-oriented individuals and need to see and understand what you are presenting to them. They will need to not only understand the compensation algorithm, but also to receive, in a timely manner, summary and detailed reports for them to monitor their progress. Businesses that do not have the capacity to track clinical activity and produce reports in a timely manner should not attempt to develop complex compensation formulas. Providers will doom them to extinction. Review and consider your own data capabilities as you begin to develop your plans with the providers.

Changes in compensation systems always should be modeled using actual historical practice data before implementing the plan. This time-consuming effort lays the foundation for the sanity check on whether the plan allows for adequate coverage of practice overhead expenses, including return on investment, as well as to review physician compensation. Physicians will be keenly aware of models that result in decreased personal income. In some instances, particularly in dealing with underproductive providers, that is the desired outcome. In other situations, the model needs to demonstrate that the system will work in all its dimensions.

First and foremost is the soundness of the model from a regulatory perspective. Once the concept has passed legal review for compliance with relative statutes on fraud and abuse and antireferral issues, the application of the model begins. One key issue is the maintenance of the concept of FMV in dealing with employed physician compensation. In application, the prior year's financial and operating data should be applied to the proposed model to determine how the practice operations and physician compensation would have resulted if the model were in place during the prior year. Do not forget to adjust benefits and employment taxes when applying the model to the practice's overall financial performance.

Indications of weaknesses in the model become apparent when using the prior year's data. Changes may be adjusted to correct the model, or a new direction for compensation may be determined.

Be aware also of the provider complement from your capacity analysis (Chapter 2). Compensation is highly affected by capacity of providers and staff (indeed all overhead expenses). Be sure that you understand your complement of providers and staff before trying to make some model fit where it hasn't a chance of working. As needed, approach these issues carefully when indicating the results of capacity analysis as it impacts compensation, especially when making recommendations about certain provider's ability to accept greater workloads to even out capacity.

AUTOMATING COMPENSATION ALGORITHMS

Compensation algorithms may be created using a simple Excel spreadsheet. Recall the exercise from Chapter 2 in reviewing the financial model case study. Different compensation amounts may easily be entered into overall pro formas and budgets as long as care is given in the design of the spreadsheet. It is difficult to create one single template whereby different compensation scenarios may be interchanged with a few keystrokes. The reason for this is twofold. Circular references are often created when compensation models are based in part on a pool of available income necessitating the development of compensation formulas in an unrelated spreadsheet. Second, using basic software such as Excel makes it difficult and time-consuming to format a table to operate as essentially an add-on piece of software. It would require a reasonably complex formula to create a completely integrated spreadsheet that would switch different, complex compensation models in and out. There are ways to do this within Excel, even by using some presentation formats to show specifically the overall pro forma performance under different models. It is only difficult to set it up and still show business profit and loss in conventional presentations.

Building Flexibility into Financial Models for Varying Compensation

Compensation expenses can be modeled as in the example from Chapter 1 in which total provider compensation is calculated in a detail table that points to the annual pro forma under its own category. Taxes and benefits can be driven off this number through calculation within the monthly pro forma. More detailed compensation modeling should exclude the provider's benefits from the annual pro forma unless they are fully identified and not related to total compensation. Retirement or profit-sharing plan contributions are commonly based on total direct compensation; other plans are based on contributions up to a specified level of compensation. The more detail that is available, the better to guide you in setting up the pro forma and to avoid missing or duplicating expenses. Analysts may choose to set up one entire spreadsheet that links all data from the annual pro forma except items impacted by provider compensation and choose to run lines at the bottom of the analysis related to compensation only.

The goal is to create a model that suits your needs and allows you to represent the activity of your business in a manner that is logical from an analytical perspective and conveys understanding to the reader. Above all, take your time to understand the underlying issues affecting business operations prior to evaluating the options for compensation. Once done, these assumptions will guide the analyst to suggest certain models suited to the business goals.

NOTES

1. Letter from D. McCarty Thornton, Chief Counsel to the Inspector General. Impact of the Anti-Kickback Statute and the Stark Amendment on Vertically Integrated Delivery Systems in the Health Care Industry, January 20, 1995.
2. 42 U.S.C. § 1320a-7b(b).
3. *Hanlester Network* v. *Shalala,* 51 F.3d 1390 (9th Cir. 1995).
4. Ibid.
5. 760 F.2d 68 (3d Cir. 1985), cert. denied, 474 U.S. 988 (1985).
6. 871 F.2d 105 (9th Cir. 1989).
7. 42 U.S.C. § 1395nn.
8. Ibid.
9. 60 Fed. Reg. 41,914 (1995) (to be codified at 42 C.F.R. pt. 411).
10. HCFA Aims to Curb Medicare Fraud with new Provider Application Form, in 5 Health L. Rep. (BNA) No. 33, at 1215 (August 15, 1996).
11. Ibid.
12. Ibid. at 41,931. The final regulations for Stark I set forth a methodology for calculating this measurement. *Patient care services* is defined as any task performed by a group practice member that addresses the medical needs of specific patients, regardless of whether they involve direct patient encounters. Patient care services are measured by the total patient care time each member spends on the services. If eight members of a 10-member group practice devote 100% of their patient care time to the group practice, one devotes 80% of his time to the group practice, and the other physician devotes only 10% of his time to the group practice, then the 10 participants devote a total of 890% of their total time to the group. That percentage is then divided by the number of physicians in the group, or 890/10, for a quotient reflecting that 89% of the patient care services are provided through the group. This requirement applies unless the group practice is located in a health professional shortage area. If members of an urban practice devote a portion of their medical services to a shortage area, then that amount of time is not calculated in determining whether the group meets the "substantially all" test.
13. 60 Fed. Reg. 41,914 (1995) (to be codified at 42 C.F.R. pt. 411).
14. 42 U.S.C. § 1395ww(d)(2)(D).
15. 60 Fed. Reg. 41,914, 41,981 (1995) (to be codified at 42 C.F.R. pt. 411). The final regulation clarifies that the physician being recruited must not be precluded from establishing staff privileges at another hospital or referring business to another entity.
16. 800 F.Supp. 1451 (E.D. Tex. 1992).
17. 60 Fed. Reg. 41,914, 41,960 (1995) (to be codified at 42 C.F.R. pt. 411).

18. 985 F.2d 1210, 1215 (3d Cir. 1993), aff'd, 30 F.3d 494 (3d Cir. 1994).

19. Rev. Rul. 69-545, 1969-2 C.B. 117.

20. Gen. Couns. Mem. 37,789 (Dec. 18, 1978).

21. Gen. Couns. Mem. 39,862 (Nov. 21, 1991). 22 Gen. Couns. Mem. 39,498 (Apr. 24, 1986). 23 Ibid.

22. IRS Ann. 95-25, 1995-14 I.R.B. (Apr. 3, 1995).

23. Gen. Couns. Mem. 39,862 (Nov. 21, 1991).

24. Ibid.

25. P.L. 104-168.

26. Ibid.

27. See Rev. Proc. 93-19, 1993-1 C.B. 526; Rev. Proc. 82-15, 1982-1 C.B. 460.

28. Ibid.

29. Velasquez, M. (1992). *Business Ethics: Concepts and Cases.* Prentice-Hall: Englewood Cliffs, N.J., 91.

5
CHAPTER

Selected Issues in Medical Practice Operations

"Success is most appropriately measured not by what we have accomplished but by the difficulty of the questions we are willing to address."

Paul Hawken

WHAT WILL IT TAKE TO BE SUCCESSFUL AS AN ORGANIZATION PROVIDING MEDICAL SERVICES?[1]

Delivery of medical services will be customer focused

Healthcare will always be delivered between one provider and one patient at a time. The increase in knowledge and willingness to question the historical culture of the doctor-patient relationship has changed how patients interact with the healthcare system. Patients and family members ask more questions and expect to be answered with cogent and direct answers. For the foreseeable future, patients will not be able to evaluate and judge the quality of care they receive due to the lack of technical knowledge; however, patients will continue to judge the quality of care based largely on the growing amount of consumer and technical data that are becoming available. The use of the Internet and World Wide Web as tools for the dissemination of information is expanding rapidly and many consumers are using them to gain information about their healthcare choices. Practical matters remain related to contracting for services, health plan participation, and the real ability to choose providers, which will continue to limit the choices of some consumers. Ultimately, providers, both individual and institutional, will need to cater to their individual patient customers as well as their employer customers in order to remain effective and viable in the competing marketplace.

There will be a fully linked system of medical excellence that outperforms its competition in quality, cost, accessibility, and service

The complexity and competitive nature of delivering healthcare has contributed substantially to the consolidation among institutional and individual providers. The ability to earn substantial return on investment has also driven the consolidation for those with great foresight. In markets of extreme competition and in the development of regionally and nationally linked organizations, developing the ability to deliver superior quality care, in all its dimensions, at competitive rates resulting in return on investment, will determine which provider organizations survive. The dimensions of superior quality care include not only the provision of the right amount of clinical service provided at the right time, but also that it is provided in a manner which the customer (e.g., patient, family, employer) deems it to be of such quality that they would seek no other resource. They view the clinical delivery of service as exactly what they had in mind, to whatever degree they perceive to be complete care. They perceive the care delivery coming not only from the physician or other clinical provider, but also from the administrative structure with which they interface. Although it may not appear to be a fair assessment of their clinical satisfaction, it is well believed that the patient's perceived clinical satisfaction is affected by their interaction with clinical administrative staff and how their health plan functions administratively in the ease of obtaining clinical services.

From an administrative position, the care delivery must be provided in the correct, most cost effective setting based on the clinical severity of the episode. While this will always be fraught with some level of inefficiency, the delivery of healthcare must consider the patient's clinical needs first, based on the severity of presentation.

The larger issue then is the ability for the system to provide this level of care in a system-wide cost-effective manner in the face of competitors large and small. In many markets, health systems have sought market share at the expense of operating plan losses and have funded them with system arbitrage; they covered losses with gains from other markets. As systems regionalize and margins get smaller, systems cannot afford such tactics. Recent criticism of Medicare+Choice HMO rates have forced many health plans to stop providing the HMO plan due to inadequate funding. At some point, the arbitrage has to stop, and it has in many markets.

How health systems position themselves through growth, financial and operational management, and relationships will determine which ones will survive and remain leaders in their markets. The retrenching of many systems and hospitals have led them to focus on their core competencies. Physician groups and larger physician networks are in the same position; only physicians tend to feel the bite even more. Physician groups, which have not been accustomed to retaining capital, must examine the real issues involved in taking less money, taking on debt at the appropriate time, and for the right reasons, in order to remain competitive. It will be the relationships between the institutional and individual providers that will allow systems to remain successful in all dimensions.

The organization will surpass the performance of competitors on a per-member, per-month basis for the cost of medical services, while being able to pay physicians at premium levels for value received

Successful systems, through excellent financial and operational management, and with sufficient resources, will be able to outperform their competitors from a pure cost basis and, in doing so, will gain initial access to the markets they desire. Employers and consumers, as a whole, still choose their healthcare plans and providers based on cost as the primary criterion. Employers remain unlikely to pay for services of higher quality unless the plan design carves out the incremental cost to the patient, which many plans do, and which many patients accept. To remain competitive in contracting for groups of covered health plan lives, systems need to be competitive on a cost side first, or they will be excluded from the start. Not that even getting to the table with a competitive offer is an easy task; it's just that until organizations develop the understanding, the data, and the analysis capacity to contract effectively, the point is moot.

Once baseline ability to participate from a cost-effective delivery of care position, relationships with physicians will become vitally important in order to compete as a group or accept global contracting arrangements. In many markets, global contracting for the physician and hospital components (as well as the rest of the care continuum) are expected. Hospitals without physician group relationships find it very difficult to compete. Hospitals with physician relationships must examine how to compensate the physicians for the services they provide and create a means to share earnings at appropriate and, where applicable, legal levels. Successful systems will recognize the physicians' unique role in assessing and maintaining high quality of care and will reward the physician for the administrative services they provide in executing the delivery of care. Physicians must be compensated fairly for what they bring to the entire operation. This includes their role in administration, delivery design, cost-saving opportunities, and actual cost-savings performance. Many systems have put in place cost savings performance measures to reward physicians in the delivery of episodic care, the actual one-on-one patient-physician interaction. These are made typically through evaluation of length of stay, ancillary usage, and location of care delivery. Fewer systems have taken the leap toward using physician administrative input to assist in broader cost-saving initiatives. Such initiatives are found in compensating the physician for participation, tangible results, quality and clinical protocol, care pathway development, and other forms of cost-saving measures where the physician-administrator team creates mechanisms for delivery of care that results in high quality of care delivered at a cost savings.

Recent decisions by the Office of the Inspector General of the Department of Health and Human Services have found that such gainsharing arrangements are illegal when involving Medicare and Medicaid beneficiaries and are considered as a payment for referrals to the participating physicians, for which the federal government is responsible to pay. Gainsharing activities will not fade away in respect to non-Medicare and non-Medicaid populations, and it will remain an effective system to involve physicians in cost reduction efforts. At the end of the day, it will be the ability of the system to reduce its costs of delivery while maintaining its provider relationships that will prove successful.

The patient care system will serve the community

Patients continue to consider themselves the basis of the healthcare system. In the last ten years, the provision of healthcare has become an expected right of the people of the United States. This is an important turning point. In the early 1980s, the public perception was one of questioning whether healthcare was a right or a privilege. Societal expectations, clinical developments, and the aging of the ever-growing cohort of Medicare beneficiaries led ultimately to the decision that it was a responsibility of the government to provide healthcare to its citizens. The entire debate is far from finished. Should healthcare, beyond emergency care, be provided to illegal aliens while being funded by the government? Should primary care, not episodic urgent or emergency care, be available to all citizens regardless of their ability to pay?

The law related to not-for-profit status of hospitals indicates that emergency care must be provided; however, the hospital may adjust its charges to remain financially viable.[2] The Internal Revenue Service held that the promotion of health is a charitable purpose under I.R.C. §501(c)(3) in Revenue Ruling 69-545. Specifically, a hospital is engaged in the promotion of health if it meets the "community benefit" test, as follows.

1. The class of persons benefiting from the hospital's activities must be reasonably broad;
2. The hospital must operate an emergency room open to all persons without regard to their ability to pay;
3. The hospital must provide hospital care to everyone in the community who is able to pay directly or through private or public reimbursement;
4. The hospital must be governed by a board of trustees composed of independent civic leaders, as opposed to physicians or others with a private interest in the organization; and

5. The hospital must maintain a medical staff open to all qualified physicians.

Other factors, which the Internal Revenue Service has considered since the 1969 ruling, include the following.

1. Whether the hospital provides specialized services if it does not operate an emergency room;

2. The hospital's provision of charity care, medical research, and educational activities;

3. The hospital's compliance with other laws, such as the Stark anti-referral laws and EMTALA—the Emergency Medical Treatment and Active Labor Act.

The entity must also be operated exclusively for charitable purposes. No private benefit is permitted—no more than an insubstantial portion of its activities may further non-exempt purposes. No private inurement is permitted—no part of the entity's net earnings may inure to the benefit of an "insider." Any private benefit conferred by the organization must be qualitatively and quantitatively incidental to the charitable purpose of the activity or arrangement. To be qualitatively incidental, the private benefit must occur only as a necessary concomitant of the activity that benefits the public—the benefit to the public cannot be achieved without necessarily benefiting private individuals. To be quantitatively incidental, the private benefit must be insubstantial when viewed in relation to the public benefit conferred by the activity.

Hospitals organized under such charitable missions have a responsibility to provide such service—which constitute those provided generally by hospitals—including nursing care, nutritional care, pharmaceuticals, and emergency medical services. Relating these issues to the subject analysis, a hospital is required to provide emergency medical services to patients in the community and must ensure that qualified physicians are available to direct and provide professional patient-care services.

With the proliferation of investor-owned (for-profit) organizations, local governments are increasingly scrutinizing the conversion of not-for-profit (NFP) facilities into investor-owned organizations. It has been reported in several studies that the cost of care appears to increase when NFP facilities are converted to for-profits. While some accounting issues may be debated, the public is expressing concern over the resources available to serve the public.

The system for distributing primary care will include locations convenient to the patient members

Outperforming the competition in quality, cost, accessibility, and service while serving the community comes from being in the community and available to patients. Geographically dispersed networks of providers will be the delivery sites of choice for patients and employer groups. Patients will vote with their feet when they can. The continual stresses on family life and free time are making it difficult for many families to enjoy life. Gone are the days of the single wage earner, unless you count single-parent families. The demands on the personal time of most people is so great that they seek convenience over quality, even in healthcare. If providers strive to make it easy for the patient to access the system, they will be rewarded with business. The philosophy should be the same with patients as between the physician seeing the patient and the referring physician. Both the patient and the referring physician are trying to put money in your pocket; you should not make that process difficult. Indeed, you should be doing everything you can to make it easy and rewarding for them to do so, when you can. The lifeline of any business is its revenue source. The public will demand easy access and will pay for it with the choices it makes.

The practice will include linkage with (or ownership of) capabilities for medical research with a focus on performing activities that lead to the improvement in quality and efficiency of care and the creation of preventive avenues to enhance health

Patients and payors expect that physicians and hospitals will provide technically correct services. When a patient visits a laboratory to provide a sample for a test, he or she does not consider whether the test is being performed correctly; this is a given assumption. What they perceive as a quality interaction is the process by which they were referred to the lab, the lab visit itself, the demeanor of the staff at the lab, and their overall impression of the lab encounter. Patients and payors do, however, look favorably upon, or perceive to be of great value, continual education, including proximity to and participation in research. They do not currently hold such activity to be of significant tangible value (they will not necessarily pay for it), but they report that it is nevertheless valuable to them.

Physicians and systems that participate in basic science, clinical research and in research related to the provision of clinical services will have not only a perceived edge on the competition but will also have the opportunity to translate such research into practical application. The transfer of basic science technology and of improved clinical practices will result in better care for the patient, and may result in improved efficiency in the delivery of care. New clinical practices tend to insinuate themselves in the standard of care slowly, often upon the completion of scientific research that has been deemed to be statistically significant. In some cases, new technologies become available, new drugs and treatment modalities are created and while the benefit to the patient may be positive, the cost and practicality of implementation may have yet to be determined.

Patients and payors tacitly expect that physicians and hospitals are paragons of the knowledge of medical care. Despite untoward outcomes that occur, some with seemingly blatant disregard for the human condition, the public demands—sometimes weakly—that medical research and the transfer of knowledge continue. What systems have begun to realize is that this is in their best interests also. The problem lies in the mechanism to conduct such research, its funding, and the transfer of putting it into practice.

KEY ASSUMPTIONS

- Reforms of healthcare will continue informally and/or formally.
- The competition will send their patients for care primarily to sites they own or control.
- Cost pressures on healthcare will increase significantly.
- The competitors will be both vertically integrated systems and networks of deeply discounting independent providers.
- Managed care and managed competition in the marketplace will spread.

KEY FINANCIAL AREAS TO EXAMINE

Profit-Loss Statements

Each annual profit-loss (P/L) statement is examined on an individual basis and then compared to previous years. P/L statements can be formatted in a variety of ways with the first number column showing the most recent month, the most recent quarter, or most recent year. The comparison column typically shows either the fiscal year to date (FYTD) or last fiscal year (FY). Helpful columns might show percentages of each category as well as percentage change from year to year.

Monitoring the P/L statement is extremely important to understand because it shows how your expenses increase from period to period. For groups that do not prepare and operate by a budget, quarterly and annual review of the P/L statement gives some indication of trends and increasing or decreasing costs.

One of the key issues in P/L statement analysis is the posting of amounts correctly. Smaller businesses seem to get away with grouping expenses based on a top-of-mind awareness, although not always in a logical manner or one that would facilitate clear understanding of the item categories. A good rule to adopt is to create general ledger categories or a chart of accounts that facilitates a clear understanding of the cost and revenue items associated with it. Recall Exhibit 1–2, Sample Income Statement Input Worksheet. It breaks down categories into readily understandable areas. Your computer system may allow you to code items in subcategories below these as well.

Only through a clear understanding of the numbers behind the category titles will the analyst be able to discern any relationships, trends, or patterns.

Additionally, as mentioned in Chapter 1, using common categories facilitates the use of national comparative data as operational benchmarks as well.

Financial Management

The ability to integrate general ledger (income/expense) information into the information system allows practices to expand their opportunities for meaningful data analysis. The ongoing profile of individual categories of expense—usually highly variable categories—helps practices keep tabs on their expenses. Items such as office or clinical supplies, laboratory expenses/fees, patient refunds, write-offs, bad debt, and other disbursements should be monitored on a regular basis. The ability to compare these data elements against a budget or prior year is essential, as discussed above.

Businesses should create a financial management committee with responsibility for overseeing and reporting on the financial structure of the business. In smaller businesses, the business owner and accountant usually complete this, if done at all. In many small businesses, the owner keeps this information private.

Accounts Receivable Aging (Aged Trial Balance)

The accounts receivable aging is important to identify the amounts of billings that are outstanding and to help prevent too many accounts from growing old enough that their ultimate collection becomes unlikely. It is valuable to see total accounts receivable aged in the following standard categories: current (0–30 days), 31–60 days, 61–90 days, 90–120 days, and greater than 120 days. The reasons for these divisions are many, including tradition, comparison with national comparative data sets such as MGMA, and the historical likelihood of collection of accounts that tend to fall into these categories. In addition, integrating current collection ratios (ratio of gross charges to net collections) helps practices examine the likelihood of collection.

Accounts receivable aging is also very valuable on a payor basis. Knowing the total aging (by above categories) of all Medicare accounts tells you something very different than the total aging of individual commercial accounts. Knowing that a particular payor is contractually bound to pay the practice within a certain period of time helps keep track of income. The key here is having access to both the total accounts receivable aging as well as payor-specific accounts receivable aging. Exhibits 5–1 and 5–2 show an accounts receivable aging by category and by payor with subsequent valuation.

Seek to continually reduce accounts receivable from the perspective of account turnover. Increasing amounts of total accounts receivable are essential in a growing business and reflect increased billings. Increased days in accounts receivable (turnover) is indicative of a breakdown in the collection process. As indicated earlier, accounts receivable days in the 40s are indicative of industry best practices. Achieving this amount requires a concerted effort and collections plan. Establish business policies in writing that you share not only with all employees (as emissaries of the firm) but with patients as well. Insist on collecting copayments at the time of service and offer discounts for up-front payment. Filing insurance for patients has become a standard, although some practices do not provide this service. Accepting credit card payments is another route to rapid payments, although businesses need to be careful about vendor fees. Any strategy you employ to bring payments in sooner will help your business, from both a cash flow perspective and other aspects of operations. While the focus of business must be on the patient, the practical matter is that you need to remain solvent in order to operate.

Productivity Reports

Productivity reports comprise the greatest variety of reports of value to small businesses for operations purposes. The following reports provide some insight into examining data from different perspectives to yield information on specific and overall business performance.

Charges by Location

It is valuable to be able to see the sources (office, hospital, ancillaries, etc.) of charge by percentage, but this tends to make tables excessive without adding significant information. Manual calculation is sufficient on an annual basis just to give analysts an idea of charge distribution. This also is valuable when planning business expansion (new providers, new facilities, etc.) Breakdowns of charges by location and by provider also yields insight into practice patterns and clinical variation. In capitated payment systems, this analysis is vital to examine opportunities to practice more efficiently across the entire business.

Charges by Visit and/or Procedure

Generally the top 20 or 25 outpatient visit CPT codes are a mix between office visits, laboratory orders, and procedures. Remove all the ancillary visits to obtain a clean picture of what takes up your providers' time (Exhibit 5–3). Knowing the top 10 to 20 CPT codes in each subcategory is useful to monitor changes in the practice over a period of time. In addition, profiling individual physicians within the practice also is useful to examine practice patterns, coding, and other individual aspects of performance. This is particularly helpful when allocating overhead in complex or multispecialty practices or in setting provider compensation algorithms. In many practices, the top 25 provider codes (excluding ancillaries) account for 60% to 70% of all operations. Beyond the top 25, the number of individual procedures becomes so small that it yields little immediate benefit from this type of analysis.

E X H I B I T   5–1

Accounts Receivable Comparative Analysis
Anytown OB/GYN: All Accounts as of: 12/31/98

Notes	Payor	Number of Active Accts	Total A/R	Current	30–60
1, 2	Blue Cross	483	29,156	24,199	1,067
	Cancer Program	49	14,616	14,109	109
	Collections (CA & CB)	160	130,159	4,259	42
	Collections (all other)	141	64,878	11,365	1,329
	Medicaid Only	615	77,358	75,604	1,101
	Medicaid/Private	31	3,713	3,422	0
	Medicare	64	2,496	2,251	97
	Medicare/Medicaid	51	4,650	4,650	0
	Medicare/Private	266	11,534	11,441	14
	Private Insurance	1,133	101,544	91,395	3,597
	Self Pay	292	13,467	10,571	244
	All Other	88	23,672	14,308	1,876
	Total:	**3,373**	**477,243**	**267,574**	**9,476**
	Percent of Total:		100%	56%	2%

Assumptions: AR was examined and valued based on a payor class. The following summary indicates the gross payor classes examined and their respective aged accounts. Some rounding may occur.

Unbilled amounts are a portion of the total A/R which have been billed to third parties and not yet assigned to patient responsibility.

Notes:

1. YTD Historical Collection Rate derived by ratio of YTD Payments divided by YTD Charges. While not a pure reflection of charges billed and collected within a discrete time period (YTD), this is regarded generally as a reasonable estimate in a going concern unless billing anomalies occur in the sample period (e.g., Medicaid/Private collection rate exceeding 100%).

2. FMV Collection Estimate based on normal practice historical collections given the business as a going concern with appraisal adjustments for apparent anomalies. Collections (all other) was adjusted to the Private Insurance rate as these are current patients on internal billing arrangements with the practice. Considering a sale of Medicaid/Private was reduced to the Private insurance rate of 80%.

61–90	91–120	121+	Unbilled Amounts	YTD Historical Collection Rate	FMV Est. Collection Rate
1,688	39	2,163	28,503	70%	70%
353	45	0	14,119	49%	49%
1,033	511	124,314	4,168	18%	18%
6,718	4,601	40,865	9,362	107%	80%
305	240	108	76,885	53%	53%
227	0	64	3,702	117%	80%
127	3	18	2,005	63%	63%
0	0	0	4,650	38%	38%
25	11	43	11,098	38%	38%
2,563	424	3,565	92,858	80%	80%
869	149	1,634	5,641	59%	59%
744	3,790	2,954	7,994	25%	25%
14,652	**9,813**	**175,728**	**260,985**		
3%	2%	37%			

EXHIBIT 5–2

Valuation of Accounts Receivable

Method 1	A/R Category by Aging times FMV Collection Estimate					
	Total A/R	Current	30–60	61–90	91–120	121+
	477,243	267,574	9,476	14,652	9,813	175,728
Using gross FMV factors:	257,762	227,438	7,107	9,524	4,907	8,786
		@85%	@75%	@65%	@50%	@5%

Method 2	Total A/R by Payor Class times Historical Collection Estimate
Using historical collection factors:	268,256

Method 3	Total A/R by Payor Class times FMV Collection Estimate
Using payor-specific FMV factors:	249,650

CONCLUSION: Fair Market Value of Accounts Receivable: 249,650
Liquidation Value Estimate of Accounts Receivable @40%: 99,860

Breakdown by Payor

Knowing the total number of charges, total patient visits, and the number of individual patients by each payor helps practices examine their dependence on each source of income. By examining the difference between these numbers, providers gain insight into the average number of visits made by each patient, which is an essential utilization component to consider when presented with a capitation arrangement for your established patient base. By stratifying the ages of your patients, you can further evaluate the use patterns of different populations of patients within a single payor. Overall payor mix based on charges is commonly a quick way of analyzing your income sources. This information should be in sufficient detail to provide meaningful use, although for some analyses fine detail may be more desirable.

Patient Visits

The total number of patient visits is important for both capitated and noncapitated patient bases. Productivity is measured in part by the number of patients seen by all types of providers. Knowing the number of individual patients also is valuable, as mentioned above, to establish utilization comparisons. Total number of individual patients, as mentioned above, allows businesses to review

EXHIBIT 5-3

Top CPT Office Codes by Charges
Anytown Family Practice: All Physicians—10/1/97–9/30/98

Description	CPT Code	Volume	Total Charges	Percent of Practice Total
Estab. patient office visit level 3	99213	3,666	$170,719	15,89%
Estab. patient office visit level 2	99212	4,494	$166,660	15.51%
Estab. patient office visit level 5	99215	445	$ 43,465	4.05%
Estab. patient office visit level 4	99214	568	$ 40,286	3.75%
Well patient visit age 4	99396	376	$ 24,440	2.27%
New patient office visit level 2	99202	317	$ 18,376	1.71%
New patient office visit level 3	99203	193	$ 15,708	1.46%
New patient office visit level 4	99204	123	$ 12,913	1.20%
Reg periodic screening	W8010	159	$ 12,346	1.15%
Aspiration of large joint	20610	104	$ 11,024	1.03%
ThinPrep Pap test	88142	168	$ 6,545	0.61%
Well patient visit age 1	99395	92	$ 5,704	0.53%
EKG stress test	93015	16	$ 4,688	0.44%
Estab. patient office visit level 1	99211	167	$ 4,168	0.39%
Interpretation only EKG	93010	212	$ 3,392	0.32%
New patient office visit level 5	99205	3	$ 408	0.04%
New patient office visit level 1	99201	1	$ 44	0.00%
Percent of total charges—top CPT office codes:				**50.35%**

the size of the patient base, the average number of visits by classes of patients, and allows analysts to develop a better picture on whether their business serves a more stable customer base or a more transient base. Each of these last two issues has important marketing, retention, and business growth concerns.

Demographics of Service Population

Profiling the demographics of the practice's patients is valuable for business marketing and evaluation. For reasons discussed above, the more detail analysts have about their customer base, the better they can understand the flow of customers and income and position themselves for growth into market areas or segments of particular strength or where opportunities exist.

Top CPT Office Code Fee Analysis
Anytown Family Practice: All Physicians—10/1/97–9/30/98

Description	CPT Code	Volume	Current Fee
New patient office visit level 1	99201	1	$ 44
New patient office visit level 2	99202	317	$ 58
New patient office visit level 3	99203	193	$ 81
New patient office visit level 4	99204	123	$ 105
New patient office visit level 5	99205	3	$ 136
Estab. patient office visit level 1	99211	167	$ 25
Estab. patient office visit level 2	99212	4,494	$ 37
Estab. patient office visit level 3	99213	3,666	$ 47
Estab. patient office visit level 4	99214	568	$ 71
Estab. patient office visit level 5	99215	445	$ 98
Thin Prep Pap test	88142	168	$ 39
Well patient visit age 4	99396	376	$ 65
Well patient visit age 1	99395	92	$ 62
EKG stress test	93015	16	$ 293
Reg periodic screening	W8010	159	$ 78
Aspiration of large joint	20610	104	$ 106
Interpretation–only EKG	93010	212	$ 16

Total gross potential lost from undercharged top CPT office codes:

Zip Code Analysis
Zip code analysis allows providers to examine the market sources and drawing area of their practice. Accurate patient referral patterns are established by zip code analysis and providers can begin to target growing areas of their community by examining areas of key importance, such as housing developments or new schools. Zip code analysis may be used quite effectively in establishing the geographic boundaries for provider restrictive covenants as well.

Fee Schedule Analysis

Gross charges are almost meaningless in today's managed care world. They are valuable for use with health plans that evaluate a practice's fee schedule to indicate which fees they will accept and which of the practice's fees fall above their fee

National Fee Comparison Regionally Adjusted Fees—1998			Calculated Diff. from Current and 50th	Potential Lost Revenue
50th	75th	90th		
$ 42	$ 51	$ 60	$ 2	$ —
$ 56	$ 68	$ 80	$ 2	$ —
$ 78	$ 94	$ 109	$ 3	$ —
$ 113	$ 137	$ 162	$ (8)	$ 966
$ 147	$ 177	$ 208	$ (11)	$ 34
$ 22	$ 27	$ 33	$ 3	$ —
$ 35	$ 42	$ 49	$ 3	$ —
$ 47	$ 56	$ 66	$ (1)	$ 2,756
$ 69	$ 83	$ 96	$ 2	$ —
$ 106	$ 127	$ 148	$ (8)	$ 3,509
$ —	$ —	$ —	$ 39	$ —
$ 101	$ 136	$ 177	$ (36)	$13,540
$ 92	$ 125	$ 162	$ (30)	$ 2,752
$ 236	$ 302	$ 365	$ 57	$ —
N/A	N/A	N/A	N/A	$ —
$ 64	$ 83	$ 102	$ 42	$ —
$ 27	$ 35	$ 44	$ (11)	$ 2,396
				$ 25,953

schedule. A practice whose fees are routinely accepted by a health plan is a practice whose fees are too low. The ability to profile, by payor, the gross fees next to the plan fees, by CPT code, with a percentage difference gives practices valuable information in negotiation and for internal planning purposes. Evaluating fee schedules for balance and appropriateness within a given community is a bit more complex, requiring the use of external sources of data and may raise antitrust concerns of price fixing (Exhibit 5–4).

Coding Analysis

A profile of CPT codes experienced (similar to charges by visit or procedure, discussed above) is valuable in examining historical coding patterns and identifying areas for miscoding. Medicare has defined miscoding as de facto fraud. It is imperative that practices begin to evaluate their coding and billing practices and put in place a system of corporate compliance to reduce the likelihood of fraud. Coding is usually profiled for evaluation and management codes (e.g., new vs. established office visits) and for procedures (Exhibits 5–5 and 5–6).

Medical Group Management Association (MGMA) extracted data from its Physician Services Practice Analysis Comparison Service for the period 1995–1997 examining CPT coding practices. Exhibit 5–7 indicates the results of the most frequently requested CPT codes for family practice physicians for the period from July–December 1997.[3]

This issue cannot be stressed highly enough. Businesses providing service to Medicare and Medicaid beneficiaries *must* set up internal corporate compliance plans to ensure appropriate billings and antifraud procedures. Numerous books, manuals, and seminars are being distributed to educate businesses on this issue. Practices should contract with external, independent parties to conduct coding reviews of the providers. External review by a certified coding expert is the only way to ensure that providers keep current with changes in coding practice.

Appointment Scheduling

Automated appointment scheduling creates greater opportunity for examining the internal operations of the practice. If the patient appointment times are also compared with the patient waiting times and the lengths of visits, valuable data are gleaned on the throughput of the practice. Patient waiting times are quantified and lengths of appointments are monitored. This can be valuable to communicate to payors demonstrative effective operations and some aspect of patient satisfaction.

Scheduling and referral tracking is valuable within the appointment scheduling module because it provides the practice with the ability to monitor where it is sending business. In areas of increasing managed care, this module may contain payor-specific, approved referral sources. This information also is useful in more advanced markets and in negotiating subcapitation arrangements with other providers.

COST ISSUES—COST PER UNIT CALCULATIONS

Activity-Based Costing

Activity-based costing (ABC) and activity-based management (ABM) principles, while well established in manufacturing and other industries, are fairly new to healthcare. The concept behind activity based perspectives is to examine the causes of actions, not simply the financial ramifications on a retrospective basis. ABC focuses on cost objects such as services, patients, physicians, and staffing,

E X H I B I T 5–5

CPT Code Approximate Expected Distribution

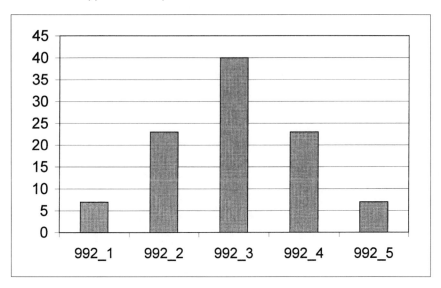

E X H I B I T 5–6

CPT Code Distribution
Established Patient Visits—All Physicians (10/1/97–9/30/98)

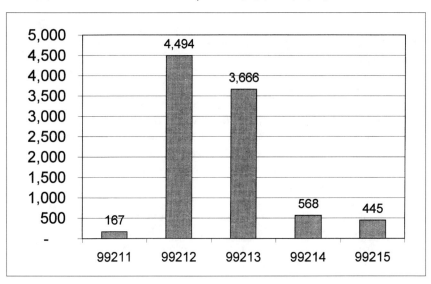

EXHIBIT 5–7

CPT Code Distribution
Percent of Patient Visits (Comparative Data—Family Practice)

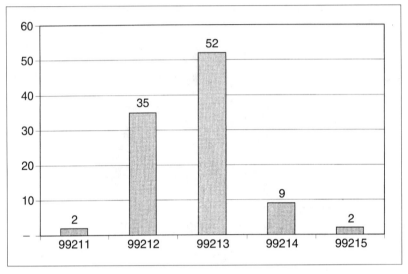

Source: Medical Group Management Association.

whereas ABM focuses on activities such as "why are our costs so much for these activities?"

The Consortium for Advanced Manufacturing—International (CAM-I) is the leading international group responsible for forwarding the concept of ABC and ABM principles around the globe. The CAM-I Cross (Exhibit 5–8) describes the interplay between cost drivers and resource drivers for the identification of cost objects and performance.

ABC and ABM principles represent the current state of the art in operating cost analysis in the healthcare industry. Devotees of these concepts see it as the best means to approach the analysis of difficult issues and a means to identify costs and improve performance when the quick fixes have already been tried. Structurally, the process works as follows. Activity-based systems are a cost management systems approach to identifying where costs exist and the reasons behind them. Costs may be incurred as a result of physical plan layout, practice styles and desires of physicians, administrative mechanisms employed by managers, and the more tangible elements, such as supply costs and equipment costs. The goal is to understand and examine what resources are consumed by what activities in order to produce your work product.

Resource drivers, those elements such as staff time and equipment use, are associated with activities to create a clear picture of where these resources are

The CAM-I Cross

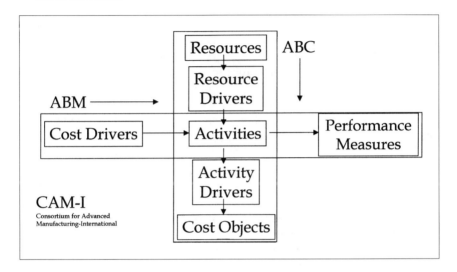

expended. Activity drivers are measures of intensity of demand, which drive the amount or frequency at which resources are expended, such as taking x-rays. Cost drivers are factors that cause changes in the performance of activities. Allocated costs are those elements of overhead that are attributed to certain activities as a result of a general allocation, though often incorrectly. Performance measures are the targets for analysis—benchmarked activities to which the business is aspiring to meet. These measures may be developed as internal targets or based on national comparative data.

The activity-based process identifies the elements of activity that then contributes to the flow of identified actions resulting in costs. Perhaps one of the most exciting opportunities may be the application of activity-based concepts with relative value unit analysis.

RELATIVE VALUE UNITS AND THEIR PRACTICAL USE

Over the past 2 years, dozens of articles have appeared in industry journals on the application of relative value unit (RVU) analysis in the operation of medical practice and in physician compensation. This section will discuss briefly the concept and application of RVUs, although the reader is directed to review the last 12 months of *Healthcare Financial Management, Medical Group Management Journal*, and the *Medical Group Management Update*. These two journals and one periodical contain nearly all of the information needed to effectively understand the application of RVUs in the analysis of medical practice operations and for use in provider compensation models. As a result, this section has been reduced to mere mention of the technique.

RVUs are standardized measures of work effort attached to CPT codes under several different systems, most notably the Healthcare Financing Administration's (HCFA) Resource Based Relative Value Scale (RBRVS). While other RVU scales have gained some prominence (McGraw-Hill for one), the industry tends to be leaning on the RBRVS developed for Medicare and Medicaid payments. The RBRVS is available through many practice office management software systems, for purchase from software vendors, for free from HCFA's website.

The general process is that all practice activity can be accounted by a CPT code with accompanying RVUs reflecting relative work effort. Each physician's productivity may then be compared not just in dollars or patients seen, but also by RVUs generated. The combination of these productivity measures is what is valuable to examine. Analysts know that a variety of issues may skew productivity measures, such as dollars billed or collected or patients seen; but in combination with RVUs generated, a good picture of provider productivity can be generated. RVUs can be used to evaluate mid-level provider productivity also. MGMA reports RBRVS RVUs in its Physician Compensation and Production Survey for various specialties.

RVU analysis should be undertaken for the purpose of a deeper understanding of provider productivity, but can also be used to address overhead and operational costs of the practice as well. The combination of RVU and activity-based principles yields a particularly clear indication of the sources of costs and the reimbursement associated with each activity. RVU analysis can clearly demonstrate the profit or loss, by CPT code, of a particular payor. It is a sobering event when a physician thought to be a big producer, finds that he has been maximizing a procedure that causes the group to lose money each time he does it.

Groups should absolutely take advantage of RVU and activity-based analyses to identify opportunities for improvement. The RVU modeling is quite simple and yields immediate results. The addition of activity-based analysis is much more time-consuming, but is one of the best means to truly understand the relationship between activities and the costs associated with them.

AGENTS OF CHANGE[4]

You must think about how your competitors are positioning for the purpose of taking your business away. They want your market share and will use various tactics. Battlefield thinking and organization may be helpful. During turbulent times, *The Art of War,* by Sun-tzu (translated by Sawyer in 1994), offers timely considerations. This historic text emphasizes that winning any battle requires the need for rationality and self-control. It stresses the need to avoid any conflict not based upon thorough analysis, a review of all options, and one's own capabilities.

Examples are listed below.

- Your competitors will draw your patients to them with the exciting promise of better service. They will dominate your marketplace with excellence.
- Your competitors will develop innovative products and services in your areas of strength. Move quickly to meet needs. Where you are vulnerable, your competitors will emphasize the advantages of their products.
- They will confuse you with constant innovation and superior service. Innovation is the one weapon that cannot be defended against.
- If you appear arrogant, your competitors will be humble. They will find out why you are currently favored by your constituents. Your competitors will be patient and, with careful questions, will uncover your weaknesses.
- They will wear you out with unrelenting attention to the needs of your constituents.
- When your creativity is dulled, your commitment dampened, your enthusiasm drained, and your financing depleted, competitors will take advantage of your weakness. When that happens, no executive, however wise, can prevent the decline of his career and the loss of business.
- While we know that hastily executed competitive operations can be troublesome, we have never seen successful competitive operations that wasted time. A successful competitive operation need not be complicated. To win, do simple things well . . . and quickly!
- Strategies that waste time and exhaust resources never work.
- Physicians who cannot balance risk with opportunity cannot profit in today's business environment. Speed and innovation are the keys. Only those comfortable with the pitfalls and ambiguities of rapid execution can profitably manage new products and services. Only those who appreciate the knowledge gained from quick failure can achieve lasting success.
- Skillful physicians do not hesitate to utilize the resources at their command. They engage the competition immediately and gain precious information from direct contact with constituents. They do not waste time talking to corporate staff who are farther removed from the competitive situation than they are. Being one step ahead of the competition is worth more than anything else to the success of the practice. Gaining that step is the wise physician's greatest desire.
- Skillful physicians build the strongest possible team from the people in a practice. They let the competition show them how to serve better. In

this way, they are always increasing their share of constituents. They build the practice through outstanding performance.

- Timely, accurate information is the lifeblood of successful competition. When obtained from outside sources, information is expensive. Expensive information wastes the company's resources.
- The most expensive information is that which is out of date. Resources spent to gather yesterday's data are wasted. Maintaining yesterday's data consumes large portions of available money and human resources.
- The wise physician harvests timely information from constituents and competitors. The accumulated data is analyzed from a product possibility perspective. One new product idea generated from discussion with a real customer is worth any number of ideas generated by consultants.
- In order to dominate, you and your medical group – from top to bottom – must be passionate about the services you provide and the products you represent.
- To capture the spirits of your employees, you must give them clearly defined and valuable rewards. You should reward the group for gaining customer share, but people should also be able to get rewards based on individual merit.
- When someone provides outstanding service to a customer, reward that person openly. Make that service an example for others to follow by providing sure and meaningful rewards for excellence.
- Treat your employees well and train them thoroughly. The success of the organization is built on the individual success of its members.
- The important thing in competitive operations is quick results, not prolonged activity. The physician who understands how to excite the staff and dominate the marketplace will become the foundation for progress of that medical group.
- The ideal strategy is to make a competitor's products or services obsolete next to your innovation.
- The next best strategy is to market yourself more effectively.
- The worst strategy is to attack a competitor's reputation or product directly. This sort of strategy is a matter of desperation. It often results in the ruin of all parties involved.
- To engage in destructive competition is ultimately self-defeating. Your aim is to provide superior service that generates high opinions among your constituents. How can you do this by ruining competitors' reputations and perhaps destroying your own in the process?
- If physicians are unable to control their impatience and seek to destroy their competitors by direct attacks, they will waste at least one-third of

their resources without accomplishing much. The impact of such a strategy is disaster.

- Skillful physicians conquer with knowledge and imagination. They create better products; they uncover unmet needs; they provide greater satisfaction. They outflank their competitors in the constituent's mind, without resorting to head-to-head battles or lengthy campaigns.
- Your aim is to take over a group of constituents intact by appearing as superior in their minds. Thus, your resources will be preserved and your profit will be greater. This is the art of an effective competitive strategy.
- The philosophy of competitive strategy is this: If your customer base is already five to ten times larger than your competitor's, press the competition hard through aggressive service. Dominate the situation with your presence. Spend your resources on research and innovation.
- If you have twice as many customers, make sure you understand why they are choosing your medical services and why they might choose your competitors'. Talk with your constituents. Redefine and differentiate yourself. How are you different? How are you superior?
- Five indicators predict who will dominate:

  Who knows when to fight and when to retreat will win

  Who uses resources appropriate to the challenge at hand will win

  Who is enthusiastic and innovative will win

  Who uses accurate, timely information to make decisions will win

  Who is not burdened by onerous rules or troublesome staff will win

- If you know your constituents, your competitors, and yourself, your strategies will not fail, even if you are challenged a hundred times.
- If you know yourself only, but are ignorant of your constituents or your competitors, you can expect to fail as often as you succeed.
- If you are ignorant of yourself in addition to your constituents and competitors, you will fail.

MEDICAL STAFF PLANNING

Readers interested in larger system-wide physician need planning are encouraged to review the sample plan in the Appendix. In earlier sections, the need and capacity concept was introduced. In the Appendix readers can review the components of a comprehensive medical staff development plan that was developed for a client about 5 years ago and remains a current approach to the issue. Although dates have been updated to reflect a plan year from 2000–2004, newer plans would address physician need based on current managed care penetration. Some supporting tables and maps are excluded, as well as the detailed calculations on physician need. The text sections address the concepts in each of these cases. Readers may notice some reference to the strategies of practice acquisition and the creation of an MSO. These issues were relevant when this plan was first prepared, and they may still be relevant in certain markets. The key to medical staff development planning is the market in which it is being done, as well as all the factors that influence the market. The issues you end up with will always be unique, and you cannot cookie-cutter the outcome.

NOTES

1. Sommers, P. (1998) *Medical Group Management in Turbulent Times.* Binghampton, NY: The Haworth Press, p. 154. Although the main points were expanded by the author, this section outline was taken from Dr. Sommers's excellent text.

2. Internal Revenue Code Revenue Ruling 69-545, 1969-2 C.B. 117.

3. Glass, K.P. E&M coding comparisons for office visits in high demand, *Medical Group Management Update,* June 15, 1999, p 2.

4. Ibid., Sommers, pp. 176–179. This entire section is taken from Dr. Sommers's text. Readers should begin to think of these things in the financial planning process, particulary in identifying variables.

6
CHAPTER

Modeling Mergers

"Misery aquaints a man with strange bedfellows."

Shakespeare

Conventional wisdom in merging medical practices and strategic business units seems to indicate that the initial focus should be on addressing the cultural issues of the entities rather than on the benefits gained, such as reduced overhead, operational efficiencies, and better provider call schedules. In small business merger forums you are likely to hear more about the difficulties involved in bringing two similar groups together than the benefits achieved. These difficulties stem from basic human and professional instincts inherent in human nature. The following summary denotes key areas that are the underpinnings of medical practice business, professional, and personal relationships. While much of the following discussion is presented from a medical practice merger perspective, attention to these detail items are likely to be the only way that a successful merger will occur across any autonomous business unit.

MERGER Q & A

Q. Why do separate groups, practices, or businesses entertain a merger?

A. The answer must be addressed in the context of small autonomous units such as medical practices and healthcare businesses versus larger organizations such as hospitals, physician groups, and health plans. Small groups or businesses may lack confidence about their ability to compete given the rapidly changing marketplace. Concern over the predomination of group practice, the increasing business aspect of medicine, the burden to forecasting business growth, and the general picture of risk leads most physicians to link up with larger, presumably more stable groups. Sharing call, relief of isolation in solo practice, having a colleague in the office, and small scale overhead control round out the list of prevalent reasons.

Larger entities seek mergers for some of the same reasons, although mostly on a larger scale. Hospital mergers may stem from immediate or imminent financial loss in one example to the adoption of a proactive position to avoid competitor ingress into an otherwise stable market. In some cases, mergers seem to make sense, given the regulatory approvals, or in the landmark case of Memorial Mission and St. Joseph's Hospital in Asheville, N.C., the hospitals found state immunity from federal antitrust under a state Certificate of Public Benefit. Many of the investor-owned entities, large and small, use mergers as a means for rapid growth and capital acquisition. Emphasis on service delivery, cost, quality, utilization, and convenience also are driving factors.

Q. What are some of the precipitating factors that drive groups to merger?

A. Increasing overhead expenses and reduced per physician earnings are among the most frequently cited reasons. With expenses approaching 70% in some practices, there is not much room left for provider income. High dollar specialties cannot afford too much inefficiency in the system, and there appears to be no readily apparent change. Fees and reimbursement keep dropping and cutting overhead is difficult. Increasing discounted fees and the initial experiences with capitation gives most physicians cause for concern in less developed managed care areas. The need for a partner to weather the storm is also a compelling reason for solo physicians and smaller groups, citing safety in numbers.

Q. Why are so many groups finding difficulty with merging?

A. There are myriad of reasons why different groups have difficulties merging their economic and cultural business components. Economic issues are daunting enough: Fee schedules, physician compensation, employment and buy-sell agreements, business and real estate valuation, and financial projections may be extremely sensitive issues to resolve between two different groups. Cultural issues including new practice styles and expectations, personnel management, interpersonal relationships, and the blending of practice patients create tensions that most groups neglect to consider in light of the vast economic benefits perceived. Lack of vision, leadership and effective governance, choosing the wrong partners, failure to make good on needs of clinical and economic consolidation, working through the tough points between members, and generally not completing the merger details.

Q. What are some of the myths of economic savings in mergers?

A. The first myth is that the pooling of resources on a small scale is unlikely to gain significant economic advantages. Bringing less than approximately 10 physicians into one group (plus several extenders) will not yield much in the way of savings in overhead control. The complexity added with slightly less that this number warrants more practice or business management horsepower than either of the individual groups, and the expense will likely be about the same, if not higher.

The second myth is that capturing and maximizing ancillary services from a larger group will be an ongoing significant revenue source. While indeed ancillary services will continue to be a strong revenue source, increasing prohibitions are scaling back the potential that groups once enjoyed and corporate systems may well need to capture these services outside of the practice setting. This creates concern for physician bonus pools and requires careful planning. In addition, physician compensation plans, in private or corporate systems, cannot directly or indirectly tie physician compensation to ancillary revenues (gross distributions of total practice revenues is legal; careful structuring of distribution plan is advised).

The small healthcare business world is significantly different than it was five or ten years ago. Changing patient volumes and patterns of care, ever-increasing regulatory issues, new and emerging (pervasive) lifestyle concerns among physicians, and the power shift to a gatekeeper mentality makes specialists reluctant partners for multispecialty arrangements. Issues on income distribution, especially mixing primary care and specialists, are more difficult in lean times. Topping all of it off is a greater fear of loss of autonomy than ever before.

Q. What are the best reasons to consider a merger?

A. Among the best are the following reasons.

1. To create a group of substantial size for managed care contracting

2. To gain or retain a significant market share/geographic coverage or presence

3. To add primary care (or selected specialty care), building clout for all types of future negotiations (managed care/practice sales)

4. To achieve demonstrable economies through significant overhead reduction

5. Physical facility consolidation—improvement from inadequate facilities (Most important are the compelling conditions that make a business merger the correct choice.)

Exhaustive study should precede the go-ahead decision on behalf of each group to ensure a commonality of need, interest, desire, and strength to achieve a successful merger.

Q. Does the value of each business automatically increase by merging?

A. Automatically increase, no. A successful merger of two strong groups will most likely have a positive impact on the economic value of the entity, although valuation less than about one year postmerger will give the best indication. An unsuccessful merger will be readily apparent to the appraiser and be reflected in the opinion of fair market value (FMV). Value is not simply added by creating one large semidysfunctional group or one with significant risk of dissolving. The increased market power of the merged group may neutralize some of this when being pursued by a buyer seeking a group of sufficient mass for vertical integration or strategic partnership, such as in the case of a specialty or multispecialty group partnering with a primary care group. Nonetheless, the FMV of the entity should reflect the desirability and marketability of the subject group in relation to the universe of comparable entities in the geographic market—all things held equal, a well-functioning and strong merged group will be more valuable than a poorly merged group.

FACILITATING A MERGER: PRACTICAL EXPERIENCES AND SELF-ASSESSMENT

Deciding to Merge

Considerations to evaluate include the following.

- Why are we considering a merger? (i.e., What are our objectives in pursuing this merger? What are the compelling reasons and conditions that would make this the strategy of choice?)
- Are there alternatives? Will they create similar, positive outcomes?
- Who are the potential partners and why are they being considered?
- What do they add to this group and will they allow us to achieve our objective?
- Why are we compatible partners and what potential advantages and impediments are foreseen?

- Will there be significant governance and management challenges caused by dissimilarities (group size, incomes, overhead, practice style, etc.)?
- Can we afford to merge ($10,000 per physician or $500,000 to $1,000,000 for medium-sized hospital—external costs only)?
- Can we afford not to merge? Are there compelling factors in the marketplace that would force you into a negative bargaining positions or, at worst, cause your business to fail?
- Are there anticipated regulatory (chiefly antitrust) and due diligence issues?
- Time frame: Most practice and small business mergers should be completed in six to twelve months after initial conversation with a potential partner to avoid changing minds, disillusionment, and disruption. Expect about three months for the leading group to discuss, educate, and make the decision to pursue potential partners and an additional one to three months to evaluate potential partners before approaching them. From here, plan about three months to discuss, educate within your group, evaluate compatibility and practice styles, discuss governance and management. Only after these issues have been framed should you approach compensation. Larger entities (e.g., large physician networks and hospitals) may require significantly more time to work through community benefit issues (as appropriate), business plan development, due diligence and regulatory review, document preparation, transition planning and preparation, and final implementation.

Merger Planning

Visioning and strategic planning may well be the only ways that organizations can blend economic operations and cultures. As mentioned above, the organization leading the process must develop a clear understanding and imperative that a merger is required as the first step.[1] Once the leading (read: initiating) group decides on the merger path, the next step is to evaluate potential partners. The following section elaborates on merger planning, citing examples of do's and don'ts when evaluating the likelihood for merger success with a potential candidate.

Feasibility—Opportunity To Determine Likelihood Of Merger

- Signing the Letter of Confidentiality and Premerger Discussions
  The Letter of Confidentiality creates in each group the understanding that each party can explore, in confidence, the potential relationship. These need not be exhaustive documents but should be executed before formal discussions begin.

- Role of Merger Facilitator

  The merger facilitator is an outside disinterested perspective to the merger process. The facilitator should be engaged jointly by each party to the merger or in the case of a merger of numerous groups, such as in a large multispecialty organization engaged after presentation to an organizing membership of the parties. The facilitator is the main coordinator of effort; they keep people on schedule for accomplishing the tasks each group must perform along the way. This role is vital to the success of the merger. It is difficult for any party with a vested interest (i.e., ownership interest) not to appear overbearing when it comes to coordinating project work. An independent outside professional can ride the issues with practices and physicians without creating personal ill feelings that may negatively affect working relationships after the merger. The merger facilitator also is the main point of contact for all issues in the merger process.

- Commitment

  Each group must be committed to the group practice environment as the preferred choice of practice. The reason you are considering a merger in the first place is because you do not want to go it alone or sell out and become an employee without control (some of the physician management company equity models are offering aspects of control and investment, and although true equity is rare, expect this to increase). Each group needs to realize that they need greater strength to withstand competitor and market conditions than remaining in their current structure. Each group must desire to control costs, utilization, risk, and maintenance of a commitment to high quality care. Groups must understand the need to retain capital and reduce expenses, remembering that operating margins are identified in advance and that equity is built through retaining earnings and developing a value-creating organization. Recall Richard Normann and Rafael Ramirez: The secret of creating value lies in an organization's ability to build a "value creating system, within which different economic actors—suppliers, business partners, allies, customers—work together to co-produce value."[2] Each group must realize that a merger will require somewhat less autonomy than in their existing practice, but much more than in any other long-term alternative—you have to give up power to get power. Last, each party must agree and sign a statement of purpose or objectives for discussion (not intent). Remember, we are still in the early stages of determining whether partners are right for each other. Groups should begin to outline their objectives as individual physicians, delineating their own personal and professional aspirations before each group comes to a general consensus of the personal and professional issues that are important to them. The facilitator discusses (and assists each group, as necessary) these areas of concern and coordinates discussion of the areas of commitment as they relate to common objectives and potential conflicting objectives.

Negotiation on Key Areas of Concern

Key areas of concern will include common issues in business governance, management, operations, compensation, and other factors as well as unique issues identified in the previous commitment assessment.

- Governance

  The guiding principle is that you should seek balance in power, authority, and the mutual respect of each party (a merger is when each party retains some facets of the their own identity; a takeover or acquisition results in one party being subsumed into the other). Groups should take guidance from their key areas of concern and not seek to covet, but to expand each other's wealth. As the old saying goes, you have to give up something to get something. In the process, not everyone can play the role of the leader. A lead (coordinating) physician or principal from each organization should be elected to represent that group; in the event of larger numbers of shareholders, several members may be worthwhile. That leaders should lead and followers should follow is a good maxim. Once each group has decided on its representative, work through him or her, raising your issues as needed, but don't micromanage the process. Everyone is busy enough with clinical and other duties, and the merger process is time-consuming as it is. Groups coming together should create allowances for dissimilar group size. It is natural that a smaller party may feel overwhelmed or undervalued (not from a financial sense, although this applies as well) when partnering with a larger group. Not only does the smaller group sense this disparity, but one can immediately envision the postmerger governance dynamics when the smaller merged group still retains a minority voting position. One way to address this, maintaining parity for the larger group, is to allow some votes based on majority (i.e., greater than 50% of the voters), some votes based on a supermajority (i.e., greater or equal to 66%), and/or some based comajorities among operating boards or divisions of the group. A resourceful facilitator can work with each group and the merger attorney to create a win-win relationship if differing group size is the most significant issue. Last, maintain formality in governance without undue burden.

- Management and Personnel

  How management is envisioned and what level is required depends on group size and complexity. The merging of two medical practices with three physicians each may not significantly increase the complexity of the new group, depending of course on individual circumstances. The ultimate merging of 30 physicians is another matter entirely. Either existing manager, in the case of two groups merging, or any of the existing managers in the case of a larger merger may not be appropriate for the new group. The groups should work with their merger facilitator to develop the conditions under which the new group would see the management function, and what knowledge, skills, and abilities are important for the administrator of the new group. In bringing two groups with competent administrative staff together, pick one to lead; team management seldom works. Evaluate needs and skills for the role and refer the departing manager(s) to a qualified outplacement counselor. Regarding major financial operations decisions, identify charitable care issues, write-offs, and courtesy policies of each group to determine whether they may be in potential conflict. In these times of decreasing reimbursement and increased risk, it is important that everyone understand the implications of charitable contribution. Evaluate capital needs and the strategy for developing a base (remember, equity models build equity, partially by not distributing reserves back to the physicians) or identify the means to acquire capital from outside resources. Identify means, and plan for asset depreciation and amounts for replacement reserves. Reevaluate staffing needs (provider and support staff) and supervisory responsibilities for all employees and functional units. Flatten and downsize should be the general idea. Mergers begin to save real money only by eliminating duplicative services, most important, duplicative staffing. Identify differences in staff cultures and begin to think of how the merger will necessarily affect changes in operations and staff culture. Prune and groom should be the goal. Now is the time to create a new organization and leave all the excess baggage behind, not necessarily staff; leave behind outmoded practices and bring in new ones that you've wanted to for years but couldn't. Now is the ideal time to make all types of positive changes.

- Blending of Processes and Cultures
  Blending personnel in organizations requires a critical analysis of practice or professional styles, compatibility, and autonomy. Individuals who have become accustomed to one style of conducting business may find it difficult to assimilate into the new environment. These issues become one of the greatest obstacles to successful merging, and they are common causes for merged organizations splitting. These cultural issues should be examined very carefully to ensure that a common understanding is present before moving ahead. Work schedules and

habits, especially related to use of personnel, should be discussed. Just because Sadie leaves early on Fridays and has always taken one hour and fifteen minutes for lunch doesn't mean that it can continue in the new organization. Similarly, most smaller practices and businesses operate without time clocks, but few organizations with more than 30 staff do. The technical proficiency of providers should be examined, not only the physicians, but the physician extenders as well. In most professional practice mergers, it is difficult to exclude a given physician (or dentist, counselor, or therapist) on the grounds of lack of technical proficiency. Preferably these issues are identified by each group and dealt with prior to and outside of merger discussions. In the event that one party questions the inclusion of a specific individual, tactful, professional discussion should rule, recognizing that this may become a sticking point. Other technical staff such as laboratory, radiology, and so on should be evaluated with appropriate action taken where needed.

The range of expertise within specialties (e.g., GI procedures, minor surgery, urgent/injury care, occupational medicine) should be determined, and the groups should jointly decide on a plan of recruitment if a given specialty or technical proficiency is desired. The groups also should analyze referral patterns, hospital privileges, and identify after-hours call coverage concerns, especially as they relate to insurance and managed care participation. Groups that are able to evaluate utilization should do so, although this is typically beyond the scope of most practices and small healthcare businesses. Demand management, the ability to maximize the use of all business resources to their optimum utility should be embraced, not only for the coordination of administrative and support services, but also for scheduling and provision of clinical care. For example, supply inventories should be examined to ensure that adequate amounts are available on site and that replacements are available on short notice (delivered within 48 hours). By reducing the inventory, cash flow is enhanced; by negotiating timely delivery—and many suppliers have geared up to support demand management—overall resource utility is improved. Demand management concepts can extend as well into staff scheduling, administrative processing, patient scheduling (determining historical peak periods), and other areas of business limited only by your imagination.

All types of healthcare businesses should make the commitment to continuing education and quality improvement in all facets of their work. In the new era of differentiation of health services, high quality, high functioning teams are of greater value (to the marketplace and to the ongoing business) than other "me too" businesses. Related to examining and creating a better business environment is the willingness of individuals and groups to modify personal or parochial habits for the good of the group. No one group or person has the monopoly on good ideas and the overall success of the business and satisfaction of its members should require each member to adapt to the activity or style of practice that most benefits the organization. While some accommodation should be expected, not everything can be resolved. Compatibility of personal ethics, lifestyles, and religious affiliation are among the greatest differences to overcome in interpersonal and business relationships. Potential partners should openly discuss any and all of these areas that they believe may cause personal or professional conflict for them.

- Name of the Practice or Business

Selecting the new name of the entity also is an area of considerable difficulty (readers might wonder why, but it is). No single group should dominate the discussion or force its name onto the new entity. At a minimum, groups should evaluate and discuss their beliefs on an appropriate name for the new group. In some circumstances, the groups may know intuitively that they will be selecting one of the existing names, as in the case of a smaller group joining a slightly larger group with better location, name recognition, and so on. One method to delay the naming (if there is some concern that it may take some time) is to establish a transition period of six to twelve months after merging to work on potential names for the new group. This method allows the principals to keep focused on clinical care as well as all the other issues of merging and deal with the name issue last. Culturally, allow the new identity time to develop—do not attempt to create it all at once. Cultural shock, an appropriate term, occurs when individuals (principals and staff) are thrown into a new, somewhat unknown environment causing confusion and frustration. Some aspects of business operations can and should be changed immediately, especially those that relate to administrative processes and key areas that the groups agree should change immediately. But don't bite off more than you can chew; changes in organizations are similar to the body's prioritization system right after a big meal: after this significant event, you can't jump up and run a marathon. Take your time, but plan your time, and prioritize the actions that need completion first.

- Physician Compensation And Employment Agreements

Groups should make a commitment to leveling the income field among providers by some equitable means of distribution. In the merged environment, a greater likelihood exists for income disparity, especially in multispecialty groups. These groups should make a commitment to supporting primary care development and network participation to ensure the adequate flow of patients into the practice. Groups must be particularly careful in treating ancillary income; create effective and legal ancillary distribution methods. Establish a system for mutual respect and reward within appropriate risk sharing. Groups and members should be rewarded for their share of activity and how that activity benefits the group. For example, an otolaryngology group with one member who specializes in pediatrics (read: sees almost all the pediatric cases) has a significantly different pattern than his partners. In the income distribution method, this may prove to be a significant issue. Likewise, the percentage of total income from capitated patients and other payor sources may be different between physicians. These also should be addressed.

Consider the effect of ownership on partner recruitment and retirement. Do not create impossible buy-ins and pay-outs for the group or you will not be able to recruit new partners, and exiting partners may seriously impact cash operations, physician salaries, and bonuses. Consider deferred compensation and cash value policies where feasible.

· Valuation of Practices

Define tangible and intangible assets of each group and whether significant disparity exists. Should goodwill be considered? Typically it is not included, although it may exist in varying degrees between the groups. Frank discussion should be coordinated by the merger facilitator on the handling of intangible assets including a definition, by group, of what each brings and how its importance relates in the marketplace. From here the groups can choose to include all or part of the intangible assets. Further discussion includes what other assets are included or excluded from valuation, for example, automobiles owned by one practice, original or personal artwork, heirloom private furnishings, and so on. The main issue is to determine what might stay and what might not and attach value estimates to the sum of each group's assets. Discuss also the impact or need for real estate usage, purchase, or divestiture. Recognize economic value of each party aside from hard asset value. This may be thought of as the strategic value of merging two or more specific groups. This concept gets back to your earliest premerger internal discussions: Who are our potential partners and why? Along each step of the merger process, greater and greater validation of the concept is made, for without it, reservations exist and the potential for differences to force the merger apart (which may be okay, the decision not to merge with another party may end up to be the best decision, and if not, you had good reasons).

- Pension/Retirement Plan (Partially Funded Plans vs. Fully Funded)

  Analyze and determine equitable pay-out or rollover for each party's pension or retirement plan for employees and partners. Each party's accountant should be able to reconcile the statements and guide the principals through the best way to maximize benefit from each plan. In some cases, maintenance of individual plans is possible and works out best for the group as long as equity is maintained in business contributions to the plan. Stock issues—redemption, dissolution, new values, taxes—should be coordinated through each group's accounting counsel with assistance from the merger attorney and merger facilitator. In the case of large mergers or the merging of two groups of different sizes, different classes of stock may be issued with defined voting rights to balance the governing decisions of the newly merged organization. As mentioned previously, requiring a majority, supermajority, or comajority vote on certain issues may obviate the need for different classes of ownership. Again, be careful how ownership is structured and how it affects the ability to recruit new potential partners.

- Leasing, Purchasing, Building Arrangements

  Merger planning should include an evaluation on what real property will be required to operate the new organization. Many smaller mergers can be implemented successfully by remaining in existing facilities but larger ones may need to divest one or more buildings, or remodel, lease, or build new space to maximize efficient operations. Real estate usage should be examined carefully to identify opportunities for savings and new purchase, building, or divestiture should really be based on a unanimous consensus of the partners (in reality this may be impossible; the group has to go with the most sound decision and move on).

- Signing of Letter of Intent to Merge

  The letter of intent to merge establishes the time frame and confidence among the parties that a strong potential exists for a merger. It establishes the merger schedule and plan (see Exhibit 5–1) and allows each party to clearly see that progress is being made, not simply more discussion. Last, it establishes that major issues are already resolved—baseline discussions on governance, operations, facilities, and financial matters. The fine points are yet to come.

DECISION AND IMPLEMENTATION

- Role of Merger Attorney

  The merger attorney is a neutral participant who processes papers and transactions regarding the merger of the parties. It should be a health law specialist with experience in these types of business transactions. The merger attorney advises on matters related to the transaction only, focusing on facilitating the arrangement and explaining each suggested approach to each party's attorney.

- (New) Practice Administrator

  The practice administrator is the key individual in creating the new environment (culture) of the merged group. While practice administrators often move heaven and earth to make sure that everything gets done correctly, they serve three primary functions related to the merger. As a facilitator, they assure and encourage all information processing needed by the new group, not limited only to physician, group, and business licenses and regulatory/administrative requirements (new plan numbers, contract changes, etc.), but they also coordinate the numerous pieces of information required by the principals, the merger attorney, merger facilitator, and all external groups. They are the ones who know where everything is and without whom, almost everything would be lost. The practice administrator serves, therefore as a point of coordination before and after the merger. They also serve as a confidant for providers and staff to provide discussion about the future, how they will survive, how existing operations will be affected, and how to make the process run tolerably well, if not smoothly.

PREMERGER OPERATIONAL ASSESSMENT

The following areas should be examined in the form of an operational assessment.

- Management and personnel

  Which, if any, employees will be leaving

  New position descriptions and performance standards

  Benefits coordination and resolution of disparities

  - Listing by name, age distribution, sex
  - Documents on file (I-9, W-4, employment applications, etc.)
  - Salary histories, benefits records, sick/vacation time schedules
  - Training received, cross training

- Business operations and systems

  Patient relations and marketing

  Formal marketing plans, service area of practice

  Age/sex distribution of patients, population analysis

  Scope of accounts (payor mix, industrial accounts, etc.)

Telephone operations
- Number of phone lines/extensions/fax
- Answering machine/services
- Emergency procedures/logs/messages/pages
- Patient difficulties/satisfaction

Management information systems
- Comprehensive practice management software
- Financial software
- Hardware issues

Appointment scheduling
- Day/date/time analysis
- Manual/computerized/method
- Reserved slots, walk-ins, extenders, follow-up policy

Medical records
- Number of active charts, completeness, legibility
- Filing system, pull tabs, outguides
- Office notes, loose filing, backlogs

Insurance
- Frequency of filing
- Manual/electronic, superbill
- Data backup, systematic monitoring, tracking
- Denials, claim refiling, time frames
- Third-party participation, contractual adjustments tracking

Financial management
- Prospective operating budget established
- Education/training of staff
- Accountancy services/frequency of reporting
- Cost containment/inventory control

Collections
- Written and working policies
- Readability of bills/frequency/time of service
- Phone calls, collections referral service
- Deposits required for procedures/cash collections

Internal control
- Charge and payments posting and canceling, deposits, bonding
- Petty cash maintenance, change fund
- Recording disbursements

- Physical facility
    Renovations, parking, updates
    Interior/exterior appearance
    Ingress/egress
    CLIA/OSHA
- Real estate
    Owned/leased (how much/fair value rent)
    Mortgage or lease terms
    Leasehold improvements
    Immediate improvements required

DEAL BREAKERS

Deal-breaking issues should occur only very early in the process, typically in the feasibility stage in which parties are identifying compatibility and likelihood of a similar view of the practice of medicine. In some cases deal breakers are surfaced early in the negotiations of key areas of concern phase, often after governance and into compensation issues. Compensation continues to be one of the most difficult issues to overcome in merging two entities. It is advisable to identify potential deal breakers for each group early in the process to decide whether partnership compatibility exists. While it sounds somewhat defeatist, the sooner two groups decide they are not suited to each other the better they both are. Mergers are difficult, time-consuming efforts, and fewer than half of the original negotiations result in completed mergers.[3] Both organizations benefit by identifying incompatibility early so they may continue with their partner searches.

NOTES

1. Kelly, T.L. (1995). What it Takes to Consummate a Merger. *Medical Economics,* January 9:30.
2. Normann, R., Ramirez, R. (1993). From Value Chain to Value Constellation: Designing Interactive Strategy. *Harvard Business Review* 71(4):65–77.
3. Slomski, A.J. (1994). Got the Urge to Merge? You're Not Alone. *Medical Economics,* April 11:50.

7

C H A P T E R

Operational and Legal Issues in Healthcare Network Development

"Think like a man of action; act like a man of thought."

Henri Bergson

This final chapter will take the reader through a discussion on issues in developing healthcare provider networks, the structural, the legal, and the practical representation of the network. Much of the discussion will be more on structure and less on financial modeling.

DEVELOPING INTEGRATED PHYSICIAN RELATIONSHIPS

Whether it is a developing, mid-stage, or nearly mature integrated delivery system (IDS), creating pluralistic physician relationships (a.k.a. physician integration) will remain arguably an important area for developing systems. The strategies are vastly different by stage of the system, managed care penetration, market readiness, and other factors, but the relationships must continue to be developed, nurtured, formalized, and solidified. Much of this text has discussed the need to partner with physicians and other community care providers in order to create a healthcare system with sufficient infrastructure to manage the clinical and administrative components demanded in the delivery systems of today. Developing integrated physician relationships means not only bringing together the clinicians to render care, but also means true partnership, win-win relationships, equal and proportional risk sharing for common and individual benefit. Few communities will develop successful, sustaining delivery systems without true partnering behavior. It is true that some markets are created by strong-arming the physicians into a given structure but these strategies are not lasting. Primary care physicians can relocate so many places that they may be bound only by contracts. Specialists may have to make tough personal decisions about their practice locations in order to find the right mix of professional and personal contentment.

CREATING A SHARED SENSE OF PURPOSE WITHIN THE SYSTEM

Aligning incentives within the IDS infrastructure is much easier in a single eco-nomic entity (i.e., a mature system) than in a developing or mid-stage IDS. As capitation has its own way of aligning physician incentives, albeit with some real problems in the absence of quality indicators, a shared sense of purpose must be developed by all components of the IDS to effect substantive, sustaining change. Physicians must begin to understand one another and share responsibility and risk proportionate to their individual, group, and system goals within the scope of good clinical medicine. In the academic environment, many autonomous faculty believe they have no immediate superior; they function and make decisions on their own and without responsibility to any person, department, or institution. They are simply treating patients. Helping the cardiovascular surgeon understand that he or she is truly an economic partner with the cardiologist, internist, and family physician often takes more than sharing the same incentive risk pools. The location of care (turf) is secondary to the delivery of appropriate care, at the ap-propriate time, in the appropriate setting. Unless physicians are given the oppor-tunity and resources to look past their own wallets, incentives are not aligned among them.

Bringing together the elements of the system, hospital services, physician services, health plan or risk-bearing capacity, and all other supplemental (carved-out) services requires each entity to be incentivized so that the whole succeeds. How is that effected? On the macro level, focusing on the inflow of premium dol-lars identifies the first part of the equation. Administrative details, such as pay-ment periods, claims periods, and interest payments, are negotiated to full advan-tage. System elements, as discussed under health plans above, must create incentives for distinct populations of physicians based on their ability to control costs and make substantive changes in the system, but these physicians must also believe that the total system orientation is one of cooperation and support of common goals. For obvious reasons, the incentive mechanism for a primary care physician is likely to be very different from a cardiologist or pathologist. The issue is to examine what the environment is dictating and what can reasonably be accomplished in your given system. As an example, in any given system the con-tracting mechanisms may vary from discounted fee-for-service to capitation to patient premium or a percentage of premium for specified services. The approach to creating a shared sense of purpose addresses the impact of each constituent group on their ability to effect meaningful change. In most health plans, the majority of expenses fall into the hospital services pool, followed by the specialist physician pool, followed by the primary care pool and carve-outs. Allowing the hospital to manage its expenses based on certain elements of cost and utilization (over which it has no control) is one beginning. Specialists can accept risk through capitation, although only when developed quality standards are in place to prevent the natural ill consequences of delivering care under capitation. Recognizing that most physicians will do the right thing for the patient regardless of the mechanism for payment, IDS organizations, physician networks, and health plans should make the development of quality standard a top priority in order to assist the fringe physicians and ensure continuous improvement in the whole system. Unfortunately, for many developing systems, it may be several years before enough covered lives are in the system to effectively capitate the specialist component. Specialists also can accept risk through other mechanisms such as payment drafts against risk pools. Obviously, the more narrow the risk pools the more comfortable the physicians will feel that they are able to manage care because they are more likely to see the result of their efforts. Grouping small numbers of physicians of similar specialties together, provided with appropriate data, is one means of assisting these self-managed teams to higher levels of managed care operations. Primary care physicians lend themselves well to either of the techniques outlined for specialists, although because the volume of lives needed for a primary care physician is considerably less than for specialists, capitation works well, again, only after appropriate quality standards are in place.

Administrative functions also must be aligned to a common purpose within the system. Senior management must feel empowered to make decisions by a supportive board and understand that the environment is flat, fluid, and fast. Physicians are going to go along with making major cultural changes on their behalf only if they perceive the same type of pressure is not on administration. Administration must bend over backwards and recognize that physicians are in the driver's seat. Successful integration will occur only when hospital and system leadership recognizes this imperative. As healthcare delivery moves toward assumption of the health status of a community (a defined geographical area such as a county), the shared sense of purpose is facilitated by total system economic alignment and systems of rewards shared by all.

INSURANCE LAWS

State insurance laws concern any entity that involves itself in "the business of insurance." Accordingly, such laws typically regulate insurance companies, HMOs, and third-party administrators (TPAs). Some states also are beginning to regulate third-party utilization review companies as well. The difficulty with IDSs is ascertaining whether an entity has assumed an insurance-type risk, and if so, which of the entities in the integrated system has actually assumed that risk.

On the other hand, the federal Employee Retirement Income Security Act of 1974 (ERISA) regulates the self-funded employee benefit plans structured by employers.[1] ERISA preempts state insurance laws that relate to employee benefit plans, but not state laws regulating the business of insurance.[2] State laws cannot deem employee benefit plans to be the business of insurance under ERISA.

Insurance Risks

Insurance-type risks are not easily susceptible to a bright-line definition. However, it is recognized that insurance generally involves four elements.

1. The insured has an interest in his health that can be measured in dollar terms.
2. That interest is subject to a risk of loss through disease or accident.
3. An insurer can assume the risk as part of a program to share or distribute losses among a large group that bears similar risks in exchange for a premium.
4. Neither the insurer nor the insured have any substantial control over the risk.[3] State insurance codes are concerned with entities that indemnify or reimburse insureds for the expenses incurred in sustaining a loss.

Under the traditional fee-for-service reimbursement system, a state-licensed insurance company assumed the risk that losses would exceed its receipts; however, under managed care, new reimbursement methods have evolved that have shifted the risk onto different types of entities. Under a capitated payment system, an individual physician or hospital assumes the risk that excess care must be provided; however, such risk is not always pooled. Thus, some state insurance regulators view capitated payments as not an insurance-type risk. It is only when integrated organizations pool risk that some state insurance regulations apply. On the other hand, other state regulators view capitation as involving an insurance-type risk. Withholds are typically viewed as a financial risk, not an insurance risk.

Hospitals reimbursed under the per diem or per case systems are not viewed as assuming an insurance-type risk, nor are physicians reimbursed under a global fee program, nor entities paid under a bundled fee arrangement. These reimbursement methodologies are more typically viewed as creative compensation arrangements and merely the financial-type risks of doing business. In *Group Life & Health Ins. Co.* v. *Royal Drug Co.*, for example, the Supreme Court held that negotiated fee contracts with pharmacies participating in a network were not the business of insurance.[4] Likewise in *NGS American, Inc.* v. *Barnes*, the court held that claims processing and other administrative services were not the business of insurance because they were not part of the underlying contract with the insured.[5] In *Varol* v. *Blue Cross & Blue Shield*, the court held that a fee-for-service psychiatric program using Blue Cross' provider network, in which the employer retained the risk for paying claims, was not an insurance product offered by Blue Cross but merely a cost management function.[6]

Risk Bearers

Under the insurance laws of most states, insurance companies and HMOs are permitted to assume insurance risk if they comply with the respective state insurance laws. Preferred provider organizations (PPOs) are not regulated under state insurance rules because they do not assume risk but broker services, and point-of-service (POS) plans are regulated through the HMOs that sponsor them.

IDSs, on the other hand, obtain cost savings by joining forces to pool resources and risk and thus may incur regulation under state insurance laws. A key issue is whether there is a regulated entity involved in the integrated system that is permitted under state law to assume or transfer insurance risk. Until state insurance regulations catch up with current movements in the healthcare industry, payment arrangements must be structured carefully to avoid the high reserve requirements and regulatory burdens imposed by the state insurance laws. Creative payment arrangements might include the use of bonuses for efficient service, which provide an upside risk but not a downside risk; charging losses to future management fees of the physician-hospital organization (PHO); assumption of risk providers in an individual capacity; organizing the physician group as a professional corporation; and setting up joint ventures with insurance companies and HMOs. These payment arrangements may trigger application of other regulations and thus must be analyzed carefully.

Insurance Laws

If an entity is in the business of insurance, it will fall under a state's insurance laws governing insurance companies, HMOs, or health service organizations. Such laws typically require the entity to set aside financial reserves of a specific amount and to submit insurance contracts to state regulators for approval.

Reimbursement and Payment Issues

Medicare is the largest third-party payor of health services in the country. As such, its rules for reimbursement percolate down to other payors in many instances. Because the reimbursement protocols for other payors are highly varied and subject to state insurance laws, only the Medicare program will be covered here.

The Medicare program was enacted in 1965 as Title XVIII of the Social Security Act to provide a national health insurance program for the aged. Generally, Medicare covers medical services that are "reasonable or necessary" for the diagnosis or treatment of a disease or malformation; however it does not cover experimental treatments. While in recent years the Health Care Financing Administration (HCFA) has encouraged Medicare beneficiaries to enroll in managed care plans through risk contracts with HMOs, Medicare is still primarily a fee-for-service reimbursement system.

Part A of the Medicare program covers care provided by or in institutional providers, such as inpatient hospital services, hospice care, skilled nursing facility care, and home healthcare, subject to an annual deductible. Medicare Part B pays for services provided by healthcare professionals and suppliers, as well as outpatient hospital services, home care, durable medical equipment, ambulance services, dialysis, and ambulatory surgery center services, subject to an annual deductible and a 20% coinsurance requirement.

Medicaid is a combination federal-state program that provides healthcare assistance to low-income persons who are aged, blind, or disabled, and to categorically needy persons.[7] States have the option to receive federal funding to help cover medically needy persons as well as those who may have slightly higher incomes.[8] In the past, reimbursement under Medicaid was very similar to that under Medicare. As it relates to other third-party payors, Medicaid is intended to be the payor of last resort. However, since 1981, states have been permitted to develop their own reimbursement programs and methodologies within certain federal limits, and thus their Medicaid reimbursement methodologies are becoming more widely varied.[9]

Institutional Provider Participation in Medicare

Hospitals electing to participate in Medicare must comply with the program's Conditions of Participation and enter into a participation agreement with the HCFA agreeing to accept Medicare assignment.[10] Assignment is mandatory for Part A services, which means that Medicare's payment is payment in full for all services rendered to all Medicare patients. Most hospitals are currently reimbursed under Medicare Part A for most services on a prospective payment system (PPS) basis, but other institutional providers must meet various conditions of participation and are generally reimbursed on a reasonable cost basis subject to cost or target rate limits. Certain specific services also are excluded from the PPS rate as well. HCFA sets the PPS reimbursement rates for hospitals, which it calculates to account for not only costs related to patient care, but also the overhead costs of the facility, necessary and proper interest costs related to patient care, and certain other specific categories of costs. By the year 2001, capital costs are scheduled to be fully included in the PPS rate as well.

Certain patient care services are not reimbursable at all, and certain other services are reimbursable on a non-PPS basis, typically calculated on a retrospective reasonable cost basis.[11]

Fiscal intermediaries, under contract with HCFA, process claims and make PPS payments to hospitals based on the diagnosis related group (DRG) in which a patient is categorized based on the diagnosis at admission. The DRG reimbursement may vary for specific patients when their length of stay or costs exceeds the norm by a certain factor—day outliers and cost outliers. In addition, one component of the DRG rate is adjusted for differences in area wages, thus payments for the same DRG will vary for hospitals in different areas. Finally, reimbursement rates vary for special categories of institutional providers, such as public hospitals, cancer hospitals, rural referral centers, hospitals in Alaska or Hawaii, disproportionate share hospitals, and sole community hospitals.[12]

Physician Participation in Medicare

Individual physicians may participate in Medicare and bill for their services under Part B in two different ways. First, the physician may elect to become a participating provider, whereby he or she signs a yearly contract agreeing to accept Medicare assignment. Assignment means that Medicare's payment is payment in full for all services rendered to all Medicare patients. Physicians may charge patients only a 20% copayment amount and may not balance bill for excess charges. On the other hand, physicians also may participate in Medicare as nonparticipating providers whereby they accept assignment on a claim-by-claim basis. However, nonparticipating physicians are reimbursed 5% less than participating providers.

If the physician belongs to a group practice or is a member of a hospital medical staff, and that entity submits bills in its own name, then one participation agreement binds all physicians who work for that entity as to any services furnished for that entity.[13] However, if the physicians bill in their own names, they may decide individually whether to participate. In the case of university medical centers, individual departments can decide whether to participate.

Prior to 1992, Medicare carriers under contract with HCFA reimbursed physicians on a reasonable-charge basis. A physician's reasonable charge was determined based on several factors: the physician's actual charge, the physician's customary charge, and the prevailing charges in the area for like services. Customary charges were based on the amount the physician charged in the majority of cases for a specific service to all third-party payors. If the physician was in a group practice, the group had a group customary charge if each physician in the group charged the same as the other physicians for the same services, otherwise the physician had his or her own customary charge.

As of January 1, 1992, the Medicare program began to phase in the use of a fee schedule for reimbursement of physician services, to be completely in place by 1996. The Medicare program eliminated reimbursement based on customary charges and now reimburses physicians based on the lesser of the physician's actual charge for the service or the amount determined under the Medicare fee schedule.[14] The fee schedule has three cost components: 1) the physician's time and the intensity of the work, 2) overhead costs, and 3) malpractice insurance expenses. Each of these three components has its own relative value unit (RVU), each of which is adjusted for geographic differences. These adjusted RVUs are then multiplied by a conversion factor to ascertain the payment amount. There are three conversion factors based on the type of services provided—surgical services, nonsurgical services, and primary care services. These conversion factors currently do not take into account any other specialty services.

Other services and items provided incident to a physician's services also are reimbursable under the Medicare program. Patient treatment supplies furnished incident to physician services are reimbursed as part of the fee schedule if they represent an actual expense to the physician, and the charges for supplies must be included in the physician's bills. Charges for drugs and biologicals that cannot be self-administered, which are provided incident to physician services and which represent an expense to the physician, are reimbursed as the lesser of the acquisition cost of the drug or the national average wholesale price of the drug as long as the charges are included on the physician's bill.[15]

The services of other medical paraprofessionals, such as physician assistants and nurse practitioners, also are reimbursable if commonly provided incident to a physician's services. However, such professionals must be employed by the physician or his or her clinic in order for the clinic to bill for their services. On the other hand, if these paraprofessionals perform tasks normally performed only by the physician, such as minor surgery or conducting physicals, then such services are not reimbursable because they are not provided incident to a physician's services unless they are performed under the supervision of a physician in a hospital or nursing facility.

As with the services of physician assistants and nurse practitioners, the services of physical, occupational, and speech therapy providers also may be reimbursable under Medicare under several different arrangements. First, they are reimbursable if they are furnished incident to a physician's services, the physician or clinic employs the therapist, the physician personally supervises the therapy, and the physician's bills include such charges. Second, physical therapy and speech pathology services also may be provided under arrangement by an outside service organization with a written contract. In such a case, they are reimbursable under Medicare if the clinic or physician bills for the services, if the clinic is qualified to provide such services under state law and assumes responsibility for their provision, and if receipt of payment by the clinic discharges the beneficiary's obligation to pay for the service. Finally, physical and occupational therapists in independent practice also may be reimbursed under Medicare up to an annual limit per patient of $1,500 in billed charges apart from therapy services furnished incident to a physician's services.[16]

Diagnostic tests are usually reimbursable under the physician's fee schedule if furnished by a physician, by the physician's employees under the physician's supervision, or incident to a physician's services.[17] However, diagnostic services performed under arrangement with an outside supplier, regardless of where they are performed, are reimbursable only at the physician's cost of purchasing those outside services, not at a marked-up cost.[18] All claims now must be submitted with documentation on purchased services or a statement to the effect that the claim includes no purchased services.

UNAUTHORIZED CORPORATE PRACTICE OF MEDICINE

Most states permit only natural persons to hold a license to practice medicine. Thus, general business corporations are prohibited from practicing medicine, and, in most states, also are prohibited from employing physicians to practice medicine on their behalf. This restriction also can apply to acquisitions of physician practices, prohibiting the transfer of assets such as patient medical records and practice goodwill.

Violations of the corporate practice of medicine doctrine can result in fines and imprisonment in some states, or loss of licensure. On the other hand, most states permit professional corporations to practice medicine or to employ physicians if all shareholders of the professional corporation are licensed physicians. Some states permit hospitals to practice medicine under the hospital licensing statutes as well.

Although this doctrine has been in existence for some time, its persuasive hold on courts is diminishing in many states because pervasive changes affect the healthcare landscape. Originally, the rationales for the prohibition were to prohibit lay control over professional medical judgment, to avoid commercial exploitation of medical practice, and to avoid conflicts of interest between a physician's duty to the patient and to the physician's employer. Few states today strictly enforce the doctrine, or they statutorily decree that certain entities, such as hospitals and HMOs, are permitted to employ physicians. Where it is enforced, however, physicians typically enter into extensive contractual arrangements with corporations to work around the restriction. Primarily, the doctrine is seen as an obstacle to managed care initiatives, particularly in light of the fraud and abuse safe harbors protecting employment relationships.

SPECIAL LEGAL ISSUES

Independent Contractors, Vicarious Liability, and Ostensible Agency

The general rule under common law is that an employer is not liable for the neg-ligence of independent contractors. An exception to this rule is the nondelegable duty doctrine, which holds that the employer cannot avoid liability by delegating certain functions to independent contractors.

Under the vicarious liability doctrine, an employer organization will be li-able under the *respondeat superior* theory for the malpractice of its employed physicians. The physician's employment status is ascertained under common law, which typically focuses on the organization's legal right to control the ends and the means of the employee's work. The label given to the relationship in a con-tract is not controlling.[19] Most courts have held that the vicarious liability doctrine applies to staff model HMOs, however some courts have held that HMOs them-selves do not render medical services and are thus not liable.[20,21] Other courts also have held that HMOs are liable for the negligent treatment of consulting physi-cians who are independent contractors.[22]

A substantial number of jurisdictions follow the ostensible agency doctrine, which holds that hospitals or HMOs are liable for the malpractice of their inde-pendent contractors if the hospital holds the contractor out to the public as its agent and a member of the public believes that the contractor is the hospital's agent.[23,24] Cases relying on this argument typically involve services provided in the hospital's emergency department and perhaps other hospital-based services.

Corporate Negligence

The corporate negligence doctrine, effective in a substantial number of states, im-poses a direct obligation upon hospitals to properly hire and credential physicians on its medical staff.[25] Depending on the jurisdiction, this doctrine also may re-quire hospitals and managed care organizations to ensure that patients receive quality care, to maintain safe and adequate facilities and equipment, and to for-mulate and enforce policies to ensure quality care.[26,27] It also covers negligent uti-lization review, negligent benefit determinations, improper denials of coverage, and bad faith.

Financial Disincentives and Duty to Disclose

Most courts hold that managed care organizations are not liable for physician negli-gence by virtue of the financial disincentives to provide care in their compensation arrangements.[28] While managed care organizations may not have a duty to disclose their compensation arrangements under common law, many state legislatures are now requiring managed care organizations at least to disclose other forms of treat-ment that may be useful but are not covered under the patient's benefit plan.[29]

Special Considerations for Tax-Exempt Organizations

Tax-exempt hospitals confront additional legal issues in the process of affiliation. Under the tax-exemption rules, exempt entities may not use their assets for substantial private benefit, nor may they permit private inurement of their resources. They also must operate primarily for a charitable purpose. Exempt entities that enter into joint ventures with non-exempt entities risk losing their exempt status if they engage in substantial activities that do not further their charitable purposes.

Exempt entities may serve as general partners in a limited partnership with a taxable entity if they meet a two-pronged test.[30]

1. The partnership arrangement should be closely scrutinized to ensure that the exempt entity's duties under the Internal Revenue Code do not conflict with the objectives of the partnership. In essence, the exempt entity must be serving a charitable purpose through the partnership.
2. The partnership arrangement must permit the exempt entity to act exclusively in furtherance of its charitable purposes and only incidentally for the benefit of the taxable entity.

Because most exempt hospitals are also nonprofit entities under state law, additional concerns are raised when they are sold to for-profit entities. In addition, if they are sold, exempt entities must normally contribute their assets to a nonprofit foundation under state law. Particularly, the concern centers around whether community assets held by the hospital, which were obtained in the form of tax deductions, are being properly valued and distributed at the time of sale.

PHYSICIAN ORGANIZATIONS AND PHYSICIAN RELATIONSHIPS

Organizational Issues

Physicians collaborate in several different models of integrated systems.[31] Depending on the form of the organization and the services offered, collaborating physicians may be able to contract directly with employers to provide care, because many employers are self-funded and prefer one-stop shopping.

Traditionally, a physician participated in an integrated system by entering into a group practice with other physicians. Although there are typically few practice sites, the group practice is completely economically integrated into a single legal entity. It may have additional subsidiaries that provide specialized services, such as a real estate partnership or a management services company, which are separate for tax reasons.

A group practice without walls is made up of physicians at different sites who are shareholders and/or employees of a corporation in which they share overhead expenses but retain the individual assets of their own medical practices. Such groups typically permit physicians to remain independent practitioners while providing them with the stronger negotiating power of a group. On the other hand, such groups lack the legal protections that a single entity would have under the antitrust laws, which prohibit collusive activity between two or more parties, and under the fraud and abuse and antireferral laws, which provide safe harbor protections to organizations legally organized as a single-entity group practice. Multientity groups that merge their assets and employ physicians usually have such protections. Furthermore, where physician organizations share risk, they are under less scrutiny under the antitrust laws because it is assumed that they do not have financial incentives to violate the antitrust laws or fraud and abuse laws.

An independent practice (or physician) association (IPA) is another integration model. In an IPA, physicians practice independently but partially integrate their practices to contract more effectively with third-party payors, including managed care contracting. IPAs are attractive to third-party payors because they provide one-stop shopping for either a single or multi specialty group. An IPA can serve as the messenger of fee information to avoid antitrust risks, and it can assume economic risk by entering into capitation arrangements on behalf of the participating physicians. If the IPA does assume risk, it generally must comply with state insurance laws at some level.

IPAs can be formed as a business corporation, nonprofit corporation, professional corporation, or a limited liability form of corporation. If the IPA is formed as a business corporation, then it may sell shares of stock, but it must also comply with securities laws unless an exemption applies. If it is formed as a professional corporation, then all of its shareholders must be physicians. If it is formed as a nonprofit corporation and obtains tax-exempt status, then it must comply with private inurement restrictions. Another model may involve minimal integration in the form of sharing overhead costs, such as leases, staffing, and equipment costs.

Physician organizations (POs) are another form of physician integration. A PO provides the contract negotiation functions of an IPA combined with other functions. A PO may handle group purchasing and consolidate the billing functions of a group of physicians. A PO may be set up in the same corporate formats as an IPA with the same advantages and disadvantages.

Governance of the integrated practice will depend in part on the corporate form of the practice. If it is a corporation, governance is vested in the board of directors with approval on fundamental corporate changes reserved to shareholders. If it is a partnership, a managing partner typically handles governance. Ownership of shares in a corporation need not correspond to each shareholder's voting rights, however.

Legal and Regulatory Issues

Integration of physician practices raises several legal issues. First, the antitrust laws are implicated when the participants begin negotiations on the process of integration because such discussions could be viewed as an attempt to monopolize depending on the size of the market. Antitrust laws are also implicated if such discussions involve market allocation or collective discussions on fees. Although most of the models discussed are not sufficiently integrated to avoid antitrust scrutiny, the group practice without walls may be sufficiently integrated to avoid scrutiny, such as when it contracts on a capitated basis, depending on its actual structure.

Referrals of patients between affiliated entities also may raise fraud and abuse issues. Fraud and abuse concerns arise when the integrated practice provides designated health services but does not meet the requirements of a group practice under the safe harbors. Under the Stark antireferral law, a group practice is defined as a group of two or more physicians legally organized as a partnership, professional corporation, foundation, nonprofit corporation, or similar association. Services provided must be provided through the joint use of shared office space, equipment, and staff, and substantially all of the services of the physician members must be provided through the group practice and billed under the group's billing number. Income must be treated as income to the group, not the individual physicians, although the physicians may be paid based on the services they personally perform. The Department of Health and Human Services' Office of the Inspector General has opined that a group practice without walls may be deemed a sham structure, formed to avoid restrictions on joint ventures for ancillary services.

The form of the new entity also will determine where liability ultimately rests. If the integrated practice is a corporation, then liability will be limited to the corporation's assets in most cases. If the groups are integrated and formed as partnerships, then individual partners are personally liable for the partnership's debts. Securities laws are implicated if the integrated entity is formed as a corporation and seeks sources of outside capital, unless an exemption applies.

Physician integration also may implicate corporate practice of medicine restrictions. These restrictions limit the types of entities that may practice medicine and thus limit the forms of organizations that can be used for physician integration. State law may require physicians to practice in and be employed only by professional corporations or HMOs as opposed to general business corporations.

The formation of an integrated physician practice also raises tax implications depending on whether a separate entity is formed or whether existing entities are merged.

Special Considerations for Tax-Exempt Organizations

Although physician groups are not typically formed as tax-exempt entities, they may be formed as such if they are organized and operated exclusively for charitable purposes and if they comply with the rules governing tax-exempt entities.

Additional issues arise if one merging entity is tax exempt and the other is not or even if a joint venture is formed between such entities. In a merger situation, the tax-exempt entity is prohibited from selling a portion of its gross or net revenue stream.[32] However, a tax-exempt entity may engage in insubstantial profit-making activities unrelated to its charitable purpose as long as it pays the unrelated business income tax on such activities.

PHYSICIAN-HOSPITAL ORGANIZATIONS

Organizational Issues

Physician-hospital affiliations are quickly becoming prevalent in the healthcare delivery system. Generally, in these affiliations, physician and hospital services are integrated to provide more comprehensive services to patients and perhaps to provide capital to physicians. A physician-hospital affiliation may take several forms, including direct employment of physicians by hospitals, a separate physician practice entity owned or controlled by the hospital, or a PHO. Such affiliations provide the same advantages of IPAs in negotiating third-party payor arrangements, and because they include hospital services, they can provide more comprehensive services to payors.

Direct employment of physicians by hospitals is one form of affiliation between physicians and hospitals. Hospitals may seek direct employment of physicians to develop a more extensive primary care base or to penetrate new markets. However, direct employment may pose a problem under state corporate practice of medicine prohibitions in some states. In other states, hospitals are authorized to practice medicine under their licensing statutes and thus are exempt from this prohibition. Direct employment of physicians does have the benefit of avoiding referral problems under the Medicare fraud and abuse rules and related state statutes. It also may avoid private inurement problems if the hospital is tax exempt.

Another form of affiliation may be a separate practice entity formed as a subsidiary of the hospital or as a subsidiary of a parent corporation over both the hospital and the practice entity. The physician practice entity may be formed as a nonprofit, tax-exempt subsidiary of the hospital, but it must meet certain criteria under IRS rules.

In a PHO, a hospital integrates with its medical staff to negotiate and provide services under third-party payor contracts. The medical staff may be represented by a PO or an IPA, which would deal directly with the PHO. The PHO structure permits the hospital and medical staff to manage utilization review, peer review, and quality assurance functions, and it may handle management services functions as well. A PHO is appealing to payors because it provides one-stop shopping for comprehensive services. A PHO is often an intermediate step to more complete integration of medical services.

PHOs typically are legal entities separate from the hospital and physician group. They may be organized in several forms, including for-profit business corporations, nonprofit corporations, partnerships, or limited liability companies. A for-profit business corporation structure will require that the PHO comply with federal and state securities laws if stock is offered to numerous individuals, but it may be the most practical if the shareholders will hold their interests as an investment to be sold at a later date perhaps. If the PHO is set up as a nonprofit entity, then the members obtain financial benefits through their contractual arrangements. If the PHO is structured as a corporation, it will incur double taxation at the entity and individual shareholder levels, and thus compensation arrangements must be structured carefully. Most PHOs are not tax-exempt entities, even though they may be nonprofit corporations.

If the PHO is set up as a limited liability company, then it will have the advantages of taxation as a partnership and limited liability, although it still may need to comply with securities laws unless an exemption applies. As a partnership, the PHO would be taxed as a partnership but the partners would have joint and several liability.

One common form of the PHO is the foundation model. Under this form, the hospital establishes a separate corporation, usually a tax-exempt organization, that builds or acquires all assets of a medical group clinic facility and then owns and operates the facility. If the foundation is tax exempt, then the medical group cannot obtain an ownership interest in it. The PHO either employs or contracts with the medical group to provide the clinical services, depending on the state's corporate practice of medicine prohibition. Unlike a management services organization (MSO), a foundation-model PHO is the provider of care and can bill for medical services rendered.

The Medicare billing rules applicable to MSO arrangements also may apply to the foundation model. Under these rules, a group medical practice may bill Medicare for services rendered by medical personnel only if those services are performed under the supervision of the physician. The group may reassign its right to payment only to an employer or to an organization in whose facilities the physician practices exclusively. To qualify under the supervision requirement, the services must be performed by the physician directly, by employees of the physician, or by ancillary personnel who have a common employer with the physician. Thus, if the physicians are independent contractors with the foundation, the medical group may not assign its payment rights to the foundation, and the foundation may not bill directly for the group's services. The foundation may provide billing services, but it must do so as a billing agent. As a billing agent, the foundation may not be compensated based on collections or billable amounts. Although HCFA is currently reviewing this issue, there are some approaches to solving it. One is to treat the physicians as employees, in which case HCFA will approve the transfer of a provider number to the foundation. However, this approach implicates the corporate practice of medicine prohibition.

The fully integrated model is a variant of the foundation model. In a fully integrated model, a corporate parent is created over the hospital and physician group subsidiaries. The parent may or may not be jointly governed by the hospital and physician group. This model may provide increased access to tax-exempt funding for all subsidiary organizations if the parent is tax exempt. A fully integrated organization enjoys substantial power in the marketplace through its ability to provide one-stop shopping and better control over costs. It also enjoys less scrutiny under the fraud and abuse laws if the entity employs the physicians, because there is only one entity, and it cannot refer to itself.[33] This single-entity status likewise applies to private inurement and antitrust concerns. But corporate practice, licensure, and certificate of need (CON) issues may arise. If the physicians are employed, the entity also may need to employ auxiliary personnel and to lease physician space in order to obtain reimbursement for auxiliary services provided incident to a physician's services without requiring the physician's direct supervision.

Legal and Regulatory Issues

There are several legal issues relating to who will own, control, and govern the joint organization. Antitrust is a chief concern with nearly all forms of IDSs in which there is more than one legal entity involved in the system. If the system involves a parent-subsidiary relationship and the subsidiary is wholly owned, then generally no antitrust issues arise because there can be no conspiracy without two separate entities. An exception is when monopolization claims arise with a large system because monopolization can be a unilateral activity.

The Justice Department has been particularly concerned with activities involving price-fixing, boycotts, and monopolization. Price-fixing issues arise when two separate entities agree to set rates for specific services, or even discuss the rates they charge. Boycott issues arise when the ability of physicians to obtain medical staff membership at the hospital is limited because the medical staff is closed to new members. There are also significant antitrust issues if physicians are on the board of a PHO and the PHO is involved in managed care network activity, such as setting fee schedules.

Fraud and abuse issues also are a concern for most managed care activities involving hospitals now that Stark II is in effect. One of the designated health services that triggers application of Stark II is inpatient and outpatient hospital services. If the physicians are employees or independent contractors of the hospital or the PHO, then the arrangement generally will fall under a safe harbor if the compensation is reasonable and is not based on the volume of referrals between the parties. However, an employment relationship may trigger the corporate practice of medicine prohibition in some states. If the integration process involves the merger or acquisition of physician practices, then the transaction must comply with the safe harbor requiring a single transaction not based on the value of referrals. It should be noted, however, that the safe harbor for practice purchases does not cover hospitals at all, only physician-physician purchases from a retiring physician.

Insurance issues also are implicated in hospital-physician affiliations. If the PHO assumes risk, it must be regulated in some form by state insurance laws, either as a preferred provider or as an HMO. In addition, its utilization review functions also may be regulated under state laws.

Special Considerations for Tax-Exempt Organizations

The IRS set forth the tax-exemption requirements for hospital-affiliated medical practices in its rulings on the Friendly Hills Health Care Foundation and the Facey Medical Foundation in 1993 and 1994, respectively, which reiterate and expand the community benefit standard applicable to tax-exempt hospitals.

1. The hospital and the physician practice entity must provide an open emergency room to all persons regardless of their ability to pay.
2. The medical staff should be open to all qualified applicants.
3. The board of directors must represent a fair cross-section of the community, and no more than 20% of the board can be comprised of physicians with a financial interest in the organization.
4. Covenants not to compete must be limited so as not to limit the community's access to medical care if the physicians leave.
5. Physicians must participate in Medicare and Medicaid programs in a nondiscriminatory manner.
6. The organization must comply with other tax-exempt requirements, such as operating for a charitable purpose and providing a community benefit, including a certain level of charity care.
7. Physician compensation must be reasonable and must not violate private inurement restrictions.
8. The acquisition of any medical practices must be done at fair market value (FMV) according to approved IRS methodologies.[34]

There also are private inurement concerns if the hospital capitalizes the PHO in an amount that is disproportionate to the physician investors' share or if it engages in other activities that would expose the hospital's assets to a risk of loss that is greater than the physician investors' risk. Generally, the tax-exempt participant may not capitalize the PHO disproportionate to its profits, nor may it assume risks disproportionate to its interest in the PHO, and all services provided by or paid for by the exempt entity must be at FMV. In addition, the exempt participant must be permitted to veto actions by the PHO, such as those implicating private inurement, that would jeopardize the exempt participant's tax-exempt status.

Physician recruitment is another area that implicates tax-exempt issues. Traditional recruitment incentives include loans, relocation assistance, income guarantees, malpractice insurance assistance, office and equipment leasing, and the provision of billing and support services. These recruitment incentives also create legal issues under the fraud and abuse rules because such incentives can be viewed as inducements to refer.

In 1994 the IRS issued guidance in the area of physician recruitment with its publication of the Hermann Hospital closing agreement. This closing agreement specified the parameters within which recruiting would be permitted for tax-exempt hospitals.

1. The hospital must show a demonstrable community need for the physician's services. For example, the physician's specialty is deficient in the hospital's service area, there is a demand for service and long waiting periods, the area has been designated a health professional shortage area by the Department of Health and Human Services, physicians are reluctant to relocate to the hospital because of its location; a physician is expected to retire, or there is a documented lack of physicians serving indigent or Medicaid patients in the service area.

2. Incentives used to retain existing physicians who are nonemployee physicians with staff privileges are prohibited.

3. Hospital subsidization of salary and benefit costs for support staff of nonemployee physicians in their private practices is prohibited.

4. Income guarantees cannot exceed two years.

Tax-exempt status is now more difficult to obtain for a foundation model PHO, and the IRS limits physician participation on the foundation board to 20%. Medicare also is concerned about granting provider numbers to the foundation entity because physicians may assign their rights to payment only to an organization in which facilities the physician practices—typically a hospital. Thus, the foundation may not be able to bill for physicians' services. Other IRS concerns include private use of tax-exempt bonds as well as acquisition of physician practices at FMV.

MANAGEMENT SERVICES ORGANIZATIONS

Organizational Issues

MSOs can provide a broad range of management support and administrative services to physician practices. Such support may include staffing and recruiting, billing, record keeping and information systems, equipment leasing, contract negotiation, consultation services, and the use of facilities. An MSO may have the capacity to provide all nonclinical services to medical practices. It also may purchase all of the assets of a physician practice and then contract with the physician practice to provide management services for a set fee. MSOs allow physician autonomy while providing centralized practice management and centralized managed care contract negotiations for physicians. MSOs are commonly used when enforcement of the corporate practice of medicine doctrine is strong and thus prohibits employment of physicians.

MSOs may be set up in various ways. Commonly, they are owned and governed by hospitals, less commonly by physicians, but they also may be jointly owned and governed in some instances. MSOs may function as a division or subsidiary of a hospital, or as a joint venture between the hospital and its medical staff, or as a separate entity. In a separate entity, its corporate form will depend on whether any of its participants are tax-exempt entities, but it may be set up as a business corporation, a nonprofit corporation, a partnership, or a limited liability version of those. The MSO itself normally does not qualify for tax-exempt status because it does not provide medical care services and thus does not have a charitable purpose. If it is a division of a tax-exempt hospital, then income from the MSO's operations is unrelated business income that is taxable to the hospital. In addition, the activities of the MSO division cannot be more than a substantial part of the hospital's operations, otherwise the hospital will jeopardize its tax-exempt status. On the other hand, the MSO may be set up as a separate limited liability company, in which case income can be passed through to the participants including to a tax-exempt hospital. Private inurement restrictions will still apply in relation to physician contracts where a tax-exempt hospital is involved, however.

Hospitals also can be involved by contracting with a large group of physicians, although they remain separate entities with the hospital providing many management services to the group, such as managed care contract negotiations, group purchasing, information systems, office management, provision of support staff, and leasing of space and equipment.

The MSO is typically a separate legal entity and perhaps is co-owned by the hospital and the physician group. The physician group may be a part-owner of the entity outright or through another entity, such as a PHO. It may purchase the tangible assets of the group and lease them back to the group. Intangible assets, such as patient records, managed care contracts, and the practice goodwill, might not be acquirable because of state corporate practice restrictions, which may require these assets to be held by a professional corporation. In addition, asset appraisals are required if the MSO is affiliated with a tax-exempt entity or generally for fraud and abuse concerns that excess payments are inducements to refer.

Medicare has special billing rules applicable to MSO arrangements. A group medical practice may bill Medicare for services rendered by medical personnel only if those services are performed under the supervision of the physician. To qualify under the supervision requirement, the services must be performed by the physician directly, by employees of the physician, or by ancillary personnel who have a common employer with the physician. Thus, even where the MSO provides comprehensive services, ancillary personnel normally are employed by the physician or his or her group practice as opposed to being employed by the MSO. If the MSO provides billing services, it must do so as a billing agent and may not bill directly for the physician's services under Medicare reassignment rules.

Legal and Regulatory Issues

Antitrust considerations come into play with MSOs that are a separate legal entity. If the MSO employs the physicians, then it is a competitor with the hospital in the area of outpatient services. Antitrust risks will include price-fixing, concerted refusals to deal, and market allocation.

The corporate practice of medicine prohibition is implicated with MSOs in relation to both organizational and operational issues. In regard to organizational issues, this doctrine will determine whether the MSO can employ the physicians. In regard to operational issues, the physicians should retain the ability to exercise independent clinical judgment in which the corporate practice prohibition is enforced.

Fraud and abuse issues also arise with MSOs. If an MSO is owned by a provider that might receive referrals from medical practices that the MSO services, then the arrangement must comply with fraud and abuse safe harbors. Although the MSO does not provide medical services, an indirect referral may exist when physicians own the MSO. Generally, the arrangement must comply with the safe harbors under the anti-kickback and antireferral laws for employment and management services contracts. These safe harbors require that the contract be in writing and specify the services to be provided and that it have a minimum term of one year. Compensation under the agreement must not be referral-based, it must be set in advance, and it must be based on the FMV of the services. In addition, ancillary service personnel should remain employees of the medical practice in order to qualify as a group practice under the antireferral laws.

Special Considerations for Tax-Exempt Organizations

Private inurement concerns arise when the MSO deals with a tax-exempt entity. In particular, private inurement is an issue if a tax-exempt hospital capitalizes the MSO in an amount that is disproportionate to its ownership interest or if the MSO undercharges the physicians for the services it renders. In addition, if a tax-exempt hospital receives services from the MSO, it must pay for them at FMV.

NOTES

1. 29 U.S.C. § 1001 et seq.
2. 29 U.S.C. § 1144.
3. See Couch on Insurance 3d § 1 (1995).
4. 440 U.S. 205 (1979), reh. denied, 441 U.S. 917 (1979).

5. 805 F. Supp. 462 (W.D. Tex. 1992), aff'd, 998 F.2d 296 (5th Cir. 1993); see also *Insurance Bd. of Bethlehem Steel Corp. v. Muir,* 819 F.2d 408 (3d Cir. 1987).

6. 708 F.Supp. 826 (E.D. Mich. 1989).

7. See Social Security Act § 1902(a)(10)(A).

8. See Social Security Act § 1902(a)(10)(C).

9. See, e.g., Social Security Act § 1915 (permitting a gatekeeper arrangement).

10. See 42 C.F.R. pt. 42.

11. See Social Security Act § 1862; 42 C.F.R. § 411.

12. See Social Security Act § 1886(d)(5) and 42 C.F.R. § 412.106.

13. Gen. Couns. Mem. 39,005 (Jun. 28, 1983); see also Priv. Ltr. Rul. 95-17-029 (Jan. 27, 1995) (regarding use of the limited liability company form).

14. See generally Grant, P.N. (1993). Forming Integrated Delivery Systems: Legal Issues Related to the Formation and Restructuring of Integrated Medical Groups and New Models in Hospital-Medical Group Affiliation, in 2 American Academy of Hospital Attorneys 26th Annual Meeting, § 10; Stukes, T.S. (1995). Overview of Integrated Delivery Systems and Selected Regulatory Issues in North Carolina, in 1995 Health Law Primer, Dec. 15 (North Carolina Bar Foundation).

15. Gen. Couns. Mem. 39,862 (Nov. 21, 1991).

16. See Medicare Compliance Alert, Sept. 27, 1993 (safe harbor may not be needed where a parent-subsidiary relationship is involved, since there is not a referral to be protected).

17. See IRS Continuing Professional Education Technical Instruction Manual for Exempt Organizations, 1995 and 1996.

18. See Social Security Act § 1842(n).

19. *Keller v. Missouri Baptist Hospital,* 800 S.W.2d 35 (Mo. Ct. App. 1990).

20. See, for example, *Sloan v. The Metropolitan Health Council of Indianapolis, Inc.* 516 N.E.2d 1104 (Ind. Ct. App. 1987).

21. See, e.g., *Mitts v. H.I.P. of Greater New York,* 104 A.D.2d 318 (N.Y. App. Div. 1984); *Williams v. Good Health Plus,* 743 S.W.2d 373 (Tex. Ct. App. 1987).

22. *Schleier v. Kaiser Foundation Health Plan,* 876 F.2d 174 (D.C. Cir. 1989).

23. See *Uhr v. Lutheran General Hosp.,* 589 N.E.2d 723 (Ill. App. Ct. 1992).

24. *Boyd v. Albert Einstein Medical Center,* 547 A.2d 1229 (Pa. Super. 1988); but see *Raglin v. HMO Illinois, Inc.,* 595 N.E.2d 153 (Ill. App. Ct. 1992).

25. See, e.g., *Darling v. Charleston Community Memorial Hosp.,* 211 N.E.2d 253 (Ill. 1965), cert. denied, 383 U.S. 946 (1966); *Elam v. College Park Hosp.,* 132 Cal. App. 3d 332 (1982); *Rule v. Lutheran Hospitals & Home Society of America,* 835 F.2d 1250 (8th Cir. 1987); *Johnson v. Misericordia Community Hosp.,* 301 N.W.2d 156 (Wis. 1981).

26. *Candler General Hosp., Inc. v. Purvis,* 181 S.E.2d 77 (Ga. Ct. App. 1971).

27. *Wood v. Samaritan Institution,* 161 P.2d 556 (Cal. Ct. App. 1945).

28. See, e.g., *Swede v. Cigna HealthPlan of Delaware, Inc.* 1989 WL 12608 (Del. Super. 1989); *Pulvers v. Kaiser Foundation HealthPlan,* 99 Cal. App. 3d 560 (1979). But see *Bush v. Dake,* No. 86-25767 (Saginaw County, Mich., 1989) (unpublished opinion).

29. *Teti* v. *U.S. Healthcare,* 1989 WL 143274 (E.D. Pa. 1989).

30. Gen. Couns. Mem. 39,005 (Jun. 28, 1983); see also Priv. Ltr. Rul. 95-17-029 (Jan. 27, 1995) (regarding use of the limited liability company form).

31. See generally Grant, P.N. (1993). Forming Integrated Delivery Systems: Legal Issues Related to the Formation and Restructuring of Integrated Medical Groups and New Models in Hospital-Medical Group Affiliation, in 2 American Academy of Hospital Attorneys 26th Annual Meeting, § 10; Stukes, T.S. (1995). Overview of Integrated Delivery Systems and Selected Regulatory Issues in North Carolina, in 1995 Health Law Primer, Dec. 15 (North Carolina Bar Foundation).

32. Gen. Couns. Mem. 39,862 (Nov. 21, 1991).

33. See Medicare Compliance Alert, Sept. 27,1993 (safe harbor may not be needed where a parent-subsidiary relationship is involved, since there is not a referral to be protected).

34. See IRS Continuing Professional Education Technical Instruction Manual for Exempt Organizations, 1995 and 1996.

PART THREE

CASE STUDIES IN FINANCIAL FEASIBILITY

The following case studies are provided as an example of how to address real-life feasibility analyses. The examples provided were taken from actual client projects with the names and locations changed. In each case, detailed discussions of the environment have been eliminated because they would have accounted for many pages of this book. The studies represent one approach to each issue. They are, by no means, the only approach, or even the best approach. Time and money, as has been stressed on numerous occasions in this book, always limits the level of detail in analysis. Some of these studies are very detailed in their assumptions, others less detailed. The reader should have gained enough insight by this point to understand where detail is warranted and where additional information would prove valuable to present in analyses.

As with any analyst, the client often dictates what level of detail is desired. Your goal should be to exceed your client's expectations on the work product, while not presenting or being consumed with the unnecessary and the irrelevant. Readers should understand that every number or assumption represents a decision point. Decisions are not always documented in the assumptions, but they should always be made consciously. In some cases, small analyses or calculations may be processed "off the spreadsheet" where the analyst may combine numbers or other aspects of the study that do not appear in the presented report.

The following studies represent the results of many hours of thought and decision on behalf of physicians, healthcare executives, clinical and technical experts, and consultants to derive the models presented. Each of these studies therefore represents the best understanding of the current situation to which the study was commissioned. Applying the same assumptions to other situations is not likely to be completely appropriate, however many of the basic tenets are transferable.

The author would like to acknowledge his colleagues in The Health Service Group, Inc., for their contribution to the studies presented here. F. Gene DePorter, CHE, Terry Dixon, CHE, and Jeffrey Shovelin have provided much of the environmental analysis, approach, external data analysis, and presentation and have helped refine the assumptions and conclusions. The studies therefore, are largely inclusive of their efforts.

CASE ONE STUDY NOTES

Case Study:
Acquisition of Dr. Grahame

Dr. Grahame was a senior internal medicine physician in a rural area who approached the hospital to acquire his practice and hire him until his retirement in three years. The goal was to keep Dr. Grahame serving the community for the rest of his years of practice and to recruit his replacement to keep the practice in the community. The hospital commissioned The Health Service Group, Inc. to perform an independent appraisal of the practice and subsequently to assist in the development of a compensation model and postsale operational pro forma.

The valuation portion of the engagement and other issues were discussed earlier in Chapter 6. The following pro forma is the result of planning for the acquisition of the practice and operating it under the umbrella of a hospital-based physician practice. From a Stark law perspective, this falls into the employee exception.

The general plan was to compensate Dr. Grahame consistent compensation observed from national comparative data and relate it to his status as an employee physician. The physician compensation plan that follows indicates simply a model for requiring Dr. Grahame to attain certain revenue targets based on physician professional services only, no ancillaries. Given the circumstances of this engagement, it was not anticipated that Dr. Grahame would gain collections greater than that which was projected. Other items of note included an adjustment for improved billing and collection related to Dr. Grahame's old and outdated fee schedule. It was clear that his fees should have been increased. Second, the practice was to assume a greater amount of Medicaid patients under the hospital ownership than was previous under Dr. Grahame. This was not expected to change the nature of the practice other than reduced reimbursement of approximately $10,000.

The hospital was to use its own MSO practice management services that was arranged on a cost-plus basis, the net result was to provide adequate management oversight for about $12,000 per year, a bargain given other competitive services.

The remainder of the pro forma modeling is fairly straightforward. The goal was to operate the practice at very near the net income amount projected in the valuation in order to assure that excess benefit was not conferred to Dr. Grahame in the form of overpayment for his practice. The net result is that the hospital is able to provide for a reasonable return on its investment while covering the costs of the acquisition over reasonable terms.

ANYTOWN MEDICAL CENTER: OPERATIONAL PRO FORMA ASSUMPTIONS Acquisition of Dr. Grahame (January 5, 1998)

EXECUTIVE SUMMARY

The following operating assumptions and attached pro forma financial statements represent the projected operational pro forma for Dr. Grahame practice for Anytown Medical Center (ABC). The following indicates the notable initial findings and key indicators of operation.

- The pro forma cash flow projections indicate amortization of $157,196 as start-up expenses carried at 5% interest over 5 years. Year 3 includes the addition of $25,000 to recruit and relocate a physician to replace Dr. Grahame upon his retirement. These second year expenses are added to the amortization schedule, which is completely repaid by the end of Year 5.

- The pro forma projections allow for Dr. Grahame to earn compensation consistent with, but not exceeding, Medical Group Management Association (MGMA) survey data. This condition should satisfy Medicare Anti-kickback laws and Stark laws. It appears from discussion with legal counsel that the IRS's Intermediate Sanctions legislation is not applicable. Total compensation is capped at $200,000 and may not exceed a compensation to production ratio greater that 46% (practice operations are unlikely to attain such conditions).

- The practice maintains positive cash flow. The elements of greatest concern are:

  Revenue Targets—The pro forma and compensation plan are based on attaining minimum levels of production based on historical productivity and readily identifiable practice changes. Attainment of pro forma income targets is required before payment of any incentive. Modeling has not presumed capitated income streams;

  Contractual Adjustments—Based on historical operations billing allowable amounts with a $10,000 reduction for increasing Medicaid participation; and

Anytown Medical Center: Operational Pro Forma Assumptions Continued

Operating Expenses—Expenses are based on historical expenses and the adoption of best industry practices in operations of medical practices including maximum cross-training of staff, use of electronic methods of operation, and elimination of redundant functions.

The following table highlights selected performance indicators under the current set of assumptions.

Selected Operating Indicators

Initial Capital Investment	$ 157,196
Net Income Year 1	$ 35,242
Net Income Year 2	$ 41,770
Net Income Year 3	$ 41,372
Interest Rate on Investment	5.0%
Principal Return in Year 1	$ 29,871
Interest Return in Year 1	$ 6,437
Capital Expenditures Per Year	$ 2,000

To assist in the refinement of this model, attention should be given to identifying any areas of inconsistency in the assumptions.

OPERATING ASSUMPTIONS

Overview

The following initial assumptions are used in the development of an operating pro forma for a planned medical practice acquisition by Anytown Medical Center. The categories of items for discussion include income assumptions and operating expense assumptions.

1.0 INCOME ASSUMPTIONS

   1.1 Income—Professional fees have been estimated based on historical operation with adjustments made for readily identifiable changes to the practice. Ancillary amounts are estimated because the current practice does not separate ancillary charges from physician charges. All income reflects collections.

Historic Production Last Year:	421,255
Less Ancillaries @ 15%:	(63,188)
Adjusted MD Production:	358,067
Long Term Growth Rate:	4.0%

Anytown Medical Center: Operational Pro Forma Assumptions Continued

	YEAR 1	YEAR 2	YEAR 3
Indicated Collections MD Services	372,389	387,285	402,776
Projected Changes			
Improved Coding & Fee Schedule	15,000	15,600	16,224
Increased Medicaid Mix	(10,000)	(10,400)	(10,816)
Collections MD Services	377,389	392,485	408,184
Plus Ancillaries @ 15%	56,608	58,873	61,228
Total Collections	**433,998**	**451,358**	**469,412**

1.2 Income—Ancillary and technical are estimated at 15% of revenue. It is estimated that the present level of laboratory will continue to be provided on site.

2.0 PROVIDER EXPENSES

2.1 Salary Draw—Dr. Grahame is based on the compensation and incentive plan (attached). Monthly salary draw is equal to 80% of the ABC base income target of $140,000 for internal medicine. Salary rates increase 3% annually for modeling purposes.

2.2 Salary Withhold—Paid includes amounts paid based on attainment of production targets in the compensation plan. Amounts are paid monthly. Goals are reviewed quarterly. If Dr. Grahame does not attain 100% of his goals at these points, compensation is adjusted.

2.3 Incentive plan payments is included but not modeled within the pro forma itself. Incentive is available based on the excess of income over physician revenue targets. It is not anticipated that Dr. Grahame will attain this level of production. In the event he does, he could be paid his incremental revenue (collections) less the practice overhead rate (inclusive of employer taxes) up to a maximum compensation to production ratio of 46% and not exceeding $200,000 annually.

2.4 Provider benefits are estimated at 23% of salary draw and salary withhold compensation. Additional benefits such as CME and journals are carried in operating expenses.

2.5 Malpractice insurance is estimated at $12,000 in Year 1, increasing 5% annually.

3.0 OPERATING EXPENSES

3.1   All expenses increase 3% annually unless otherwise indicated.

3.2   Support staff salaries are based on estimates of practice needs and Anytown Medical Center's current personnel management system. The following tables indicate the staffing complement during Years 1–3. All salary rates increase 3% annually.

Anytown Medical Center: Operational Pro Forma Assumptions Continued

Support Staff Salaries	Hourly	YEAR 1 Salary	FTE	Total
BC–Accts. Mgr.	$ 11.75	35,000	1.0	35,000
AL–MOA	$ 11.00	22,880	1.0	22,880
Bookeeper	$ 10.00	20,800	1.0	20,800
BJ–Typist/Transcrip	$ 8.48	17,638	0.5	8,819
Additional MOA	$ 11.00	22,880	0.5	11,440
Total				87,499
Benefits at	23%			20,125
		Total	4.0	107,624
MGMA Staff per FTE MD (Family Practice):			4.6	

3.3   Staff benefits are estimated at 23% of salaries.

3.4   Repairs and maintenance is estimated at $5,000 in Year 1, increasing 3% annually.

3.5   Office supplies and services are estimated at $5,000 in Year 1 increasing 3% annually.

3.6   Telephone is estimated at $3,500 in Year 1, increasing 3% annually.

3.7   Travel, dues, and subscriptions are estimated at $4,000, increasing 3% annually.

3.8   Clinical and laboratory supplies are estimated at $6,000, increasing 5% annually.

3.9   Business insurance provides coverage for fire, theft, and vandalism estimated at $2,000, increasing 3% annually.

3.10 Promotion and marketing is estimated at $2,000 for Year 1, increasing 3% annually.

3.11 Accounting and legal fees are estimated at $2,000 for Year 1, increasing 3% annually.

3.12 Rent includes utilities, based on the current lease arrangement for the office space at $21,240 for Year 1, increasing 3% annually.

3.13 ABC management fee is estimated at $12,000 for Year 1, increasing 3% annually.

3.14 All other expenses include amounts for other operating expenses not included elsewhere, estimated at $7,000 for Year 1, increasing 3% annually.

3.15 Depreciation is based on GAAP straight line of 10 years on all equipment, presently valued at $72,421 for an annual amount of $7,242 for Years 1-5.

3.16 Capital expenditures are estimated at $2,000 annually.

Anytown Medical Center: Operational Pro Forma Assumptions Concluded

3.17   Amortization of start-up includes the total amounts expensed to the acquisition carried over 5 years at 5% interest. The amounts include $127,196 as the net practice purchase price, $10,000 for computer conversion expenses, $10,000 for consulting to include compensation and incentive plan development and preparation of the operational pro formas, $5,000 for legal services related to the acquisition, and $5,000 for signage, printing, and other changes required prior to opening for a total amount of $157,196.

4.0 SUMMARY OPERATIONS

4.1   Expenses as a percentage of net revenue is maintained for provider expenses and operating expenses.

4.2   Profit/(loss) indicates funds flow from all activities.

4.3   Profit margin provides each year's operating performance.

Income Assumptions

Internal Medicine Productivity based on MGMA Median: | $ 336,833

Source: MGMA Physician Compensation and Production Survey: 1996 Report–Family Practice, A&T Excluded Table 12 Charges inflated 4% per year to 9/98

Historic Production Last Year:	421,255
Less Ancillaries @ 15%:	(63,188)
Adjusted MD Production:	358,067
Long Term Growth Rate:	4.0%

	YEAR 1	YEAR 2	YEAR 3
Indicated Collections MD Services	372,389	387,285	402,776
Projected Changes			
Improved Coding & Fee Schedule	15,000	15,600	16,224
Increased Medicaid Mix	(10,000)	(10,400)	(10,816)
Collections MD Services	377,389	392,485	408,184
Plus Ancillaries @ 15%	56,608	58,873	61,228
Total Collections	**433,998**	**451,358**	**469,412**

Operating Expense Assumptions

Support Staff Salaries

	Hourly	Year 1			Year 2			Year 3		
		Salary	FTE	Total	Salary	FTE	Total	Salary	FTE	Total
BC–Accts. Mgr.	$ 11.75	35,000	1.0	35,000	36,050	1.0	36,050	37,132	1.0	37,132
AL–MOA	$ 11.00	22,880	1.0	22,880	23,566	1.0	23,566	24,273	1.0	24,273
Bookeeper	$ 10.00	20,800	1.0	20,800	21,424	1.0	21,424	22,067	1.0	22,067
BJ–Typist/Transcrip	$ 8.48	17,638	0.5	8,819	18,168	0.5	9,084	18,713	0.5	9,356
Additional MOA	$ 11.00	22,880	0.5	11,440	23,566	0.5	11,783	24,273	0.5	12,137
Total			**4.0**	**87,499**		**4.0**	**90,124**		**4.0**	**92,828**
Benefits at	23%			20,125			20,729			21,350
Total				**107,624**			**110,853**			**114,178**
MGMA Staff per FTE MD (Family Practice):	4.6									Continued

Financing and Start-Up Costs

Purchase Price	127,196	= $161,000–$33,804 in cash/net AR
Computer Conversion Expenses	$10,000	per CompuSystems
Consulting	$10,000	
Legal	$5,000	
Signage, Printing, Etc.	$5,000	
Acquisition/Conversion Cost:	**$ 157,196**	

Financing Terms: Total Cash Price Startup financed 100% from reserves at 5.0% over 5 years

	Year 1		Year 3	
Total Payment Years 1 & 2:	$ 35,450	**Additional Year 3 Expenses:**	$ 25,000	MD Recruitment @ $20,000 and Relocation @ $5,000
Based on Total Purchase Price		**New Payment for Years 3–5:**	$ 42,735	Total remaining costs over 3 years

Depreciation Base—GAAP/SL

FMV of Depreciable Assets:	72,421	depreciated over 10 years
Depreciation Years 1–10:	7,242	

Compensation Plan Example: Dr. Grahame
TARGET COMPENSATION–Year 1

ABC Base Income Target–Internal Medicine: $140,000

Baseline Production Expectations for the Practice

Gross Revenue Last Fiscal Year: $421,255

Physician Production Amount: $358,067   Estimated based on 15% ancillaries

	Month 3	Month 6	Month 9	Month 12	TOTAL
Forecasted Cumulative Revenue Targets:	$ 94,347	$188,695	$283,042	$377,389	$377,389
Percentage Revenue Target Attained:	100%	100%	100%	100%	100%
Salary Withhold Paid @ 20% of Base Income Target:	7,000	7,000	7,000	7,000	28,000

Withhold Paid Monthly–Reviewed Quarterly

Monthly Salary Draw @ 80%: $ 9,333

Total Draw: $112,000

At Risk Element of Base Compensation
20.00%

Total Payment of Base Compensation: **$140,000**

Dr. Grahame Comp. to Production Ratio: 37.10%

232

Compensation Plan Example: Dr. Grahame Concluded

NATIONAL COMPARATIVE DATA SUPPORT

PRODUCTION

			Compensation to Production Ratio
Our Practice (Revenue):	358,067		
MGMA Median Production (Est. Revenue):			
TC/PE Excluded			
	255,800	Eastern	55.75%
	299,473	General Category	46.52%
	366,745	Single Specialty	42.02%
	411,000	Eastern Single Specialty	42.12%
	321,000	18+ Years	46.19%
Mean	**330,804**		**46.52%**
		Mean	
		Mean w/o outlier	44.21%

Compensation:		
	142,600	Eastern
	139,320	General Category
	154,115	Single Specialty
	173,098	Eastern Single Specialty
	148,261	18+ Years
Mean	**151,479**	

Pre-Sale Compensation Data

Dr Grahame's 1997 Compensation	165,000	@ $154,115 MD comp, it leaves
Dr. Grahame's 1997 Production	358,067	$10,885 as owner comp = 2.6%
Total Practice Revenue	421,255	Standard is 4%–5% or $16,850–$21,063
Dr. Grahame's 1997 Comp to Production Ratio	46.08%	**RESULT:**
as an Owner, not employee		**Difficult to support paying a 46% ratio**

Financial Analysis: Postsale Pro Forma—Acquisition of Dr. Grahame
Page 1

Year 1	Month 1	Month 2	Month 3	Month 4	Month 5	Month 6
Income						
Income–Professional Fees	31,449	31,449	31,449	31,449	31,449	31,449
Income–Ancillary & Technical	4,717	4,717	4,717	4,717	4,717	4,717
Total Net Revenue	**36,166**	**36,166**	**36,166**	**36,166**	**36,166**	**36,166**
Provider Expenses						
Salary Draw–Dr. Grahame	9,333	9,333	9,333	9,333	9,333	9,333
Salary Withhold–Paid	2,333	2,333	2,333	2,333	2,333	2,333
Incentive Plan Payments	0	0	0	0	0	0
Provider Benefits	2,683	2,683	2,683	2,683	2,683	2,683
Malpractice Insurance	375	375	375	375	375	375
Subtotal	**14,725**	**14,725**	**14,725**	**14,725**	**14,725**	**14,725**
Expenses as % of Net Revenue	41%	41%	41%	41%	41%	41%
Operating Expenses						
Support Staff Salaries	7,292	7,292	7,292	7,292	7,292	7,292
Staff Benefits	1,677	1,677	1,677	1,677	1,677	1,677
Repairs and Maintenance	417	417	417	417	417	417
Office Supplies and Services	417	417	417	417	417	417
Equipment Rental	0	0	0	0	0	0
Telephone	292	292	292	292	292	292
Travel, Dues and Subscriptions	333	333	333	333	333	333
Clinical and Laboratory Supplies	500	500	500	500	500	500
Business Insurance	500	0	0	500	0	0
Advertising	167	167	167	167	167	167
Accounting and Legal Fees	167	167	167	167	167	167
Rent–Includes Utilities	1,770	1,770	1,770	1,770	1,770	1,770
ABC Management Fee	1,000	1,000	1,000	1,000	1,000	1,000
All Other Expenses	583	583	583	583	583	583
Depreciation	604	604	604	604	604	604
Capital Expenditures	167	167	167	167	167	167
Amortization of Start-up	2,954	2,954	2,954	2,954	2,954	2,954
Subtotal	**18,838**	**18,338**	**18,338**	**18,838**	**18,338**	**18,338**
Expenses as % of Net Revenue	52%	51%	51%	52%	51%	51%
Total All Expenses	**33,563**	**33,063**	**33,063**	**33,563**	**33,063**	**33,063**
Profit/(Loss)	2,603	3,103	3,103	2,603	3,103	3,103
Profit Margin	7%	9%	9%	7%	9%	9%

	Month 7	Month 8	Month 9	Month 10	Month 11	Month 12	EOY 1	% of Total Revenue	Year 1 Monthly Average
	31,449	31,449	31,449	31,449	31,449	31,449	**377,389**	87.0%	31,449
	4,717	4,717	4,717	4,717	4,717	4,717	**56,608**	13.0%	4,717
	36,166	**36,166**	**36,166**	**36,166**	**36,166**	**36,166**	**433,998**	100%	**36,166**
								Percent of Revenue	
	9,333	9,333	9,333	9,333	9,333	9,333	**112,000**	25.8%	9,333
	2,333	2,333	2,333	2,333	2,333	2,333	**28,000**	6.5%	2,333
	0	0	0	0	0	0	**0**	0.0%	0
	2,683	2,683	2,683	2,683	2,683	2,683	**32,200**	7.4%	2,683
	375	375	375	375	375	375	**4,500**	1.0%	375
	14,725	**14,725**	**14,725**	**14,725**	**14,725**	**14,725**	**176,700**	40.7%	**14,725**
	41%	41%	41%	41%	41%	41%	**41%**		
	7,292	7,292	7,292	7,292	7,292	7,292	**87,499**	20.2%	7,292
	1,677	1,677	1,677	1,677	1,677	1,677	**20,125**	4.6%	1,677
	417	417	417	417	417	417	**5,000**	1.2%	417
	417	417	417	417	417	417	**5,000**	1.2%	417
	0	0	0	0	0	0	**0**	0.0%	0
	292	292	292	292	292	292	**3,500**	0.8%	292
	333	333	333	333	333	333	**4,000**	0.9%	333
	500	500	500	500	500	500	**6,000**	1.4%	500
	500	0	0	500	0	0	**2,000**	0.5%	167
	167	167	167	167	167	167	**2,000**	0.5%	167
	167	167	167	167	167	167	**2,000**	0.5%	167
	1,770	1,770	1,770	1,770	1,770	1,770	**21,240**	4.9%	1,770
	1,000	1,000	1,000	1,000	1,000	1,000	**12,000**	2.8%	1,000
	583	583	583	583	583	583	**7,000**	1.6%	583
	604	604	604	604	604	604	**7,242**	1.7%	604
	167	167	167	167	167	167	**2,000**	0.5%	167
	2,954	2,954	2,954	2,954	2,954	2,954	**35,450**	8.2%	2,954
	18,838	**18,338**	**18,338**	**18,838**	**18,338**	**18,338**	**222,056**	51.2%	
	52%	51%	51%	52%	51%	51%	**51%**		
	33,563	**33,063**	**33,063**	**33,563**	**33,063**	**33,063**	**398,756**		
	2,603	3,103	3,103	2,603	3,103	3,103	**35,242**		
	7%	9%	9%	7%	9%	9%	8%		

Financial Analysis: Postsale Pro Forma—Acquisition of Dr. Grahame
Page 2

Year 2	Month 13	Month 14	Month 15	Month 16	Month 17	Month 18
Income						
Income–Professional Fees	32,707	32,707	32,707	32,707	32,707	32,707
Income–Ancillary & Technical	4,906	4,906	4,906	4,906	4,906	4,906
Total Net Revenue	**37,613**	**37,613**	**37,613**	**37,613**	**37,613**	**37,613**
Provider Expenses						
Salary Draw–Dr. Grahame	9,613	9,613	9,613	9,613	9,613	9,613
Salary Withhold–Paid	2,403	2,403	2,403	2,403	2,403	2,403
Incentive Plan Payments	0	0	0	0	0	0
Provider Benefits	2,764	2,764	2,764	2,764	2,764	2,764
Malpractice Insurance	394	394	394	394	394	394
Subtotal	**15,174**	**15,174**	**15,174**	**15,174**	**15,174**	**15,174**
Expenses as % of Net Revenue	40%	40%	40%	40%	40%	40%
Operating Expenses						
Support Staff Salaries	7,510	7,510	7,510	7,510	7,510	7,510
Staff Benefits	1,727	1,727	1,727	1,727	1,727	1,727
Repairs and Maintenance	429	429	429	429	429	429
Office Supplies and Services	429	429	429	429	429	429
Equipment Rental	0	0	0	0	0	0
Telephone	300	300	300	300	300	300
Travel, Dues and Subscriptions	343	343	343	343	343	343
Clinical and Laboratory Supplies	525	525	525	525	525	525
Business Insurance	515	0	0	515	0	0
Advertising	172	172	172	172	172	172
Accounting and Legal Fees	172	172	172	172	172	172
Rent–Includes Utilities	1,823	1,823	1,823	1,823	1,823	1,823
ABC Management Fee	1,030	1,030	1,030	1,030	1,030	1,030
All Other Expenses	601	601	601	601	601	601
Depreciation	604	604	604	604	604	604
Capital Expenditures	167	167	167	167	167	167
Amortization of Start-up	2,954	2,954	2,954	2,954	2,954	2,954
Subtotal	**19,301**	**18,786**	**18,786**	**19,301**	**18,786**	**18,786**
Expenses as % of Net Revenue	51%	50%	50%	51%	50%	50%
Total All Expenses	**34,476**	**33,961**	**33,961**	**34,476**	**33,961**	**33,961**
Profit/(Loss)	**3,137**	**3,652**	**3,652**	**3,137**	**3,652**	**3,652**
Profit Margin	**8%**	**10%**	**10%**	**8%**	**10%**	**10%**

Month 19	Month 20	Month 21	Month 22	Month 23	Month 24	EOY 2	% of Total Revenue	Year 2 Monthly Average
32,707	32,707	32,707	32,707	32,707	32,707	**392,485**	87.0%	32,707
4,906	4,906	4,906	4,906	4,906	4,906	**58,873**	13.0%	4,906
37,613	**37,613**	**37,613**	**37,613**	**37,613**	**37,613**	**451,358**	100%	**37,613**
							Percent of Revenue	
9,613	9,613	9,613	9,613	9,613	9,613	**115,360**	25.6%	9,613
2,403	2,403	2,403	2,403	2,403	2,403	**28,840**	6.4%	2,403
0	0	0	0	0	0	**0**	0.0%	0
2,764	2,764	2,764	2,764	2,764	2,764	**33,166**	7.3%	2,764
394	394	394	394	394	394	**4,725**	1.0%	394
15,174	**15,174**	**15,174**	**15,174**	**15,174**	**15,174**	**182,091**	40.3%	15,174
40%	40%	40%	40%	40%	40%	**40%**		
7,510	7,510	7,510	7,510	7,510	7,510	**90,124**	20.0%	7,510
1,727	1,727	1,727	1,727	1,727	1,727	**20,729**	4.6%	1,727
429	429	429	429	429	429	**5,150**	1.1%	429
429	429	429	429	429	429	**5,150**	1.1%	429
0	0	0	0	0	0	**0**	0.0%	0
300	300	300	300	300	300	**3,605**	0.8%	300
343	343	343	343	343	343	**4,120**	0.9%	343
525	525	525	525	525	525	**6,300**	1.4%	525
515	0	0	515	0	0	**2,060**	0.5%	172
172	172	172	172	172	172	**2,060**	0.5%	172
172	172	172	172	172	172	**2,060**	0.5%	172
1,823	1,823	1,823	1,823	1,823	1,823	**21,877**	4.8%	1,823
1,030	1,030	1,030	1,030	1,030	1,030	**12,360**	2.7%	1,030
601	601	601	601	601	601	**7,210**	1.6%	601
604	604	604	604	604	604	**7,242**	1.6%	604
167	167	167	167	167	167	**2,000**	0.4%	167
2,954	2,954	2,954	2,954	2,954	2,954	**35,450**	7.9%	2,954
19,301	**18,786**	**18,786**	**19,301**	**18,786**	**18,786**	**227,497**	50.4%	
51%	50%	50%	51%	50%	50%	**50%**		
34,476	**33,961**	**33,961**	**34,476**	**33,961**	**33,961**	**409,588**		
3,137	**3,652**	**3,652**	**3,137**	**3,652**	**3,652**	**41,770**		
8%	10%	10%	8%	10%	10%	9%		

Financial Analysis: Postsale Pro Forma—Acquisition of Dr. Grahame
Page 3

Year 3	Month 25	Month 26	Month 27	Month 28	Month 29	Month 30
Income						
Income–Professional Fees	34,015	34,015	34,015	34,015	34,015	34,015
Income–Ancillary & Technical	5,102	5,102	5,102	5,102	5,102	5,102
Total Net Revenue	**39,118**	**39,118**	**39,118**	**39,118**	**39,118**	**39,118**
Provider Expenses						
Salary Draw–Dr. Grahame	9,902	9,902	9,902	9,902	9,902	9,902
Salary Withhold–Paid	2,475	2,475	2,475	2,475	2,475	2,475
Incentive Plan Payments	0	0	0	0	0	0
Provider Benefits	2,847	2,847	2,847	2,847	2,847	2,847
Malpractice Insurance	413	413	413	413	413	413
Subtotal	**15,637**	**15,637**	**15,637**	**15,637**	**15,637**	**15,637**
Expenses as % of Net Revenue	40%	40%	40%	40%	40%	40%
Operating Expenses						
Support Staff Salaries	7,736	7,736	7,736	7,736	7,736	7,736
Staff Benefits	1,779	1,779	1,779	1,779	1,779	1,779
Repairs and Maintenance	442	442	442	442	442	442
Office Supplies and Services	442	442	442	442	442	442
Equipment Rental	0	0	0	0	0	0
Telephone	309	309	309	309	309	309
Travel, Dues and Subscriptions	354	354	354	354	354	354
Clinical and Laboratory Supplies	551	551	551	551	551	551
Business Insurance	530	0	0	530	0	0
Advertising	177	177	177	177	177	177
Accounting and Legal Fees	177	177	177	177	177	177
Rent–Includes Utilities	1,878	1,878	1,878	1,878	1,878	1,878
ABC Management Fee	1,061	1,061	1,061	1,061	1,061	1,061
All Other Expenses	619	619	619	619	619	619
Depreciation	604	604	604	604	604	604
Capital Expenditures	167	167	167	167	167	167
Amortization of Start-up	3,561	3,561	3,561	3,561	3,561	3,561
Subtotal	**20,386**	**19,856**	**19,856**	**20,386**	**19,856**	**19,856**
Expenses as % of Net Revenue	52%	51%	51%	52%	51%	51%
Total All Expenses	**36,024**	**35,493**	**35,493**	**36,024**	**35,493**	**35,493**
Profit/(Loss)	3,094	3,624	3,624	3,094	3,624	3,624
Profit Margin	8%	9%	9%	8%	9%	9%

	Month 31	Month 32	Month 33	Month 34	Month 35	Month 36	EOY 3	% of Total Revenue	Year 3 Monthly Average
	34,015	34,015	34,015	34,015	34,015	34,015	**408,184**	87.0%	34,015
	5,102	5,102	5,102	5,102	5,102	5,102	**61,228**	13.0%	5,102
	39,118	**39,118**	**39,118**	**39,118**	**39,118**	**39,118**	**469,412**	100%	**39,118**
								Percent of Revenue	
	9,902	9,902	9,902	9,902	9,902	9,902	**118,821**	25.3%	9,902
	2,475	2,475	2,475	2,475	2,475	2,475	**29,705**	6.3%	2,475
	0	0	0	0	0	0	**0**	0.0%	0
	2,847	2,847	2,847	2,847	2,847	2,847	**34,161**	7.3%	2,847
	413	413	413	413	413	413	**4,961**	1.1%	413
	15,637	**15,637**	**15,637**	**15,637**	**15,637**	**15,637**	**187,648**	40.0%	**15,637**
	40%	40%	40%	40%	40%	40%	**40%**		
	7,736	7,736	7,736	7,736	7,736	7,736	**92,828**	19.8%	7,736
	1,779	1,779	1,779	1,779	1,779	1,779	**21,350**	4.5%	1,779
	442	442	442	442	442	442	**5,305**	1.1%	442
	442	442	442	442	442	442	**5,305**	1.1%	442
	0	0	0	0	0	0	**0**	0.0%	0
	309	309	309	309	309	309	**3,713**	0.8%	309
	354	354	354	354	354	354	**4,244**	0.9%	354
	551	551	551	551	551	551	**6,615**	1.4%	551
	530	0	0	530	0	0	**2,122**	0.5%	177
	177	177	177	177	177	177	**2,122**	0.5%	177
	177	177	177	177	177	177	**2,122**	0.5%	177
	1,878	1,878	1,878	1,878	1,878	1,878	**22,534**	4.8%	1,878
	1,061	1,061	1,061	1,061	1,061	1,061	**12,731**	2.7%	1,061
	619	619	619	619	619	619	**7,426**	1.6%	619
	604	604	604	604	604	604	**7,242**	1.5%	604
	167	167	167	167	167	167	**2,000**	0.4%	167
	3,561	3,561	3,561	3,561	3,561	3,561	**42,735**	9.1%	3,561
	20,386	**19,856**	**19,856**	**20,386**	**19,856**	**19,856**	**240,392**	51.2%	
	52%	51%	51%	52%	51%	51%	**51%**		
	36,024	35,493	35,493	36,024	35,493	35,493	**428,040**		
	3,094	3,624	3,624	3,094	3,624	3,624	**41,372**		
	8%	9%	9%	8%	9%	9%	**9%**		

CASE TWO STUDY NOTES
Case Study:
Obstetrics Service Feasibility

Anytown Medical Center (AMC) had not operated an obstetrics (OB) service for over 20 years. Recent market share and patient origin data had indicated a substantial amount of OB care going out of county to a neighboring hospital for normal vaginal deliveries and cesarean sections. AMC engaged The Health Service Group, Inc., to conduct a feasibility study to re-open an obstetrics service.

After examination of the marketplace opportunity for the service, it was determined that the hospital could support a 5-bed unit combining labor and delivery, recovery, and postpartum (LDRP) beds. An exhaustive analysis of patient origin and physician referral patterns was performed as well as a fee survey for hospital and ancillary charges. The availability of a local foundation's hospital cost study provided peer hospital comparison on days of care, charges, collections, and other related operating data. The pro forma modeling itself was fairly simple; the hospital, along with the consultants, decided on the overhead structure for the unit and outlined the financing assumptions and alternatives. Ultimately the project would need to obtain a Certificate of Need (CON) and the feasibility study would be required to support the CON application.

This study was an example of taking a service line application and reasoning through the market opportunity, gathering data, and applying the financial modeling to the facts. There are many instances in which managers could make changes in the assumptions, particularly in allocating overhead costs from the hospital. Whether a given project represents reality may or may not be that important. Remember that there are often strategic reasons for pursuing business ventures. From a CON perspective, each state will have its own requirements on what types of overhead must be carried and when other aspects might be left out. If the goal were to allocate as much cost as possible to a given venture, then many projects would not warrant continuation. On the other hand, inclusion of certain costs in the Medicare Cost Report might be advantageous. Address each project logically and make decisions based on good business sense, taking into account the whole picture.

The pro forma income and production assumptions use a case-based ramp-up rate to drive the income. The staffing and other costs are modeled on an annual basis. Remember that there is never an end to the level of detail you can model, but time is important too. Do not spend too much time on details that will tell you very little (think return on investment: Is it worth the effort?). In this study, the goal was to evaluate the market opportunity using reasonable market-based assumptions—Can we do this without losing money? Does this service complement our service vision, even if it is a loss leader?

ANYTOWN HOSPITAL: OBSTETRICS SERVICE FEASIBILITY STUDY
February 24, 1997

EXECUTIVE SUMMARY

The following operating assumptions and attached *pro forma* financial statements represent our understanding of the proposed Obstetrics Service for Anytown Hospital. These statements cover the development and operation of a 5-unit facility combining labor and delivery, recovery, and postpartum (LDRP) beds.

Notable Initial Findings

- The pro forma cash flow projections indicate a minimum of 2 years of operation before independent cash flow. Under the current fee structure, independent cash flow begins in Year 3 with an annual contribution to payback for future years.

- The two elements of greatest impact are the adjustments to income (projected at Anytown's 1997-budgeted amount of 47%) and the average charge per case ($4,350). Anytown Hospital will need to decide on its pricing position given Next County Hospital's comparative average charge per case of approximately $4,000. It appears that the market could well sustain a higher price, perhaps as high as $4,500 per case. The median adjusted revenue per case in a 1995 Anystate Foundation study for similarly sized hospitals was $4,800 (Next County Hospital's and Anystate Foundation figures are inflated to 1997–1998 dollars).

To assist in the refinement of this model, attention should be given to identifying any areas of inconsistency in the assumptions and tightening of the assumptions relevant

Anytown Hospital: Obstetrics Service Feasibility Study Continued

to local market pricing of goods and services. It should be noted also that certain issues of income, expense, and financing have yet to be resolved. Estimates and assumptions based on previous experience have been made in the following categories:

1. Financing for project has been projected at 100% financing (from reserves) @ 5% over 10 years. Principal payments only are deducted.
2. Amounts for replacement reserve and capital expenditures should be reviewed, as well as the preferred method of handling of any amortized expenses.

These issues should be resolved in order to complete the most realistic projections of project start-up and operation.

OPERATING ASSUMPTIONS

Overview

The following initial assumptions are used in the development of operating *pro formas* for a planned Obstetrics Service by Anytown Hospital. The categories of items for discussion include Income and Occupancy Assumptions, Operating Expense Assumptions, and Financing Assumptions. Actual amounts may cause rounding error to appear in column totals.

1.0 Income and Occupancy Assumptions

    1.1 The current analysis examines the creation of 3 postpartum beds and 2 LDRP beds.

    1.2 The following comparative data were used to determine the pricing structure for this study.

Comparative Revenue and Expense Data (1994–1995)

Hospital A			Anystate Foundation Study Peer Group		
	Avg. Expense*	**Avg. Revenue**		**Avg. Expense***	**Avg. Revenue**
Nursing	$ 1,130	$ 1,774	Nursing	$ 1,044	$ 1,966
Delivery	$ 822	$ 1,317	Delivery	$ 1,132	$ 2,006
Newborn	$ 478	$ 616	Newborn	$ 367	$ 520
Total:	$ 2,430	$ 3,707	Total:	$ 2,543	$ 4,492

*Inflating these revenue amounts to 1997–1998 dollars makes Hospital A total revenue approximately $4,000 and the Anystate Foundation Group 6, approximately $4,800. Extending this to Anytown Hospital projections, we project the following charge and case distribution, increasing 3% annually:

1997–1998 Charges		No. of Cases	Percent of Cases	Percent of Income
C-Section:	$ 6,200	35	35%	51%
Spontaneous Delivery:	$ 3,400	50	50%	38%
Low Forceps Delivery:	$ 3,200	15	15%	11%
Average Per Case:	$ 4,350			

Anytown Hospital: Obstetrics Service Feasibility Study Continued

1.3 The occupancy assumptions include the addition of two OB/GYN physicians with reasonable time for patient acquisition. Detailed occupancy assumptions are included with the *pro forma* statements. Please note that cases are projected cyclically to estimate natural birthing patterns.

1.4 Contractual adjustments are carried at 36% as indicated in Anytown's 1997 budget.

1.5 Bad debt is carried at 8% as indicated in Anytown's 1997 budget.

1.6 Other adjustments are carried at 3% as indicated in Anytown's 1997 budget.

2.0 Operating Expense Assumptions

2.1 Unless otherwise indicated, all expenses increase 5% annually.

2.2 Support staff salaries are based on comparative hospital staffing levels for postpartum and LDRP units to include, for Year 1, the following FTE complement: 4.5 registered nurses, 1.0 LPN, 0.5 nursing assistant, and 1.0 clerical support. Staffing complement increases with the number of cases. Detailed staffing assumptions are included with the *pro forma* statements. Support staff salaries increase 4% annually.

2.3 Staff benefits are projected at 25% representing Anytown's actual expenses.

2.4 Recruitment expenses—New MDs are projected at $60,000 to include $20,000 per physician for recruitment fees paid to a professional recruiter and $10,000 per physician to accommodate site visits, travel, moving and other expenses. The full amount is carried in Month 1, Year 1 to reflect expenses incurred prior to opening of the unit.

2.5 Repairs and maintenance are projected at $2,400 given the new facility and equipment.

2.6 Telephone and utilities are estimated at $10,000 based on Anytown's historical expenses.

2.7 Travel, dues, and subscriptions are estimated at $6,000 as continuing education expenses for the unit patient care staff.

2.8 Clinical supplies are estimated at $200 per case as referenced from comparative hospitals for a Year 1 total of $20,000. Clinical supplies are projected equally throughout the year rather than cyclically as cases are projected.

2.9 Promotion and marketing are estimated at $20,000 for Year 1 increasing annually at 5% to reflect an aggressive informational campaign designed to support case projections.

2.10 Capital expenditures are included at $10,000 annually beginning Year 2. This assumption should be reviewed to determine whether this expense should be carried at all given the full complement of new equipment.

Anytown Hospital: Obstetrics Service Feasibility Study Concluded

2.11 Depreciation is carried on equipment purchases of $600,304 over 8 years and on building and construction expenses of $585,000 over 20 years. After Year 1, new capital expenditures are depreciated over 10 years.

2.12 All other expenses category includes any expenses not included elsewhere. Carried at $20,000 for Year 1.

3.0 Financing Assumptions

3.1 Depreciation is added back to income and replacement reserve is subtracted. The replacement reserve, $60,030 in Year 1, is estimated at a flat 10% of the equipment costs, increasing annually with capital expenditures.

3.2 Principal payment is estimated at $74,467 for Year 1 reflecting the principal amount from the $1,185,304 total project cost. Should Anytown choose alternative financing, these amounts may change significantly. At the present time, no interest or carrying cost of money has been included.

3.3 Cash flow represents owner's discretionary income when positive and loss when negative.

3.4 Profit margin represents the relationship between net income and cash flow.

3.5 Outstanding balance from start-up indicates the total project expenses at any given time.

Financial Analysis: Anytown Hospital
Obstetrical Unit: Income and Production Assumptions (Page 1)

Production Volume Detail

Post Partum Beds: 3
LDRP Beds: 2

	Fiscal Year Ending September 30				
	1998	1999	2000	2001	2002
Avg. Per Case Charge:	$ 4,350	$ 4,481	$ 4,615	$ 4,753	$ 4,896
Total Charges:	$435,000	$896,100	$1,153,729	$1,426,009	$1,586,292
Rate of Fee Increase:	—	3%	3%	3%	3%
Rate of Case Growth:	—	8%	8%	8%	8%
ALOS:	2.5	2.4	2.3	2.2	2.1
Number of Cases:	100	200	250	300	324

	Fiscal Year Ending September 30, 1998				
	1st Qtr	2nd Qtr	3rd Qtr	4th Qtr	Total
OB:					
Cases	8	20	35	37	100
Days	20	50	88	93	250
ALOS	2.5	2.5	2.5	2.5	2.5
Charges	34,800	87,000	152,250	160,950	435,000

	Fiscal Year Ending September 30, 1999				
	1st Qtr	2nd Qtr	3rd Qtr	4th Qtr	Total
OB:					
	40	67	53	40	200
Cases	96	160	128	96	480
Days	2.4	2.4	2.4	2.4	2.4
ALOS	179,220	298,670	238,945	179,220	896,100

	Fiscal Year Ending September 30, 2000				
	1st Qtr	2nd Qtr	3rd Qtr	4th Qtr	Total
OB:					
Cases	50	83	67	50	250
Days	115	192	153	115	575
ALOS	2.3	2.3	2.3	2.3	2.3
Charges	230,746	384,538	307,642	230,746	1,153,729

1997–1998 Charges		# of Cases	% of Cases	% of Income
C-Section:	$ 6,000	35	35%	51%
Spontaneous Delivery:	$ 3,100	50	50%	38%
Low Forceps Delivery:	$ 2,800	15	15%	11%
Average Per Case:	$ 4,070			

Comparative *Revenue*   (Adjusted for 1997–1998)

Anystate Foundation Study Peer Group: $ 4,800   Hospital A: $ 4,000

	Fiscal Year Ending September 30, 2001				
	1st Qtr	2nd Qtr	3rd Qtr	4th Qtr	Total
OB:					
Cases	60	100	80	60	300
Days	132	220	176	132	660
ALOS	2.2	2.2	2.2	2.2	2.2
Charges	285,202	475,289	380,245	285,202	1,426,009

	Fiscal Year Ending September 30, 2002				
	1st Qtr	2nd Qtr	3rd Qtr	4th Qtr	Total
OB:					
Cases	65	108	86	65	324
Days	136	227	181	136	680
ALOS	2.1	2.1	2.1	2.1	2.1
Charges	317,258	528,711	422,985	317,258	1,586,292

Financial Analysis: Anytown Hospital
Obstetrical Unit: Income and Production Assumptions (Page 2)

Comparative Revenue and Expense Data (1994–1995)

Hospital A			Anystate Foundation Study Peer Group		
	Expense*	Revenue		Expense*	Revenue
Nursing	$ 1,130	$ 1,774	Nursing	$ 1,044	$ 1,966
Delivery	$ 822	$ 1,317	Delivery	$ 1,132	$ 2,006
Newborn	$ 478	$ 616	Newborn	$ 367	$ 520
Total:	$ 2,430	$ 3,707	Total:	$ 2,543	$ 4,492

*Total Per Case Expense for Nursing Salaries, Benefits and Clinical Supplies

Expenses Applied to Anytown Hospital's Expected Cases

Year	1998	1999	2000	2001	2002
Cases	100	200	250	300	324
Hospital A	262,800	525,600	657,000	788,400	851,472
Study	275,100	550,200	687,750	825,300	891,324

Staffing & Clinical Expenses

	Year 1			Year 2			Year 3		
	Salary	FTE	Total	Salary	FTE	Total	Salary	FTE	Total
RN	34,000	4.5	153,000	35,360	5.5	194,480	36,774	6.0	220,646
LPN	21,000	1.0	21,000	21,840	2.0	43,680	22,714	2.0	45,427
NA	13,520	0.5	6,760	14,061	1.0	14,061	14,623	1.0	14,623
Clerk	13,520	1.0	13,520	14,061	1.0	14,061	14,623	1.5	21,935
	Total:	7.0	194,280	Total:	9.5	266,282	Total:	10.5	302,632
Benefits @ 25%			48,570	Benefits @ 25%		66,570	Benefits @ 25%		75,658
Clinical Supplies			20,000	Clinical Supplies		40,000	Clinical Supplies		50,000
		Total:	262,850		Total:	372,852		Total:	428,290

Expenses Inflated to 1997–1998 Year

Hospital A	Anystate Foundation Study
Expense*	Expense*
$ 2,628	$ 2,751

	Year 4			Year 5	
Salary	FTE	Total	Salary	FTE	Total
38,245	6.5	248,595	39,775	6.0	238,651
23,622	2.0	47,244	24,567	2.0	49,134
15,208	1.0	15,208	15,816	1.0	15,816
15,208	1.5	22,812	15,816	2.0	31,633
Total:	11.0	333,860	Total:	11.0	335,235
Benefits @ 25%		83,465	Benefits @ 25%		83,809
Clinical Supplies		60,000	Clinical Supplies		64,800
Total:		477,325	Total:		483,843

Financial Analysis: Anytown Hospital—Obstetrics Service Feasibility Study
Page 1

Year 1	Month 1	Month 2	Month 3	Month 4	Month 5	Month 6
Income						
Income–Labor and Delivery	11,600	11,600	11,600	29,000	29,000	29,000
Total Gross Income	**11,600**	**11,600**	**11,600**	**29,000**	**29,000**	**29,000**
Contractual Adjustments	4,176	4,176	4,176	10,440	10,440	10,440
Bad Debt	928	928	928	2,320	2,320	2,320
Other	348	116	116	290	290	290
Total Adjustments	5,452	5,220	5,220	13,050	13,050	13,050
Total Net Income	**6,148**	**6,380**	**6,380**	**15,950**	**15,950**	**15,950**
Operating Expenses						
Support Staff Salaries	16,190	16,190	16,190	16,190	16,190	16,190
Staff Benefits @ 25%	4,048	4,048	4,048	4,048	4,048	4,048
Recruitment Expenses–New M.D.s	60,000	0	0	0	0	0
Repairs and Maintenance	200	200	200	200	200	200
Telephone and Utilities	833	833	833	833	833	833
Travel, Dues and Subscriptions	500	500	500	500	500	500
Clinical Supplies	1,667	1,667	1,667	1,667	1,667	1,667
Promotion and Marketing	2,000	1,000	6,000	1,000	1,000	2,000
Capital Expenditures	0	0	0	0	0	0
Depreciation	8,691	8,691	8,691	8,691	8,691	8,691
All Other Expenses	1,667	1,667	1,667	1,667	1,667	1,667
Total Operating Expenses	**95,795**	**34,795**	**39,795**	**34,795**	**34,795**	**35,795**
Expenses as % of Net Income	1558%	545%	624%	218%	218%	224%
Add Back: Depreciation	8,691	8,691	8,691	8,691	8,691	8,691
Minus: Replacement Reserve	5,003	5,003	5,003	5,003	5,003	5,003
Minus: Principal Payment	6,206	6,206	6,206	6,206	6,206	6,206
Total All Expenses	**98,312**	**37,312**	**42,312**	**37,312**	**37,312**	**38,312**
Cash Flow	(92,164)	(30,932)	(35,932)	(21,362)	(21,362)	(22,362)
Profit Margin	−1499.1%	−484.8%	−563.2%	−133.9%	−133.9%	−140.2%
Outstanding Balance from Start-up	1,277,468	1,308,401	1,344,333	1,365,695	1,387,058	1,409,420
Annual Return on Investment	−7.8%	−2.6%	−3.0%	−1.8%	−1.8%	−1.9%

Month 7	Month 8	Month 9	Month 10	Month 11	Month 12	EOY 1	% of Gross Revenue	Monthly Average
50,750	50,750	50,750	53,650	53,650	53,650	**435,000**	100%	36,250
50,750	**50,750**	**50,750**	**53,650**	**53,650**	**53,650**	**435,000**	100%	**36,250**
18,270	18,270	18,270	19,314	19,314	19,314	**156,600**	36.0%	13,050
4,060	4,060	4,060	4,292	4,292	4,292	**34,800**	8.0%	2,900
508	508	508	537	537	537	**4,582**	1.1%	382
22,838	22,838	22,838	24,143	24,143	24,143	**195,982**	45.1%	16,332
27,913	**27,913**	**27,913**	**29,508**	**29,508**	**29,508**	**239,018**	55%	**19,918**
							% of Total Revenue	Monthly Average
16,190	16,190	16,190	16,190	16,190	16,190	**194,280**	81.3%	16,190
4,048	4,048	4,048	4,048	4,048	4,048	**48,570**	20.3%	4,048
0	0	0	0	0	0	**60,000**	25.1%	NM.
200	200	200	200	200	200	**2,400**	1.0%	200
833	833	833	833	833	833	**10,000**	4.2%	833
500	500	500	500	500	500	**6,000**	2.5%	500
1,667	1,667	1,667	1,667	1,667	1,667	**20,000**	8.4%	1,667
2,000	2,000	2,000	500	500	0	**20,000**	8.4%	1,667
0	0	0	0	0	0	**0**	0.0%	0
8,691	8,691	8,691	8,691	8,691	8,691	**104,288**	43.6%	8,691
1,667	1,667	1,667	1,667	1,667	1,667	**20,000**	8.4%	1,667
35,795	35,795	35,795	34,295	34,295	33,795	**485,538**	203.1%	**40,462**
128%	128%	128%	116%	116%	115%	**203%**		
8,691	8,691	8,691	8,691	8,691	8,691	**104,288**		
5,003	5,003	5,003	5,003	5,003	5,003	**60,030**		
6,206	6,206	6,206	6,206	6,206	6,206	**74,467**		
38,312	**38,312**	**38,312**	**36,812**	**36,812**	**36,312**	**515,748**		
(10,400)	(10,400)	(10,400)	(7,305)	(7,305)	(6,805)	**(276,730)**		
−37.3%	−37.3%	−37.3%	−24.8%	−24.8%	−23.1%	−115.8%		
1,419,820	1,430,219	1,440,619	1,447,924	1,455,229	1,462,034	1,462,034	Year 1	
							Balance Forward	
−0.9%	−0.9%	−0.9%	−0.6%	−0.6%	−0.6%	−23.3%		

Financial Analysis: Anytown Hospital—Obstetrics Service Feasibility Study
Page 2

Year 2	Month 1	Month 2	Month 3	Month 4	Month 5	Month 6
Income						
Income–Labor and Delivery	59,740	59,740	59,740	99,557	99,557	99,557
Total Gross Income	**59,740**	**59,740**	**59,740**	**99,557**	**99,557**	**99,557**
Contractual Adjustments	21,506	21,506	21,506	35,840	35,840	35,840
Bad Debt	4,779	4,779	4,779	7,965	7,965	7,965
Other	1,792	1,792	1,792	2,987	2,987	2,987
Total Adjustments	28,078	28,078	28,078	46,792	46,792	46,792
Total Net Income	**31,662**	**31,662**	**31,662**	**52,765**	**52,765**	**52,765**
Operating Expenses						
Support Staff Salaries	22,190	22,190	22,190	22,190	22,190	22,190
Staff Benefits @ 25%	5,548	5,548	5,548	5,548	5,548	5,548
Repairs and Maintenance	210	210	210	210	210	210
Telephone and Utilities	875	875	875	875	875	875
Travel, Dues and Subscriptions	525	525	525	525	525	525
Clinical Supplies	3,333	3,333	3,333	3,333	3,333	3,333
Promotion and Marketing	2,000	1,000	6,000	1,000	1,000	2,000
Capital Expenditures	833	833	833	833	833	833
Depreciation	8,774	8,774	8,774	8,774	8,774	8,774
All Other Expenses	1,750	1,750	1,750	1,750	1,750	1,750
Total Operating Expenses	46,038	45,038	50,038	45,038	45,038	46,038
Expenses as % of Net Income	145%	142%	158%	85%	85%	87%
Add Back: Depreciation	8,774	8,774	8,774	8,774	8,774	8,774
Minus: Replacement Reserve	877	877	877	877	877	877
Minus: Principal Payment	6,516	6,516	6,516	6,516	6,516	6,516
Total All Expenses	**44,658**	**43,658**	**48,658**	**43,658**	**43,658**	**44,658**
Cash Flow	(12,995)	(11,995)	(16,995)	9,107	9,107	8,107
Profit Margin	−41.0%	−37.9%	−53.7%	17.3%	17.3%	15.4%
Outstanding Balance from Start-up	1,475,029	1,487,024	1,504,020	1,494,912	1,485,805	1,477,698
Annual Return on Investment	−1.1%	−1.0%	−1.4%	0.8%	0.8%	0.7%

Month 7	Month 8	Month 9	Month 10	Month 11	Month 12	EOY 2	% of Gross Revenue	Monthly Average
79,648	79,648	79,648	59,740	59,740	59,740	**896,055**	100%	74,671
79,648	**79,648**	**79,648**	**59,740**	**59,740**	**59,740**	**896,055**	100%	**74,671**
28,673	28,673	28,673	21,506	21,506	21,506	**322,580**	36.0%	26,882
6,372	6,372	6,372	4,779	4,779	4,779	**71,684**	8.0%	5,974
2,389	2,389	2,389	1,792	1,792	1,792	**26,882**	3.0%	2,240
37,435	37,435	37,435	28,078	28,078	28,078	**421,146**	47.0%	35,095
42,214	**42,214**	**42,214**	**31,662**	**31,662**	**31,662**	**474,909**	53%	**39,576**

							% of Total Revenue	Monthly Average
22,190	22,190	22,190	22,190	22,190	22,190	**266,282**	56.1%	22,190
5,548	5,548	5,548	5,548	5,548	5,548	**66,570**	14.0%	5,548
210	210	210	210	210	210	**2,520**	0.5%	210
875	875	875	875	875	875	**10,500**	2.2%	875
525	525	525	525	525	525	**6,300**	1.3%	525
3,333	3,333	3,333	3,333	3,333	3,333	**40,000**	8.4%	3,333
2,000	2,000	2,000	500	500	0	**20,000**	4.2%	1,667
833	833	833	833	833	833	**10,000**	2.1%	833
8,774	8,774	8,774	8,774	8,774	8,774	**105,288**	22.2%	8,774
1,750	1,750	1,750	1,750	1,750	1,750	**21,000**	4.4%	1,750
46,038	46,038	46,038	44,538	44,538	44,038	**548,460**	115.5%	45,705
109%	109%	109%	141%	141%	139%	**115%**		
8,774	8,774	8,774	8,774	8,774	8,774	**105,288**		
877	877	877	877	877	877	**10,529**		
6,516	6,516	6,516	6,516	6,516	6,516	**78,191**		
44,658	**44,658**	**44,658**	**43,158**	**43,158**	**42,658**	**531,891**		
(2,444)	(2,444)	(2,444)	(11,495)	(11,495)	(10,995)	**(56,982)**		
−5.8%	−5.8%	−5.8%	−36.3%	−36.3%	−34.7%	−12.0%		
1,480,142	1,482,585	1,485,029	1,496,525	1,508,020	1,519,016	1,519,016	Year 2	
							Balance Forward	
−0.2%	−0.2%	−0.2%	−1.0%	−1.0%	−0.9%	−4.8%		

Financial Analysis: Anytown Hospital—Obstetrics Service Feasibility Study
Page 3

Year 3	Month 1	Month 2	Month 3	Month 4	Month 5	Month 6
Income						
Income–Labor and Delivery	76,915	76,915	76,915	128,179	128,179	128,179
Total Gross Income	**76,915**	**76,915**	**76,915**	**128,179**	**128,179**	**128,179**
Contractual Adjustments	27,689	27,689	27,689	46,145	46,145	46,145
Bad Debt	6,153	6,153	6,153	10,254	10,254	10,254
Other	2,307	2,307	2,307	3,845	3,845	3,845
Total Adjustments	36,150	36,150	36,150	60,244	60,244	60,244
Total Net Income	**40,765**	**40,765**	**40,765**	**67,935**	**67,935**	**67,935**
Operating Expenses						
Support Staff Salaries	25,219	25,219	25,219	25,219	25,219	25,219
Staff Benefits @ 25%	6,305	6,305	6,305	6,305	6305	6,305
Repairs and Maintenance	221	221	221	221	221	221
Telephone and Utilities	919	919	919	919	919	919
Travel, Dues and Subscriptions	551	551	551	551	551	551
Clinical Supplies	4,167	4,167	4,167	4,167	4,167	4,167
Promotion and Marketing	2,000	1,000	6,000	1,000	1,000	2,000
Capital Expenditures	833	833	833	833	833	833
Depreciation	8,857	8,857	8,857	8,857	8,857	8,857
All Other Expenses	1,838	1,838	1,838	1,838	1,838	1,838
Total Operating Expenses	**50,909**	**49,909**	**54,909**	**49,909**	**49,909**	**50,909**
Expenses as % of Net Income	125%	122%	135%	73%	73%	75%
Add Back: Depreciation	8,857	8,857	8,857	8,857	8,857	8,857
Minus: Replacement Reserve	886	886	886	886	886	886
Minus: Principal Payment	6,516	6,516	6,516	6,516	6,516	6,516
Total All Expenses	**49,454**	**48,454**	**53,454**	**48,454**	**48,454**	**49,454**
Cash Flow	(8,689)	(7,689)	(12,689)	19,481	19,481	18,481
Profit Margin	−21.3%	−18.9%	−31.1%	28.7%	28.7%	27.2%
Outstanding Balance from Start-up	1,527,704	1,535,393	1,548,082	1,528,600	1,509,119	1,490,638
Annual Return on Investment	−0.7%	−0.6%	−1.1%	1.6%	1.6%	1.6%

Month 7	Month 8	Month 9	Month 10	Month 11	Month 12	EOY 3	% of Gross Revenue	Monthly Average
102,547	102,547	102,547	76,915	76,915	76,915	**1,153,671**	100%	96,139
102,547	**102,547**	**102,547**	**76,915**	**76,915**	**76,915**	1,153,671	100%	**96,139**
36,917	36,917	36,917	27,689	27,689	27,689	**415,322**	36.0%	34,610
8,204	8,204	8,204	6,153	6,153	6,153	**92,294**	8.0%	7,691
3,076	3,076	3,076	2,307	2,307	2,307	**34,610**	3.0%	2,884
48,197	48,197	48,197	36,150	36,150	36,150	**542,225**	47.0%	45,185
54,350	**54,350**	**54,350**	**40,765**	**40,765**	**40,765**	**611,446**	53%	**50,954**
							% of Total Revenue	Monthly Average
25,219	25,219	25,219	25,219	25,219	25,219	**302,632**	49.5%	25,219
6,305	6,305	6,305	6,305	6,305	6,305	**75,658**	12.4%	6,305
221	221	221	221	221	221	**2,646**	0.4%	221
919	919	919	919	919	919	**11,025**	1.8%	919
551	551	551	551	551	551	**6,615**	1.1%	551
4,167	4,167	4,167	4,167	4,167	4,167	**50,000**	8.2%	4,167
2,000	2,000	2,000	500	500	1,000	**21,000**	3.4%	1,750
833	833	833	833	833	833	**10,000**	1.6%	833
8,857	8,857	8,857	8,857	8,857	8,857	**106,288**	17.4%	8,857
1,838	1,838	1,838	1,838	1,838	1,838	**22,050**	3.6%	1,838
50,909	**50,909**	**50,909**	**49,409**	**49,409**	**49,909**	**607,914**	99.4%	**50,659**
94%	94%	94%	121%	121%	122%	**99%**		
8,857	8,857	8,857	8,857	8,857	8,857	**106,288**		
886	886	886	886	886	886	**10,629**		
6,516	6,516	6,516	6,516	6,516	6,516	**78,191**		
49,454	**49,454**	**49,454**	**47,954**	**47,954**	**48,454**	**590,445**		
4,896	4,896	4,896	(7,189)	(7,189)	(7,689)	**21,001**		
9.0%	9.0%	9.0%	−17.6%	−17.6%	−18.9%	3.4%		
1,485,742	1,480,845	1,475,949	1,483,138	1,490,326	1,498,015	1,498,015	Year 3 Balance Forward	
0.4%	0.4%	0.4%	−0.6%	−0.6%	−0.6%	1.8%		

Financial Analysis: Anytown Hospital—Obstetrics Service Feasibility Study
Page 4

Year 4	Month 1	Month 2	Month 3	Month 4	Month 5	Month 6
Income						
Income–Labor and Delivery	95,067	95,067	95,067	158,430	158,430	158,430
Total Gross Income	**95,067**	**95,067**	**95,067**	**158,430**	**158,430**	**158,430**
Contractual Adjustments	34,224	34,224	34,224	57,035	57,035	57,035
Bad Debt	7,605	7,605	7,605	12,674	12,674	12,674
Other	2,852	2,852	2,852	4,753	4,753	4,753
Total Adjustments	44,682	44,682	44,682	74,462	74,462	74,462
Total Net Income	**50,386**	**50,386**	**50,386**	**83,968**	**83,968**	**83,968**
Operating Expenses						
Support Staff Salaries	27,822	27,822	27,822	27,822	27,822	27,822
Staff Benefits @ 25%	6,955	6,955	6,955	6,955	6,955	6,955
Repairs and Maintenance	232	232	232	232	232	232
Telephone and Utilities	965	965	965	965	965	965
Travel, Dues and Subscriptions	579	579	579	579	579	579
Clinical Supplies	5,000	5,000	5,000	5,000	5,000	5,000
Promotion and Marketing	2,000	1,000	6,000	1,000	1,000	2,000
Capital Expenditures	833	833	833	833	833	833
Depreciation	8,941	8,941	8,941	8,941	8,941	8,941
All Other Expenses	1,929	1,929	1,929	1,929	1,929	1,929
Total Operating Expenses	**55,255**	**54,255**	**59,255**	**54,255**	**54,255**	**55,255**
Expenses as % of Net Income	110%	108%	118%	65%	65%	66%
Add Back: Depreciation	8,941	8,941	8,941	8,941	8,941	8,941
Minus: Replacement Reserve	894	894	894	894	894	894
Minus: Principal Payment	6,516	6,516	6,516	6,516	6,516	6,516
Total All Expenses	**53,725**	**52,725**	**57,725**	**52,725**	**52,725**	**53,725**
Cash Flow	(3,339)	(2,339)	(7,339)	31,243	31,243	30,243
Profit Margin	−6.6%	−4.6%	−14.6%	37.2%	37.2%	36.0%
Outstanding Balance from Start-up	1,501,354	1,503,693	1,511,032	1,479,789	1,448,546	1,418,303
Annual Return on Investment	−0.3%	−0.2%	−0.6%	2.6%	2.6%	2.6%

Month 7	Month 8	Month 9	Month 10	Month 11	Month 12	EOY 4	% of Gross Revenue	Monthly Average
126,748	126,748	126,748	95,067	95,067	95,067	1,425,937	100%	118,828
126,748	126,748	126,748	95,067	95,067	95,067	1,425,937	100%	118,828
45,629	45,629	45,629	34,224	34,224	34,224	513,337	36.0%	42,778
10,140	10,140	10,140	7,605	7,605	7,605	114,075	8.0%	9,506
3,802	3,802	3,802	2,852	2,852	2,852	42,778	3.0%	3,565
59,572	59,572	59,572	44,682	44,682	44,682	670,191	47.0%	55,849
67,177	67,177	67,177	50,386	50,386	50,386	755,747	53%	62,979
							% of Total Revenue	Monthly Average
27,822	27,822	27,822	27,822	27,822	27,822	333,860	44.2%	27,822
6,955	6,955	6,955	6,955	6,955	6,955	83,465	11.0%	6,955
232	232	232	232	232	232	2,778	0.4%	232
965	965	965	965	965	965	11,576	1.5%	965
579	579	579	579	579	579	6,946	0.9%	579
5,000	5,000	5,000	5,000	5,000	5,000	60,000	7.9%	5,000
2,000	2,000	2,000	1,000	1,000	1,000	22,000	2.9%	1,833
833	833	833	833	833	833	10,000	1.3%	833
8,941	8,941	8,941	8,941	8,941	8,941	107,288	14.2%	8,941
1,929	1,929	1,929	1,929	1,929	1,929	23,153	3.1%	1,929
55,255	55,255	55,255	54,255	54,255	54,255	661,065	87.5%	55,089
82%	82%	82%	108%	108%	108%	87%		
8,941	8,941	8,941	8,941	8,941	8,941	107,288		
894	894	894	894	894	894	10,729		
6,516	6,516	6,516	6,516	6,516	6,516	78,191		
53,725	53,725	53,725	52,725	52,725	52,725	642,697		
13,452	13,452	13,452	(2,339)	(2,339)	(2,339)	113,050		
20.0%	20.0%	20.0%	−4.6%	−4.6%	−4.6%	−15.0%		
1,404,852	1,391,400	1,377,948	1,380,287	1,382,626	1,384,965	1,384,965	Year 4	
							Balance Forward	
1.1%	1.1%	1.1%	−0.2%	−0.2%	−0.2%	9.5%		

Financial Analysis: Anytown Hospital—Obstetrics Service Feasibility Study
Page 5

Year 5	Month 1	Month 2	Month 3	Month 4	Month 5	Month 6
Income						
Income—Labor and Delivery	105,753	105,753	105,753	176,237	176,237	176,237
Total Gross Income	**105,753**	**105,753**	**105,753**	**176,237**	**176,237**	**176,237**
Contractual Adjustments	38,071	38,071	38,071	63,445	63,445	63,445
Bad Debt	8,460	8,460	8,460	14,099	14,099	14,099
Other	3,173	3,173	3,173	5,287	5,287	5,287
Total Adjustments	49,704	49,704	49,704	82,831	82,831	82,831
Total Net Income	**56,049**	**56,049**	**56,049**	**93,406**	**93,406**	**93,406**
Operating Expenses						
Support Staff Salaries	27,936	27,936	27,936	27,936	27,936	27,936
Staff Benefits @ 25%	6,984	6,984	6,984	6,984	6,984	6,984
Repairs and Maintenance	243	243	243	243	243	243
Telephone and Utilities	1,013	1,013	1,013	1,013	1,013	1,013
Travel, Dues and Subscriptions	608	608	608	608	608	608
Clinical Supplies	5,400	5,400	5,400	5,400	5,400	5,400
Promotion and Marketing	2,000	1,000	6,000	1,000	1,000	2,000
Capital Expenditures	833	833	833	833	833	833
Depreciation	9,024	9,024	9,024	9,024	9,024	9,024
All Other Expenses	2,026	2,026	2,026	2,026	2,026	2,026
Total Operating Expenses	**56,067**	**55,067**	**60,067**	**55,067**	**55,067**	**56,067**
Expenses as % of Net Income	100%	98%	107%	59%	59%	60%
Add Back: Depreciation	9,024	9,024	9,024	9,024	9,024	9,024
Minus: Replacement Reserve	902	902	902	902	902	902
Minus: Principal Payment	6,516	6,516	6,516	6,516	6,516	6,516
Total All Expenses	**54,462**	**53,462**	**58,462**	**53,462**	**53,462**	**54,462**
Cash Flow	1,587	2,587	(2,413)	39,944	39,944	38,944
Profit Margin	2.8%	4.6%	−4.3%	42.8%	42.8%	41.7%
Outstanding Balance from Start-up	1,383,377	1,380,790	1,383,202	1,343,258	1,303,314	1,264,370
Annual Return on Investment	0.1%	0.2%	−0.2%	3.4%	3.4%	3.3%

	Month 7	Month 8	Month 9	Month 10	Month 11	Month 12	EOY 5	% of Gross Revenue	Monthly Average
	140,995	140,995	140,995	105,753	105,753	105,753	**1,586,213**	100%	132,184
	140,995	**140,995**	**140,995**	**105,753**	**105,753**	**105,753**	**1,586,213**	100%	**132,184**
	50,758	50,758	50,758	38,071	38,071	38,071	**571,037**	36.0%	47,586
	11,280	11,280	11,280	8,460	8,460	8,460	**126,897**	8.0%	10,575
	4,230	4,230	4,230	3,173	3,173	3,173	**47,586**	3.0%	3,966
	66,268	66,268	66,268	49,704	49,704	49,704	**745,520**	47.0%	62,127
	74,727	**74,727**	**74,727**	**56,049**	**56,049**	**56,049**	**840,693**	53%	**70,058**
								% of Total Revenue	Monthly Average
	27,936	27,936	27,936	27,936	27,936	27,936	**335,235**	39.9%	27,936
	6,984	6,984	6,984	6,984	6,984	6,984	**83,809**	10.0%	6,984
	243	243	243	243	243	243	**2,917**	0.3%	243
	1,013	1,013	1,013	1,013	1,013	1,013	**12,155**	1.4%	1,013
	608	608	608	608	608	608	**7,293**	0.9%	608
	5,400	5,400	5,400	5,400	5,400	5,400	**64,800**	7.7%	5,400
	2,000	2,000	2,000	1,500	1,500	1,100	**23,100**	2.7%	1,925
	833	833	833	833	833	833	**10,000**	1.2%	833
	9,024	9,024	9,024	9,024	9,024	9,024	**108,288**	12.9%	9,024
	2,026	2,026	2,026	2,026	2,026	2,026	**24,310**	2.9%	2,026
	56,067	56,067	56,067	55,567	55,567	55,167	**671,907**	79.9%	55,992
	75%	75%	75%	99%	99%	98%	**80%**		
	9,024	9,024	9,024	9,024	9,024	9,024	**108,288**		
	902	902	902	902	902	902	**10,829**		
	6,516	6,516	6,516	6,516	6,516	6,516	**78,191**		
	54,462	**54,462**	**54,462**	**53,962**	**53,962**	**53,562**	**652,638**		
	20,266	20,266	20,266	2,087	2,087	2,487	**188,055**		
	27.1%	27.1%	27.1%	3.7%	3.7%	4.4%	22.4%		
	1,244,104	1,223,838	1,203,573	1,201,485	1,199,398	1,196,910	1,196,910	Year 5	
								Balance Forward	
	1.7%	1.7%	1.7%	0.2%	0.2%	0.2%	15.9%		

CASE THREE STUDY NOTES

Case Study: Indigent Free Pharmacy Feasibility

This study was based on a hospital attempting to contain its rapidly escalating costs for providing drugs and other pharmacy items to indigent patients. The hospital engaged The Health Service Group, Inc., to assist in the development of the model to determine how to slow the rate of growth of its pharmacy expenses and work with the community to maximize the effectiveness of limited resources.

The study evaluated all of the community resources that were providing some form of free pharmacy services to indigent patients to determine how patients get these services, the eligibility criteria of various agencies, and how the hospital could complement these services. Over a dozen model programs were evaluated, visited, and interviewed to learn lessons in fund raising, pharmacy and drug manufacturer networking, and program operation. The resulting study indicates a bottom-line level of support for the sponsor hospital. Viewing the cash flow as negative means only that this amount is what the hospital would put into the program to sustain it. As a benchmark, the hospital was spending well over $100,000 annually in all its areas to support this service prior to commencing the feasibility study.

Ultimately, free pharmacies must be self-sufficient but derive their operating income from a variety of sources of donations. The role of the executive director is crucial. This is the person with the drive to locate sources of funds and supplies. This is the person who makes or breaks the project. Support from foundations, grants, and trusts are time-limited by nature. Securing a regular stream of contributions should be a key long-term goal for the pharmacy.

Donations of drugs and supplies, in general, have no bearing on the fixed or variable costs of the service if the assumption is that all drugs and supplies are donated. If the assumption is that some amount of the drugs or supplies are purchased to provide a baseline level of service, the initial and par-level amounts must be defined and modeled.

Lastly, this pro forma is based on simplicity. It does not contain monthly cash flow or expense projections, only annual projections with detail for five years and a 10-year summary. The goal was to examine general project feasibility before moving into fund raising, budget setting, and implementation.

ANYTOWN MEDICAL CENTER: INDIGENT FREE PHARMACY FEASIBILITY STUDY Financial Analysis (September 23, 1997)

EXECUTIVE SUMMARY

The following operating assumptions and attached pro forma financial statements represent our understanding of the proposed Free Pharmacy for Anytown Medical Center (AMC). The following indicates the notable initial findings and key indicators of operation.

- The pro forma cash flow projections indicate a minimum of 3 years of major funding from foundations, grants, and trusts. The pro forma profiles a minimum base of $10,000 of ongoing foundation, grant, and trust funding for remaining years.

- The two elements of greatest impact are the amount of support received from AMC that is profiled as covering the negative cash flow, and the amount of financial support available in the community. To a lesser extent, the location of the clinic and the amount of in-kind services provided also play a role in minimizing operating expenses.

- The one key element of ongoing financial success will be the ability of the program Executive Director to locate ongoing financial support from foundations, grants, and trusts to make up for pro forma shortfalls.

The following table highlights selected performance indicators under the current set of assumptions.

Cash Flow Years 1–5	Total Staffing Expense Years 1–5	Start-Up Expense		Total Equipment Expense	
Year 1 ($75,254)	Year 1 $84,588	Salaries	$ 7,049	Computers	$17,000
Year 2 ($47,703)	Year 2 $87,126	Equip. & Furniture	$23,500	Leasehold Improve.	$ 2,000
Year 3 ($51,075)	Year 3 $89,739			Equipment	$ 2,500
Year 4 ($84,911)	Year 4 $92,432			Shelving	$ 1,000
Year 5 ($88,321)	Year 5 $95,205			Furniture	$ 1,000
		Total	$30,549	Total	$23,500

Anytown Medical Center: Indigent Free Pharmacy Feasibility Study
Continued

To assist in the refinement of this model, attention should be given to identifying any areas of inconsistency in the assumptions, the planned location of the clinic, the level of in-kind operating support from various organizations, and the amounts of direct financial support from community agencies.

OPERATING ASSUMPTIONS

Overview

The following initial assumptions are used in the development of an operating pro forma for a planned Free Pharmacy service by Anytown Medical Center. The categories of items for discussion include income assumptions and operating expense assumptions.

1.0 Income Assumptions

1.1 Revenue amounts have been estimated based on income estimates from similar programs. Please review the detail assumptions found under the section "Pro Forma Assumptions Detail" at the end of this report.

1.2 Donations—church groups are estimated at $4,000 for Year 1, increasing 10% annually. Programs visited reported slightly higher amounts ($8,000–$10,000) however some adjustment is considered given the size of these comparison communities vs. Anytown. It is likely that these amounts would be higher, however, conservative planning indicates that a lower estimate should be used, then modified as donations are received.

1.3 Donations—individuals are estimated at $10,000 for Year 1, increasing 10% annually. Programs visited reported slightly higher amounts ($15,000), however, a downward adjustment has been made for the same reasons as outlined in 1.2 above.

1.4 Donations—civic groups/businesses are estimated at $10,000 for Year 1, increasing 10% annually. Programs visited reported slightly higher amounts ($15,000), however, a downward adjustment has been made for the same reasons as outlined in 1.2 above.

1.5 Donations—drugs/supplies are not included because these items have no direct bearing on the fixed costs of providing services. This category of in-kind support plays the most significant role in determining the number of clients that may be served, however, for the purposes of this study, the volume of clients served will be modeled based on the overall impact on the fixed costs of providing services.

1.6 Operating support amounts are not included because initial assumptions are that operating shortfalls will become the amounts of support provided by AMC. Additionally, the amount of direct financial support available in the community is unknown at present. The detail assumptions found under

Anytown Medical Center: Indigent Free Pharmacy Feasibility Study Continued

the section "Pro Forma Assumptions Detail" at the end of this report indicate an initial estimate of approximately $14,000 of additional financial support available from identified community resources. These amounts are not included in accounting for operational deficits. These amounts are estimated to be limited because most community-based programs have limited resources, and the persistence of these resources is questionable due to anticipated changes in Medicaid funding levels as the result of the Anystate Medicaid Program. The net result is that additional financial resources are available to assist this venture, but these amounts are likely to be limited and are projected to be even more limited in future years.

1.7 Grants and trusts income is estimated at a base amount of $40,000 for Years 1–3. This amount was chosen as a conservative estimate based on the start-up funds other community programs have received from these sources. It is widely held that most support of this nature is intended for program start-up and not for sustaining ongoing operations. This is not entirely the case, as Anycounty Medical Ministries is in its sixth year of operation and still receives approximately $110,000 in support from foundations, grants, and trusts. The key to ongoing financial success will be the ability of the Executive Director to locate ongoing financial support from foundations, grants, and trusts to make up operating shortfalls. For the purposes of profiling reasonable operations, grants and trusts income normalizes to $10,000 in Year 3, increasing 10% annually thereafter.

1.8 Other income is estimated at $4,000 in Year 1, increasing 10% annually.

2.0 Operating Expense Assumptions

2.1 Expenses increase 3%–5% annually unless otherwise noted.

2.2 Support staff salaries are included in the detail assumptions found at the end of this report. Categories of staff include 1.0 FTE Executive Director @ $35,000; 0.25 FTE Pharmacist @ $28.00 per hour; and .75 FTE Pharmacy Technician/Administrative Assistant @ $9.00 per hour. All salaries increase 3% annually.

2.3 Staff benefits are projected at 33% representing AMC's actual expenses.

2.4 Office supplies are estimated at $750 in Year 1, increasing 5% annually.

2.5 Telephone expense is estimated at $1,200 in Year 1, increasing 5% annually.

2.6 Printing/publications expense is estimated at $750 in Year 1, increasing 5% annually. This is a category of expense that might be eliminated by finding a printer willing to donate in-kind services.

2.7 Postage is estimated at $750 in Year 1, increasing 5% annually.

2.8 Copier/copies expense is estimated at $1,200 in Year 1, increasing 5% annually.

Anytown Medical Center: Indigent Free Pharmacy Feasibility Study Concluded

2.9 Purchased drugs include those items that are consistent with the scope of services provided by the free pharmacy but are not available through donated sources. The Year 1 amount is estimated at $15,000, increasing 20% annually to reflect overall program growth.

2.10 Rent is estimated based on the assumption that the free pharmacy will be located in the Anytown Downtown Clinic. The three rooms available for use in the clinic total approximately 420 square feet. An estimate of 500 square feet @ $10.00 per sq. ft. is used for Year 1, increasing 3% annually. It should be noted that this represents the minimum amount of space for clinic start-up. An ideal amount is more likely to be in the 1,000–1,500 square foot range, depending on location of client waiting areas and storage. In addition, the opportunity to locate the pharmacy within other community resources should be evaluated and adjustments to this expense made.

2.11 Utilities and maintenance are estimated at $950 in Year 1, increasing 3% annually.

2.12 Housekeeping expenses are estimated at $420 in Year 1, increasing 3% annually.

2.13 Repairs are projected at $500 in Year 1, increasing 5% annually.

2.14 Volunteer expenses are amounts designated for volunteer recognition and other volunteer costs, estimated at $1,000 in Year 1, increasing 5% annually.

2.15 Accounting expenses are estimated at $500 in Year 1, increasing 3% annually. These services also might be donated as an in-kind contribution.

2.16 Start-up expenses of $30,549 are included in Year 1 alone, based on items indicated in the detail assumptions found at the end of this report.

2.17 Capital expenditures are estimated at $2,000 in Year 1, increasing 5% annually.

2.18 Depreciation and amortization are estimated on an asset base of $23,000 of equipment and furnishings identified in the start-up expense profile plus the $2,000 in capital expenditures. Amounts are estimated based on an 8-year straight-line method. The amount in Year 9 is provided as an estimate of the remaining assets not fully depreciated.

2.19 Miscellaneous amounts are included as expenses not included elsewhere, with a Year 1 estimate of $2,000, increasing 3% annually.

2.20 Add back: depreciation and amortization and replacement reserve reflect the actual cost of asset replacement. Replacement reserve is estimated at 75% of annual amounts of depreciation and amortization.

2.21 Cash flow indicates overall program outcome.

10-Year Pro Forma: Anytown Medical Center—Indigent Free Pharmacy
Feasibility Study

	Dec-98 Month 12	Dec-99 Month 24	Dec-00 Month 36	Dec-01 Month 48
Income and In-Kind Donations				
Total Donations—Cash	24,000	26,400	29,040	31,944
Grants & Trusts	40,000	40,000	40,000	10,000
Other Income	10,000	11,000	12,100	13,310
Gross Income	**74,000**	**77,400**	**81,140**	**55,254**
Operating Expenses				
Staff Salaries	84,588	87,126	89,739	92,432
Benefits @ 33%	20,988	21,618	22,266	22,934
Office Operations	4,450	4,673	4,906	5,151
Purchased Drugs	15,000	18,000	21,600	25,920
Rent—500 sq. ft. @ $10.00	5,000	5,150	5,305	5,464
Utilities and Maintenance	950	979	1,008	1,038
Housekeeping	420	433	446	459
Repair	500	525	551	579
Volunteer Expenses	1,000	1,050	1,103	1,158
Accounting	500	515	530	546
Start-up Expenses	30,549	0	0	0
Capital Expenditures	2,000	2,100	2,205	2,315
Depreciation & Amortization	3,063	3,325	3,601	3,890
Miscellaneous	2,000	2,060	2,122	2,185
Total Operating Expenses	**150,020**	**125,934**	**133,115**	**141,137**
Net Income	(76,020)	(48,534)	(51,975)	(85,883)
Add Back: Deprec. & Amort.	3,063	3,325	3,601	3,890
Minus: Replacement Reserve	2,297	2,494	2,700	2,918
Cash Flow	(75,254)	(47,703)	(51,075)	(84,911)
Operating Margin	−102%	−62%	−63%	−154%
Outstanding Balance from Start-up	(75,254)	(122,957)	(174,032)	(258,943)

Dec-02 Month 60	Dec-03 Month 72	Dec-04 Month 84	Dec-05 Month 96	Dec-06 Month 108	Dec-07 Month 120
35,138	38,652	42,517	46,769	51,446	56,591
11,000	12,100	13,310	14,641	16,105	17,716
14,641	16,105	17,716	19,487	21,436	23,579
60,779	**66,857**	**73,543**	**80,897**	**88,987**	**97,886**
95,205	98,061	101,002	104,033	107,154	110,368
23,622	24,331	25,061	25,813	26,587	27,385
5,409	5,950	6,545	7,199	7,919	8,711
31,104	37,325	44,790	53,748	64,497	77,397
5,628	5,796	5,970	6,149	6,334	6,524
1,069	1,101	1,134	1,168	1,203	1,240
473	487	502	517	532	548
608	638	670	704	739	776
1,216	1,276	1,340	1,407	1,477	1,551
563	580	597	615	633	652
0	0	0	0	0	0
2,431	2,553	2,680	2,814	2,955	3,103
4,194	4,513	4,848	5,200	4,000	4,388
2,251	2,319	2,388	2,460	2,534	2,610
150,149	**184,929**	**197,527**	**211,826**	**226,564**	**245,252**
(89,370)	(118,072)	(123,984)	(130,928)	(137,577)	(147,366)
4,194	4,513	4,848	5,200	4,000	4,388
3,145	3,385	3,636	3,900	3,000	3,291
(88,321)	(110,174)	(115,500)	(121,829)	(130,577)	(139,687)
−145%	**−165%**	**−157%**	**−151%**	**−147%**	**−143%**
(347,264)	(457,438)	(572,938)	(694,767)	(825,344)	(965,031)

Pro Forma Assumptions Detail: Anytown Medical Center—Indigent Free Pharmacy
Feasibility Study
Page 1

	Dec-98 Month 12	Dec-99 Month 24	Dec-00 Month 36	Dec-01 Month 48	Dec-02 Month 60	Annual % Increase
Income and In-Kind Donations						
Donations						
Donations—Church Groups	4,000	4,400	4,840	5,324	5,856	10%
Donations—Individuals	10,000	11,000	12,100	13,310	14,641	10%
Donations—Civic Groups/						
Businesses	10,000	11,000	12,100	13,310	14,641	10%
Donations—Drugs and Supplies	—	—	—	—	—	—
Total Donations	24,000	26,400	29,040	31,944	35,138	10%
Operating Support—See Note	—	—	—	—	—	
Grants & Trusts	40,000	40,000	40,000	10,000	11,000	—
Other Income	10,000	11,000	12,100	13,310	14,641	10%
Gross Income	**74,000**	**77,400**	**81,140**	**55,254**	**60,779**	
Operating Expenses						
Staffing Expenses						
Salary—Executive Director						
1.0 FTE	35,000	36,050	37,132	38,245	39,393	3%
Salary—Pharmacist .25 FTE	14,560	14,997	15,447	15,910	16,387	3%
Salary—Tech/Admin. Asst.						
.75 FTE	14,040	14,461	14,895	15,342	15,802	3%
Benefits @ 33%	20,988	21,618	22,266	22,934	23,622	—
Total Staffing Expenses	**84,588**	**87,126**	**89,739**	**92,432**	**95,205**	
Office Operations						
Office Supplies	750	788	827	868	912	5%
Telephone	1,200	1,260	1,323	1,389	1,459	5%
Printing/Publications	750	788	827	868	912	5%
Postage	750	788	827	868	912	5%
Copier/Copies	1,000	1,050	1,103	1,158	1,216	5%
Total Office Operations	**4,450**	**4,673**	**4,906**	**5,151**	**5,409**	
Purchased Drugs	15,000	18,000	21,600	25,920	31,104	20%
Rent—500 sq. ft. @ $10.00	5,000	5,150	5,305	5,464	5,628	3%
Utilities and Maintenance	950	979	1,008	1,038	1,069	3%
Housekeeping	420	433	446	459	473	3%
Repair	500	525	551	579	608	5%
Volunteer Expenses	1,000	1,050	1,103	1,158	1,216	5%
Accounting	500	515	530	546	563	3%
Start-up Expenses	30,549	—	—	—	—	—
Capital Expenditures	2,000	2,100	2,205	2,315	2,431	5%
Depreciation & Amortization	3,063	3,325	3,601	3,890	4,194	—
Miscellaneous	2,000	2,060	2,122	2,185	2,251	3%
Total Operating Expenses	**150,020**	**125,934**	**133,115**	**141,137**	**150,149**	
Net Income	**(76,020)**	**(48,534)**	**(51,975)**	**(85,883)**	**(89,370)**	
Add Back: Deprec. & Amort.	3,063	3,325	3,601	3,890	4,194	
Minus: Replacement Reserve	2,297	2,494	2,700	2,918	3,145	
Cash Flow	**(75,254)**	**(47,703)**	**(51,075)**	**(84,911)**	**(88,321)**	
Operating Margin	−102%	−62%	−63%	−154%	−145%	

Pro Forma Assumptions Detail: Anytown Medical Center—Indigent Free
Pharmacy Feasibility Study
Page 2

Potential Sources of Operating Support—Not Reflected in Income Projections

NOTE: All amounts are estimated based on existing community resources but not
necessarily indicative of actual amounts which may be received.

DSS—Emergency Assistance Program	$ 7,500	$300.00	multiplied by	25	qualified clients
County Health Services	$ 1,250	$ 50.00	multiplied by	25	qualified clients
Operation Help	$ 5,000	$ 50.00	per Rx for	100	qualified Rxs
Total Other Community Support:	**$13,750**				

Start-up Expenses

Pre-Opening Salaries

Executive Director @ 1 month	2,917	May want to consider a 2–3 month
Pharmacist @ 1 month	1,213	lead on the Exec. Director
Tech/Admin Asst @ 1 month	1,170	
Benefits @ 33%	1,749	
Total Pre-Opening Salaries	**7,049**	

Equipment & Furnishings

Pharmacy Computer

Computer w/ tape backup, modem, label & ink jet printers, power backup & software (QS-1)	10,000	Jones Data Services has made donations of both hardware and software for similar programs.
Office Computer	7,000	
File server with 3 terminals, modem, tape backup, (3) ink jet printers, power backup, all connections		
Wiring for Computers, Phone, Outlets	2,000	
Pharmacy Equipment	1,500	
Pharmacy Shelving	1,000	
Office Furniture—donated	—	
Office Furniture—purchased	1,000	
Misc. small office equipment	1,000	
Total Start-up	**30,549**	

CASE FOUR STUDY NOTES
Case Study: Multispecialty Primary Care Start-Up Feasibility

This study was commissioned with the intention of expanding physician service presence into a growing area of a hospital's county. The hospital operated one internal medicine practice and sought to expand by adding family practice, OB/GYN, pediatrics, and an urgent care function in a new facility.

The study began with market demographics and the determination of the best location for the 15,000–square foot facility. The hospital chose to pursue building a much larger building and renting out space to other physicians and professionals.

Income was modeled based on the number of providers on board each year. Medical Group Management Association physician compensation and production data were used as a baseline for the practice. All costs including physician recruitment, consulting, preopening, marketing, and construction-related costs were carried.

This model is a fairly complex pro forma. It includes most variables that one would normally associate with a new business start-up. The model is based on accrual accounting, which most hospitals use. All decisions on costs, modeling, equipment, and other aspects of performance were determined jointly with the hospital. Some analysts or hospitals might choose to use alternative equipment, configurations, or change the scope of the practice. These decisions will always be made on a project-by-project basis. This model should provide significant assistance to healthcare managers examining the issues of expansion, merger, or acquisition. Simply take what you have learned and apply it to your situation.

ANYTOWN MEDICAL CENTER: PRIMARY CARE PRACTICE AND URGENT CARE CENTER FEASIBILITY STUDY
Financial Analysis (January 19, 1998)

EXECUTIVE SUMMARY

The following operating assumptions and attached pro forma financial statements represent our understanding of the proposed Primary Care Practice and Urgent Care Center for Anytown Medical Center (AMC). The following indicates the notable initial findings and key indicators of operation.

1. The pro forma cash flow projections indicate a minimum of 2 years of major working capital needs, with a cumulative total of $787,521 required as of Month 21 in Year 2, when sustainable cash flow begins.

2. The elements of greatest impact are:
   - *Revenue Targets*—The pro forma is based on attaining minimum levels of production based on Medical Group Management Association median productivity for each specialty, with estimates used for the Urgent Care Center. These physician-specific targets should be considered the minimum level for physician competency. Dollar amounts are used, which may be interpolated into visit volume, as need dictates. Modeling has not presumed capitated income streams;
   - *Contractual Adjustments*—Based on similar hospital-based primary care practices billing allowable amounts;
   - *Physician Compensation and Incentive Plan*—If the current plan does not hold the physicians at risk for production levels, attainment of pro forma may not result. In addition, consideration should be given to gainsharing with physicians and practice staff;
   - *Operating Expenses*—Expenses are based on the adoption of best industry practices in operations of medical practices including maximum cross training of staff, use of electronic methods of operation, and elimination of redundant functions; and
   - *Employee Fringe Benefit Rate*—The pro forma was modeled using a 25% rate, which should be consistent with comparable practices in the community.

The following table highlights selected performance indicators under the current set of assumptions.

Selected Operating Indicators

Initial Capital Investment	$ 1,775,763	
Capital Investment—End of Month 12	$ 2,301,706	
Greatest Working Capital Exposure	$ 787,521	—Month 21
Positive Cash Flow Begins	Year 2	—Month 22
Return on Invested Capital Begins	Year 2	—Month 21

Anytown Medical Center: Primary Care Practice and Urgent Care Center Feasibility Study Continued

OPERATING ASSUMPTIONS

Overview

The following initial assumptions are used in the development of an operating pro forma for a planned Primary Care Practice and Urgent Care Center to be located in Anytown County by Anytown Medical Center. The categories of items for discussion include Income Assumptions and Operating Expense Assumptions.

1.0 Income Assumptions

1.1 Revenue amounts have been estimated based on income estimates from similar practices and based on Medical Group Management Association (MGMA) median productivity for each specialty. Please review the detail assumptions attached to the pro forma statements at the end of this report.

1.2 *Charges—Professional Fees* are estimated at $1,515,142 for Year 1 increasing with the maturation of new practices and addition of new physicians. The following table indicates the provider complement for the planned practice and urgent care center.

Provider Complement	Year 1	Year 2+
Internal Medicine	2	2
Family Practice	1	1
OB/GYN	1	2
Pediatrics	0	1
Urgent Care Physician	1	1
Extender (PA)	1	1
Total Provider FTE	**6.0**	**8.0**

Please refer to the attached "Income Assumptions" for the provider-specific ramp-up rates and revenue projections. It is presumed that the existing providers will be at the MGMA median by the end of Year 1. All revenue is projected to increase 4% annually once a full practice is attained. Full practice is defined as the median production from MGMA. Note also that this category excludes ancillary charges.

1.3 *Charges—Ancillary and Technical* are estimated at 16% of revenue. It is estimated that a CLIA moderate laboratory will be used on site, with mail out to reference labs as necessary. Routine radiography is planned. Similar practices have reported higher amounts; however, conservative planning is used.

1.4 *Total Adjustments* are estimated at 20% of revenue. This is an estimate of the best practices of private medical groups when billing allowable charges. IRC section 501(c)(3) allows for the exempt organization to carry on it business in a financially viable manner. To support a greater

Anytown Medical Center: Primary Care Practice and Urgent Care Center Feasibility Study Continued

contractual adjustment would prevent the project from being financially feasible on its own merit.

2.0 *Provider Expenses*

    2.1 *Direct Compensation—Providers* are based on salary rates provided by AMC in the following table. Salary rates increase 4% annually for modeling purposes. It should be noted that straight salary is not the recommended means for provider compensation. AMC is at significant risk if the compensation model used for the providers does not place them at risk for their targeted levels of production. HSG strongly recommends the use of a structured compensation and incentive model that ties the salary draw and periodic incentive payments to specific income targets. Additional incentive is then based on production that exceeds targets as well as other value-added physician services.

Provider Specialty	Year 1	Year 2	Year 3	Year 4	Year 5
Family Practice	$120,000	$ 124,800	$ 129,792	$ 134,984	$ 140,383
Internal Medicine	$120,000	$ 124,800	$ 129,792	$ 134,984	$ 140,383
Internal Medicine	$120,000	$ 124,800	$ 129,792	$ 134,984	$ 140,383
Urgent Care Center Physician	$120,000	$ 124,800	$ 129,792	$ 134,984	$ 140,383
OB/GYN # 1	$200,000	$ 208,000	$ 216,320	$ 224,973	$ 233,972
OB/GYN # 2	—	$ 208,000	$ 216,320	$ 224,973	$ 233,972
Pediatrics	—	$ 120,000	$ 124,800	$ 129,792	$ 134,984
Extender (PA is modeled)	$ 50,000	$ 52,000	$54,080	$ 56,243	$ 58,493
FTE Provider Complement	6.0	8.0	8.0	8.0	8.0
Total Direct Compensation	**$730,000**	**$1,087,200**	**$1,130,688**	**$1,175,916**	**$1,222,952**

    2.2 Provider Benefits are estimated at 25% of direct compensation. Additional benefits, such as continuing medical education (CME) and journals, are carried in operating expenses.

    2.3 *Malpractice Insurance* is estimated at $34,000 in Year 1, increasing to $49,400 in Year 2, then increasing 5% annually.

3.0 *Operating Expenses*

    3.1 All expenses increase 3% annually unless otherwise indicated.

    3.2 *Support Staff Salaries* are based on estimates of Anytown Medical Center's current personnel management system. The following tables indicate the staffing complement during Years 1-3. All salary rates increase 4% annually.

Anytown Medical Center: Primary Care Practice and Urgent Care Center Feasibility Study Continued

Support Staff Salaries	Hourly	YEAR 1 Salary	FTE	Total	YEAR 2 Salary	FTE	Total	YEAR 3 Salary	FTE	Total
Office Manager		35,000	1.0	35,000	36,400	1.0	36,400	37,856	1.0	37,856
Registered Nurse	$ 14.00	29,120	2.0	58,240	30,285	2.0	60,570	31,496	2.0	62,992
Laboratory/Radiology Techs	$ 8.50	17,680	3.0	53,040	18,387	3.0	55,162	19,123	4.0	76,491
Medical Office Assistant	$ 9.00	18,720	4.0	74,880	19,469	6.0	116,813	20,248	7.0	141,733
Ultrasound Technician	$ 9.50	19,760	0.0	—	20,550	0.5	10,275	21,372	0.5	10,686
Insurance/Billing Supervisor	$ 10.50	21,840	1.0	21,840	22,714	1.0	22,714	23,622	1.0	23,622
Insurance/Billing	$ 8.50	17,680	2.5	44,200	18,387	4.0	73,549	19,123	4.0	76,491
Receptionist/Medical Records	$ 7.50	15,600	3.5	54,600	16,224	4.0	64,896	16,873	4.0	67,492
Transcriptionist	$ 10.00	20,800	2	41,600	21,632	3	64,896	22,497	3	67,492
Total			19.0	383,400		24.5	505,274		26.5	564,855
Benefits at 25%				95,850			126,318			141,214
	Total FTE		19.0	479,250		24.5	631,592		26.5	706,068
MGMA Median Total FTE Support Staff per MD (Multispecialty—PC):		3.83								
MGMA 25th %ile Total FTE Support Staff per MD (Multispecialty—PC):		2.75								
Total Number of Providers:			6.0			8.0			8.0	
MGMA # Staff—Median Calculated:			22.98			30.64			30.64	
MGMA # Staff—25th %ile Calculated:			16.5			22			22	

Anytown Medical Center: Primary Care Practice and Urgent Care Center Feasibility Study Continued

3.3   *Staff Benefits* are estimated at 25% of salaries.

3.4   *Repairs and Maintenance* is estimated at $15,000 in Year 1, increasing 3% annually.

3.5   *Office Supplies and Services* are estimated at 2.0% of net revenue for a Year 1 estimate of $28,121.

3.6   *Telephone and Utilities* are estimated at $20,000 in Year 1, increasing 3% annually.

3.7   *Travel, Dues and Subscriptions* are estimated at $4,000 per physician and $2,000 for the Extender, increasing 3% annually.

3.8   *Clinical and Laboratory Supplies* include amounts for outside lab fees as well as in-house needs. Expenses are estimated at 7.0% of revenues for a Year 1 estimate of $98,424.

3.9   *Business Insurance* provides coverage for fire, theft and vandalism estimated at $2,000, increasing 3% annually.

3.10   *Promotion and Marketing* is estimated at $30,000 for Year 1, $20,000 for Year 2, and $15,000 for Year 3 to reflect an aggressive campaign to support the one-year new practice ramp-ups. Expenses increase 3% annually thereafter.

3.11   *Accounting and Legal Fees* are estimated at $6,000 for Year 1, increasing 3% annually.

3.12   *All Other Expenses* include amounts for real estate taxes and other operating expenses not included elsewhere, estimated at $50,000 for Year 1, increasing 10% in Year 2, then 3% annually.

4.0   Nonoperating Expenses

    4.1   *Depreciation* is based on GAAP straight line of 30 years on the building costs and 7 years on all equipment. Please refer to the Start-up Equipment List for a detailed breakdown of depreciation.

    4.2   *Interest* is carried at 6% under the assumption of financing from hospital reserves. Financing on construction costs is modeled over 30 years and all other start-up costs over 12 years.

Anytown Medical Center: Primary Care Practice and Urgent Care Center Feasibility Study Concluded

5.0 Cash Flow Statement

    5.1 *Principal Reductions* are based on financing assumptions under Interest above.

    5.2 *Capital Expenditures* are estimated at $5,000 annually based on the large amount of new equipment and funded depreciation account.

    5.3 *Funded Depreciation* is carried at 100%.

    5.4 *Cash Increase (Decrease)* reflects ultimate cash flow from all activities.

Financial Analysis: Anytown Medical Center—Multispecialty Primary Care
Start-Up Feasibility

Revenue	Sep-98 Month 12	Sep-99 Month 24	Sep-00 Month 36	Sep-01 Month 48
Net Patient Revenue	**1,406,051**	**2,437,255**	**3,028,446**	**3,149,584**
Provider Expenses				
Direct Compensation—Providers	730,000	1,087,200	1,130,688	1,175,916
Provider Benefits	182,500	271,800	282,672	293,979
Malpractice Insurance	34,000	49,400	51,870	54,464
Subtotal	946,500	1,408,400	1,465,230	1,524,358
Expenses as % of Net Revenue	67%	58%	48%	48%
Operating Expenses				
Support Staff Salaries	383,400	505,274	564,855	581,800
Staff Benefits	95,850	126,318	141,214	145,450
Repairs and Maintenance	15,000	15,450	15,914	16,391
Office Supplies and Services	28,121	48,745	60,569	62,992
Telephone and Utilities	20,000	20,600	21,218	21,855
Travel, Dues and Subscriptions	18,500	23,000	23,690	24,401
Clinical and Laboratory Supplies	98,424	170,608	211,991	220,471
Business Insurance	2,000	2,060	2,122	2,185
Promotion and Marketing	30,000	20,000	15,000	15,450
Accounting and Legal Fees	6,000	6,180	6,365	6,556
All Other Expenses	50,000	55,000	56,650	58,350
Subtotal	747,295	993,235	1,119,587	1,155,901
Expenses as % of Net Revenue	53%	41%	37%	37%
Total Operating Expenses	1,693,795	2,401,635	2,584,817	2,680,258
Contribution Margin	**(287,743)**	**35,620**	**443,629**	**469,326**
Contribution Margin %	−20%	1%	15%	15%
Non-Operating Expenses				
Depreciation	83,174	85,051	85,765	86,479
Interest	106,546	108,420	105,355	102,107
Total All Expenses	**1,883,515**	**2,595,106**	**2,775,938**	**2,868,845**
Net Income (Loss)	**(477,463)**	**(157,851)**	**252,509**	**280,740**
Cash Flow—Sources of Cash				
Net Income (Loss)	(477,463)	(157,851)	252,509	280,740
Add: Depreciation	83,174	85,051	85,765	86,479
Total Sources of Cash	**(394,289)**	**(72,800)**	**338,274**	**367,219**
Cash Flow—Uses of Cash				
Principal Reductions	43,480	51,079	54,144	57,393
Capital Expenditures	5,000	5,000	5,000	5,000
Funded Depreciation	83,174	85,051	85,765	86,479
Total Uses of Cash	**131,654**	**141,130**	**144,909**	**148,872**
Cash Increase (Decrease)	**(525,943)**	**(213,930)**	**193,365**	**218,347**
Cumulative Increase (Decrease)	(525,943)	(739,873)	(546,508)	(328,161)

Sep-02 Month 60	Sep-03 Month 72	Sep-04 Month 84	Sep-05 Month 96	Sep-06 Month 108	Sep-07 Month 120
3,275,568	**3,406,590**	**3,542,854**	**3,684,568**	**3,831,951**	**3,985,229**
1,222,952	1,271,870	1,322,745	1,375,655	1,430,681	1,487,908
305,738	317,968	330,686	343,914	357,670	371,977
57,187	60,046	63,048	66,201	69,511	72,986
1,585,877	1,649,884	1,716,480	1,785,769	1,857,862	1,932,872
48%	48%	48%	48%	48%	49%
599,254	623,225	648,154	674,080	701,043	729,085
149,814	155,806	162,038	168,520	175,261	182,271
16,883	17,389	17,911	18,448	19,002	19,572
65,511	68,132	70,857	73,691	76,639	79,705
22,510	23,185	23,881	24,597	25,335	26,095
25,133	25,887	26,663	27,463	28,287	29,136
229,290	238,461	248,000	257,920	268,237	278,966
2,251	2,319	2,388	2,460	2,534	2,610
15,914	16,391	16,883	17,389	17,911	18,448
6,753	6,956	7,164	7,379	7,601	7,829
60,100	61,903	63,760	65,673	67,643	69,672
1,193,412	1,239,653	1,287,699	1,337,621	1,389,491	1,443,388
36%	36%	36%	36%	36%	36%
2,779,289	2,889,537	3,004,179	3,123,390	3,247,353	3,376,259
496,279	**517,053**	**538,675**	**561,178**	**584,598**	**608,970**
15%	15%	15%	15%	15%	15%
87,194	78,622	79,336	51,758	49,881	49,881
98,663	95,013	91,144	87,043	82,695	78,087
2,965,146	**3,063,172**	**3,174,659**	**3,262,190**	**3,379,929**	**3,504,227**
310,422	**343,418**	**368,195**	**422,378**	**452,021**	**481,002**
310,422	343,418	368,195	422,378	452,021	481,002
87,194	78,622	79,336	51,758	49,881	49,881
397,615	422,040	447,531	474,136	501,902	530,883
60,836	64,486	68,356	72,457	76,804	81,413
5,000	5,000	5,000	5,000	5,000	5,000
87,194	78,622	79,336	51,758	49,881	49,881
153,030	148,108	152,692	129,214	131,685	136,294
244,586	**273,932**	**294,839**	**344,921**	**370,217**	**394,589**
(83,576)	190,356	485,196	830,117	1,200,334	1,594,923

Income Assumptions

Provider Complement	Year 1	Year 2+
Internal Medicine	2	2
Family Practice	1	1
OB/GYN	1	2
Pediatrics	0	1
Urgent Care Physician	1	1
Extender (PA)	1	1
Total Provider FTE	6.0	8.0

YEAR 1—Months 1–12	Month 1	Month 2	Month 3	Month 4
Charges—IM Practice # 1	50,000	50,000	50,000	55,000
Charges—Urgent Care Physician	3,000	6,000	9,000	12,000
Charges—Dr. New OB/GYN # 1	3,000	6,000	9,000	12,000
Charges—Dr. New FP	3,000	6,000	9,000	12,000
Charges—Existing Extender	11,000	12,000	14,000	15,000
Total Professional Fees	70,000	80,000	91,000	106,000
Charges—Ancillary & Technical estimated at 16% of charges	11,200	12,800	14,560	16,960
Total Adjustments estimated at 20% of total	(16,240)	(18,560)	(21,112)	(24,592)
Total Net Revenue	**64,960**	**74,240**	**84,448**	**98,368**
Total Year One Revenue	**1,406,051**	**All charges based on allowables**		

YEAR 2—Months 13–24	Month 13	Month 14	Month 15	Month 16
Charges—Dr. New Peds	2,000	4,000	6,000	8,000
Charges—Urgent Care Physician	26,567	26,567	26,567	26,567
Charges—IM Practice # 1	53,848	53,848	53,848	53,848
Charges—Dr. New OB/GYN # 1	54,778	54,778	54,778	54,778
Charges—Dr. New OB/GYN # 2	3,000	6,000	9,000	12,000
Charges—Dr. New FP	26,567	26,567	26,567	26,567
Charges—Existing Extender	16,227	16,227	16,227	16,227
Total Professional Fees	182,987	187,987	192,987	197,987
Charges—Ancillary & Technical estimated at 16% of charges	29,278	30,078	30,878	31,678
Total Adjustments estimated at 20% of total	(42,453)	(43,613)	(44,773)	(45,933)
Total Net Revenue	**169,812**	**174,452**	**179,092**	**183,732**
Total Year Two Revenue	**2,437,255**	**All charges based on allowables**		

Estimated Gross Charges based on MGMA Median:

FP:	$306,544	**IM:**	$310,663
OB/GYN:	$632,055	**PEDS:**	$331,453
Extender (PA):	$187,231		

Source: MGMA Physician Compensation and Production Survey: 1997 Report—Family Practice, Physician Extender and A&T Excluded (Tables 15, 77) Charges inflated 4% per year to 9/98 also MGMA Cost Survey: 1997 Report
(Note: These are very good data sources—Call MGMA at (303) 397-1822 to purchase.)

Estimated Ramp-Up to Median for New Providers: 12 months

Month 5	Month 6	Month 7	Month 8	Month 9	Month 10	Month 11	Month 12
55,000	55,000	55,000	55,000	55,000	55,000	55,000	51,777
14,000	16,000	18,000	20,000	22,000	24,000	25,000	25,545
15,000	20,000	26,000	33,000	40,000	45,000	50,000	52,671
14,000	16,000	18,000	20,000	22,000	24,000	25,000	25,545
15,000	15,000	15,000	15,000	15,000	15,000	15,000	15,603
113,000	122,000	132,000	143,000	154,000	163,000	170,000	171,142
18,080	19,520	21,120	22,880	24,640	26,080	27,200	27,383
(26,216)	(28,304)	(30,624)	(33,176)	(35,728)	(37,816)	(39,440)	(39,705)
104,864	**113,216**	**122,496**	**132,704**	**142,912**	**151,264**	**157,760**	**158,819**

Month 17	Month 18	Month 19	Month 20	Month 21	Month 22	Month 23	Month 24
10,000	12,000	15,000	18,000	20,000	25,000	28,000	28,726
26,567	26,567	26,567	26,567	26,567	26,567	26,567	26,567
53,848	53,848	53,848	53,848	53,848	53,848	53,848	53,848
54,778	54,778	54,778	54,778	54,778	54,778	54,778	54,778
15,000	20,000	26,000	33,000	40,000	45,000	50,000	54,778
26,567	26,567	26,567	26,567	26,567	26,567	26,567	26,567
16,227	16,227	16,227	16,227	16,227	16,227	16,227	16,227
202,987	209,987	218,987	228,987	237,987	247,987	255,987	261,491
32,478	33,598	35,038	36,638	38,078	39,678	40,958	41,839
(47,093)	(48,717)	(50,805)	(53,125)	(55,213)	(57,533)	(59,389)	(60,666)
188,372	**194,868**	**203,220**	**212,500**	**220,852**	**230,132**	**237,556**	**242,664**

YEAR 3—Months 25–36	Month 25	Month 26	Month 27	Month 28
Charges—Dr. New Peds	29,875	29,875	29,875	29,875
Charges—Urgent Care Physician	27,630	27,630	27,630	27,630
Charges—IM Practice # 1	56,002	56,002	56,002	56,002
Charges—Dr. New OB/GYN # 1	56,969	56,969	56,969	56,969
Charges—Dr. New OB/GYN # 2	56,969	56,969	56,969	56,969
Charges—Dr. New FP	27,630	27,630	27,630	27,630
Charges—Existing Extender	16,876	16,876	16,876	16,876
Total Professional Fees	271,951	271,951	271,951	271,951
Charges—Ancillary & Technical estimated at 16% of charges	43,512	43,512	43,512	43,512
Total Adjustments estimated at 20% of total	(63,093)	(63,093)	(63,093)	(63,093)
Total Net Revenue	**252,371**	**252,371**	**252,371**	**252,371**
Total Year Three Revenue	**3,028,446**	**All charges based on allowables**		

Operating Expense Assumptions

Direct Compensation—Providers	Should be Based on a Stark-Compliant Production-Based Compensation and Incentive Plan				
Provider Specialty	**Year 1**	**Year 2**	**Year 3**	**Year 4**	**Year 5**
Family Practice	$120,000	$ 124,800	$ 129,792	$ 134,984	$ 140,383
Internal Medicine	$120,000	$ 124,800	$ 129,792	$ 134,984	$ 140,383
Internal Medicine	$120,000	$ 124,800	$ 129,792	$ 134,984	$ 140,383
Urgent Care Center Physician	$120,000	$ 124,800	$ 129,792	$ 134,984	$ 140,383
OB/GYN # 1	$200,000	$ 208,000	$ 216,320	$ 224,973	$ 233,972
OB/GYN # 2	—	$ 208,000	$ 216,320	$ 224,973	$ 233,972
Pediatrics	—	$ 120,000	$ 124,800	$ 129,792	$ 134,984
Extender (PA is modeled)	$ 50,000	$ 52,000	$ 54,080	$ 56,243	$ 58,493
FTE Provider Complement	6.0	8.0	8.0	8.0	8.0
Total Direct Compensation	**$730,000**	**$1,087,200**	**$1,130,688**	**$1,175,916**	**$1,222,952**
Estimated Malpractice Premium	**$ 34,000**	**$ 49,400**	**$ 51,870**	**$ 54,464**	**$ 57,187**

Month 29	Month 30	Month 31	Month 32	Month 33	Month 34	Month 35	Month 36
29,875	29,875	29,875	29,875	29,875	29,875	29,875	29,875
27,630	27,630	27,630	27,630	27,630	27,630	27,630	27,630
56,002	56,002	56,002	56,002	56,002	56,002	56,002	56,002
56,969	56,969	56,969	56,969	56,969	56,969	56,969	56,969
56,969	56,969	56,969	56,969	56,969	56,969	56,969	56,969
27,630	27,630	27,630	27,630	27,630	27,630	27,630	27,630
16,876	16,876	16,876	16,876	16,876	16,876	16,876	16,876
271,951	271,951	271,951	271,951	271,951	271,951	271,951	271,951
43,512	43,512	43,512	43,512	43,512	43,512	43,512	43,512
(63,093)	(63,093)	(63,093)	(63,093)	(63,093)	(63,093)	(63,093)	(63,093)
252,371	**252,371**	**252,371**	**252,371**	**252,371**	**252,371**	**252,371**	**252,371**

Support Staff Salaries

	Hourly	YEAR 1 Salary	FTE	Total
Office Manager		35,000	1.0	35,000
Registered Nurse	$ 14.00	29,120	2.0	58,240
Laboratory/Radiology Techs	$ 8.50	17,680	3.0	53,040
Medical Office Assistant	$ 9.00	18,720	4.0	74,880
Ultrasound Technician	$ 9.50	19,760	0.0	—
Insurance/Billing Supervisor	$ 10.50	21,840	1.0	21,840
Insurance/Billing	$ 8.50	17,680	2.5	44,200
Receptionist/Medical Records	$ 7.50	15,600	3.5	54,600
Transcriptionist	$ 10.00	20,800	2	41,600
Total				383,400
Benefits at	**25%**			95,850
		Total FTE	**19.0**	**479,250**

MGMA Median Total FTE Support Staff per MD (Multispecialty—PC):	3.83
MGMA 25th %ile Total FTE Support Staff per MD (Multispecialty—PC):	2.75
Total Number of Providers:	6.0
MGMA # Staff—Median Calculated:	22.98
MGMA # Staff—25th %ile Calculated:	16.5

FINANCING AND START-UP COSTS

Pre-Opening Costs

MD Recruitment	$30,000	includes $10,000 for relocation
Salaries & Benefits	$59,906	1 1/2 months
Consulting	$20,000	See text
Construction Interest	$71,141	over 9 months
Property Taxes Payable	$956	at $0.60 per $1,000
Furniture, Fixtures, Equip	$268,760	See detail
Total Pre-Opening Costs	**$450,763**	
Site Development	$50,000	@ $25,000 per acre
Construction Costs	$1,275,000	15,000 sq. ft. @ $85
Total Construction	**$1,325,000**	
Total Cash Price Start-up:	**$1,775,763**	(Construction + Pre-Opening)

YEAR 2			YEAR 3		
Salary	**FTE**	**Total**	**Salary**	**FTE**	**Total**
36,400	1.0	36,400	37,856	1.0	37,856
30,285	2.0	60,570	31,496	2.0	62,992
18,387	3.0	55,162	19,123	4.0	76,491
19,469	6.0	116,813	20,248	7.0	141,733
20,550	0.5	10,275	21,372	0.5	10,686
22,714	1.0	22,714	23,622	1.0	23,622
18,387	4.0	73,549	19,123	4.0	76,491
16,224	4.0	64,896	16,873	4.0	67,492
21,632	3	64,896	22,497	3	67,492
		505,274			564,855
		126,318			141,214
	24.5	**631,592**		**26.5**	**706,068**

	8.0			8.0	
	30.64			30.64	
	22			22	

Depreciation Base—GAAP/SL

	Year 1	Years 2–5	Years 6–7	Year 8	Years 9+
Equipment:	$38,293	$40,170	$30,170	$1,877	$0
Building:	$44,167	$44,167	$44,167	$44,167	$44,167
Capital Exp:	$714	$714	$714	$714	$714
Total:	$83,174	$85,051	$78,622	$51,758	$49,881
Year 3/7	$85,765	$79,336			
Year 4	$86,479				
Year 5	$87,194				

Financing Terms: Total Cash Price Startup financed 100% from reserves at 6.0%
Construction over 30 years, **Pre-Opening Costs** over 12 years
Working Capital financed at 0% as needed

	Year 1		Year 2
Annual Construction Pmt:	$96,260	Additional Year 2 Equipment:	$18,000
Year 1 Pre-Opening Pmt:	$53,766	Additional Year 2 Expenses:	$30,000
Total Payment Year 1:	**$150,026**	MD Recruitment @ $20,000 and Relocation @ $10,000	

Financing Construction— 30 years @ 6%	Year 1	Year 2	Year 3	Year 4	Year 5	Year 6	Year 7	Year 8	Year 9	Year 10
Principal:	$16,760	$17,765	$18,831	$19,961	$21,159	$22,428	$23,774	$25,201	$26,713	$28,315
Interest:	$79,500	$78,494	$77,428	$76,299	$75,101	$73,831	$72,486	$71,059	$69,547	$67,944
All Other— 12 years @ 6%	**Year 1**	**Year 2**	**Year 3**	**Year 4**	**Year 5**	**Year 6**	**Year 7**	**Year 8**	**Year 9**	**Year 10**
Principal:	$26,720	$33,314	$35,313	$37,431	$39,677	$42,058	$44,581	$47,256	$50,092	$53,097
Interest:	$27,046	$29,926	$27,927	$25,808	$23,562	$21,182	$18,658	$15,983	$13,148	$10,142
Total Financing	**Year 1**	**Year 2**	**Year 3**	**Year 4**	**Year 5**	**Year 6**	**Year 7**	**Year 8**	**Year 9**	**Year 10**
Total Principal	$43,480	$51,079	$54,144	$57,393	$60,836	$64,486	$68,356	$72,457	$76,804	$81,413
Total Interest	$106,546	$108,420	$105,355	$102,107	$98,663	$95,013	$91,144	$87,043	$82,695	$78,087
Total Payment	**$150,026**	**$159,499**	**$159,499**	**$159,499**	**$159,499**	**$159,499**	**$159,499**	**$159,499**	**$159,499**	**$159,499**

Multispecialty Primary Care Practice Start-up Equipment List
Recommended Source: Anytown Medical Supply

Assumptions:
1. Built-in cabinetry in exam rooms.
2. Building uses central hallway with offices on each side, laboratory and administrative are centralized.
3. OB/GYN and Urgent Care—FP are on one side in Year 1 w/IM on the other side. Year 2 is OB/GYN and Peds.
4. Furniture from existing IM practice is used; essentially one new office is being furnished.
5. Providers have 2 exam rooms each; one procedure room each on side doubles as an exam room; presumes the existing practice does not have a procedure room.
6. OB/GYN exam rooms have toilets, all others have sinks only.
7. Six exam rooms furnished Year 1—Urgent Care, FP, OB/GYN.
8. Four exam rooms furnished Year 2—OB/GYN, Peds.
9. All equipment purchased—By amortizing over 12 years @ 6%, the net effect is comparable to lease/purchase.

	Common	
	Lab	IM
OB/GYN		
		FP
	Reception	
Peds	Scheduling	Urgent Care

Example

YEAR 1   3 Exam Rooms and 2 Procedure Rooms Furnished

EXAM ROOMS

Item	Quantity	Price	Total	Recovery Period	Model or Equivalent
Examination Table	4	649	2,596	7	Ritter #104
Examination Light	4	90	360	7	Ritter #157 table mounted
Power Table	2	4,500	9,000	7	DMI #250
Stool, physicians	6	175	1,050	7	Exam stool on casters
Side Chair	4	50	200	7	No side chair in exam/procedure room
Surgical Lamp	2	950	1,900	7	Burton reflector lamp for procedure room
Halogen Diagnostic Set	6	185	1,110	7	Welch Allyn Ophthalmoscope & Otoscope handpieces
Wall Transformer Unit	6	260	1,560	7	Welch Allyn power source for diagnostic set
Wall Blood Pressure Unit	7	75	525	7	Welch Allyn–1 extra needed for office triage area
Mayo Stand	2	325	650	7	Stand on casters with tray for procedure room
Hyfrecator Plus	2	800	1,600	7	
Sharps Container	8	31	248	—	SAGE–wall mounted w/ glove holder
Misc. Small Equipment	—	—	3,000		
TOTAL EXAM ROOMS			**$23,799**		

Depreciable Basis Total 7 Year Assets:	**$20,551**	**Depreciation per Year:**	**$2,936**

YEAR 1

GENERAL MEDICAL EQUIPMENT

Item	Quantity	Price	Total	Recovery Period	Model or Equivalent
Defibrillator	1	6,100	6,100	7	Burdick Medic 5
Base Station	1	850	850	7	Craftsman tool cabinet
ECG	1	3,600	3,600	7	Burdick E 350i
Spirometer	1	925	925	7	
Suction Pump	1	350	350	7	
Microscope	1	1,450	1,450	7	
Autoclave	1	1,300	1,300	7	Ritter M7 Speed Clave
Thermometer	4	260	1,040	7	Thermascan
Chemistry Analyzer	1	12,000	12,000	7	Becton Dickenson QBC Autoread or (more expensive) Coulter Counter MD II with automated disk
Pulse Oximeter	1	1,300	1,300	7	Nellcor N-100
Audiometer	1	2,126	2,126	7	Monitor Systems MI-S000B or Welch Allyn Auto Tymp TM 262 (more expensive)
Intoxilizer	1	1,825	1,825	7	
Incubator	1	2,500	2,500	7	
Ultrasound Unit	1	32,000	32,000	7	Ultramark IV or SC200 w/ 2 dual frequency probes, cart and printer
Colposcope	1	8,000	8,000	7	Prices range from $5,000–$10,000. Estimate: Zeiss Colposcope Plus/ZMS-501
Cryotherapy Unit	1	1,695	1,695	7	Leisegang LM-900 with 4 tips, cart, 20lb. N20 filled, case
Electrocautery Unit	1	3,500	3,500	7	LOOP unit. ZSI Sabre 180 w/smoke evacuator, electrodes, Graves speculum
Antepartum Monitor	1	4,695	4,695	7	ALM-210
Fetal Heart Detector	1	1,190	1,190	7	Leisegang LM-120
Cervical Biopsy Forceps	1	300	300	7	
Fetal Doppler	1	550	550	7	
Cervical Biopsy Set	2	300	600	7	One set needed for each exam room
Tall Stool for Lab	3	175	525	7	
Scale—Adult	2	195	390	7	Detecto
Scale—Pediatric	2	190	380	7	Detecto Doctors Infant Scale
Large Refrigerator	2	600	1,200	7	For clinical use only
Linen Containers	4	125	500	7	
Lab Drawing Table	2	325	650	7	Table with stand and adjustable arms
Trash Receptacles	—	—	2,000	7	Includes fireproof and biohazard trash containers
Reference Books	—	—	2,000	—	PDR, etc.
Misc. Surg. Instruments	—	—	3,000	—	For OB/GYN practice
Misc. Small Equipment	—	—	7,500	—	Includes small pediatrics equipment items

TOTAL GENERAL EQUIPMENT			**$106,041**		
Depreciable Basis Total 7 Year Assets:			**$93,541**		**Depreciation per Year: $13,363**

YEAR 1

OFFICE FURNISHINGS				Recovery	
Item	Quantity	Price	Total	Period	Model or Equivalent
Computer Hardware	—	—	30,000	5	Server, 10 workstations, modem, tape & UPS backup, concentrator, 2 laser and 5 dot matrix printers, cables
Software	—	—	20,000	5	TBD
Shredder	2	80	160	—	Fellows Powershred PS60
Security System	1	1,000	1,000	7	First Alert
Phone System	1	8,000	8,000	7	Prostar or Toshiba DK16 (plus upgrade)
File System—Records	—	—	30,000	7	Fixed 8-shelf units and 2-sided movable units
Transcription System	2	600	1,200	7	2 Base Stations plus 3 hand held units
Fax Machine	1	500	500	7	Presuming the existing office has one
TV/VCR Combo Unit	—	—	550	7	For patient education; presuming the existing office has one
Waiting Room Chairs	20	325	6,500	7	For one waiting room
Waiting Room Tables	—	—	1,500	7	Estimated for side tables or console
Office Decorating	—	—	4,000	7	Prints (15) @ $150 plus lamps, etc.—for new office
Office Task Chairs	12	280	3,360	7	
Hallway Furniture	—	—	3,000	7	Chairs (4) @ $325, plus misc. Tables, lamps
Additional Side Chairs	4	50	200	7	
Break Room Table/Chairs	—	—	600	7	
Safe	1	200	200	7	Sentry #6250 Floor Safe
Furniture—Provider Office	3	3,250	9,750	7	Laminate desk, credenza, desk chair, 2 guest chairs, bookcase, 2 drawer file cabinet, lamp, desk accessories
Office Furniture	—	—	12,000	7	Highly variable estimate. Includes all desking and file storage for space without built-in desking.
Large Refrigerator	1	600	600	7	For break room
Children's Play Area	—	—	1,000	7	Small furniture, toys, books, etc.
Break Room Accessories	—	—	300	—	Dishware, microwave, etc.
Other Office	—	—	4,500	—	Contingency

TOTAL OFFICE FURNISHINGS	**$138,920**	
Depreciable Basis Total 5 Year Assets:	**$50,000**	**Depreciation per Year:** **$10,000**
Depreciable Basis Total 7 Year Assets:	**$83,960**	**Depreciation per Year:** **$11,994**
TOTAL ALL YEAR 1 EQUIPMENT & FURNISHINGS	**$268,760**	

YEAR 2   4 Exam Rooms Furnished

Item	Quantity	Price	Total	Recovery Period	Model or Equivalent
Examination Table	4	649	2,596	7	Ritter #104
Examination Light	4	90	360	7	Ritter #157 table mounted
Stool, physicians	4	175	700	7	
Side Chair	4	50	200	7	
Halogen Diagnostic Set	4	185	740	7	Welch Allyn Ophthalmoscope & Otoscope handpieces
Wall Transformer Unit	4	260	1,040	7	Welch Allyn power source for diagnostic set
Wall Blood Pressure Unit	4	75	300	7	Welch Allyn—1 extra needed for triage area
Dictaphone	2	350	700	7	Hand held units for 3 new providers
Furniture—Provider Office	2	3,250	6,500	7	Laminate desk, credenza, desk chair, 2 guest chairs, bookcase, 2 drawer file cabinet, lamp, desk accessories
Fetal Hear Detector	1	1,190	1,190	7	Leisegang LM-120
Fetal Doppler	1	550	550	7	
Sharps Container	4	31	124	—	SAGE—wall mounted w/glove holder
Misc. Small Equipment	—	—	2,000		
Misc. Other Office	—	—	1,000		
TOTAL YEAR TWO EQUIPMENT			**$18,000**		

Depreciable Basis Total 7 Year Assets: **$13,136**   Depreciation per Year: **$1,877**

Annual Depreciation on Equipment and Furnishings Year 1: $38,293
Annual Depreciation on Equipment and Furnishings Years 2–5: $40,170
Annual Depreciation on Equipment and Furnishings Years 6–7: $30,170
Annual Depreciation on Equipment and Furnishings Year 8: $ 1,877

AMC Multispecialty Practice Start-up
Revenue and Expense Profile

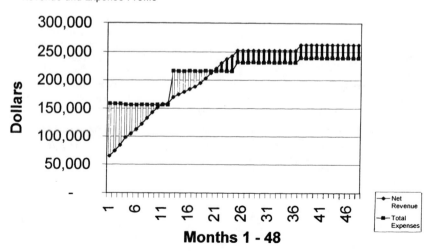

Months 1 - 48

AMC Multispecialty Practice Start-up
Cash Flow

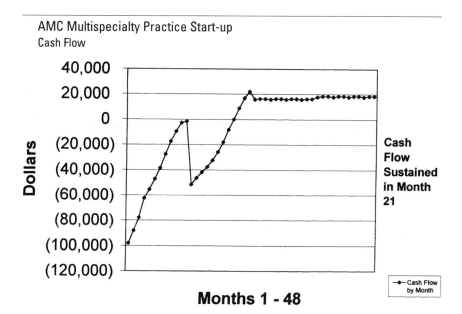

Months 1 - 48

AMC Multispecialty Practice Start-up
Working Capital

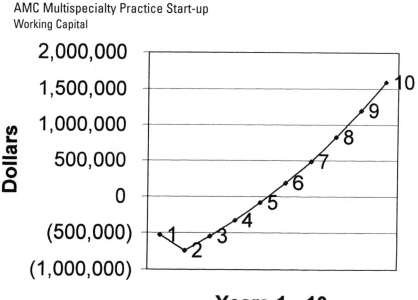

Years 1 - 10

Financial Analysis: Anytown Medical Center—Multispecialty Primary Care
Start-up Feasibility
Page 1

Year 1	Month 1	Month 2	Month 3	Month 4	Month 5	Month 6
Patient Revenue						
Charges—Professional Fees	70,000	80,000	91,000	106,000	113,000	122,000
Charges—Ancillary & Technical	11,200	12,800	14,560	16,960	18,080	19,520
Total Adjustments	(16,240)	(18,560)	(21,112)	(24,592)	(26,216)	(28,304)
Net Patient Revenue	**64,960**	**74,240**	**84,448**	**98,368**	**104,864**	**113,216**
Provider Expenses						
Direct Compensation—Providers	60,833	60,833	60,833	60,833	60,833	60,833
Provider Benefits	15,208	15,208	15,208	15,208	15,208	15,208
Malpractice Insurance	2,833	2,833	2,833	2,833	2,833	2,833
Subtotal	78,875	78,875	78,875	78,875	78,875	78,875
Expenses as % of Net Revenue	121%	106%	93%	80%	75%	70%
Operating Expenses						
Support Staff Salaries	31,950	31,950	31,950	31,950	31,950	31,950
Staff Benefits	7,988	7,988	7,988	7,988	79,88	7,988
Repairs and Maintenance	1,250	1,250	1,250	1,250	1,250	1,250
Office Supplies and Services	2,343	2,343	2,343	2,343	2,343	2,343
Telephone and Utilities	1,667	1,667	1,667	1,667	1,667	1,667
Travel, Dues and Subscriptions	1,542	1,542	1,542	1,542	1,542	1,542
Clinical and Laboratory Supplies	8,202	8,202	8,202	8,202	8,202	8,202
Business Insurance	500	0	0	500	0	0
Promotion and Marketing	4,000	4,000	4,000	2,000	2,000	2,000
Accounting and Legal Fees	500	500	500	500	500	500
All Other Expenses	4,167	4,167	4,67	4,167	4,167	4,167
Subtotal	64,108	63,608	63,608	62,108	61,608	61,608
Expenses as % of Net Revenue	99%	86%	75%	63%	59%	54%
Total Operating Expenses	**142,983**	**142,483**	**142,483**	**140,983**	**140,483**	**140,483**
Contribution Margin	(78,023)	(68,243)	(58,035)	(42,615)	(35,619)	(27,267)
Contribution Margin %	−120%	−92%	−69%	−43%	−34%	−24%
Non-Operating Expenses						
Depreciation	6,931	6,931	6,931	6,931	6,931	6,931
Interest	8,879	8,879	8,879	8,879	8,879	8,879
Total All Expenses	**158,793**	**158,293**	**158,293**	**156,793**	**156,293**	**156,293**
Net Income (Loss)	**(93,833)**	**(84,053)**	**(73,845)**	**(58,425)**	**(51,429)**	**(43,077)**
Cash Flow—Sources of Cash						
Net Income (Loss)	(93,833)	(84,053)	(73,845)	(58,425)	(51,429)	(43,077)
Add: Depreciation	6,931	6,931	6,931	6,931	6,931	6,931
Total Sources of Cash	**(86,902)**	**(77,122)**	**(66,914)**	**(51,494)**	**(44,498)**	**(36,146)**
Cash Flow—Uses of Cash						
Principal Reductions	3,623.31	3,623.31	3,623.31	3,623.31	3,623.31	3,623.31
Capital Expenditures	417	417	417	417	417	417
Funded Depreciation	6,931	6,931	6,931	6,931	6,931	6,931
Total Uses of Cash	**10,971**	**10,971**	**10,971**	**10,971**	**10,971**	**10,971**
Cash Increase (Decrease)	(97,873)	(88,093)	(77,885)	(62,465)	(55,469)	(47,117)
Cumulative Increase (Decrease)	(97,873)	(185,966)	(263,851)	(326,315)	(381,784)	(428,901)

Month 7	Month 8	Month 9	Month 10	Month 11	Month 12	EOY 1	% of Total Revenue	Year 1 Monthly Average
132,000	143,000	154,000	163,000	170,000	171,142	**1,515,142**	86.2%	126,262
21,120	22,880	24,640	26,080	27,200	27,383	**242,423**	13.8%	20,202
(30,624)	(33,176)	(35,728)	(37,816)	(39,440)	(39,705)	**(351,513)**	−20.0%	(29,293)
122,496	**132,704**	**142,912**	**151,264**	**157,760**	**158,819**	**1,406,051**	**100%**	**117,171**
							Percent of Revenue	
60,833	60,833	60,833	60,833	60,833	60,833	**730,000**	51.9%	60,833
15,208	15,208	15,208	15,208	15,208	15,208	**182,500**	13.0%	15,208
2,833	2,833	2,833	2,833	2,833	2,833	**34,000**	2.4%	2,833
78,875	**78,875**	**78,875**	**78,875**	**78,875**	**78,875**	**946,500**	67.3%	**78,875**
64%	59%	55%	52%	50%	50%	**67%**		
31,950	31,950	31,950	31,950	31,950	31,950	**383,400**	27.3%	31,950
7,988	7,988	7,988	7,988	7,988	7,988	**95,850**	6.8%	7,988
1,250	1,250	1,250	1,250	1,250	1,250	**15,000**	1.1%	1,250
2,343	2,343	2,343	2,343	2,343	2,343	**28,121**	2.0%	2,343
1,667	1,667	1,667	1,667	1,667	1,667	**20,000**	1.4%	1,667
1,542	1,542	1,542	1,542	1,542	1,542	**18,500**	1.3%	1,542
8,202	8,202	8,202	8,202	8,202	8,202	**98,424**	7.0%	8,202
500	0	0	500	0	0	**2,000**	0.1%	167
2,000	2,000	2,000	2,000	2,000	2,000	**30,000**	2.1%	2,500
500	500	500	500	500	500	**6,000**	0.4%	500
4,167	4,167	4,167	4,167	4,167	4,167	**50,000**	3.6%	4,167
62,108	**61,608**	**61,608**	**62,108**	**61,608**	**61,608**	**747,295**	53.1%	
51%	46%	43%	41%	39%	39%	**53%**		
140,983	**140,483**	**140,483**	**140,983**	**140,483**	**140,483**	**1,693,795**		
(18,487)	(7,779)	**2,429**	**10,281**	**17,277**	**18,337**	**(287,743)**		
−15%	−6%	2%	7%	11%	12%	**−20%**		
6,931	6,931	6,931	6,931	6,931	6,931	**83,174**	5.9%	
8,879	8,879	8,879	8,879	8,879	8,879	**106,546**	7.6%	
156,793	**156,293**	**156,293**	**156,793**	**156,293**	**156,293**	**1,883,515**	134.0%	
(34,297)	(23,589)	(13,381)	(5,529)	1,467	2,527	**(477,463)**		
(34,297)	(23,589)	(13,381)	(5,529)	1,467	2,527	**(477,463)**		
6,931	6,931	6,931	6,931	6,931	6,931	**83,174**		
(27,366)	(16,658)	(6,450)	**1,402**	**8,398**	**9,458**	**(394,289)**		
3,623.31	3,623.31	3,623.31	3,623.31	3,623.31	3,623.31	**43,480**		
417	417	417	417	417	417	**5,000**		
6,931	6,931	6,931	6,931	6,931	6,931	**83,174**		
10,971	**10,971**	**10,971**	**10,971**	**10,971**	**10,971**	**131,654**		
(38,337)	(27,629)	(17,421)	(9,569)	(2,573)	(1,513)	**(525,943)**		
(467,238)	(494,867)	(512,288)	(521,857)	(524,429)	(525,943)	**(525,943)**		

Financial Analysis: Anytown Medical Center—Multispecialty Primary Care Start-up Feasibility
Page 2

Year 2	Month 13	Month 14	Month 15	Month 16	Month 17	Month 18
Patient Revenue						
Charges—Professional Fees	182,987	187,987	192,987	197,987	202,987	209,987
Charges—Ancillary & Technical	29,278	30,078	30,878	31,678	32,478	33,598
Total Adjustments	(42,453)	(43,613)	(44,773)	(45,933)	(47,093)	(48,717)
Net Patient Revenue	**169,812**	**174,452**	**179,092**	**183,732**	**188,372**	**194,868**
Provider Expenses						
Direct Compensation—Providers	90,600	90,600	90,600	90,600	90,600	90,600
Provider Benefits	22,650	22,650	22,650	22,650	22,650	22,650
Malpractice Insurance	4,117	4,117	4,117	4,117	4117	4,117
Subtotal	117,367	117,367	117,367	117,367	117,367	117,367
Expenses as % of Net Revenue	69%	67%	66%	64%	62%	60%
Operating Expenses						
Support Staff Salaries	42,106	42,106	42,106	42,106	42,106	42,106
Staff Benefits	10,527	10,527	10,527	10,527	10,527	10,527
Repairs and Maintenance	1,288	1,288	1,288	1,288	1,288	1,288
Office Supplies and Services	4,062	4,062	4,062	4,062	4,062	4,062
Telephone and Utilities	1,717	1,717	1,717	1,717	1,717	1,717
Travel, Dues and Subscriptions	1,917	1,917	1,917	1,917	1,917	1,917
Clinical and Laboratory Supplies	14,217	14,217	14,217	14,217	14,217	14,217
Business Insurance	515	0	0	515	0	0
Promotion and Marketing	1,667	1,667	1,667	1,667	1,667	1,667
Accounting and Legal Fees	515	515	515	515	515	515
All Other Expenses	4,583	4,583	4,583	4,583	4,583	4,583
Subtotal	83,113	82,598	82,598	83,113	82,598	82,598
Expenses as % of Net Revenue	49%	47%	46%	45%	44%	42%
Total Operating Expenses	**200,480**	**199,965**	**199,965**	**200,480**	**199,965**	**199,965**
Contribution Margin	(30,667)	(25,512)	(20,872)	(16,747)	(11,592)	(5,096)
Contribution Margin %	−18%	−15%	−12%	−9%	−6%	−3%
Non-Operating Expenses						
Depreciation	7,088	7,088	7,088	7,088	7,088	7,088
Interest	9,035	9,035	9,035	9,035	9,035	9,035
Total All Expenses	**216,602**	**216,087**	**216,087**	**216,602**	**216,087**	**216,087**
Net Income (Loss)	**(46,790)**	**(41,635)**	**(36,995)**	**(32,870)**	**(27,715)**	**(21,219)**
Cash Flow—Sources of Cash						
Net Income (Loss)	(46,790)	(41,635)	(36,995)	(32,870)	(27,715)	(21,219)
Add. Depreciation	7,088	7,088	7,088	7,088	7,088	7,088
Total Sources of Cash	**(39,702)**	**(34,547)**	**(29,907)**	**(25,782)**	**(20,627)**	**(14,131)**
Cash Flow—Uses of Cash						
Principal Reductions	4,256.60	4,256.60	4,256.60	4,256.60	4,256.60	4,256.60
Capital Expenditures	417	417	417	417	417	417
Funded Depreciation	7,088	7,088	7,088	7,088	7,088	7,088
Total Uses of Cash	**11,761**	**11,761**	**11,761**	**11,761**	**11,761**	**11,761**
Cash Increase (Decrease)	(51,463)	(46,308)	(41,668)	(37,543)	(32,388)	(25,892)
Cumulative Increase (Decrease)	(577,406)	(623,714)	(665,382)	(702,925)	(735,314)	(761,206)

	Month 19	Month 20	Month 21	Month 22	Month 23	Month 24	EOY 2	% of Total Revenue	Year 2 Monthly Average
	218,987	228,987	237,987	247,987	255,987	261,491	**2,626,352**	86.2%	218,863
	35,038	36,638	38,078	39,678	40,958	41,839	**420,216**	13.8%	35,018
	(50,805)	(53,125)	(55,213)	(57,533)	(59,389)	(60,666)	**(609,314)**	−20.0%	(50,776)
	203,220	**212,500**	**220,852**	**230,132**	**237,556**	**242,664**	**2,437,255**	100%	**203,105**
								Percent of Revenue	
	90,600	90,600	90,600	90,600	90,600	90,600	**1,087,200**	44.6%	90,600
	22,650	22,650	22,650	22,650	22,650	22,650	**271,800**	11.2%	22,650
	4,117	4,117	4,117	4,117	4,117	4,117	**49,400**	2.0%	4,117
	117,367	**117,367**	**117,367**	**117,367**	**117,367**	**117,367**	**1,408,400**	57.8%	117,367
	58%	55%	53%	51%	49%	48%	**58%**		
	42,106	42,106	42,106	42,106	42,106	42,106	**505,274**	20.7%	42,106
	10,527	10,527	10,527	10,527	10,527	10,527	**126,318**	5.2%	10,527
	1,288	1,288	1,288	1,288	1,288	1,288	**15,450**	0.6%	1,288
	4,062	4,062	4,062	4,062	4,062	4,062	**48,745**	2.0%	4,062
	1,717	1,717	1,717	1,717	1,717	1,717	**20,600**	0.8%	1,717
	1,917	1,917	1,917	1,917	1,917	1,917	**23,000**	0.9%	1,917
	14,217	14,217	14,217	14,217	14,217	14,217	**170,608**	7.0%	14,217
	515	0	0	515	0	0	**2,060**	0.1%	172
	1,667	1,667	1,667	1,667	1,667	1,667	**20,000**	0.8%	1,667
	515	515	515	515	515	515	**6,180**	0.3%	515
	4,583	4,583	4,583	4,583	4,583	4,583	**55,000**	2.3%	4,583
	83,113	**82,598**	**82,598**	**83,113**	**82,598**	**82,598**	**993,235**	40.8%	
	41%	39%	37%	36%	35%	34%	**41%**		
	200,480	**199,965**	**199,965**	**200,480**	**199,965**	**199,965**	**2,401,635**		
	2,741	**12,536**	**20,888**	**29,653**	**37,592**	**42,699**	**35,620**		
	1%	6%	9%	13%	16%	18%	**1%**		
	7,088	7,088	7,088	7,088	7,088	7,088	**85,051**	3.5%	
	9,035	9,035	9,035	9,035	9,035	9,035	**108,420**	4.4%	
	216,602	**216,087**	**216,087**	**216,602**	**216,087**	**216,087**	**2,595,106**	106.5%	
	(13,382)	(3,587)	4,765	13,530	21,469	26,577	**(157,851)**		
	(13,382)	(3,587)	4,765	13,530	21,469	26,577	**(157,851)**		
	7,088	7,088	7,088	7,088	7,088	7,088	**85,051**		
	(6,294)	**3,501**	**11,853**	**20,618**	**28,557**	**33,664**	**(72,800)**		
	4,256.60	4,256.60	4,256.60	4,256.60	4,256.60	4,256.60	**51,079**		
	417	417	417	417	417	417	**5,000**		
	7,088	7,088	7,088	7,088	7,088	7,088	**85,051**		
	11,761	**11,761**	**11,761**	**11,761**	**11,761**	**11,761**	**141,130**		
	(18,055)	(8,260)	**92**	**8,857**	**16,796**	**21,904**	**(213,930)**		
	(779,261)	(787,521)	(787,429)	(778,573)	(761,777)	(739,873)	**(739,873)**		

Financial Analysis: Anytown Medical Center—Multispecialty Primary Care Start-up Feasibility
Page 3

Year 3	Month 25	Month 26	Month 27	Month 28	Month 29	Month 30
Patient Revenue						
Charges—Professional Fees	271,951	271,951	271,951	271,951	271,951	271,951
Charges—Ancillary & Technical	43,512	43,512	43,512	43,512	43,512	43,512
Total Adjustments	(63,093)	(63,093)	(63,093)	(63,093)	(63,093)	(63,093)
Net Patient Revenue	**252,371**	**252,371**	**252,371**	**252,371**	**252,371**	**252,371**
Provider Expenses						
Direct Compensation—Providers	94,224	94,224	94,224	94,224	94,224	94,224
Provider Benefits	23,556	23,556	23,556	23,556	23,556	23,556
Malpractice Insurance	4,323	4,323	4,323	4,323	4,323	4,323
Subtotal	**122,103**	**122,103**	**122,103**	**122,103**	**122,103**	**122,103**
Expenses as % of Net Revenue	48%	48%	48%	48%	48%	48%
Operating Expenses						
Support Staff Salaries	47,071	47,071	47,071	47,071	47,071	47,071
Staff Benefits	11,768	11,768	11,768	11,768	11,768	11,768
Repairs and Maintenance	1,326	1,326	1,326	1,326	1,326	1,326
Office Supplies and Services	5,047	5,047	5,047	5,047	5,047	5,047
Telephone and Utilities	1,768	1,768	1,768	1,768	1,768	1,768
Travel, Dues and Subscriptions	1,974	1,974	1,974	1,974	1,974	1,974
Clinical and Laboratory Supplies	17,666	17,666	17,666	17,666	17,666	17,666
Business Insurance	530	0	0	530	0	0
Promotion and Marketing	1,250	1,250	1,250	1,250	1,250	1,250
Accounting and Legal Fees	530	530	530	530	530	530
All Other Expenses	4,721	4,721	4,721	4,721	4,721	4,721
Subtotal	**93,653**	**93,122**	**93,122**	**93,653**	**93,122**	**93,122**
Expenses as % of Net Revenue	37%	37%	37%	37%	37%	37%
Total Operating Expenses	**215,755**	**215,225**	**215,225**	**215,755**	**215,225**	**215,225**
Contribution Margin	**36,615**	**37,146**	**37,146**	**36,615**	**37,146**	**37,146**
Contribution Margin %	15%	15%	15%	15%	15%	15%
Non-Operating Expenses						
Depreciation	7,147	7,147	7,147	7,147	7,147	7,147
Interest	8,780	8,780	8,780	8,780	8,780	8,780
Total All Expenses	**231,682**	**231,151**	**231,151**	**231,682**	**231,151**	**231,151**
Net Income (Loss)	20,689	21,219	21,219	20,689	21,219	21,219
Cash Flow—Sources of Cash						
Net Income (Loss)	20,689	21,219	21,219	20,689	21,219	21,219
Add: Depreciation	7,147	7,147	7,147	7,147	7,147	7,147
Total Sources of Cash	**27,836**	**28,366**	**28,366**	**27,836**	**28,366**	**28,366**
Cash Flow—Uses of Cash						
Principal Reductions	4,512.00	4,512.00	4,512.00	4,512.00	4,512.00	4,512.00
Capital Expenditures	417	417	417	417	417	417
Funded Depreciation	7,147	7,147	7,147	7,147	7,147	7,147
Total Uses of Cash	**12,076**	**12,076**	**12,076**	**12,076**	**12,076**	**12,076**
Cash Increase (Decrease)	**15,760**	**16,291**	**16,291**	**15,760**	**16,291**	**16,291**
Cumulative Increase (Decrease)	(724,113)	(707,822)	(691,532)	(675,772)	(659,481)	(643,191)

	Month 31	Month 32	Month 33	Month 34	Month 35	Month 36	EOY 3	% of Total Revenue	Year 3 Monthly Average
	271,951	271,951	271,951	271,951	271,951	271,951	3,263,412	86.2%	271,951
	43,512	43,512	43,512	43,512	43,512	43,512	522,146	13.8%	43,512
	(63,093)	(63,093)	(63,093)	(63,093)	(63,093)	(63,093)	(757,112)	−20.0%	(63,093)
	252,371	252,371	252,371	252,371	252,371	252,371	3,028,446	100%	252,371
								Percent of Revenue	
	94,224	94,224	94,224	94,224	94,224	94,224	1,130,688	37.3%	94,224
	23,556	23,556	23,556	23,556	23,556	23,556	282,672	9.3%	23,556
	4,323	4,323	4,323	4,323	4,323	4,323	51,870	1.7%	4,323
	122,103	122,103	122,103	122,103	122,103	122,103	1,465,230	48.4%	122,103
	48%	48%	48%	48%	48%	48%	48%		
	47,071	47,071	47,071	47,071	47,071	47,071	564,855	18.7%	47,071
	11,768	11,768	11,768	11,768	11,768	11,768	141,214	4.7%	11,768
	1,326	1,326	1,326	1,326	1,326	1,326	15,914	0.5%	1,326
	5,047	5,047	5,047	5,047	5,047	5,047	60,569	2.0%	5,047
	1,768	1,768	1,768	1,768	1,768	1,768	21,218	0.7%	1,768
	1,974	1,974	1,974	1,974	1,974	1,974	23,690	0.8%	1,974
	17,666	17,666	17,666	17,666	17,666	17,666	211,991	7.0%	17,666
	530	0	0	530	0	0	2,122	0.1%	177
	1,250	1,250	1,250	1,250	1,250	1,250	15,000	0.5%	1,250
	530	530	530	530	530	530	6,365	0.2%	530
	4,721	4,721	4,721	4,721	4,721	4,721	56,650	1.9%	4,721
	93,653	93,122	93,122	93,653	93,122	93,122	1,119,587	37.0%	
	37%	37%	37%	37%	37%	37%	37%		
	215,755	215,225	215,225	215,755	215,225	215,225	2,584,817		
	36,615	37,146	37,146	36,615	37,146	37,146	443,629		
	15%	15%	15%	15%	15%	15%	15%		
	7,147	7,147	7,147	7,147	7,147	7,147	85,765	2.8%	
	8,780	8,780	8,780	8,780	8,780	8,780	105,355	3.5%	
	231,682	231,151	231,151	231,682	231,151	231,151	2,775,938	91.7%	
	20,689	21,219	21,219	20,689	21,219	21,219	252,509		
	20,689	21,219	21,219	20,689	21,219	21,219	252,509		
	7,147	7,147	7,147	7,147	7,147	7,147	85,765		
	27,836	28,366	28,366	27,836	28,366	28,366	338,274		
	4,512.00	4,512.00	4,512.00	4,512.00	4,512.00	4,512.00	54,144		
	417	417	417	417	417	417	5,000		
	7,147	7,147	7,147	7,147	7,147	7,147	85,765		
	12,076	12,076	12,076	12,076	12,076	12,076	144,909		
	15,760	16,291	16,291	15,760	16,291	16,291	193,365		
	(627,431)	(611,140)	(594,850)	(579,089)	(562,799)	(546,508)	(546,508)		

Financial Analysis: Anytown Medical Center—Multispecialty Primary Care
Start-up Feasibility
Page 4

Year 4	Month 37	Month 38	Month 39	Month 40	Month 41	Month 42
Patient Revenue						
Charges—Professional Fees	282,829	282,829	282,829	282,829	282,829	282,829
Charges—Ancillary & Technical	45,253	45,253	45,253	45,253	45,253	45,253
Total Adjustments	(65,616)	(65,616)	(65,616)	(65,616)	(65,616)	(65,616)
Net Patient Revenue	**262,465**	**262,465**	**262,465**	**262,465**	**262,465**	**262,465**
Provider Expenses						
Direct Compensation—Providers	97,993	97,993	97,993	97,993	97,993	97,993
Provider Benefits	24,498	24,498	24,498	24,498	24,498	24,498
Malpractice Insurance	4,539	4,539	4,539	4,539	4,539	4,539
Subtotal	**127,030**	**127,030**	**127,030**	**127,030**	**127,030**	**127,030**
Expenses as % of Net Revenue	48%	48%	48%	48%	48%	48%
Operating Expenses						
Support Staff Salaries	48,483	48,483	48,483	48,483	48,483	48,483
Staff Benefits	12,121	12,121	12,121	12,121	12,121	12,121
Repairs and Maintenance	1,366	1,366	1,366	1,366	1,366	1,366
Office Supplies and Services	5,249	5,249	5,249	5,249	5,249	5,249
Telephone and Utilities	1,821	1,821	1,821	1,821	1,821	1,821
Travel, Dues and Subscriptions	2,033	2,033	2,033	2,033	2,033	2,033
Clinical and Laboratory Supplies	18,373	18,373	18,373	18,373	18,373	18,373
Business Insurance	546	0	0	546	0	0
Promotion and Marketing	1,288	1,288	1,288	1,288	1,288	1,288
Accounting and Legal Fees	546	546	546	546	546	546
All Other Expenses	4,862	4,862	4,862	4,862	4,862	4,862
Subtotal	**96,689**	**96,143**	**96,143**	**96,689**	**96,143**	**96,143**
Expenses as % of Net Revenue	37%	37%	37%	37%	37%	37%
Total Operating Expenses	**223,719**	**223,173**	**223,173**	**223,719**	**223,173**	**223,173**
Contribution Margin	**38,746**	**39,293**	**39,293**	**38,746**	**39,293**	**39,293**
Contribution Margin %	15%	15%	15%	15%	15%	15%
Non-Operating Expenses						
Depreciation	7,207	7,207	7,207	7,207	7,207	7,207
Interest	8,509	8,509	8,509	8,509	8,509	8,509
Total All Expenses	**239,435**	**238,888**	**238,888**	**239,435**	**238,888**	**238,888**
Net Income (Loss)	**23,031**	**23,577**	**23,577**	**23,031**	**23,577**	**23,577**
Cash Flow—Sources of Cash						
Net Income (Loss)	23,031	23,577	23,577	23,031	23,577	23,577
Add: Depreciation	7,207	7,207	7,207	7,207	7,207	7,207
Total Sources of Cash	**30,237**	**30,784**	**30,784**	**30,237**	**30,784**	**30,784**
Cash Flow—Uses of Cash						
Principal Reductions	4,782.72	4,782.72	4,782.72	4,782.72	4,782.72	4,782.72
Capital Expenditures	417	417	417	417	417	417
Funded Depreciation	7,207	7,207	7,207	7,207	7,207	7,207
Total Uses of Cash	**12,406**	**12,406**	**12,406**	**12,406**	**12,406**	**12,406**
Cash Increase (Decrease)	**17,831**	**18,378**	**18,378**	**17,831**	**18,378**	**18,378**
Cumulative Increase (Decrease)	(528,677)	(510,299)	(491,922)	(474,090)	(455,713)	(437,335)

	Month 43	Month 44	Month 45	Month 46	Month 47	Month 48	EOY 4	% of Total Revenue	Year 4 Monthly Average
	282,829	282,829	282,829	282,829	282,829	282,829	3,393,949	86.2%	282,829
	45,253	45,253	45,253	45,253	45,253	45,253	543,032	13.8%	45,253
	(65,616)	(65,616)	(65,616)	(65,616)	(65,616)	(65,616)	(787,396)	−20.0%	(65,616)
	262,465	262,465	262,465	262,465	262,465	262,465	3,149,584	100%	262,465
								Percent of Revenue	
	97,993	97,993	97,993	97,993	97,993	97,993	1,175,916	37.3%	97,993
	24,498	24,498	24,498	24,498	24,498	24,498	293,979	9.3%	24,498
	4,539	4,539	4,539	4,539	4,539	4,539	54,464	1.7%	4,539
	127,030	127,030	127,030	127,030	127,030	127,030	1,524,358	48.4%	127,030
	48%	48%	48%	48%	48%	48%	48%		
	48,483	48,483	48,483	48,483	48,483	48,483	581,800	18.5%	48,483
	12,121	12,121	12,121	12,121	12,121	12,121	145,450	4.6%	12,121
	1,366	1,366	1,366	1,366	1,366	1,366	16,391	0.5%	1,366
	5,249	5,249	5,249	5,249	5,249	5,249	62,992	2.0%	5,249
	1,821	1,821	1,821	1,821	1,821	1,821	21,855	0.7%	1,821
	2,033	2,033	2,033	2,033	2,033	2,033	24,401	0.8%	2,033
	18,373	18,373	18,373	18,373	18,373	18,373	220,471	7.0%	18,373
	546	0	0	546	0	0	2,185	0.1%	182
	1,288	1,288	1,288	1,288	1,288	1,288	15,450	0.5%	1,288
	546	546	546	546	546	546	6,556	0.2%	546
	4,862	4,862	4,862	4,862	4,862	4,862	58,350	1.9%	4,862
	96,689	96,143	96,143	96,689	96,143	96,143	1,155,901	36.7%	
	37%	37%	37%	37%	37%	37%	37%		
	223,719	223,173	223,173	223,719	223,173	223,173	2,680,258		
	38,746	39,293	39,293	38,746	39,293	39,293	469,326		
	15%	15%	15%	15%	15%	15%	15%		
	7,207	7,207	7,207	7,207	7,207	7,207	86,479	2.7%	
	8,509	8,509	8,509	8,509	8,509	8,509	102,107	3.2%	
	239,435	238,888	238,888	239,435	238,888	238,888	2,868,845	91.1%	
	23,031	23,577	23,577	23,031	23,577	23,577	280,740		
	23,031	23,577	23,577	23,031	23,577	23,577	280,740		
	7,207	7,207	7,207	7,207	7,207	7,207	86,479		
	30,237	30,784	30,784	30,237	30,784	30,784	367,219		
	4,782.72	4,782.72	4,782.72	4,782.72	4,782.72	4,782.72	57,393		
	417	417	417	417	417	417	5,000		
	7,207	7,207	7,207	7,207	7,207	7,207	86,479		
	12,406	12,406	12,406	12,406	12,406	12,406	148,872		
	17,831	18,378	18,378	17,831	18,378	18,378	218,347		
	(419,503)	(401,126)	(382,748)	(364,917)	(346,539)	(328,161)	(328,161)		

Financial Analysis: Anytown Medical Center—Multispecialty Primary Care
Start-up Feasibility
Page 5

Year 5	Month 49	Month 50	Month 51	Month 52	Month 53	Month 54
Patient Revenue						
Charges—Professional Fees	294,142	294,142	294,142	294,142	294,142	294,142
Charges—Ancillary & Technical	47,063	47,063	47,063	47,063	47,063	47,063
Total Adjustments	(68,241)	(68,241)	(68,241)	(68,241)	(68,241)	(68,241)
Net Patient Revenue	**272,964**	**272,964**	**272,964**	**272,964**	**272,964**	**272,964**
Provider Expenses						
Direct Compensation—Providers	101,913	101,913	101,913	101,913	101,913	101,913
Provider Benefits	25,478	25,478	25,478	25,478	25,478	25,478
Malpractice Insurance	4,766	4,766	4,766	4,766	4,766	4,766
Subtotal	**132,156**	**132,156**	**132,156**	**132,156**	**132,156**	**132,156**
Expenses as % of Net Revenue	48%	48%	48%	48%	48%	48%
Operating Expenses						
Support Staff Salaries	49,938	49,938	49,938	49,938	49,938	49,938
Staff Benefits	12,484	12,484	12,484	12,484	12,484	12,484
Repairs and Maintenance	1,407	1,407	1,407	1,407	1,407	1,407
Office Supplies and Services	5,459	5,459	5,459	5,459	5,459	5,459
Telephone and Utilities	1,876	1,876	1,876	1,876	1,876	1,876
Travel, Dues and Subscriptions	2,094	2,094	2,094	2,094	2,094	2,094
Clinical and Laboratory Supplies	19,107	19,107	19,107	19,107	19,107	19,107
Business Insurance	563	0	0	563	0	0
Promotion and Marketing	1,326	1,326	1,326	1,326	1,326	1,326
Accounting and Legal Fees	563	563	563	563	563	563
All Other Expenses	5,008	5,008	5,008	5,008	5,008	5,008
Subtotal	**99,826**	**99,263**	**99,263**	**99,826**	**99,263**	**99,263**
Expenses as % of Net Revenue	37%	36%	36%	37%	36%	36%
Total Operating Expenses	**231,983**	**231,420**	**231,420**	**231,983**	**231,420**	**231,420**
Contribution Margin	**40,981**	**41,544**	**41,544**	**40,981**	**41,544**	**41,544**
Contribution Margin %	15%	15%	15%	15%	15%	15%
Non-Operating Expenses						
Depreciation	7,266	7,266	7,266	7,266	7,266	7,266
Interest	8,222	8,222	8,222	8,222	8,222	8,222
Total All Expenses	**247,471**	**246,908**	**246,908**	**247,471**	**246,908**	**246,908**
Net Income (Loss)	25,493	26,056	26,056	25,493	26,056	26,056
Cash Flow—Sources of Cash						
Net Income (Loss)	25,493	26,056	26,056	25,493	26,056	26,056
Add: Depreciation	7,266	7,266	7,266	7,266	7,266	7,266
Total Sources of Cash	**32,759**	**33,322**	**33,322**	**32,759**	**33,322**	**33,322**
Cash Flow—Uses of Cash						
Principal Reductions	5,069.68	5,069.68	5,069.68	5,069.68	5,069.68	5,069.68
Capital Expenditures	417	417	417	417	417	417
Funded Depreciation	7,266	7,266	7,266	7,266	7,266	7,266
Total Uses of Cash	**12,752**	**12,752**	**12,752**	**12,752**	**12,752**	**12,752**
Cash Increase (Decrease)	**20,007**	**20,570**	**20,570**	**20,007**	**20,570**	**20,570**
Cumulative Increase (Decrease)	(308,154)	(287,585)	(267,015)	(247,008)	(226,438)	(205,868)

	Month 55	Month 56	Month 57	Month 58	Month 59	Month 60	EOY 5	% of Total Revenue	Year 5 Monthly Average
	294,142	294,142	294,142	294,142	294,142	294,142	3,529,707	86.2%	294,142
	47,063	47,063	47,063	47,063	47,063	47,063	564,753	13.8%	47,063
	(68,241)	(68,241)	(68,241)	(68,241)	(68,241)	(68,241)	(818,892)	−20.0%	(68,241)
	272,964	272,964	272,964	272,964	272,964	272,964	3,275,568	100%	272,964
								Percent of Revenue	
	101,913	101,913	101,913	101,913	101,913	101,913	1,222,952	37.3%	101,913
	25,478	25,478	25,478	25,478	25,478	25,478	305,738	9.3%	25,478
	4,766	4,766	4,766	4,766	4,766	4,766	57,187	1.7%	4,766
	132,156	132,156	132,156	132,156	132,156	132,156	1,585,877	48.4%	132,156
	48%	48%	48%	48%	48%	48%	48%		
	49,938	49,938	49,938	49,938	49,938	49,938	599,254	18.3%	49,938
	12,484	12,484	12,484	12,484	12,484	12,484	149,814	4.6%	12,484
	1,407	1,407	1,407	1,407	1,407	1,407	16,883	0.5%	1,407
	5,459	5,459	5,459	5,459	5,459	5,459	65,511	2.0%	5,459
	1,876	1,876	1,876	1,876	1,876	1,876	22,510	0.7%	1,876
	2,094	2,094	2,094	2,094	2,094	2,094	25,133	0.8%	2,094
	19,107	19,107	19,107	19,107	19,107	19,107	229,290	7.0%	19,107
	563	0	0	563	0	0	2,251	0.1%	188
	1,326	1,326	1,326	1,326	1,326	1,326	15,914	0.5%	1,326
	563	563	563	563	563	563	6,753	0.2%	563
	5,008	5,008	5,008	5,008	5,008	5,008	60,100	1.8%	5,008
	99,826	99,263	99,263	99,826	99,263	99,263	1,193,412	36.4%	
	37%	36%	36%	37%	36%	36%	36%		
	231,983	231,420	231,420	231,983	231,420	231,420	2,779,289		
	40,981	41,544	41,544	40,981	41,544	41,544	496,279		
	15%	15%	15%	15%	15%	15%	15%		
	7,266	7,266	7,266	7,266	7,266	7,266	87,194	2.7%	
	8,222	8,222	8,222	8,222	8,222	8,222	98,663	3.0%	
	247,471	246,908	246,908	247,471	246,908	246,908	2,965,146	90.5%	
	25,493	26,056	26,056	25,493	26,056	26,056	310,422		
	25,493	26,056	26,056	25,493	26,056	26,056	310,422		
	7,266	7,266	7,266	7,266	7,266	7,266	87,194		
	32,759	33,322	33,322	32,759	33,322	33,322	397,615		
	5,069.68	5,069.68	5,069.68	5,069.68	5,069.68	5,069.68	60,836		
	417	417	417	417	417	417	5,000		
	7,266	7,266	7,266	7,266	7,266	7,266	87,194		
	12,752	12,752	12,752	12,752	12,752	12,752	153,030		
	20,007	20,570	20,570	20,007	20,570	20,570	244,586		
	(185,861)	(165,292)	(144,722)	(124,715)	(104,145)	(83,576)	(83,576)		

CASE FIVE STUDY NOTES

Case Study: Assisted Living Facility Feasibility

The last of the case studies is also the most complex of those presented. The development of assisted living (a.k.a. residential care) facilities has been increasing steadily as a means of gaining additional income in the healthcare industry or in ensuring a continuum of care for health systems.

This study examined the opportunity to develop either a 50-bed or 100-bed unit for a hospital. Several issues bear remark. Certain aspects of this study were deemed to contain fixed positions on program scope, location, and cost of the facility. The 50-unit facility under these assumptions was not financially feasible; the 100-unit facility was, providing positive cash flow in Year 2, with ultimate payback of all start-up costs anticipated after about 20 years. Under other circumstances and program scope, 50-unit facilities are feasible. Again, it is the assumptions (and scope) that affect everything.

The study contains reference to classes of residents under a managed care plan and optional supplemental (state-supported) plan. The hospital had an existing multiyear managed care contract for a certain number of residents. A limited amount of double occupancy units is considered (this is one key area where money is made, or lost).

ANYTOWN MEDICAL CENTER: ASSISTED LIVING FACILITY FEASIBILITY STUDY*

EXECUTIVE SUMMARY

The following operating assumptions and attached financial pro forma represent a statement of financial feasibility for an assisted living facility targeted to the middle income elderly and potentially sponsored by Anytown Medical Center (AMC). This resource is being considered for the continuum of geriatric services offered by AMC and in response to maintaining quality and cost-efficiency associated with managed care clients. This executive summary provides a brief overview of key issues raised by the assumptions and pro forma statements associated with a 50- or 100-unit assisted living model.

Estimates and assumptions based on previous experience, best practices, and survey of the local market have been made in the following categories:

- Private pay income (monthly charges for private pay units)
- Disposition of contract management of the facility and contract expenses
- Payment rate for property taxes and estimates of insurance premiums
- Amount of equipment to be leased instead of purchased
- Financing for project (estimated at 80% debt financing @ 5% over 30 years)
- Policy and method of depreciation, replacement reserve, and handling of amortized expenses
- Acceptable contingency amount

These issues must be resolved in order to complete the most realistic projections of project start-up and operation. In addition, final refinement of program scope will further impact these projections.

SUMMARY

100 Units—Full Financing Model

Key Issues

- UNIT AND PAYOR DISTRIBUTION
- Efficiency Units; 36 Managed Care, 11 Optional Supplemental, 11 Private Pay
- 1-Bedroom Units, Private Pay
- PROPERTY TAXES
- Per annum (mil rate of 0.2938) on $4,146,672 base of real property and $209,908 base of personal property
- FINANCING
- Total project cost estimate: $5,750,655

---

*The information in this section assesses the feasibility of developing a heavy care assisted living facility as part of the Anytown Medical Center geriatric service mix. The basis of the information contained herein is the best practices of the assisted living industry and the assisted living planning and facility development experience of staff of The Health Service Group. The viability of any model is a function of the program to be offered, level of service and staffing, development costs in the local market, competitiveness of the local market, and other factors.

Anytown Medical Center: Assisted Living Facility Feasibility Study
Continued

- Interest expense at 5% over 30 years, 80% debt financing, base of $4,600,524
- Interest and principal payments estimated each year

- DEPRECIATION, AMORTIZATION, AND REPLACEMENT
- Depreciation on real property base, straight line over 40 years
- Depreciation on furniture and fixtures, straight line over 8 years
- Estimated applicable expenses amortized over 3 years
- Depreciation and amortization added back below the line to cash flow
- Replacement reserve estimated and taken before cash flow

- RESULTS
- Cash flow in Year 2
- Estimated Payback horizon: 20–25 years
- Amount of original investment still outstanding at end of year 10: $4,260,000

OPERATING ASSUMPTIONS

Overview

The following assumptions are used in the development of operating pro formas for determining the feasibility of Anytown Medical Center developing an assisted living facility. The categories of items for discussion include income and occupancy assumptions, operating expense assumptions, and construction and financing assumptions. These assumptions are based on fifteen (15) years of geriatric services and assisted living/skilled nursing facility experience of the staff of The Health Service Group, Inc., as well as research and statistics from the assisted living and long-term care industries.

1.0 Income and Occupancy Assumptions

    1.1 The current analysis examines both 50- and 100-unit facilities.

        Under the 50-unit model, the suggested unit distribution is the following:

- 35 units will be constructed as "heavy care" units, 10 efficiencies, and 5 will be 1-bedroom units.

  All 35 heavy care units will be designated for managed care residents

  All 10 efficiencies and 1-bedroom units will be designated for private pay residents, 3 of which will ultimately be double occupancy

Under the 100-unit model, suggested unit distribution is the following:

- 58 units will be constructed as efficiency units (36 units will be designated for managed care residents; 11 efficiency units will be designated for optional supplemental residents; and 11 efficiency units will be designated for private pay residents)
- 42 units will be constructed as 1-bedroom units occupied exclusively by private pay residents
- Five of the 1-bedroom units will ultimately be double occupancy

Anytown Medical Center: Assisted Living Facility Feasibility Study
Continued

1.2 The AMC Geriatric Services Director has indicated an ability to occupy 36 units with managed care clients, at opening. These MC clients are currently residing in leased beds in other facilities. In addition, potential SNF patient transfers, and local 65+ discharge rates from AMC (that are non-MC clients) will create additional demand for short- to long-term use. It is estimated that an additional 3 alcove units will be occupied by managed care residents by end of year. Private pay resident occupancy is scaled manually to reflect reasonable occupancy rates based on industry experience and market observation. The industry experience of an ALF Resident Turnover Rate is 10% per year and is assumed in fill-up projections.

1.3 The occupancy rate for the center at full capacity is presumed to be 96% to allow for unit turnover. Unit turnover is calculated as two alcove units for the 50-unit model and four units in the 100-unit model. In reality, turnover in all units will comprise the overall occupancy rate. The tables on page 307 indicate projected occupancy fill-up rates.

1.4 Unless otherwise indicated, all income categories increase 5% annually.

1.5 The following unit charges by payor class are presumed:
   • Occupied efficiency units—managed care @ $1,250 per month
   • Occupied efficiency units—optional supplemental @ $740 per month
   • Occupied efficiency units—private pay @ $1,200 per month
   • Occupied 1-bedroom units—private pay @ $1,500 per month
   • Additional resident charge for double occupancy in a 1-bedroom unit @ $350 per month. Double occupancy is anticipated at 5% for each model; i.e., 3 additional residents in 1-bedroom units in the 50-unit model and 5 additional residents in the 100-unit model.

1.6 Optional services are estimated at $18 per month per non-MC resident. This includes personal supportive services (companion and shopping service) and out-of-ordinary personal services (ostomy or incontinence care).

1.7 Beauty shop revenue, dietary income, and laundry income are based on experience from other ALF projects, both planned and operational. The resident use of services including beautician services, snack shops, vending and other extracurricular foodstuffs, laundry and cleaning services, and assistance beyond the scope of normal residential care services constitute this category.

2.0 Operating Expense Assumptions

2.1   Unless otherwise indicated, all expenses increase 5% annually.

2.2   Dietary Expenses are divided into salary and wages, contract services, food and patient variable costs, and dietary equipment. Salary and wages are estimated under the following assumptions:

Text continued on p. 308

Anytown Medical Center: Assisted Living Facility Feasibility Study
Continued

Assisted Living Facility 50-UNIT MODEL	Sep-97 Month 1	Oct-97 Month 2	Nov-97 Month 3	Dec-97 Month 4	Jan-98 Month 5	Feb-98 Month 6	Mar-98 Month 7	Apr-98 Month 8	May-98 Month 9	Jun-98 Month 10	Jul-98 Month 11	Aug-98 Month 12
Total Units	50	50	50	50	50	50	50	50	50	50	50	50
Occupied Effic. Units—Managed Care	30	30	30	30	30	30	31	31	32	32	33	33
Occupied Effic. Units—Other	0	0	0	0	0	0	0	0	0	0	0	0
Occupied 1-BR Units—Private Pay	3	5	6	7	8	9	9	10	11	11	12	12
Number of Residents*	33	35	37	38	39	41	42	43	45	45	48	48
Percent Occupancy**	66%	70%	72%	74%	76%	78%	80%	82%	86%	86%	90%	90%

*The number of residents is greater than number of units because of second-person occupancy.
**The percent occupancy is based on number of occupied units, not number of residents.

Assisted Living Facility 100-UNIT MODEL	Sep-97 Month 1	Oct-97 Month 2	Nov-97 Month 3	Dec-97 Month 4	Jan-98 Month 5	Feb-98 Month 6	Mar-98 Month 7	Apr-98 Month 8	May-98 Month 9	Jun-98 Month 10	Jul-98 Month 11	Aug-98 Month 12
Total Units	100	100	100	100	100	100	100	100	100	100	100	100
Occupied Effic. Units—Managed Care	30	31	32	33	33	34	34	34	34	34	34	34
Occupied Effic. Units—Optional Suppl.	2	3	4	4	5	6	6	7	8	9	9	10
Occupied Effic. Units—Private Pay	2	3	4	4	5	6	6	7	8	9	9	10
Occupied 1-BR Units—Private Pay	8	17	20	22	23	23	26	28	32	32	37	38
Occupied 2-BR Units—Private Pay	0	0	0	0	0	0	0	0	0	0	0	0
Number of Residents	43	57	63	66	70	73	78	81	87	89	94	97
Percent Occupancy	42%	54%	60%	63%	66%	69%	74%	77%	82%	84%	89%	92%

Anytown Medical Center: Assisted Living Facility Feasibility Study
Continued

	Hourly Rate	50-Unit Model	100-Unit Model
Cooks	$ 8.35	2.8 FTE @ $48,630	2.8 FTE @ $48,630
Cook's Helper	$ 6.00	2.8 FTE @ $34,944	2.8 FTE @ $34,944
Food Prep/Dsh Wsh.	$ 6.50	1.4 FTE @ $18,928	2.8 FTE @ $37,856

Food and other variable costs are estimated using a per resident day modifier (developed from industry experience with other operating programs) to determine cost of providing a nutritious meal plan, other food costs, dietary and kitchen supplies, and operational expenses. Contract services (dietitian, nutrition) and equipment replacement are estimated at $100 and $150 monthly in the 50-unit model and $200 and $250 monthly in the 100-unit model, respectively.

2.3   Laundry and linens expense is estimated at $400 monthly in the 50-unit model and $600 monthly in the 100-unit model for replacement linens, equipment, repair, and supplies.

2.4   Housekeeping supplies are estimated at $400 monthly in the 50-unit model and $750 monthly in the 100-unit model. Salary and wages are estimated as follows:

	Hourly Rate	50-Unit Model	100-Unit Model
Housekeepers	$ 6.50	1.4 FTE @ $18,928	2.5 FTE @ $27,243
Janitor	$ 6.50	1.4 FTE @ $18,928	1.4 FTE @ $18,928

2.5   Activities expenses include a variable entertainment amount of $400 monthly in the 50-unit model and $600 monthly in the 100-unit model plus salary and wages as follows:

	Hourly Rate	50-Unit Model	100-Unit Model
Activities Coordinators	$ 8.50	1.4 FTE @ $24,752	1.4 FTE @ $24,752
Drivers	$ 7.00	1.4 FTE @ $20,384	1.4 FTE @ $20,384

2.6   Plant operations are estimated based on a minimum usage of utilities and support services including grounds maintenance, elevator services (in the 100-unit model), pest control, and service contracts. Variable expenses based on resident days include expense modifiers for electricity, gas, and water. Salary and wages are estimated as follows:

	Hourly Rate	50-Unit Model	100-Unit Model
General Maintenance	$ 11.50	1.4 FTE @ $33,488	1.4 FTE @ $33,488
Security Guards	$ 6.50	1.4 FTE @ $18,928	1.4 FTE @ $18,928

2.7   Promotion and marketing expenses are deemed to be $0 for the 50-unit model, given the number of MC clients to be transferred, existing patients in leased beds in other facilities, and local 65+ discharge rates from AMC. Routine news articles and hospital publicity should be sufficient to

Anytown Medical Center: Assisted Living Facility Feasibility Study
Continued

fill the private pay units. Promotion and marketing expenses in the 100-unit model are essential to accommodate the rapid fill-up projections demanded by the financing of the project. It is estimated that these costs would be $100,000+ for units not planned for occupancy by managed care clients. The preopening marketing expense is carried in the development budget and reflected in debt financing. Annual recurring marketing expense is estimated at $25,000 (these funds are necessary to establish name recognition and develop a waiting list).

2.8 Employee benefits are estimated at a flat 28% of payroll for taxes and employee benefits.

2.9 Personal care expenses include $400 monthly in the 50-unit model and $750 monthly in the 100-unit model to reflect dispensing patient medicine (not purchasing medications) and disposable supplies, etc. Nursing technicians are estimated at 7.0 FTE @ $14,019 for the 50-unit model and 12.5 FTE for the 100-unit model (this number remains constant because it is anticipated that no more than 35 units will be used for heavy care).

	Hourly Rate	50-Unit Model	100-Unit Model
Nursing Technicians	$ 6.74	7.0 FTE @ $98,133	12.5 FTE @ $175,238

2.10 Administration and general expenses include salary and wages for administration and office staff as follows:

	Hourly Rate	50-Unit Model	100-Unit Model
Director (RN-9 level)	—	1.0 FTE @ $40,000	1.0 FTE @ $40,000
Secretary/Receptionist	$ 7.80	1.4 FTE @ $22,714	1.4 FTE @ $22,714
Business Manager	$ 11.00	1.0 FTE @ $22,880	1.0 FTE @ $22,880

2.11 Management fees are estimated at 5% of gross revenue for the 50-unit model and 5% of gross revenue with a "not to exceed" of $4,500 per month for the 100-unit model. The services of a professional management firm would cover development of operational policies, establishing rent/charge structures, development of informational material, ensure regulatory compliance, maintain equipment and facilities repair schedule and reports, bookkeeping and accounting, develop annual business plan and operating budget, provide the owner with monthly and quarterly financial reports, open checking accounts, payment of facilities expenses, distribution of facility net cash flow, payment of facility debt service expenses, hire/train/direct/terminate employees, develop/maintain/review ancillary service contracts, purchase supplies and noncapital equipment, coordinate legal matters

Anytown Medical Center: Assisted Living Facility Feasibility Study
Continued

and proceedings, issue/bill/collect monies owed, obtain and maintain the necessary insurance coverage, oversee operations, and advise the center director on marketing efforts and other activities that are mutually agreed upon between ownership and management.

2.12   Postage, office supplies, telephone and communication, travel, auto expenses, bank charges, and accounting and audit fees and expenses are estimated at $1,800 monthly in the 50-unit model and increase to $2,025 for the 100-unit model.

2.13   Property taxes and insurance are estimated based on prevailing rates. Property taxes (6% per annum of assessed value times the mill rate of 0.2938) would be dropped if we seek nonprofit status. Insurance for building and contents is estimated at $1,860 annually for the 50-unit model and $3,540 annually for the 100-unit model.

2.14   Lease and rental expense includes an estimate of healthcare and facility equipment and furnishings not purchased due to cost and favorable lease terms. A detailed breakdown should be performed prior to final pro forma preparation. An initial estimate of $8,000 monthly is made for the 50-unit model and $10,000 monthly for the 100-unit model.

3.0 Construction and Financing Assumptions

3.1   Interest expense is calculated on the deductible portion of all interest paid from mortgage and lease or lease purchase sources. It is presumed that an initial financing plan will include an 80% debt financing of the entire project at a below market rate (5%) over 30 years. Final estimates will be made once project scope and financing have been established.

3.2   Depreciation and amortization is taken on buildings, furniture/fixtures, and deferred financing costs. Final estimates will be made once project scope, financing, and preferred depreciation method are established.

3.3   Contingency amount of $1,500 monthly is included in the 50-unit model for the first year only. In the 100-unit model, $1,500 monthly is budgeted for first year and $2,000 monthly each year thereafter. If there is an accumulated reserve after 3 years, this amount may be reduced.

3.4   Replacement reserve is estimated based on actual need for replacement equipment and furnishings. Final estimates will be made once project scope has been established.

Anytown Medical Center: Assisted Living Facility Feasibility Study Concluded

Assisted Living Facility: Selected Operating Expenses

100 Unit Model	Sep-98 Month 12	Sep-99 Month 24	Sep-00 Month 36	Sep-01 Month 48	Sep-02 Month 60
Personnel @ hourly rate					
Cooks—2.8 FTE @ $8.35	48,630	51,062	53,615	56,295	59,110
Cook's Helper—					
2.8 FTE @ $6.00	34,944	36,691	38,526	40,452	42,475
F. Prep/Dsh Wash—					
2.8 FTE @ $6.50	37,856	39,749	41,736	43,823	46,014
Housekeepers—					
2.5 FTE @ $6.50	27,243	28,605	30,035	31,537	33,114
Janitor—1.4 FTE @ $6.50	18,928	19,874	20,868	21,912	23,007
Activities Coord.—					
1.4 FTE @ $8.50	24,752	25,990	27,289	28,654	30,086
Drivers—1.4 FTE @ $7.00	20,384	21,403	22,473	23,597	24,777
General Maint.—					
1.4 FTE @ $11.50	33,488	35,162	36,921	38,767	40,705
Security Guards—					
1.4 FTE @ $6.50	18,928	19,874	20,868	21,912	23,007
Nursing Techs—					
12.5 FTE @ $6.74	175,238	183,998	193,198	202,858	213,000
Director (RN-9)—					
1.0 FTE @ $40,000 a.	40,000	42,000	44,100	46,305	48,620
Business Manager—					
1.0 FTE @ $11.00	22,880	24,024	25,225	26,486	27,811
Secretary/Recep.—					
1.4 FTE @ $7.80	22,714	23,850	25,042	26,294	27,609
Benefits & Payroll Taxes					
@ 28%	147,276	154,639	162,371	170,490	179,014
Total Personnel	673,261	706,921	742,268	779,381	818,350
Non-Salary Costs					
Dietary Costs	140,748	193,583	207,247	217,869	228,763
Plant Operations	83,540	97,510	102,689	107,482	112,856
Promotion & Marketing	29,244	30,708	32,244	33,864	35,557
Lease & Rental	25,008	25,008	25,008	25,008	26,258
Contingency	18,000	18,000	18,000	18,000	18,000
All Other Costs	770,642	779,135	786,196	770,588	777,928
Total Operating Expenses	1,740,442	1,850,865	1,913,652	1,952,192	2,017,712

Assisted Living Facility: Full Financing Model 10-Year Pro Forma

100 Unit Model	Sep-98 Month 12	Sep-99 Month 24	Sep-00 Month 36	Sep-01 Month 48
Operating Income				
Occupied Efficiency Units—M. Care	496,250	535,704	562,632	590,784
Occupied Efficiency Units—Opt. Suppl.	54,020	93,240	97,920	102,840
Occupied Efficiency Units—Private Pay	87,600	151,200	158,760	166,680
Occupied 1 BR Units—Private Pay	463,500	771,750	833,616	875,448
Occupied 2 BR Units—Private Pay	0	0	0	0
Second Person Differential	16,100	18,400	23,160	24,300
Optional Services	9,018	14,820	16,080	16,884
Other Income	22,488	33,531	36,126	37,936
Gross Income	**1,142,652**	**1,607,567**	**1,716,226**	**1,802,206**
Operating Expenses				
Dietary	262,176	321,083	341,121	358,437
Laundry & Linen	7,200	7,560	7,944	8,352
Housekeeping	51,645	56,073	59,019	61,933
Activities	52,332	54,949	57,702	60,586
Plant Operations	135,956	152,546	160,478	168,160
Promotion & Marketing	29,244	30,708	32,244	33,864
Employee Benefits	147,276	154,639	162,371	170,490
Personal Care	184,236	193,454	203,122	213,274
Administrative & General	168,396	176,828	185,666	194,956
Property Tax & Insurance	80,338	84,358	88,570	92,995
Lease & Rental	25,008	25,008	25,008	25,008
Depreciation & Amort.	152,628	152,628	152,628	129,912
Interest Expense	426,009	423,031	419,779	416,225
Contingency	18,000	18,000	18,000	18,000
Total Operating Expenses	1,740,442	1,850,865	1,913,652	1,952,192
Net Income	(597,790)	(243,298)	(197,425)	(149,986)
Add Back: Deprec. & Amort.	152,628	152,628	152,628	129,912
Minus: Replacement Reserve	48,000	48,000	419,779	48,000
Minus: Principal Payment	(32,150)	(35,127)	(38,380)	(41,934)
Cash Flow	(429,312)	(77,797)	(35,177)	(14,007)

Sep-02 Month 60	Sep-03 Month 72	Sep-04 Month 84	Sep-05 Month 96	Sep-06 Month 108	Sep-07 Month 120
620,323	651,339	683,906	718,102	754,007	791,707
107,982	113,381	119,050	125,003	131,253	137,815
175,014	183,765	192,953	202,601	212,731	223,367
919,220	965,181	1,013,440	1,064,113	1,117,318	1,173,184
0	0	0	0	0	0
25,515	26,791	28,130	29,537	31,014	32,564
17,728	18,615	19,545	20,523	21,549	22,626
39,833	41,825	43,916	46,112	48,418	50,838
1,892,317	**2,000,897**	**2,100,942**	**2,205,989**	**2,316,288**	**2,432,103**
376,359	395,177	414,936	435,683	457,467	480,340
8,770	9,208	9,668	10,152	10,660	11,192
65,030	68,282	71,696	75,280	79,045	82,997
63,615	66,796	70,136	73,643	77,325	81,191
176,568	185,396	194,666	204,399	214,619	225,350
35,557	37,335	39,202	41,162	43,220	45,381
179,014	187,965	197,363	207,231	217,593	228,473
223,937	235,134	246,891	259,235	272,197	285,807
204,704	214,939	225,686	236,970	248,819	261,260
97,645	102,527	107,654	113,036	118,688	124,623
26,258	27,571	28,950	30,397	31,917	33,513
129,912	129,912	129,912	129,912	103,668	103,668
412,342	408,099	403,464	398,399	398,399	386,819
18,000	18,000	18,000	18,000	18,000	18,000
2,017,712	2,086,342	2,158,223	2,233,501	2,291,616	2,368,614
(125,395)	(85,445)	(57,281)	(27,512)	**24,672**	**63,489**
129,912	129,912	129,912	129,912	103,668	103,668
48,000	48,000	48,000	48,000	48,000	48,000
(45,817)	(50,059)	(54,695)	(59,760)	(65,293)	(71,414)
6,700	**42,408**	**65,936**	**90,641**	**111,047**	**143,743**

Assisted Living Facility: Full Financing Model 5-Year Income and Expense Profile
Page 1

100 Unit Model	Sep-98 Month 12	Sep-99 Month 24	Sep-00 Month 36	Sep-01 Month 48	Sep-02 Month 60
Total Units	100	100	100	100	100
Occupied Efficiency Units—M. Care	34	34	34	34	34
Occupied Efficiency Units—Opt. Suppl.	10	10	10	10	10
Occupied Efficiency Units—Private Pay	10	10	10	10	10
Occupied 1 BR Units—Private Pay	38	42	42	42	42
Occupied 2 BR Units—Private Pay	0	0	0	0	0
Number of Residents	97	101	101	101	101
Percent Occupancy	92%	96%	96%	96%	96%
Resident Days	27,343	36,136	36,865	36,865	36,865
Occupied Efficiency Units—M. Care	496,250	535,704	562,632	590,784	620,323
Occupied Efficiency Units—Opt. Suppl.	54,020	93,240	97,920	102,840	107,982
Occupied Efficiency Units—Private Pay	87,600	151,200	158,760	166,680	175,014
Occupied 1 BR Units—Private Pay	463,500	771,750	833,616	875,448	919,220
Occupied 2 BR Units—Private Pay	0	0	0	0	0
Second Person Differential	16,100	18,400	23,160	24,300	25,515
Optional Services	9,018	14,820	16,080	16,884	17,728
Beauty Shop Revenue	2,694	3,742	4,012	4,218	4,429
Dietary Income	10,776	14,969	16,035	16,835	17,676
Laundry Income	2,694	3,742	4,012	4,218	4,429
Total Income	**1,142,652**	**1,607,567**	**1,716,226**	**1,802,206**	**1,892,317**
Expenses:					
Dietary Expenses					
Salary and Wages	121,428	127,499	133,874	140,568	147,596
Contract Services	2,400	2,520	2,652	2,784	2,923
Meat & Fish	87,498	121,417	130,133	136,769	143,608
Dairy Products	24,609	34,329	36,865	38,708	40,644
Fruit & Vegetable	8,203	11,383	12,165	12,903	13,548
Other Food Costs	8,203	11,383	12,165	12,903	13,548
Dietary Supplies	6,836	9,395	9,954	10,322	10,838
Equipment & Replacement	3,000	3,156	3,312	3,480	3,654
Total Dietary Expense	262,176	321,083	341,121	358,437	376,359

Assisted Living Facility: Full Financing Model 5-Year Income and Expense Profile
Page 2

100 Unit Model	Sep-98 Month 12	Sep-99 Month 24	Sep-00 Month 36	Sep-01 Month 48	Sep-02 Month 60
Laundry & Linen					
Linen Replacement	3,600	3,780	3,972	4,176	4,385
Equipment & Repair	3,600	3,780	3,972	4,176	4,385
Total Laundry & Linen	7,200	7,560	7,944	8,352	8,770
Housekeeping					
Salary & Wages	46,176	48,485	50,909	53,454	56,127
Housekeeping Supplies	5,469	7,589	8,110	8,479	8,903
Total Housekeeping	51,645	56,073	59,019	61,933	65,030
Activities					
Salary & Wages	45,132	47,389	49,758	52,246	54,858
Entertainment	7,200	7,560	7,944	8,340	8,757
Total Activities	52,332	54,949	57,702	60,586	63,615
Plant Operations					
Gas	9,900	10,392	10,908	11,448	12,020
Electricity	31,475	39,068	41,100	42,792	44,932
Sewer/Water	6,895	8,501	8,998	9,455	9,928
Garbage	3,600	3,780	3,972	4,176	4,385
Cable Television	7,790	10,689	11,383	11,951	12,548
Salary & Wages—Maintenance	52,416	55,037	57,789	60,678	63,712
Grounds Maintenance	4,800	5,040	5,292	5,556	5,834
Repair & Maint. Supplies	7,800	8,196	8,604	9,036	9,488
Repair & Maint. Purchased Svcs.	4,800	5,040	5,292	5,556	5,834
Elevator Services	2,100	2,208	2,316	2,436	2,558
Pest Control	780	816	852	900	945
Service Contracts	3,600	3,780	3,972	4,176	4,385
Total Plant Operations	135,956	152,546	160,478	168,160	176,568

Assisted Living Facility: Full Financing Model 5-Year Income and Expense Profile
Page 3

100 Unit Model	Sep-98 Month 12	Sep-99 Month 24	Sep-00 Month 36	Sep-01 Month 48	Sep-02 Month 60
Promotion & Marketing					
Contract Fees	12,996	13,644	14,328	15,048	15,800
Advertising	16,248	17,064	17,916	18,816	19,757
Total Promotion & Marketing	29,244	30,708	32,244	33,864	35,557
Employee Benefits					
Benefits & Payroll Taxes	147,276	154,639	162,371	170,490	179,014
Total Employee Benefits	147,276	154,639	162,371	170,490	179,014
Personal Care Expenses					
Salary & Wages	175,236	183,998	193,198	202,858	213,000
Supplies/Other	9,000	9,456	9,924	10,416	10,937
Total Personal Care Exp.	184,236	193,454	203,122	213,274	223,937
Administration & General					
Director and Business Manager	62,880	66,024	69,325	72,791	76,431
Salary & Wages—Office	22,716	23,852	25,044	26,297	27,611
Management Fee	54,000	56,700	59,532	62,508	65,633
Postage	1,500	1,572	1,656	1,740	1,827
Office Supplies	2,700	2,832	2,976	3,120	3,276
Telephone & Communication	6,000	6,300	6,612	6,948	7,295
Travel	3,000	3,156	3,312	3,480	3,654
Auto & Van Expenses	4,200	4,416	4,632	4,860	5,103
Dues & Subscriptions	900	948	996	1,044	1,096
Bank Charges	900	948	996	1,044	1,096
Accounting & Audit Fees	6,000	6,300	6,612	6,948	7,295
Other	3,600	3,780	3,972	4,176	4,385
Total Admin. & General	168,396	176,828	185,666	194,956	204,704

Assisted Living Facility: Full Financing Model 5-Year Income and Expense Profile
Page 4

100 Unit Model	Sep-98 Month 12	Sep-99 Month 24	Sep-00 Month 36	Sep-01 Month 48	Sep-02 Month 60
Property Taxes & Insurance					
Real Property Tax	73,098	76,753	80,591	84,620	88,851
Personal Property Tax	3,700	3,885	4,079	4,283	4,497
Insurance	3,540	3,720	3,900	4,092	4,297
Total Taxes & Insurance	80,338	84,358	88,570	92,995	97,645
Lease & Rental Expense					
Lease & Rental Equipment	12,504	12,504	12,504	12,504	13,129
Rentals—Miscellaneous Equipment	12,504	12,504	12,504	12,504	13,129
Total Lease & Rental	25,008	25,008	25,008	25,008	26,258
Depreciation & Amortization					
Depreciation—Buildings	103,668	103,668	103,668	103,668	103,668
Depreciation—Furniture & Fixtures	26,244	26,244	26,244	26,244	26,244
Amort.—Deferred Financing Costs	3,204	3,204	3,204	0	0
Amort.—Deferred Pre-Opening	15,396	15,396	15,396	0	0
Amort.—Construction Int. & Taxes	4,116	4,116	4,116	0	0
Total Depreciation & Amort.	152,628	152,628	152,628	129,912	129,912
Interest Expense					
Interest Expense	426,009	423,031	419,779	416,225	412,342
Total Interest Expense	426,009	423,031	419,779	416,225	412,342
Contingency	18,000	18,000	18,000	18,000	18,000
Total Expenses	**1,740,442**	**1,850,865**	**1,913,652**	**1,952,192**	**2,017,712**
Net Income	**(597,790)**	**(243,298)**	**(197,425)**	**(149,986)**	**(125,395)**

Assisted Living Facility: Full Financing Model 5-Year Income and Expense Profile
Page 5

100 Unit Model	Sep-98 Month 12	Sep-99 Month 24	Sep-00 Month 36	Sep-01 Month 48	Sep-02 Month 60
Add Back: Deprec. & Amort.	152,628	152,628	152,628	129,912	129,912
Minus: Replacement Reserve	48,000	48,000	419,779	48,000	48,000
Minus: Payment on Principal	(32,150)	(35,127)	(38,380)	(41,934)	(45,817)
Cash Flow	(429,312)	(77,797)	(35,177)	(14,007)	6,700

Assisted Living Facility: Selected Operating Expenses

100 Unit Model	Sep-98 Month 12	Sep-99 Month 24	Sep-00 Month 36	Sep-01 Month 48	Sep-02 Month 60
Personnel @ hourly rate					
Cooks—2.8 FTE @ $8.35	48,630	51,062	53,615	56,295	59,110
Cook's Helper—2.8 FTE @ $6.00	34,944	36,691	38,526	40,452	42,475
F. Prep/Dsh Wash—2.8 FTE @ $6.50	37,856	39,749	41,736	43,823	46,014
Housekeepers—2.5 FTE @ $6.50	27,243	28,605	30,035	31,537	33,114
Janitor—1.4 FTE @ $6.50	18,928	19,874	20,868	21,912	23,007
Activities Coord.—1.4 FTE @ $8.50	24,752	25,990	27,289	28,654	30,086
Drivers—1.4 FTE @ $7.00	20,384	21,403	22,473	23,597	24,777
General Maint.—1.4 FTE @ $11.50	33,488	35,162	36,921	38,767	40,705
Security Guards—1.4 FTE @ $6.50	18,928	19,874	20,868	21,912	23,007
Nursing Techs—12.5 FTE @ $6.74	175,238	183,998	193,198	202,858	213,000
Director (RN-9)—1.0 FTE @ $40,000	40,000	42,000	44,100	46,305	48,620
Business Manager—1.0 FTE @ $11.00	22,880	24,024	25,225	26,486	27,811
Secretary/Recep.—1.4 FTE @ $7.80	22,714	23,850	25,042	26,294	27,609
Benefits & Payroll Taxes @ 28%	147,276	154,639	162,371	170,490	179,014
Total Personnel	673,261	706,921	742,268	779,381	818,350
Non-Salary Costs					
Dietary Costs	140,748	193,583	207,247	217,869	228,763
Plant Operations	83,540	97,510	102,689	107,482	112,856
Promotion & Marketing	29,244	30,708	32,244	33,864	35,557
Lease & Rental	25,008	25,008	25,008	25,008	26,258
Contingency	18,000	18,000	18,000	18,000	18,000
All Other Costs	770,642	779,135	786,196	770,588	777,928
Total Operating Expenses	1,740,442	1,850,865	1,913,652	1,952,192	2,017,712

The operating pro forma begins on p. 320.

Assisted Living Facility: Full Financing Model—Operating Pro Forma
Page 1

	First Year Operations				
100 Unit Model	**Sep-97** **Month 1**	**Oct-97** **Month 2**	**Nov-97** **Month 3**	**Dec-97** **Month 4**	**Jan-98** **Month 5**
Total Units	100	100	100	100	100
Occupied Efficiency Units—M. Care	30	31	32	33	33
Occupied Efficiency Units—Opt. Suppl.	2	3	4	4	5
Occupied Efficiency Units—Private Pay	2	3	4	4	5
Occupied 1 BR Units—Private Pay	8	17	20	22	23
Occupied 2 BR Units—Private Pay	0	0	0	0	0
Number of Residents	43	57	63	66	70
Percent Occupancy	42%	54%	60%	63%	66%
Resident Days	1,290	1,767	1,890	2,046	2,170
Income					
Occupied Efficiency Units—M. Care	37,500	38,750	40,000	41,250	41,250
Occupied Efficiency Units—Opt. Suppl.	1,480	2,220	2,960	2,960	3,700
Occupied Efficiency Units—Private Pay	2,400	3,600	4,800	4,800	6,000
Occupied 1 BR Units—Private Pay	12,000	25,500	30,000	33,000	34,500
Occupied 2 BR Units—Private Pay	0	0	0	0	0
Second Person Differential @ $350	350	1,050	1,050	1,050	1,400
Optional Services	234	468	558	594	666
Beauty Shop Revenue	129	171	189	198	210
Dietary Income	516	684	756	792	840
Laundry Income	129	171	189	198	210
Total Income	**54,738**	**72,614**	**80,502**	**84,842**	**88,776**
Expenses:					
Dietary Expenses					
Salary and Wages @ 8.4 FTE	10,119	10,119	10,119	10,119	10,119
Contract Services	200	200	200	200	200
Meat & Fish	4,128	5,654	6,048	6,547	6,944
Dairy Products	1,161	1,590	1,701	1,841	1,953
Fruit & Vegetable	387	530	567	614	651
Other Food Costs	387	530	567	614	651
Dietary Supplies	323	442	473	512	543
Equipment & Replacement	250	250	250	250	250
Total Dietary Expense	**16,955**	**19,316**	**19,925**	**20,697**	**21,311**

First Year Operations

Feb-98 Month 6	Mar-98 Month 7	Apr-98 Month 8	May-98 Month 9	Jun-98 Month 10	Jul-98 Month 11	Aug-98 Month 12	EOY Total
100	100	100	100	100	100	100	**100**
34	34	34	34	34	34	34	**34**
6	6	7	8	9	9	10	**10**
6	6	7	8	9	9	10	**10**
23	28	29	32	32	37	38	**38**
0	0	0	0	0	0	0	**0**
73	78	81	87	89	94	97	**97**
69%	74%	77%	82%	84%	89%	92%	**92%**
2,044	2,418	2,430	2,697	2,670	2,914	3,007	**27,343**
42,500	42,500	42,500	42,500	42,500	42,500	42,500	**496,250**
4,440	4,440	5,180	5,920	6,660	6,660	7,400	**54,020**
7,200	7,200	8,400	9,600	10,800	10,800	12,000	**87,600**
34,500	42,000	43,500	48,000	48,000	55,500	57,000	**463,500**
0	0	0	0	0	0	0	**0**
1,400	1,400	1,400	1,750	1,750	1,750	1,750	**16,100**
702	792	846	954	990	1,080	1,134	**9,018**
219	234	243	261	267	282	291	**2,694**
876	936	972	1,044	1,068	1,128	1,164	**10,776**
219	234	243	261	267	282	291	**2,694**
92,056	**99,736**	**103,284**	**110,290**	**112,302**	**119,982**	**123,530**	**1,142,652**
10,119	10,119	10,119	10,119	10,119	10,119	10,119	**121,428**
200	200	200	200	200	200	200	**2,400**
6,541	7,738	7,776	8,630	8,544	9,325	9,622	**87,498**
1,840	2,176	2,187	2,427	2,403	2,623	2,706	**24,609**
613	725	729	809	801	874	902	**8,203**
613	725	729	809	801	874	902	**8,203**
511	605	608	674	668	729	752	**6,836**
250	250	250	250	250	250	250	**3,000**
20,687	**22,538**	**22,598**	**23,919**	**23,786**	**24,993**	**25,454**	**262,176**

Assisted Living Facility: Full Financing Model—Operating Pro Forma
Page 2

	First Year Operations				
100 Unit Model	Sep-97 Month 1	Oct-97 Month 2	Nov-97 Month 3	Dec-97 Month 4	Jan-98 Month 5
Laundry & Linen					
Linen Replacement	300	300	300	300	300
Equipment & Repair	300	300	300	300	300
Total Laundry & Linen	600	600	600	600	600
Housekeeping					
Salary & Wages @ 3.9 FTE	3,848	3,848	3,848	3,848	3,848
Housekeeping Supplies	258	353	378	409	434
Total Housekeeping	4,106	4,201	4,226	4,257	4,282
Activities					
Salary & Wages @ 2.8 FTE	3,761	3,761	3,761	3,761	3,761
Entertainment	600	600	600	600	600
Total Activities	4,361	4,361	4,361	4,361	4,361
Plant Operations					
Gas	825	825	825	825	825
Electricity	2,000	2,275	2,400	2,475	2,525
Sewer/Water	450	505	530	545	555
Garbage	300	300	300	300	300
Cable Television	400	510	560	590	610
Salary & Wages @ 2.8 FTE	4,368	4,368	4,368	4,368	4,368
Grounds Maintenance	400	400	400	400	400
Repair & Maint. Supplies	650	650	650	650	650
Repair & Maint. Purchased Svcs.	400	400	400	400	400
Elevator Services	175	175	175	175	175
Pest Control	65	65	65	65	65
Service Contracts	300	300	300	300	300
Total Plant Operations	10,333	10,773	10,973	11,093	11,173

First Year Operations

Feb-98 Month 6	Mar-98 Month 7	Apr-98 Month 8	May-98 Month 9	Jun-98 Month 10	Jul-98 Month 11	Aug-98 Month 12	EOY Total
300	300	300	300	300	300	300	**3,600**
300	300	300	300	300	300	300	**3,600**
600	600	600	600	600	600	600	**7,200**
3,848	3,848	3,848	3,848	3,848	3,848	3,848	**46,176**
409	484	486	539	534	583	601	**5,469**
4,257	4,332	4,334	4,387	4,382	4,431	4,449	**51,645**
3,761	3,761	3,761	3,761	3,761	3,761	3,761	**45,132**
600	600	600	600	600	600	600	**7,200**
4,361	4,361	4,361	4,361	4,361	4,361	4,361	**52,332**
825	825	825	825	825	825	825	**9,900**
2,575	2,700	2,750	2,850	2,875	3,000	3,050	**31,475**
565	590	600	620	625	650	660	**6,895**
300	300	300	300	300	300	300	**3,600**
630	680	700	740	750	800	820	**7,790**
4,368	4,368	4,368	4,368	4,368	4,368	4,368	**52,416**
400	400	400	400	400	400	400	**4,800**
650	650	650	650	650	650	650	**7,800**
400	400	400	400	400	400	400	**4,800**
175	175	175	175	175	175	175	**2,100**
65	65	65	65	65	65	65	**780**
300	300	300	300	300	300	300	**3,600**
11,253	11,453	11,533	11,693	11,733	11,933	12,013	**135,956**

Assisted Living Facility: Full Financing Model—Operating Pro Forma
Page 3

100 Unit Model	*First Year Operations*				
	Sep-97 Month 1	Oct-97 Month 2	Nov-97 Month 3	Dec-97 Month 4	Jan-98 Month 5
Promotion & Marketing					
Contract Fees	1,083	1,083	1,083	1,083	1,083
Advertising	1,354	1,354	1,354	1,354	1,354
Total Promotion & Marketing	2,437	2,437	2,437	2,437	2,437
Employee Benefits					
Benefits & Payroll Taxes @ 28%	12,273	12,273	12,273	12,273	12,273
Total Employee Benefits	12,273	12,273	12,273	12,273	12,273
Personal Care Expenses					
Salary & Wages @ 12.5 FTE	14,603	14,603	14,603	14,603	14,603
Supplies/Other	750	750	750	750	750
Total Personal Care Exp.	15,353	15,353	15,353	15,353	15,353
Administration & General					
Director/Manager @ 2.0 FTE	5,240	5,240	5,240	5,240	5,240
Salary & Wages—Office @ 1.4 FTE	1,893	1,893	1,893	1,893	1,893
Management Fee	4,500	4,500	4,500	4,500	4,500
Postage	125	125	125	125	125
Office Supplies	225	225	225	225	225
Telephone & Communication	500	500	500	500	500
Travel	250	250	250	250	250
Auto & Van Expenses	350	350	350	350	350
Dues & Subscriptions	75	75	75	75	75
Bank Charges	75	75	75	75	75
Accounting & Audit Fees	500	500	500	500	500
Other	300	300	300	300	300
Total Admin. & General	14,033	14,033	14,033	14,033	14,033

First Year Operations

	Feb-98 Month 6	Mar-98 Month 7	Apr-98 Month 8	May-98 Month 9	Jun-98 Month 10	Jul-98 Month 11	Aug-98 Month 12	EOY Total
	1,083	1,083	1,083	1,083	1,083	1,083	1,083	**12,996**
	1,354	1,354	1,354	1,354	1,354	1,354	1,354	**16,248**
	2,437	2,437	2,437	2,437	2,437	2,437	2,437	**29,244**
	12,273	12,273	12,273	12,273	12,273	12,273	12,273	**147,276**
	12,273	12,273	12,273	12,273	12,273	12,273	12,273	**147,276**
	14,603	14,603	14,603	14,603	14,603	14,603	14,603	**175,236**
	750	750	750	750	750	750	750	**9,000**
	15,353	15,353	15,353	15,353	15,353	15,353	15,353	**184,236**
	5,240	5,240	5,240	5,240	5,240	5,240	5,240	**62,880**
	1,893	1,893	1,893	1,893	1,893	1,893	1,893	**22,716**
	4,500	4,500	4,500	4,500	4,500	4,500	4,500	**54,000**
	125	125	125	125	125	125	125	**1,500**
	225	225	225	225	225	225	225	**2,700**
	500	500	500	500	500	500	500	**6,000**
	250	250	250	250	250	250	250	**3,000**
	350	350	350	350	350	350	350	**4,200**
	75	75	75	75	75	75	75	**900**
	75	75	75	75	75	75	75	**900**
	500	500	500	500	500	500	500	**6,000**
	300	300	300	300	300	300	300	**3,600**
	14,033	14,033	14,033	14,033	14,033	14,033	14,033	**168,396**

Assisted Living Facility: Full Financing Model—Operating Pro Forma
Page 4

100 Unit Model	First Year Operations				
	Sep-97 **Month 1**	**Oct-97** **Month 2**	**Nov-97** **Month 3**	**Dec-97** **Month 4**	**Jan-98** **Month 5**
Property Taxes & Insurance					
Real Property Tax—Estimated	6,092	6,092	6,092	6,092	6,092
Personal Property Tax—Estimated	308	308	308	308	308
Insurance	295	295	295	295	295
Total Taxes & Insurance	6,695	6,695	6,695	6,695	6,695
Lease & Rental Expense					
Lease & Rental Equipment	1,042	1,042	1,042	1,042	1,042
Rentals—Miscellaneous Equipment	1,042	1,042	1,042	1,042	1,042
Total Lease & Rental	2,084	2,084	2,084	2,084	2,084
Depreciation & Amortization					
Depreciation—Buildings	8,639	8,639	8,639	8,639	8,639
Depreciation—Furniture & Fixtures	2,187	2,187	2,187	2,187	2,187
Amort.—Deferred Financing Costs	267	267	267	267	267
Amort.—Deferred Pre-Opening	1,283	1,283	1,283	1,283	1,283
Amort.—Construction Int. & Taxes	343	343	343	343	343
Total Depreciation & Amort.	12,719	12,719	12,719	12,719	12,719
Interest Expense					
Interest Expense	35,501	35,501	35,501	35,501	35,501
Total Interest Expense	35,501	35,501	35,501	35,501	35,501
Contingency	1,500	1,500	1,500	1,500	1,500
Total Expenses	138,949	141,846	142,679	143,602	144,321
Net Income	(84,211)	(69,232)	(62,177)	(58,760)	(55,545)
Add Back: Deprec. & Amort.	12,719	12,719	12,719	12,719	12,719
Minus: Replacement Reserve	4,000	4,000	4,000	4,000	4,000
Minus: Payment on Principal	(2,679)	(2,679)	(2,679)	(2,679)	(2,679)
Cash Flow	(70,171)	(55,192)	(48,137)	(44,721)	(41,505)

First Year Operations

	Feb-98 Month 6	Mar-98 Month 7	Apr-98 Month 8	May-98 Month 9	Jun-98 Month 10	Jul-98 Month 11	Aug-98 Month 12	EOY Total
	6,092	6,092	6,092	6,092	6,092	6,092	6,092	**73,098**
	308	308	308	308	308	308	308	**3,700**
	295	295	295	295	295	295	295	**3,540**
	6,695	6,695	6,695	6,695	6,695	6,695	6,695	**80,338**
	1,042	1,042	1,042	1,042	1,042	1,042	1,042	**12,504**
	1,042	1,042	1,042	1,042	1,042	1,042	1,042	**12,504**
	2,084	2,084	2,084	2,084	2,084	2,084	2,084	**25,008**
	8,639	8,639	8,639	8,639	8,639	8,639	8,639	**103,668**
	2,187	2,187	2,187	2,187	2,187	2,187	2,187	**26,244**
	267	267	267	267	267	267	267	**3,204**
	1,283	1,283	1,283	1,283	1,283	1,283	1,283	**15,396**
	343	343	343	343	343	343	343	**4,116**
	12,719	12,719	12,719	12,719	12,719	12,719	12,719	**152,628**
	35,501	35,501	35,501	35,501	35,501	35,501	35,501	**426,009**
	35,501	35,501	35,501	35,501	35,501	35,501	35,501	**426,009**
	1,500	1,500	1,500	1,500	1,500	1,500	1,500	**18,000**
	143,752	145,878	146,020	147,555	147,456	148,913	149,472	**1,740,442**
	(51,696)	(46,142)	(42,736)	(37,265)	(35,154)	(28,931)	(25,942)	**(597,790)**
	12,719	12,719	12,719	12,719	12,719	12,719	12,719	**152,628**
	4,000	4,000	4,000	4,000	4,000	4,000	4,000	**48,000**
	(2,679)	(2,679)	(2,679)	(2,679)	(2,679)	(2,679)	(2,679)	**(32,150)**
	(37,656)	(32,102)	(28,696)	(23,225)	(21,114)	(14,891)	(11,902)	**(429,312)**

Crossroads Hospital Medical Staff Development Plan
The Changing Organization and Management of Healthcare Delivery

1.0 EXECUTIVE SUMMARY

The healthcare framework, as we know it, has begun a significant metamorphosis. As a nation we are moving away from the paradigm of diagnosis and care to a predict-and-prevent model. The primary participants will be the same, but their place in the hierarchy will change as physicians and hospitals are pushed to the lower end of the food chain. This change is precipitated by national trends related to the following:

- The growth in managed care,
- The potentials of healthcare reform, and
- Increased costs and decreased revenues.

However, these and other trends create opportunities as they create change. The primary opportunity is for physicians and hospitals to pool their abilities through new organizational structures that produce win-win benefits for consumers, business, insurers, physicians, and hospitals.

The **Crossroads Hospital Medical Staff Development Plan** is an important step into a new future. The Plan offers the following goal, strategies and tactics to continue to positively position physicians and the hospital as significant players in healthcare delivery.

GOAL

Establish and maintain physician/hospital equality in satisfying community healthcare needs through a healthcare delivery system that fosters trust, interdependence and positive positioning through; communications, strategic decision making, governance, finance and strategic planning.

This section represents the work of The Health Service Group, Inc., and F. Gene DePorter, CHE, its president. It is a fine example of how to attack such a problem and I thank him for letting me include it here.

Short-term Strategies (1 to 3 Years)

- Establish a physician/hospital development committee to collaboratively determine alternate structures for future physician/hospital efforts.
- Develop a Management Services Organization (MSO) capability.
- Expand opportunities for physician participation in hospital and medical staff boards and committees.
- Develop a joint physician/hospital marketing program.
- Recruit needed physicians into three environments: a hospital primary care practice, intercity settings and outlying service area zip codes.
- Initiate an in-house recruiting program targeted for 10 physicians in 2001 and 11 in 2002.
- Initiate a "Physician Succession Planning" program.
- Develop an intra-referral network among the CH medical staff.
- Develop satellite ambulatory care sites.

Long-term Strategies (5 Years and Beyond)

- Satisfy the community need for physicians through an active recruiting program bringing in 53 new physicians by the end of calendar year 2005.
- Link the hospital and the medical staff in a long-term "value added" partnership with its own corporate identity by 2002.
- Develop long-term programs of centralized support services to enhance physician operating efficiency through 2005 and beyond.
- Develop a long-term hospital/medical staff marketing campaign to promote beneficial services to the community and cross sell services within the medical staff and between hospital and medical staff.
- Apply a "30% of projected physician need" recruiting strategy for 2001 through 2005.
- Actively involve the medical staff in the development of a "community care network" and the organization of a vertically and horizontally integrated system for the service area.
- Develop primary care clinics in the region and anchor with existing medical staff and recruited physicians through 2005.
- All joint activities should achieve parity for participation related to incentives, financial risk and reward by 2003 and be Medicare-compliant.

Strategic Initiatives and Tactics

Strategy-Communications

- Create a common understanding of marketplace forces and competitive activity.

Tactics

- Develop a video tape education series from the office of Medical Affairs and hospital management that would be distributed to core medical staff and provide monthly updates on key business issues. Implement by January 2002.
- Involve existing and younger physician leadership in outside education experiences that track managed care impacts as well as aspects of hospital finance and management. Implement by January 2002.
- Bring in outside experts on a quarterly basis for presentations, along with the hospital president, to the medical staff, management and board on issues affecting all three constituencies. Implement by April 2001.
- Benchmark "Medical Staff/Hospital Best Communication" techniques. Implement January 2002.
- Develop "Medical Staff Support Teams" that assume ongoing responsibility for the preceding tactics. Implement June 2001.
- Work with hospital senior management to develop a "Communications Tree" to maintain monthly contact with five physicians per administrative team member. These five physicians should include existing and emerging medical staff leadership. Implement April 2002.
- Meet with high volume physician utilizers of inpatient/outpatient services on a quarterly basis to discuss services, issues and opportunities. Implement April 2001.
- Offer physician office management seminars on a quarterly or as needed basis through the hospital continuing education department. Implement April 2003.
- Develop a joint physician/hospital marketing committee by Fall of 2002. Use contract marketing support to the MSO to provide the following; cross selling of medical staff and hospital, focused direct mailings, patient education, etc.

Strategy—Decision Making

- CH in conjunction with the medical staff should jointly develop structures and policies that produce collaborative decision making through early and continuous involvement of physicians.

Tactics

- Establish a development committee with equal representation of physicians (younger emerging leaders) and management to identify potential areas of development, their feasibility, and implementation by 2001/2002.
- Expand physician participation in CH Board activities by Fall of 2001.
- All joint program development should be supported by applying the following decision points by FY 2001/2002:

  New services evaluated for strategic and technical advantage,
  collaborative services must be based upon a two year break-even point,
  activity must not compromise tax exempt status and must be in compliance
  with federal and state regulations,

All service initiatives must reinforce a positive Physician/Hospital relationship and community benefit,
Service initiatives should enhance existing revenues or secure new revenue streams for physicians and the hospital.

Strategy—Planning

- Short- and long-term planning should be jointly conducted by physicians and hospital to benefit community need. A planning orientation toward wellness and prevention should dominate all health delivery approaches for the foreseeable future.

Tactics

- CH and medical staff should develop a managed services organization (MSO) as an initial step toward a more formalized structure, by June 2001. The MSO should provide the following core services at start-up:
    Practice Marketing and Promotion,
    Group Purchasing Services,
    Office Staff Education and Training Programs,
    Practice Management Consulting,
    Additional services should be added in late 2001 or by the first quarter of 2002.
- Every physician/hospital planning effort must include sub plans for marketing, finance, staffing and resource allocation, starting in 2002.
- All planning should include time frames and accountability and be monitored on a quarterly basis for achievement of critical success factors.
- *Physician Recruiting:* Physicians and hospitals should agree to apply the "20% projected need rule" for total physician need for 2001 recruiting. Based upon the success of '01 recruiting and environmental factors, the organization should evaluate recruiting by using the "30% projected need rule" for 2002 through 2005. Recruitment should be based upon "community need," compliance, and a managed care point of view.
- The following physician recruitment by specialty is recommended:

	'01	'02	'03	'04	'05
Anesthesiology			1	1	1
Emergency Medicine	1		1		
Family Practice	3	2	3	2	3
Dermatology		1			1
Internal Medicine	3	2	2	2	2
Neurology			1		
Cardiology				1	
Psychiatry	2	2	1	1	1
Pathology		1		1	
Surgery General	1	1	1	1	2
Plastic		1		1	
Urology			1		
Gastroenterology				1	
Total	10	11	10	11	10

- Develop a hospital-based primary care and E.R. physicians' group by recruiting two physicians by Fall of 2001 and one each in '03 and '04. These physicians would be responsible for unassigned patients.
- Eliminate access concerns by anchoring future primary care physicians in satellite clinics using a split approach of development in the city of Crossroads and placement in outlying zip codes that are in need. Utilize this approach from 2001 to 2005 with at least one to two physician placements in key zip codes until need is satisfied, that is:

2001-Physician/Zip code	99901	99902	99903	99904	99905	99906
Family Practice	1		1	1		
Surgery—Gen.	1					
Internal Medicine		1	1	1		
Psychiatry	1			1		
2002-Physician/Zip code						
Family Practice		1			1	
Surgery—Gen.					1	1
Internal Medicine					1	1
Psychiatry			1			1
Dermatology				1		

- Work with selected medical staff to develop part time satellite ambulatory care sites in under-served and core outlying zip codes. Combine this with primary care physician recruitment and support with physician assistants and nurse practitioners.
- Initiate a "Physician Succession Planning" program in the Fall of 2001 using the following approaches:
  Practice assessment,
  Work with retiring physicians—one on one,
  Retain third party support resources where needed,
  Allow 2 to 5 years for succession planning turnover,
  Implement a mentoring program,
  Request letters from physicians over the age of 55 that would reference their projected year of retirement,
  Provide practice valuation services as part of succession recruitment.
- CH as part of an MSO should underwrite "Succession Recruitment," though the ultimate decision for services to be provided to private physicians should be determined by legal counsel.
- Develop an "Intra-Referral Network" among CH primary and specialty care physicians by 2002. Utilize a marketing and communications effort that increases awareness and preference within the service area for physicians affiliated with CH.

- CH medical staff through a MSO structure, should evaluate direct contracting opportunities as well as existing managed care contracting and determine the feasibility of a direct contracting program by June 2001.
- CH and the medical staff should take the lead in developing a "Community Care Network" that represents vertical and horizontal integration of healthcare resources regionally. This effort should include the Acme Community Health Center, Crossroads Department of Public Health and other providers of healthcare services. Efforts should be taken to establish a meeting of these organizations by 4/01 and to develop an action plan by mid summer of 2001.
- CH and the medical staff should serve as a catalyst to assist the merger and possible acquisition of practices.
- Establish a "Director of Physician Services" position within the Office of Medical Affairs by 2003. This individual would be responsible for communication, education (nonclinical), practice support, and physician recruitment.
- Develop information systems for management and physician recruitment that will enhance decision making for the Office of Medical Affairs. This activity should be initiated in January 2003 with a basic system operational by June 2004.

Strategy—Governance
- Joint activities of medical staff and CH should have board and executive committee parity. Existing medical staff committees should expand where possible to accommodate emerging leadership of the medical staff and provide an orientation for younger physicians by 2004.

Tactics
- Encourage interaction and relationship building among board, medical staff, and management through reorganized structures.
- Expand medical staff executive committee to include nonvoting positions targeted to younger physicians on the medical staff by 2003.
- Develop a balanced mix of primary and specialty care physicians whenever possible.
- Require problem solving at the lowest level of medical staff development.

Strategy—Finance
- Improve relations with physicians by economically aligning physician and hospital risk and incentives within the parameters provided by "safe harbors" and the IRS.

Tactics
- Expand physician participation in the financing of alternative care structures and a physician/hospital organization by 2003.

- Develop a financial strategy for physicians and hospital that assists risk sharing and discounted fee structure in pursuit of managed care/direct contracting opportunities by 2003.
- Those physicians whose utilization of the hospital's resources is 2% of total charges or admissions should be supported through every legal means possible.
- Develop a program of cost saving for physicians through centralized support services with stringent cost-containment requirements.

2.0 PROLOGUE

Newspaper and Magazine Headlines—2000

"Nationally, Number Of Physicians Available Exceeds Need"

"Payment For Medical Services Continues To Decline"

"Health Services Shift Dramatically From 'Diagnose And Treat' To 'Predict And Prevent'"

"The World That Young Doctors Face Today Is Far Cry From The One Their Role Models Knew"

The healthcare framework, as we have known it, has made a significant metamorphosis. As a nation, we are moving away from the paradigm of diagnosis and care to a model of prediction and prevention through advances in genomics, genetics, nanotechnology, DNA chips, angiogenesis, and a plethora of tools not previously available.

The primary participants in this shifting health service infrastructure will continue to be the government, business, consumers, insurers, physicians and hospitals. The difference from then to now is that the structure is being turned upside down with the result that physicians and hospitals will be moving to the lower end of the food-chain.

Throughout the country the healthcare environment is undergoing rapid and broad change, change that is precipitated by three national trends:

- The growth in managed care and the necessity for hospitals and physicians to gain as many managed care contracts as possible. An additional consequence of managed care growth is the emphasis on wellness, prevention, and outpatient services,
- The rewards of billions of dollars invested in the Human Genome Project, quantum physics, and information and computer processing technologies, and
- The increasing desire of many physicians to leave the concerns of operating a practice and devote themselves to practicing medicine.

Change is opportunity, and Stephen Shortell, in his book, *Effective Hospital-Physician Relationships,* indicates that as healthcare resources become more limited, physicians and hospitals will find themselves in a no-win competition unless they develop beneficial linkages.[1] Shortell identifies several factors that will challenge the development of successful linkages; however, if they can be overcome, the opportunities will be numerous. The challenges identified by Shortell are:

- Expectation about involvement will be quite different between the hospital leadership and the medical staff.
- There will be limitations in terms of the medical staff leadership speaking for the majority of physicians on staff.
- Physicians and hospital managers are trained differently and therefore have very different attitudes and views toward the same subject.

A highly competitive and potentially more-regulated environment is driving the hospital and medical staff together in an effort to jointly transition to the new order of business for healthcare. In spite of differences and because of common external pressures, CH and the CH medical staff have initiated efforts to define a Medical Staff Development Plan (MSDP) and investigate the feasibility of a Management Service Organization (MSO). It is believed that these efforts will improve communications, develop a common vision for a successful future, and define the strategic links and next steps that will be necessary to enhance the new approaches to health and well being.

At the same time, physician/hospital support of the implementation of the recommendations contained in this plan will be the tangible evidence of a joint commitment to be successful participants in the future healthcare marketplace. The first steps in developing a proactive strategy for and by the medical staff were taken in the early summer of 1999 with the decision to develop a medical staff plan. In August interviews were held with CH's management, physician leadership and several community based practitioners concerning medical staff relations. In addition a questionnaire was structured to determine the medical staffs' position on a number of issues. In September this questionnaire was sent to 292 physicians. By the initial cut-off in October, 58% of the Attending and Associate medical staff had responded. Additional questionnaire returns have pushed the response rate to 71%. The questionnaire was paralleled with the development of a statistical profile emphasizing the demographics of the medical staff and the hospital's service area population. The statistical profile has served as the basis for determining physician need by specialty and geographic distribution.

The issues identified from the interviews, questionnaires and statistical profile present opportunities and challenges that will be apparent in the following sections of this plan. However, at this point it is important to note that Shortell's observations are on target as the following comments and observations from CH medical staff indicate:

- Physicians exhibit a low level of participation in medical staff activities. Indications are that less than 50% of the medical staff attend meetings.
- Physicians are reluctant to accept the decisions of the medical staff leadership. Because of low attendance the medical staff leadership is elected by a minority of physicians.

- Hospital management perceives that the medical staff is not speaking with one voice. Therefore management hesitates to make decisions concerning physician requests because of potential backlash and thus physicians feel the hospital is not responsive.
- The hospital management structure is perceived to be too bureaucratic and there is a lack of equity with hospital response to physicians.
- Concerns exist about the ability and future role of hospital-based marketing. Marketing is not viewed as capable of developing new product lines, business plans, anticipating the future, and working effectively to promote existing services.
- Physicians perceive some management to be adversarial toward them.
- Concerns are expressed about who would manage and operate a PHO, if it is developed.
- The medical staff and hospital management need to develop trust, open lines of communication and shared governance to better address the profound changes in healthcare.

3.0 CONTEXT

The healthcare industry is experiencing an unprecedented whirlwind of change. The Clinton presidential campaign launched an agenda of healthcare reform and now with the Clinton presidency in place that agenda became proposed legislation as of October 27, 1998.

Yesterday's standards of practice for healthcare are no longer the norm. Regardless of the negotiated outcome of federal legislation, change will occur. Physicians, hospitals, managed care plans, insurers, state governments, consumers, business and others are positioning their sector to fare well in a legislated future.

Change means transition and some of the transitions that the healthcare industry is witnessing are the following:

- *Healthcare Provider to Healthcare Delivery System:* Over the next three to five years, healthcare systems will evolve structures that represent vertically integrated seamless continuums of care. The key building blocks of such systems will be; acute care hospitals, physicians group practices, rehabilitation and psychiatric services, long-term care providers, ambulatory care centers, PPOs, HMOs, PHOs and others.
- *Fee-for-Service to Capitated Payment:* Nationally, 16% of the population is covered by managed care contracts. In sections of the country this figure ranges from 50% in Minneapolis-St. Paul to 93% in the Sacramento Valley. In areas of the Southeast, managed care market penetration is approximately 20% with significant future growth anticipated.
- *Solo Practitioner to Large Group Practice to Systems Employee:* Reduced reimbursement has physicians spending less time with patients in the hopes of

increasing volumes to off-set lost revenue. It is difficult for a solo practitioner to accomplish this result while a group practice setting increases volume potentials. In addition, managed care plans are driven by volumes so they therefore seek group practice participation versus solo practitioners. More physicians will become employees of hospitals, PHO foundations, group practices, and managed care plans.

- *Care-at-Home to Hospital Care to Outpatient Care to Home Care:* Technology and cost move care of the sick from one's home into institutional settings and now technology and cost are moving patient care from the institutional setting back to the home. Home healthcare services have been growing at a compound annual rate of 10.2% from 1986 to 1991, with similar growth projected for the future. Physicians are becoming more comfortable with home care although uncomfortable with the level of compensation for the care management of patients at home. The home care business will be important for hospitals in their efforts to establish a vertically integrated system.

- *The General Practitioner to the Era of the Specialist to the Reestablished Dominance of the Primary Care Physician:* We have run the loop from predominantly general practitioners in the 1930s and 1940s to the dominance of specialty care physicians (65% specialists and 35% primary care mix as of 1992). The emphasis now is to develop a 40% specialist to 60% primary physician mix over the next ten to fifteen years. Specialists are now returning to school or seeking certification as primary care physicians.

- *Data of Limited Usefulness to Compact High-Tech Information Systems:* Paperless medical records and standardized claim forms are but two of the many capabilities in the information age. Some states have introduced legislation to require electronic medical records and claim forms for hospitals and evolving healthcare networks. Wireless technology will shift the focus away from bedside monitors to terminals that go with the physician and nurse. Information technology is becoming more powerful and cheaper. Physicians are seeking and expecting real-time computer links with hospitals and other physicians. Information is knowledge and knowledge is power.

The consequences of these transitions are that physicians are facing increasing costs associated with practicing medicine, while managed care growth and RBRVS will hold the lid on reimbursement. As physicians continue to see their incomes under attack, competition escalating and demands on their time increasing they are starting to turn to hospitals, large group practices, practice organizations and managed care to employ them and allow them to practice medicine instead of managing a practice.

In addition to all the economic and practice issues, physicians are faced with the probability of healthcare reform that, in its current approach, is encouraging physicians and hospitals to collaborate. Such activity will accelerate the development of standards of care, allow physicians to concentrate on treating and advising patients and possibly stabilize physician income.

4.0 MEDICAL STAFF DEVELOPMENT QUESTIONNAIRE—2000

4.1 Overview

In the summer of 1999, a questionnaire was sent to 292 attending and associate medical staff of Crossroads Hospital. The questionnaire returns occurred over three months with an initial cut-off response of 168/292 (58%) and subsequent continued response totaling 208/292 (71%). This significant level of response allows for a more accurate interpretation of medical staff thinking for the topics referenced.

The objectives of the questionnaire were as follows:

- To identify areas of physician concern specific to their practice and/or relationship with CH.
- Explore the willingness of the medical staff to link or work with CH in joint ventures or managed care contract negotiations.
- Identify whether clinical and practice support training programs, implemented by CH, would be well received.
- Provide an indicator for future practice growth and hospital utilization.
- Identify the attitudes of physicians related to current and anticipated market conditions for the practice of medicine.
- Identify medical staff support programs that would be perceived by physicians to be beneficial.

4.2 Summary of Survey Findings

Questionnaire responses were grouped by age (<55 years and ≥56 years) and specialty (primary care/internal medicine, pediatrics, family practice, OB/GYN, and specialty care). A profile of the existing medical staff was developed from information provided by the office of Medical Staff Services of CH. The medical staff profile provided the following information:

- Primary care physicians make up 45% (131/292) of the medical staff. Only 18 (14%) of the 131 are over 55 years of age. The average age for primary care physicians in 42.
- Specialty care physicians make up 55% (161/292) of the medical staff. Only 26 (16%) of the 161 are over the age of 55. The average age for specialty care physicians is 45.
- Approximately 44 of the existing medical staff, who are age 55, should be the focal point of a "Succession Planning" program. Nationally, the reference point for beginning Succession Planning is for those physicians age 50+. If CH began at this point, then approximately 73 (25%) of the 292 CH medical staff are candidates for this program.
- A number of specialties will be impacted by physicians aging to retirement: 12/28 (43%) OB/GYN physicians are 50+, 6/7 (86%) general surgeons are 50+, 7/17 (41%) ophthalmologists are 50+, 3/7 (43%) plastic surgeons are

50+, 3/7 (43%) urologists are 50+, 4/9 (44%) cardiologists are 50+, 1/2 (50%)
endocrinologists are 50+, 1/2 (50%) hematologists are 50+, 1/2 (50%)
nephrologists are 50+, and 11/40 (28%) pediatricians are 50+.

The stronger the questionnaire response rate the greater the likelihood that the respondent
profile will mirror the medical staff composition as a whole. This fact holds true for this
questionnaire with the respondents being within 2-5% points of the total staff. The data indicated a 58% response rate. There were an additional 40 questionnaires received after the
October cut-off date which raises the responses to 71%.

4.3 Summary of Questionnaire Response and Implication

The following is a summary of the response to each question with an interpretation of the
implication of the response. Bear in mind that not all respondents answered each question.
Therefore, the tabulations by question often will not equal the total number of
respondents.

Survey Questions and Responses

1. **If health services were developed and offered to businesses and managed
   care providers, how should they be developed?**

   Response: 89% of the primary care and 83% of the specialty care physicians
   responded that managed care and direct contracting should be accomplished
   through a combination of efforts by the hospital and the medical staff. On
   average 86% of the respondents are in favor of sharing the development of
   services and marketing them to business and managed care.

   Implication: The medical staff and the hospital will have a stronger negotiation
   position if they link to address managed care/direct contracting, new service
   initiatives and the management and marketing of same. Neither the physicians
   nor the hospital can offer as strong a package as they can in concert.

2. **Several hospitals in the Southeast are expanding by networking with
   other hospitals and their medical staffs. What should CH do about
   networking?**

   Response: 29% indicated that they had no opinion while 67% are in favor. Of
   the 104 physicians responding to this question, 86 are under 54 years of age
   and 42% are primary care doctors.

   Implication: The younger physicians (<55) and specialists tend to support
   networking. If the hospital and physicians decide to not pursue networking
   they will become isolated, lose market share and managed care contracts.
   Networking could increase the referral base. These activities may best be
   accomplished through a separate corporate structure such as a "Physician/
   Hospital Organization" (PHO) which could be expanded to service other
   geography. An expanded PHO could incorporate medical staffs of other
   hospitals, service multi-site employers, develop group purchasing capacity
   and centralized support services.

3. **Healthcare seems to be going toward integrated delivery systems. Integrating means affiliating with various healthcare providers such as outpatient services and physicians. How do you feel about an integrated delivery system?**

   Response: 126 of 156 (81%) indicated that they agreed that integrated delivery systems are the best way to provide healthcare. 107 of 126 (85%) of the <55 physicians favor an integrated system.

   Implication: Older physicians see themselves as working out of the healthcare system and therefore tend not to respond. Younger physicians and specialists are more in line with the emerging structure of healthcare and are moving from solo to group practice or seeking a group practice setting from the beginning.

4. **In your judgment, which of the following community clinical services or programs deserve investigation and/or development at CH?**

   Response: There were 19 program options listed and the following 15 (in rank order) received the most responses: Nephrology, Neurosurgery, Dialysis Unit, Cardiac Angioplasty, Cardiac Surgery, Level 2 Nursery, Inpatient Diabetes, 24 Hour Pharmacy, New/Expanded Nursing Home, Adult Day Care, Durable Medical Equipment, Sports Medicine, Assisted Living, Women's Infertility Center and Alzheimer Unit.

   The above services received 80 or more favorable responses. The remaining four services; Burn Center, Level 3 trauma Center, Retirement Housing and HIV/AIDS Services received 58 or less supporting responses. The interest level and support for new programs and services was strongest among the <55 physicians.

   Implication: Physicians want CH to maintain a high level of clinical services and excellence while avoiding services appropriate to a tertiary level. The services supported by physicians would enhance the breadth of programs that would appeal to managed care and support the physicians in their practices. Older physicians showed less interest in new services possibly because they are aging out of their practices.

5. **Managed care will probably grow in importance. In your opinion, what do you feel is the best way to negotiate managed care contracts?**

   Response: 57% or 89 of 157 physicians feel that the hospital and the physicians should negotiate as a single unit. 79% of the 89 are primary and specialty care physicians under the age of 55.

   Implication: The medical staff support for physicians and hospital negotiating as one unit is not significant. The fact that 43% did not support this approach indicates a need for further communication with those physicians to determine their position. Some of the lack of support can be attributed to older physicians who may view themselves as moving out of the system. If it is felt that a PHO is the direction to pursue, then it should start with younger primary care physicians who represent good geographic distribution. As a second stage, other physicians, who are interested and qualify without restriction to age or specialty, should be brought into the structure. Joint efforts in a PHO should produce more effective pricing strategies. However, it should be noted that if a PHO organization is attempted the respondents do not have confidence in the current management or physician leadership to structure the PHO or operate it. It also appears that physicians may not be aware of the "How" of participation; e.g., equity, subscription and/or level of control.

6. **In your opinion, are there enough consulting physicians to support your practice?**

Response: 131 of the 156 respondents indicated that there has been no problem in locating consulting physicians. Of those that indicated there is a problem, the most common response was the lack of an infectious disease physician.

Implication: There may be a need to recruit an Infectious Disease physician, otherwise CH medical staff feel there are sufficient specialists to meet their needs. Medical staff will be concerned about any recruiting initiative that would saturate the service area by specialty.

7. **How appropriate do you feel it is for CH to enter into joint ventures with members of their medical staff?**

Response: 147 physicians responded to this question with 128 (87%) indicating that they felt it is appropriate for CH to enter into joint ventures. Eight primary care and eleven specialty care physicians felt it is not appropriate.

Implication: Physicians cautiously consider the hospital as their most likely partner to stabilize their practices and initiate new services that could develop or enhance revenue.

8. **What joint venture projects would you be willing to participate in with Crossroads Hospital?**

Response: Of the physicians who answered this question, most were interested in participating within their own specialty in a managed care system or a Physician/Hospital Organization (PHO).

Implication: Physicians are open to discussing joint ventures particularly if they answer practice needs, deal with managed care, or potentially enhance revenue. But they will require greater participation in decision making and governance of any joint effort.

9. **What changes do you anticipate in your practice or use of CH facilities within the next three to five years?**

Response: 141 of 150 (94%) of respondents stated that they anticipate their practice expanding or staying the same over the next 3-5 years. Only 9 of 150

(6%) indicated that they would be downsizing their practice. The use of CH outpatient services is anticipated to increase while 56% of the respondents indicated that they expect to increase their use of inpatient services. Those physicians indicating growth in their practice are predominantly <54 years of age.

Implication: There is unmet need in the marketplace which is indicated by a significant number of physicians indicating growth in their practice. Physician recruitment based upon need calculations should be conservatively implemented through a formula that accounts for service area location, existing practice volumes, market absorption of new practices and other factors. Older physicians see less practice growth and these physicians should be supported with "succession" planning. Younger physicians need to be groomed for leadership roles.

10. **At this time, my practice has additional patient capacity, will be full in the near future or is at capacity and unable to expand.**

Response: 72% (91) of the physicians responded that they have additional patient capacity in their practices. Of the 151 physicians that responded to this question, 126 are under age 55. There were 43 physicians who indicated that their practices are at capacity; 22 are primary care and 21 are specialty care physicians.

Implication: Refer to number 9.

11. **In your judgment is your specialty adequately represented within the community?**

Response: Of the 168 questionnaires returned, 159 (95%) responded to this question. 88% indicated that they felt their specialty was adequately represented. Those indicating a need for additional physicians were primary care physicians.

Implication: Physician recruitment needs from the perspective of the existing medical staff is for predominantly primary care physicians with some specialists as a function of aging out.

12. **More physicians are presently needed in the following specialties?**

Response: Respondents indicated that physicians are needed in the following specialties in rank order: Infectious Disease, Primary Care, Family Medicine, Gastroenterology and Endocrinology.

Implication: Refer to number 11.

13. **What is your position on managed care and the involvement of hospital and medical staff? Specifically . . .**

Should the hospital actively seek managed care contracts?

Response: 79% of the physicians responding think that CH should seek managed care contracts.

Are you interested in working with the hospital to attract managed care contracts?

Response: This question had a large number of no opinion responses. 65% of those responding indicated that they would assist.

Will the hospital and physicians lose patients without managed care?

Response: 82% of the respondents felt that the hospital and physicians would lose patients if managed care contracts were not pursued.

Implication: Physicians know that they cannot let the managed care business go by. However, they are not certain they know how to deal with it in their practice. They struggle with reduced personal incomes. The hospital needs to work with its medical staff by first offering practice support services and overlapping that with the development of managed care pricing strategies.

14. **Are there education programs that you would like to see offered through CH?**

    Response: For medical staff, they are asking for programs that would provide information on managed care and more information on healthcare reform. For office personnel it was felt that the hospital could provide centralized training to deal with OSHA rules and regulations, PALS, CPR courses, ALS courses and the new CLIA laws.

    Implication: CH should develop an ongoing physician education program that explains managed care, healthcare reform and the responses to both. CH should also develop continuing education for physician practice personnel.

15. **In your judgment, which of the following practice support programs need investigation and development through CH?**

    Response: The medical staff had the opportunity to rank order 14 areas of support that resulted in the following order; marketing and promotion (114), computer/fax link (105), patient insurance counseling (99), group purchasing services (97), office staff education (97), physician/staff recruitment (85), practice management consulting (75), practice planning (75), practice audit/evaluation/ assessment (73), billing services (69), office management support (61), practice acquisition services (60), retirement planning assistance (58), social events (44). The social events area received the most negative votes (83).

    Implication: The medical staff would welcome staff training programs jointly developed with the hospital. Such programs could be the basis for improving medical staff hospital relations and assist both groups in their drive for improved operating efficiency.

16. **Many changes are affecting healthcare. A few of those changes include RBRVS, the growth of managed care and healthcare reform. Please comment on how you think these changes will affect your practice.**

Response: The most frequent response to this question was decreased reimbursement and patient care and increased paperwork. Many felt that promoting preventive care should be encouraged.

Implication: The hospital has the opportunity to develop, in conjunction with the medical staff, a support services program for physicians.

17. **The above mentioned changes could affect practices economically. What will be the impact on your practice?**

Response: Most physicians responded that they will see a decrease in their income, an increase in administrative work and more competition for services and patients.

Implication: Refer to number 16.

18. **How do you think the hospital and physicians should meet these changes in healthcare?**

Response: Of the 148 who responded to this question 132 (89%) indicated that the hospital and physicians should join together to meet these challenges. 111 (84%) of the 132 are <55.

Implication: The physicians under 55 are better oriented toward working with the hospital in an organized fashion to position effectively for managed care. However, there is a high level of caution on the part of physicians that is related to the past history of medical staff/hospital relations and a continuing concern about the ability of management and the hospital's marketing resources to lead an organized response, PHO or otherwise.

19. **Please provide any written comments:**

Response: The written comments were compiled and listed by specialty and age.

5.0 COMMUNITY PHYSICIAN NEED—2000–2004

5.1 Medical Staff Development Environment

Prior to the advent of Medicare Fraud and Abuse Statutes and related Safe Harbor Provisions, the recruitment and retention of medical staff had been conducted on an informal and in some instances, ad hoc basis. However, as the 1990s have unfolded, the healthcare industry is being scrutinized, externally and internally. The intensity of these inquiries is not only a function of concerns related to the cost of healthcare, but concurrent to cost, are a number of critical issues related to technology, reimbursement, manpower, competition and fraud and abuse of the Medicare/Medicaid systems.

When one analyzes the issue of physician manpower, it becomes readily apparent that we are continuing to suffer from inequities associated with the mal-distribution of physicians, a current shortage of primary care doctors and the total number of physicians growing at a rate faster than the growth of the general population. In addition, because of the past inappropriate practices of a few related to Medicare/Medicaid, the relationship between medical staff and hospital has gone under the microscope of the Health Care Finance Administration (HCFA), the Internal Revenue Service (IRS) and the U.S. Attorney General's Office (AGO). The inquiries of these agencies of government have been paralleled by the development of Fraud and Abuse Statutes, Safe Harbors, General Council Memorandum, and Private Letter Rulings (PLR), all of which question the structure of the relationship and involvement of physicians and hospitals. Since the inauguration of the Clinton Administration, there have been IRS rulings that might suggest some flexibility around the organization of physicians and hospitals.

However, inurement continues to be an area of serious investigation. This theme dominates the focus of external agencies and, as such, must be appreciated and dealt with in a very forthright manner. It is because of our rapidly changing operating environment, the growth of managed care, and the demands for increased documentation of "community benefit" that activities in the area of medical staff development must be supported by a well reasoned and documented plan. Such a plan should be anchored in reasonable calculations of "community need" for physicians. The following information reflects such calculations and will serve as the basis for the Medical Staff Development Plan.

5.2 The CH Service Area and Physicians Characteristics

The Crossroads Hospital service area (as defined by CH) includes 24 zip codes and serves a 1998 population of 319,884 and a 2004 population of 350,939. The geographic distribution of the existing medical staff is not inconsistent with the norm and has 53 primary care and 100 specialty care physicians clustered around the hospital in zip code **XXXXX**. This clustering of physicians represents 53% (153/292) of the entire medical staff. The next cluster in proximity to CH is the Veterans Affairs Hospital in zip code **XXXXX** with 15 primary and 15 specialty care physicians. The Anytown Community Health Center in zip code **XXXXX** shows 16 primary and 3 specialty care physicians. In total, the zip codes that makeup the city of Crossroads represent a population base of 184,161 (2004 population) people being served by 89 primary care and 130 specialty care physicians.

Beyond Crossroads, CH medical staff clusters exist in Jones Crossing (**99902**, 30 primary and 13 specialty care physicians) and Oxmox (**99903**, 26 primary and 14 specialty care physicians—Anytown Medical Center).

5.3 Physician/Community Need Calculation

The summary of calculations comparing the existing physician availability by specialty for the CH service area against calculations for 1998 actual and 2004 projected physician need have been presented elsewhere in this report. The differences between column desired number of physicians and projected physician complement represents the "need" for 1998 and 2004. The "need" may also been adjusted for "aging out" of medical staff by specialty. The final subjective estimate is the number of physicians that can be recruited and absorbed in a community in any given year (20%). This final adjustment is based upon experience, room for growth in existing practices and the benefit of organizing and supporting the medical staff through a formal structure. This conservative calculation of adjusted physician need can range from 20-30%. This calculation also neutralizes the presence of physicians based at the Acme and Zenith schools of medicine and their outreach clinics. An adjusted 2004 need exists for 24 primary care physicians (13 family practice, 0 pediatricians, 0.4 OB/GYNs, 11 internists) and 28 specialty care physicians. The need calculations were done on the basis of zip code and for the City of Crossroads on the basis of census tracts.

An additional adjustment can be made for the growing impact of female physicians. It is important to note that research has clearly documented that female physicians have very definite practice tendencies in terms of specialties chosen, practice settings and geographic location and number of hours worked. In reference to hours worked research indicates that female physicians see approximately 9 to 17% fewer patients than their male counterparts. Female physicians are growing significantly as a percent of total physicians and currently represent 20% of all physicians nationally. Female physicians are 26% of the CH medical staff. As the CH medical staff reflects the presence of more female physicians, future physician need projections will need to be adjusted for the reduced patient volumes of female physicians.

5.4   Medical Staff Aging

Another key element of medical staff development is "Succession Planning." This area of activity acknowledges that physicians begin to age out of practice at age 55. A good succession program can take from two to five years to work up with a physician and therefore age 50 becomes the first benchmark for physicians and hospitals to jointly work with physicians preparing for retirement. This is an opportunity to begin to highlight the achievements of these physicians while also acknowledging the need to work with them to recruit their replacement and continue to satisfy community need.

Another piece of information that documents that physicians begin to age-out of practice is the "Mean Net Income" data provided by the American Medical Association in its 1998 report, "Socioeconomic Characteristics of Medical Practice." This report confirms that the earning potential for the majority of physicians peaks between ages 46 to 55 with a dramatic drop in income from age 56 to 66. As noted in Section 4, there are a number of specialties in which significant numbers of physicians are currently 50+ years of age; namely, 12/28 (43%) OB/GYN physicians, 6/7 (86%) general surgeons, 7/17 (41%) ophthalmologists, 3/7 (43%) plastic surgeons, 3/7 (43%) urologists, 4/9 (44%) cardiologists, 1/2 (50%) endocrinologists, 1/2 (50%) hematologists, 1/2 (50%) nephrologists, 11/41 (28%) pediatricians.

Another perspective on the impact of physicians aging-out is that as of fiscal '98/'99, 50% of the top 20 physician utilizers of CH are over 50 years of age and 7 of 20 are over age 55.

6.0   STRATEGIC INITIATIVES

6.1   Overview

The information provided in the preceding sections indicates that physicians want to be associated with Crossroads Hospital, desire an increased presence in the decision making process and governance of the hospital, are interested in a joint relationship to address managed care/direct contracting, and are interested in practice support services from the hospital.

Physicians no longer seek to compete with hospitals because they are facing the same environmental pressures of competition, stringent cost containment in the face of increasing operating costs, increasing utilization review/quality assurance requirements, a more-educated consumer and employer/insurer cost sensitivity. All of this is occurring against a backdrop of physician concern with meeting community healthcare needs through cost-effective, high-quality services. Physicians are seeking a "value added" partnership with hospitals and the communities they serve.

Using the body of this report as a baseline, the following strategic initiatives and tactics are listed as a CH Medical Staff Development Plan—Road Map to the Year 2000.

CROSSROADS HOSPITAL MEDICAL STAFF DEVELOPMENT PLAN (1999–2004)

6.2   Goal

Establish and maintain physician/hospital equality in healthcare delivery through mechanisms that foster trust, interdependence, and positive positioning. Specifically, the following:

- Communications
- Strategic Decision Making
- Governance
- Finance
- Strategic Planning

6.3   Strategic Initiatives and Tactics

Strategy 6.3.1—Communications
- Create a common understanding of marketplace forces and competitive activity.

Tactics
- Develop a video tape education series from the office of Medical Affairs and hospital management that would be distributed to core medical staff and provide monthly updates on key business issues. Implement by January 2000.
- Involve existing and younger physician leadership in outside education experiences that track healthcare reform as well as hospital finance and management. Implement by January 2000.

- Bring in outside experts on a quarterly basis for presentations with the hospital president to medical staff, management, and board on issues affecting all three constituencies. Implement by April 2000.
- Benchmark "Medical Staff/Hospital Best Communication techniques. Implement January 2000.
- Develop "Medical Staff Support Teams" that assume ongoing responsibility for the preceding tactics. Implement June 2000.
- Work with hospital senior management to develop a "Communications Tree" to maintain monthly contact with five physicians per administrative team member. These five physicians should not be from the existing medical staff leadership. Implement April 2000.
- Meet with high volume physician utilizers of inpatient/outpatient services on a quarterly basis to discuss services, issues and opportunities. Implement April 2000.
- Offer physician office management seminars on a quarterly or as-needed basis through the hospital continuing education department. Implement April 2000.
- Develop a joint Physician/Hospital marketing committee by Fall of 2000. Use contract marketing support through the MSO/PHO to provide the following: cross-selling of medical staff and hospital, focused direct mailings, patient education, etc.

Strategy 6.3.2—Decision Making
- CH, in conjunction with the medical staff, should develop structures and policies that produce collaborative decision making through early and continuous involvement of physicians.

Tactics
- Establish a development committee with equal representation of physicians (younger emerging leaders) and management by 2000.
- Expand physician participation in CH Board activities by Fall of 2000.
- All joint program development should be supported by applying the following decision points by FY 2000/01:
  Services evaluated by strategic and technical advantage,
  Must be based upon a two-year break-even point,
  Activity must not compromise tax-exempt status,
  All members not required to participate in all activities,
  Service initiatives must reinforce positive physician/hospital relationship,
  Service initiatives should enhance existing revenues or secure new revenue services.

Strategy 6.3.3—Planning
- Short- and long-term planning should be jointly conducted by physicians and hospital to benefit community need. A planning orientation toward wellness and prevention should dominate any planning beginning in 2001.

Tactics

- CH and medical staff should develop a managed services organization (MSO)
  as an initial step toward a more formalized structure, by June 2000. The MSO
  should provide the following services:

  Practice Marketing and Promotion
  Group Purchasing Services
  Office Staff Education and Training Programs
  Practice Management Consults

Additional services should be added in late 2000 or by the first quarter of 2001.

- Starting in 2001, every physician/hospital planning effort must include subplans
  for marketing, finance, staffing, and resource allocation.
- All planning should reflect time frames and accountability and be monitored on
  a quarterly basis.
- Physician Recruiting: Physicians and hospitals should agree to apply the "20%
  projected need rule" for total physician need for 2000 recruiting. Based upon
  the success of '00 recruiting and environmental factors, the organization should
  evaluate recruiting by using the "30% projected need rule" for 2001 through
  2004. Recruitment should be based upon a managed care point of view.

  The 20%/30% rules are applied in acknowledgment of limited financial
  resources, available personnel to implement the medical staff development plan,
  and the improbability of recruiting more than 10 to 15 physicians in any given
  year.

  In addition, the 20%/30% rules compensate for those unidentified community-
  based physicians with admitting privileges only at Acme University Medical
  Center as well as physicians from other nearby hospitals.
- The following physician recruitment by specialty is recommended:

	'94	'95	'96	'97	'98
Anesthesiology		1		1	1
Emergency Medicine	1		1		
Family Practice	3	2	3	2	3
Dermatology		1			1
Internal Medicine	3	2	2	2	2
Neurology			1		
Cardiology				1	
Psychiatry	2	2	1	1	1
Pathology		1		1	
Surgery General	1	1	1	1	2
Plastic		1		1	
Urology			1		
Gastroenterology				1	
Total	10	11	10	11	10

- Develop a hospital-based primary care and E.R. physicians' group by recruiting two physicians by Fall of 2000 and one each in '01 and '02. These physicians would take unassigned patients.
- Eliminate access concerns by anchoring future primary care physicians in satellite clinics using a split approach of development in the city of Crossroads and placement in outlying zip codes that are in need. Utilize this approach from 2000 to 2004 with at least one to two physician placements in key zip codes until need is satisfied, that is:

2000-Physician/Zip code	99901	99902	99903	99904	99905	99906
Family Practice	1		1	1		
Surgery—Gen.	1					
Internal Med.		1	1	1		
Psychiatry	1			1		

2001-Physician/Zip code	99901	99902	99903	99904	99905	99906
Family Practice		1			1	
Surgery—Gen.					1	1
Internal Medicine					1	1
Psychiatry			1			1
Dermatology				1		

- Work with selected medical staff to develop part time satellite ambulatory care sites in under-served and core outlying zip codes. Combine this with primary care physician recruitment and support with physician assistants and nurse practitioners.
- Initiate a "Physician Succession Planning" program in Fall of 2000 using the following approaches:
   Practice assessment
   Work with retiring physicians one on one
   Retain third party support resources where needed
   Allow 2 to 5 years for succession planning turnover
   Implement a mentoring program
   Secure letters of commitment from physicians specifying date of retirement.
   Provide practice valuation services as part of succession recruitment.
- CH as part of a PHO should underwrite "Succession Recruitment."
- Develop an "Intra-Referral Network" among CH primary and specialty care physicians by 2001. Utilize a marketing and communications effort that increases awareness and preference within the service area for physicians affiliated with CH.
- CH medical staff through a PHO structure, should evaluate direct contracting opportunities as well as existing managed care contracting and determine the feasibility of a direct contracting program by 6/01.

- CH and the medical staff should take the lead in developing a "Community Care Network" as part of a regional vertical and horizontal integration of healthcare resources.
- CH and the medical staff should serve as a catalyst to assist the merger and possible acquisition of practices.
- Establish a "Director of Physician Services" position within the Office of Medical Affairs by 2000. This individual would be responsible for communication, education (non-clinical), practice support and physician recruitment.
- Develop information systems for management and physician recruitment that will enhance decision making for the Office of Medical Affairs. This activity should be initiated in January 2000 with a basic system operational by June of 2000.

Strategy 6.3.4—Governance
- Joint activities of medical staff and CH should have board and executive committee parity. existing medical staff committees should expand where possible to accommodate emerging leadership of the medical staff and provide an orientation for younger physicians by 2003.

Tactics
- Encourage interaction and relationship building among board, medical staff and management through reorganized structures.
- Expand medical staff executive committee to include 5 non-voting positions targeted for younger physicians on the medical staff by 2002.
- Develop a balanced mix of primary and specialty care physicians whenever possible.
- Require problem solving at the lowest level of medical staff development.

Strategy 6.3.5—Finance
- Improve relations with physicians by economically aligning physician and hospital risk and incentives within the parameters provided by "safe harbors" and the IRS.

Tactics
- Expand physician participation in the financing of alternative care structures and a physician/hospital organization by 2003.
- Develop a financial strategy for physicians and hospital that assists risk sharing and discounted fee structure in pursuit of managed care/direct contracting opportunities by 2002.
- Those physicians whose utilization of the hospital's resources is 2% of total charges or admissions should be supported through every legal means possible.

- Develop a program of cost saving for physicians through centralized support services.
- Develop stringent cost containment requirements for physician/hospital organization, practice support programs, and all outreach initiatives by 2002.

NOTE

1. Shortell, S.M. (1991). *Effective Hospital-Physician Relationships*, Health Administration Press, Ann Arbor, pp 3-29.

ABOUT THE AUTHOR

Christopher J. Evans, FACHE, CMPE, is a senior consultant with The Health Service Group, Inc., healthcare management consulting firm with offices in Charlotte, Raleigh, and Winston-Salem, North Carolina.

Having directed community hospital referral relationships and the physician faculty outreach clinical activities at a major academic medical center, Chris brings a wealth of experience in affiliation relationships, physician compensation and benefit plans, clinical and management information systems, feasibility studies, and administrative contracting issues. With HSG, he specializes in healthcare business acquisition, merger, valuation, financial management, and related healthcare integration and planning strategies. As a former hospital administrator and regional medical practice manager, Chris has managed numerous clinical and administrative departments and assists clients in understanding operational issues and facilitating reality-based solutions.

Chris is an active national lecturer and trainer providing continuing medical education for numerous organizations including bar and professional associations, graduate schools, healthcare executive groups and trustees. He has served on the teaching and professional development faculties for the American College of Healthcare Executives, Healthcare Financial Management Association, Medical Group Management Association, the American Society of Appraisers, the American Association of Certified Public Accountants (Advanced Business Valuation) and the McGraw-Hill Healthcare Education Group. He regularly provides continuing professional education for CPAs certified by the National Association of State Boards of Accountancy.

Chris is board certified in healthcare management and is a Fellow of the American College of Healthcare Executives. He is board certified in medical practice management with the American College of Medical Practice Executives. He holds active membership in Medical Group Management Association, Healthcare Financial Management Association, the North Carolina Association of CPAs, and the Institute of Business Appraisers. He is a Candidate Member of the American Society of Appraisers. He received his B.S. in Education, his M.P.H. in Healthcare Organization and Policy from the University of Alabama at Birmingham, and completed an ACHE postgraduate fellowship in hospital administration.

A prolific writer, he is also the principal author of *"Integrated Community Healthcare: Next Generation Strategies for Developing Provider Networks,"* published by McGraw-Hill and the Healthcare Financial Management Association (1997).

INDEX